Index

TO

MINNESOTA HISTORY

VOLUME XXIII

1942

.14418

Index

The names of contributors to *Minnesota History* are printed in capitals and small capitals. The titles of all books, periodicals, articles, and papers noted are included in quotation marks. (R) indicates that the contribution is a review.

Carson, G. M., pioneer, 25

Carson, M. E., pioneer merchant, 24; postmaster, 25

CARTER, CLARENCE E., (R) Lyon's "The Man Who Sold Louisiana," 258

Cartwright, David W., author, 40

Cartwright, William H., Jr., author, 400

Carver, Jonathan, 239n., 243, 355; explorer, 212

Carver County German Reading Society, library, 294, 397

Carver County Historical Society, museum, 100, 293–295; collections, 397

Carver County War History Committee, 390

Carver's Cave, Cass expedition at, 340

Case, Maud M., 77

Case thresher, manufactured, 324

Cass, Lewis, letters, 126; report, 132; leaves Detroit, 135; negotiates with Indians, 145–147, 249n., 328, 339; proposes exploration, 244n.

Cass expedition, 75; journal, 40, 126–148, 233–252, 271, 328–348; expenses, 127, 128; personnel, 128–132, 135, 249n.; literature, 130–132; route, 138, 233; military escort, 144; mileage covered, 348

Cass Lake, Indian agency, 93; fish, 330; reached by Cass expediton, 333

Cass Lake (village), museum, 13

Cassina Lake. *See* Cass Lake

Cathcart, Mrs. A. H., 173

Cather, Willa, novelist, 116, 125, 157

Catholic church, Minnesota, 96; Eucharistic Congress, 97; educational system, 191; Grand Portage, 196; Prairie du Chien, 286; St. Nazianz colony, 286

Catholic missions, Wisconsin, 285; Red River Valley, 366; South Dakota, 383; to Sioux, 383; Ball Club, 402

Catlin, George, drawings, 181

Catlin, Dr. Hiram W., diary, 75

Catlin, Dr. John J., 75

Census, use of records, 39, 44, 167, 168; of agriculture, 326; wartime use, 367; Fillmore County, 400

Central Cooperative Oil Association, Steele County, 200

Central Park, Minneapolis, 225

Chaboillez, Charles, trader, 272

Chambliss, Charles E., author, 180

Chandler, Clayborne, pioneer, 319

Channing, William Ellery, 261

Chapin, Earl, 104

Chapman, Timothy, 322n.

Chapple, W. W., composer, 172

Charity Islands, Lake Huron, 140n.

Charlevoix, Pierre F. X. de, traveler, 239n.; historian, 243

Chase, Alexander R., with Cass expedition, 135, 239, 248, 328, 347; maps Sandy Lake, 334

Chase, Solmon P., 135n., 261

Chatelain, Verne E., author, 85, 169, 370

CHATELAIN, VERNE E., (R) Robbins' "Our Landed Heritage," 161–163; (R) Lokken's "Iowa Public Land Disposal," 357–359

Chatfield, village ordinances, 401

Chatfield Commercial Club, improves roads, 401

Cheneaux Islands, Lake Huron, 143n.

Chequamegon Point, described, 242

Chernick, Jack, author, 388

Chicago, first telephone directory, 87; in 1890's, 165; thresher factory, 324; visited by Cass party, 347, 348n.; Norwegian clubs, 381

Chicago Academy of Sciences, 370

Chicago, Burlington and Quincy Railroad, colonization history, 63–65

Chicago Road, 348n.

Child, James E., author, 303

Chinese War Relief, 21

Chippewa County Historical Society, 50, 398; activities, 100; meetings, 193, 296

Chippewa County War History Committee, 390

Chippewa Indians, 147; Cass Lake museum, 13; at Lake Bemidji, 25; treaties, 85; fur trade, 94; pictures, 94, 154; relations with British, 126; with Cass expedition, 135; Sault Ste. Marie land cession, 146; agent, 148; in St. Croix Valley, 164; food, 181, 332; culture, 188, 288; at Fond du Lac, 244; at Sandy Lake, 249, 329–332; council with Cass,

ed, 5; publications, 5, 36–38, 349, 366; manuscript collections, 6, 7, 40; war activities, 20, 23, 149–153, 292, 367, 393; in *1941*, 35–45; members, 35, 70, 168, 269, 368; executive council, 35, 50; publications fund, 37; sponsors Round Tower Museum, 39; library, 39, 40, 42; newspaper department, 39, 41, 42; manuscript division, 39, 42, 71, 167; picture collection, 42, 71, 312; WPA projects, 43; staff, 43, 168, 269, 366, 367, 368; appropriation, 44; Scandinavian collection, 190, 380; newspaper collection, 300, 368; role in organizing state library association, 386. *See also* Historical societies

Accessions, manuscripts, 74–76, 170–172, 271–273, 370–372; museum objects, 41, 76–78, 172, 273, 373; newspapers, 76, 272; genealogies, 78–81, 173–177, 274–277, 374; books, 372

Meetings, 35, 36, 376; annual, 1, 46–51, 94; summer, 167, 267

Museum, 186; visitors, 39, 71; exhibits, 71

Minnesota history, conserved in wartime, 1–23; popularized, 49; sketch, 187

"Minnesota History," in *1941*, 36; format, 70; contributors, 72–74, 168–170, 270, 287, 369

Minnesota Library Association, history, 386

Minnesota Medical Society, history, 387

Minnesota Museum of Natural History, 50

Minnesota Mutual Life Insurance Co., war activities, 292, 394

Minnesota Office of Civilian Defense, sponsors war records work, 149, 153; powers, 151

Minnesota Office of Military Defense, 149

"Minnesota Pioneer," microfilms, 368

Minnesota River, fort established, 128

Minnesota State Fair, board, 172; history, 290

Minnesota State Guard, 268, 270

Minnesota State Medical Association, publication, 95; history, 190, 289

Minnesota Supreme Court, decisions, 180

Minnesota Taxpayers Association, 266

Minnesota Territory, established, 4; first medical meeting, 190

Minnesota University. *See* University of Minnesota

Minnesota War History Committee, established, 149; program outlined, 150–153; activities, 169, 291–293, 392–394; accessions, 292, 393; local committees, 150, 390–392; conference, 392; meeting, 291

Minnesota War Records Commission, problems, 18; collections, 151

Miska, Mrs. Josephine, speaker, 398

Missions and missionaries, Northwest, 37, 366; frontier, 82, 272; to Sioux, 97. *See also* various denominations and mission stations

Mississippi River, 147, 305, 344; explored, 58; keelboats on, 62; reached by Burlington Road, 64; search for source, 126n., 233n., 328, 333; log jams, 198; source discovered, 234n.; routes to, 236, 345n.; voyage down, 328, 334–345; tributaries, 343; panorama described, 349–354; songs, 382. *See also* Bridges, Steamboats and steamboating

Mississippi Valley, French vocabulary, 84; background for fiction, 124; struggle for, 161

Mississippi Valley Historical Association, Alvord Memorial Commission, 38, 366; meeting, 83

Missouri, lead mines, 130, 344n.; protects James boys, 381

Missouri Compromise, opposed by North, 261

Missouri Expedition, reaches Fort Snelling, 339

Missouri River, scenery, 155; explored, 170

Missouri State Historical Society, library, 379

Mitchill, Samuel L., scientist, 342

Mixed bloods, at Sault Ste. Marie, 144; in fur trade, 247; art, 288; among Chippewa, 329; at Green Bay, 347

Mizpah, history, 107

Modern Woodmen, Bemidji, 32

Moline (Ill.), plow factory, 323

Monaghan, Jay, author, 281

Wright, Thomas C., 171
Wright County, museum, 14
Wright County Historical Society, organized, 195
Wright County War History Committee, 392

Yantes, Ray, 392
Yellow Medicine County, archives, 93; Norwegian settlements, 290
Yellow Medicine County War History Committee, 392
Yellowstone National Park, first winter trip, 282; established, 383
Yellowstone Valley, explored, 282

Young, Mrs. E. B., 35
Young, Harry H., journalist, 372
Young, J. Tracy, composer, 172
Youngdahl, Luther W., speaker, 194
Young Men's Christian Association, war activities, 21

Zalusky, Joseph, 391
Zavoral, James, 298
Zieglschmid, A. J. F., author, 183
Zimmermann, Dr. Harry B., 50
Zoll, Rev. Joseph, 27
Zrust, Mrs. Isabelle, 101
Zumbrota, bridge, 290
Zweiner, C. A., 149

ERRATA

Page 24, line 9, for *William Aitkin*, read *William Aitken*.
———— 40, line 11, for *Teigen*, read *Teigan*.
———— 183, line 33, for *costumes*, read *customs*.
———— 274, line 20, for *Mrs. C. E. Lindley*, read *Mrs. E. C. Lindley*.
———— 385, lines 25 and 27, for *Canadian Historical Society*, read *Canadian Geographical Society*.

MINNESOTA HISTORY

VOLUME 23 • PUBLISHED IN MARCH 1942 • NUMBER 1

Conserving Minnesota's History in Wartime

As THE EVENING session of the Minnesota Historical Society's annual meeting drew to a close, those who attended the four sessions remarked upon the fact that a single theme ran through many of the papers and talks presented. Dean Blegen's appeal for the "protection of our cultural heritage" served as a climax not only to his own survey of the vast cultural resources built up by two leading state institutions over a period of almost a century, but to the programs of the entire day. Speakers who addressed the local history conference in the morning suggested the part that can be played in time of war by county and community leaders of historical work and told how the activities of the local historical society fit into the war program. In the hope that readers of this magazine will find them useful, the address presented by Dean Blegen at the evening session and three short papers read in connection with the morning meeting are published herewith. Ed.

THE MINNESOTA HISTORICAL SOCIETY AND THE UNIVERSITY OF MINNESOTA

Theodore C. Blegen

WHEN WILLIAM WATTS FOLWELL came to Minnesota in 1869 as the first president of the University of Minnesota, he found one building on the campus — the "Old Main." It was heated by forty-three wood stoves. The narrow stairs that connected the second and third floors were so dark and winding that Dr. Folwell found it necessary to

1

station on them an "officer of the day" to prevent student collisions. This "officer of the day" was presumably our first personnel and guidance official. As Dr. Folwell surveyed the pioneer temple of learning, he was troubled by its deficiencies and bluntly told the board of regents that it was "not an exaggeration to say that the building has no system of ventilation" whatever. The fire hazards and the danger to life seemed terrible to him, with more than two hundred students — 14 freshmen and 216 preparatory students — in the building. The latter group included, in Dr. Folwell's phrase, "146 gentlemen and 70 ladies."

Notwithstanding difficulties, Dr. Folwell launched the university on its career. He believed that he and his colleagues could carry on the work, and he challenged the people of the state with his vision of a great center of learning. One thing that he never tired of calling to the attention of the regents was the need for books and of space in which to house them. "When I reported for duty in September, 1869," he wrote many years later, "the library consisted mainly of a set of sixteen volumes of an encyclopedia." Those were the beginnings of a university library that today numbers 1,200,000 accessioned volumes and is one of the half-dozen greatest university libraries in America. It places a slight strain upon the imagination to think of a university functioning with a library consisting mainly of a sixteen-volume encyclopedia. But Dr. Folwell, though of course he had to think of stairs and fire hazards and other material problems, was an educational statesman who put first things first. Not long after he arrived on the campus he declared to the regents, "The first great interest of the University is, of course, the instruction. Next to that comes the Library." In his inaugural address, a document in which he dreamed dreams of what a great university might mean to Minnesota in the future, he also envisaged a great library and said, "To such a library as will some day exist here, can resort not only the scholar, and the learned author, but the historian, the statistician, the legislator, the editor, the manufacturer and the inventor, to consult those works which are beyond reach of private means." A great dream indeed, and a dream come true — even though Dr. Folwell, in his category of users, seems to imply that the historian is a different species from the scholar.

When Dr. Folwell made his report for 1869 he was able to announce the first gift of any size to the university library. It was a gift of some seventy-odd volumes. Tonight, when the state historical society honors the university by meeting on the same, though perhaps slightly changed, campus to which Dr. Folwell came in 1869, it gives me great pleasure to report that that gift of seventy-odd volumes, made in the first year after the university opened its doors to college students, came from the Minnesota Historical Society. I believe that the precise number of volumes was seventy-four, but when I say seventy-odd volumes, I am, I think, stating the precise truth, for there were some odd books in the gift. It included such works as *Discoveries among the Ruins of Nineveh and Babylon, Peruvian Antiquities,* volume 2 of Davidson's Vergil, and volumes 6, 7, and 12 of *Explorations and Surveys for a Railroad from the Mississippi River to the Pacific Ocean.* But the university was delighted with the gift, and the Minnesota Historical Society still has in its files a letter saying how "thankfully" it was received and expressing warm appreciation of the society's "effort" in behalf of the university.

It would be interesting to go on and tell the story of the building of a great university library — how in the first year twelve hundred volumes were purchased for twelve hundred dollars from Colonel Daniel A. Robertson, a collection including a seventy-volume set of Voltaire and a six-volume edition of Charlevoix; how in 1873 the university purchased the twenty-five hundred volumes comprising the private library of former President Henry P. Tappan of the University of Michigan; how, after Dr. Folwell had been here only four years, the library had grown from a sixteen-volume encyclopedia to a collection of ten thousand books; and how Dr. Folwell himself served as librarian through many years after his presidency and helped to make his pioneer library dreams come true. He never lost his deep interest in the university library and in library matters. I may mention one small evidence of that interest when he was a very old man. In the 1920's Dr. Folwell was working on his *History of Minnesota;* I was then the assistant superintendent of the Minnesota Historical Society. Dr. Folwell had taken note of the fact that in the library catalogues his own writings were listed, under the Cutter system of numbering, with the symbol F73. Frequently he would write me cards and notes asking me to look up this or that, and almost invariably he signed them "V.t.y"—that is "Very truly yours,"—F73. To me, F73 was William Watts Folwell.

What interests me chiefly this evening, however, is not so much the story of the university library as the good will and co-operation between the society and the university, symbolized nearly three-quarters of a century ago by the pioneer gift of books. Not a few of the founders and builders of the university were also founders and builders of the society, and the reason, I think, lies in the identity of ideals motivating the two institutions. Both stood for the service of the truth and the promotion of the welfare of the people. Both stood for cultural continuity. Both, created by a free people, were institutions of a kind that, in President Ford's phrase, helps to "keep the mind free and the spirit of man aloft." Dr. Folwell, in his university inaugural, might have been speaking for the society when, addressing a people struggling with the material problems of the western frontier, he voiced the cause of education, called for perspective, and asked the state to hold fast to enduring values. "We do not cling to the past in order to reproduce it," he said, "but because we cannot spare its lessons. We cannot spare its examples of heroism, martyrdom, patriotism, valor, love. Unhappy will that nation be which cuts itself off from the past. As well might a seaman throw overboard his compass and charts, and resolve to steer his ship by chalk marks on her taffrail." Alexander Ramsey might have been speaking for the university when in 1849 he called upon Minnesotans to preserve the records of the process of building a commonwealth, advocated "history in a land of yesterday," and urged the pioneers to found a history society on the frontier rim of America.

In 1849 Minnesota Territory was established, the first newspaper of Minnesota issued, and the Minnesota Historical Society founded; two years later the University of Minnesota was chartered. Thus at the outset of the commonwealth's history the people had a free press for the dissemination of ideas and information, an organized society devoted to preserving for the future the product of that press and other records, and the charter of a university for the people of the commonwealth. It is not surprising to learn that Dr. Edward D. Neill, the chancellor of the projected university, was also, from 1851 to 1863, the secretary of the society; that Henry H. Sibley was one of the founders of both institutions, served as president of the society for a dozen years, and was also for many years president of the university board of regents. The tradition of close co-operation between the two institutions has deepened in relatively recent times, for in 1913 Dean Guy Stanton Ford was made a member of the society's executive council, and the next year Dr. Solon J. Buck of the university history department became its secretary and superintendent. In the following years he took the lead in reorganizing the society and greatly expanding its collections and services. Perhaps the most remarkable example, however, of the co-operation of the society and the university is to be found in the services of Dr. Folwell himself. Throughout the years he had been fertile in ideas for the developing society, but no one could have dreamed that in the 1920's the state society would publish a great four-volume *History of Minnesota* written by the man who in 1869 came to the frontier to head the infant University of Minnesota. In 1869 Dr. Folwell placed the scholar in one class and the historian in another, but in the 1920's he himself combined the two by giving us our best history of this state. Nothing that I could say about the society and university research could find better exemplification than the comprehensive history that this man, a man of our university classes and campus, wrote for our sister institution in St. Paul. When to all this I add that Dr. Folwell served a term as president of the state historical society, that Dean Ford also held that honored position in the 1930's, that the new president of the society is the head of our university history department, Professor Lester B. Shippee, and that the efficient superintendent of the society is Dr. Arthur J. Larsen, trained in the university history department, I think you will all agree that the tradition of friendly co-operation between the two is a vital tradition.[1]

But there is another side to the story. I have referred to the great library of the University of Minnesota, but I have not said much about that rich laboratory for the student of history — the books, newspapers, and manuscripts of the state society. Here on this campus, in a time when as never before we need to understand the meaning of our past and to appreciate our heritage — here are teachers and students engaged in studies of that past and heritage. There, in the Historical Building, are collections of priceless records. Among them are the letters, diaries, and other records left by Alexander Ramsey, the first governor of Minnesota Territory; by Henry H. Sibley, fur trader and first governor of the state; by Lawrence Taliaferro, Indian agent at old Fort Snelling; by Ignatius Donnelly, the leader of agrarian third parties; by Knute Nelson, United States senator from Minnesota; by Henry B. Whipple, bishop and friend of the Indians; by William W. Folwell, university president and historian; and by hundreds of other Minnesotans. When I say that this collection includes the personal papers of explorers, senators, governors, legislators, lawyers, doctors, engineers, architects, geologists, bankers, lumbermen, railroad builders, steamboatmen, millers, missionaries, ministers, merchants, farmers, teachers, even blacksmiths and shoemakers — all makers of Minnesota and America — I give only a hint of the treasures that make the society's collection one of the most notable in America. It stirs my imagination to think of those treasures, of their potential value to students, and of the articles and books that can be produced from them if we can but bring students and records together. And I think that nothing in my experience at the society was quite so exciting as the constant

[1] To this list of the men who have served as leaders both of the society and the university, Dean Blegen's name must be added. His connection with the society, first as assistant superintendent and then as secretary and superintendent, spanned the period from 1922 to 1939, and he continues to serve as a member of its executive council. During much of this period he served also as a member of the history faculty in the university, and in 1940 he was named dean of its graduate school. Ed.

search for and finding of old records, a game in which we called upon the people of the state to join us.

The story of the building of that collection will match the story of the university library. As early as 1860 the society acquired the manuscript journal of Stephen H. Long's narrative of a trip of exploration into the Minnesota country in 1817. In the late 1860's it got the wonderful Taliaferro diaries. Unfortunately, some volumes were missing. That was too bad, for it broke the sequence of the record. More than sixty years later a Minnesota man browsing in a St. Louis bookstore picked up an old handwritten volume and noted such familiar words as Fort Snelling, Sioux, and Chippewa. The volume, the dealer explained, had been found with some rubbish in an old St. Louis cellar. The Minnesota man bought it and sent it to the society. It was one of the missing Taliaferro diaries and it fitted neatly into an empty niche in the series. In 1893 the Sibley Papers came to the society. And so year after year, the collection was built up. But it has grown most rapidly in the past quarter century. And I am glad to say that out of our university classes has come some interesting co-operation. One of my own students found in the basement of a St. Paul building the old records of the Mississippi steamboat magnate, Commodore Davidson; another located a barrel of papers relating to the Sweetman Irish colony of southern Minnesota; and one of Professor Osgood's students brought to a class in American history an original diary kept on the Long expedition of 1823 by James E. Colhoun, a nephew of John C. Calhoun. Such records, when found, go to the Minnesota Historical Society, or if the originals cannot be secured for the society, film copies are taken.

No one who has not taught a class in history can understand the stimulus of interest that comes of putting students in actual contact with original documents. My first experience of this kind happened many years ago when I was a high-school teacher in Milwaukee. I sent my students on an attic hunt for old records and one of them brought into class a diary kept by a great-grandfather who was a forty-niner. It recorded a trip across the plains in 1849, told of hunting gold in the Sacramento Valley, and described a return to Wisconsin by way of Panama and New York. I still remember the tense interest of my class and myself as the boy read the diary to us. We were studying American history at the middle of the nineteenth century and we had been reading about the California gold rush. Well, here was the real thing. The story we had been studying became alive and convincing to us as no textbook could make it. Ever since that experience I have had a sharp interest in the discovery and use of original records.

The point I am coming to is that our Minnesota students have been and are exploring the records collected by the historical society. I have recently looked over a half hundred masters' theses written at this university, all of which are based largely upon the society's records. Their subject matter includes land policies, frontier homes, flour milling, lumbering, railroad history, immigration, politics, the church, banking, finance, the fur trade, labor, journalism, public opinion, roads and travel, the story of communities, biographies of leaders in various fields, and other topics. Similarly I find a dozen or more doctors' theses, with topics ranging from the agricultural history of Minnesota to a life of Sibley and a study of wild life conservation. It is not so much the importance of such studies to the public in terms of books and articles that I want to emphasize, though much of this research has resulted in publication, as the creative influence of the research itself upon the students, an influence carried with them into their work wherever they are.

I might also speak of the research in the collections of the society which has found its way into books published by the University of Minnesota Press. A dozen volumes readily come to my mind, including Charles M. Gates's *Five Fur Traders of the Northwest,* Lester B. Shippee's edition of *Bishop Whipple's Southern Diary,* Mildred L. Hartsough's *From Canoe to Steel Barge on the Upper Mississippi,* George M. Stephenson's *John Lind of Minnesota,* which is based primarily upon the Lind Papers, Netta W. Wilson's life of *Alfred Owre, Dentistry's Militant Educator,* Edgar B. Wesley's book on *Owatonna,* a model study of an American community, and

Helen Clapesattle's *The Doctors Mayo,* a brilliant combination of good research and good writing which drew to no small extent upon the newspaper and manuscript treasures of the society. If I had time to go on and tell of other studies, published here and in other parts of the country, which have come in considerable part out of the society's materials, I should gradually build up a description of a Northwest regional literature which in the full compass of its range and variety has made a notable contribution to our understanding of American history. Drawing upon cultural resources, scholars have added to the cultural riches of the region and the nation.

While I was thinking over my topic for this program, I received a letter from Washington asking me to serve as the chairman of a state committee on the conservation of the cultural resources of Minnesota. The request came from the President's National Resources Planning Board. It was a war and emergency request. I have already brought together the state committee and we have started work. Our problem is to survey the state to determine what irreplaceable or peculiarly valuable cultural and scientific treasures are exposed to possible damage; to formulate plans for the removal of certain treasures and to survey storage space; to take steps to guard against the destruction or damage of cultural resources, especially records and papers, as a result of urgent war work and emergency needs for space; to offer haven to treasures in coastal areas more exposed than the Middle West to possible enemy attack; and in general to protect our cultural resources as a part of the civilian defense effort.

It seems to me that this war request bears a relation to the values that I have been trying to emphasize tonight. In the midst of a gigantic war effort the government calls upon us to make plans to conserve our cultural resources. We know that, as a part of the civilization we are pledged and determined to defend and preserve, these resources are precious beyond price. What we are doing in the war is in fact to defend our cultural heritage. So, in speaking as I have done tonight about the university and the state historical society, I have been thinking about our cultural resources and our cultural heritage. I am reminded that during the first World War, in 1918, the building of the Minnesota Historical Society was dedicated, with Frederick J. Turner, the interpreter of the westward movement, as the chief speaker. We did not then, and we do not now, forget the cause of history, education, and the conserving of cultural resources amid the grim urgency of war. Turner spoke in 1918 on Middle Western democracy, and he said that the times were appropriate for erecting a new "home for history." When he said that America was fighting for historic ideals, he used words that seem to me to be vivid with truth today. "If this nation is one for which we should pour out our savings," he said, "postpone our differences, go hungry, and even give up life itself, it is not because it is a rich, extensive, well-fed, and populous nation; it is because from its early days America has pressed onward toward a goal of its own; because it has followed an ideal, the ideal of a democracy developing under conditions unlike those of any other age or country." America was then at war, he said, that the history of the United States might "not become the lost and tragic story of a futile dream." I believe Turner's words are true today, and I believe that in the national conviction of the truth they embody is the assurance of victory and of the protection of our cultural heritage.

LOCAL HISTORICAL MUSEUMS AND THE WAR PROGRAM

Bertha L. Heilbron

WHEN THE LIBRARY and museum at Hyde Park in which President Roosevelt's papers and collections are housed was opened on June 30, 1941, the chief executive appropriately included in his dedicatory address some remarks on the significance of such an institution in a democracy. "Among democracies the building of libraries and museums for the use of all the people flourishes," said the President. "That is especially true in our own land," he continued, "for we believe that people should work out for themselves, and through their own study, the determination of their best interest rather than accept such so-called information as may be handed out to them by

self-constituted leaders." And he added that "It is in keeping with
the well-considered trend in these difficult days that we are distributing historical collections more widely than ever throughout our
land."

Certainly here in Minnesota historical collections are widely distributed. In every section of our state, from Roseau on the north to
Fairmont on the south, from Moorhead on the west to Duluth and
Stillwater on the east, local historical museums are flourishing. In
the past few years, I have had an opportunity to see a number of
these collections, and I have gained impressions and made compari-
sons which I shall attempt to pass on to you today.

Of the sixty-odd historical societies now active in Minnesota, perhaps two-thirds have museum collections of one kind or another. In
addition, there are a few museums that are not affiliated with societies. They are housed in quarters that vary in suitability from the
magnificent building specially erected for the Brown County Historical Society to damp and dingy rooms in the basements of anti-
quated courthouses. I do not mean to imply that basement rooms are
always damp and dingy and inadequate. I think, for example, of the
room in the basement of the Rochester Public Library that has been
so attractively adapted to the purposes of the Olmsted County Historical Society. And there is the spacious room in the high-school
building at Hutchinson, where the McLeod County society has its
exhibits. A museum of real distinction is that in the basement of the
Cokato library. In a library also, but on an upper floor, is the museum of the Rice County society. Among other localities that provide
space in public buildings for historical museums are Roseau, Duluth, Brainerd, and St. Louis Park in Hennepin County. Museums
at Winona and Moorhead are on the campuses of state teachers'
colleges.

A few years ago a Frenchman who was traveling in the United
States remarked that "Few Americans live in or near the house
where they were born," but that "not infrequently in small towns
one sees a single stone building, standing in the midst of less permanent constructions, preserved as a specimen of the home and

dedicated to the town as a museum."[1] He could see such houses today in several Minnesota communities — in Stillwater, for example, where the old warden's residence has been recently deeded by the state to the local historical society; or in Mankato, where a mansion of the 1870's, in itself an object of no slight historical interest, has been adapted to museum purposes.

The museum has been described as the "chief agent in bringing the public and the historical society together."[2] We have plenty of evidence here in Minnesota that the public is familiar with our local museums. Two thousand people saw the museum at Hutchinson on its opening day in 1939 — a crowd equal in size to two-thirds of the city's population. The secretary of the Otter Tail County society reported recently that since its museum at Fergus Falls opened in 1934, it has received more than 30,000 visitors who registered. On a holiday a few years ago, 150 people saw the Roseau museum; and the Round Tower museum at Fort Snelling attracted over 300 visitors on a single Sunday last October. At Rochester, about 1,300 visitors were counted in the museum's first three months in 1940. After the opening day about eighty-five per cent of the visitors came from outside the county or the state. Obviously, a large number of the transients who seek medical aid in Rochester are finding their way to the Olmsted County museum and carrying away impressions of southern Minnesota's background. It has been estimated that the Crow Wing County museum at Brainerd receives about 5,000 visitors each year, many of them during the summer tourist season. It is not surprising that in many communities businessmen look upon the local museum as an important tourist attraction.

The frequent changing of exhibits helps to sustain interest in the museum, once it is firmly established. The Brown County Society at New Ulm, for example, devotes four floor cases to temporary displays that are changed every two weeks. In some of them portraits of early settlers are rotated in alphabetical order, and pioneers and

[1] Raoul de Roussy de Sales, "What Makes an American," in *The Atlantic*, 163:300 (March, 1939).
[2] Alexander J. Wall, "The Place of the Historical Society and Museum in the United States and Elsewhere," in Conference of State and Local Historical Societies, *Proceedings*, 1937, p. 10.

their descendants have come to watch for the display of pictures of their own families and to visit the museum when they may be seen. Mr. Fred W. Johnson, the moving spirit of the New Ulm museum, agrees with a local historical leader who wrote recently that "History is an abstract thing until we suddenly find that our own family had a hand in its making." [3] In building up and maintaining his collection, he appeals to family pride, believing that the children and grandchildren of pioneers will co-operate in an undertaking that helps to perpetuate the memories of their forebears.

There are some notable examples in Minnesota of co-operation between the schools and the local museums, and most of the latter have records of group visits by classes and teachers. The Hutchinson museum is not only in the school, but its entire program has been linked with school activities. Some societies have conducted local history essay contests, offering prizes for the best narratives written by school children. An unusual form of co-operation is to be found in Roseau County, where trips to the museum have been awarded by a local chapter of the American Legion to honor students in the rural schools.

The work of any local society, whether it is collecting and preserving the raw materials of history or making them available to the people of the community, must of necessity be far more specialized than the work of the state society. It has been said that "each society of energy and enterprise will find in its area some special work to do, a work pressed upon it by special circumstance." [4] Thus at Cass Lake a great Chippewa Indian collection has been assembled. Special attention has been given by the Rice County society to the commercial development of the Cannon Valley and to the growth of educational institutions in the county. An exhibit of logging camp equipment, including cooking utensils used in such camps, is the feature of the Crow Wing County museum. This exhibit typifies the northern Minnesota logging industry; it is to be hoped that

[3] Lou D. MacWethy, "Making Local History Pay," in Columbia County [New York] Historical Society, *Quarterly Bulletin*, no. 29, p. 8 (January, 1935).

[4] Louis Blake Duff, "The Problems and Opportunities of Canadian Historical Societies," in *Canadian Historical Review*, 13:256 (September, 1932).

the Washington County museum will collect logging materials for the St. Croix Valley. Two outstanding collections in the St. Louis County museum relate to North Shore history. They are the manuscripts left by Edmund F. Ely, a pioneer missionary in the Lake Superior country, and the paintings and sketches of North Shore scenes and Indians made by Eastman Johnson when he visited the region in the 1850's. The newly organized Hibbing Historical Society has an opportunity to supplement the St. Louis County museum by giving emphasis to the history of the iron mines. The author of the recently published biography of *The Doctors Mayo* found useful the collections of the Olmsted County society. The Round Tower museum at Fort Snelling specializes in the history of Minnesota's oldest military post. It is natural that the Hutchinson museum should contain much material on cultural history, for the community was founded and bears the name of three New Englanders who played an important role in the nation's musical history. An excellent example of a local concern with the folkways of the pioneers is to be found in the Cokato museum, where the collections consist largely of domestic and agricultural implements characteristic of those used by the Scandinavians who settled in Wright County. Both originals and miniature reproductions are included in this unique collection, which has been assembled and arranged by Mr. and Mrs. R. M. Peterson.

In addition to what we usually think of as museum objects, local societies in Minnesota are collecting manuscripts, newspapers, archives, business records, genealogical records, books, pamphlets, pictures, maps. Outstanding is the picture collection of the New Ulm museum, which includes more than ten thousand portraits of Brown County pioneers. There are important newspaper collections in such counties as Blue Earth, Olmsted, and Rice. A method for building up a local historical library was suggested recently by the Waseca County Historical Society, when it announced its plan "to honor the memory of each departed member with a book to be placed in the county library." In Kandiyohi County, both the society and the local officials realize that the historical society has a heavy responsibility in caring for the local archives. The society recently received from the county board an appropriation of a thousand dollars to be used in constructing a fireproof vault in its museum building, thus assuring the safe preservation of archives and other valuable records in its custody.

The success with which local museum workers make their collections available to and readily usable by the public varies greatly in Minnesota. Only a few examples can be cited. In Blue Earth County a trained librarian has carefully identified and specifically labeled every item acquired, and has instituted a system of keeping accessions records and making inventories of the museum's holdings. At Cokato, easily read, hand-lettered labels are used. The specially designed wall cases and excellent lighting of the Brown County museum represent an ideal toward which any institution might strive. A few societies, like Martin and Hennepin, are reaching the public through publications.

By looking at historical museums in all sections of Minnesota, I have learned that the local museum is a cultural asset that even the smallest community can support. It takes a large city with a wealthy population to maintain an art museum, a symphony orchestra, or a vast reference library. But a village of a few hundred people can assemble the materials for a historical museum and give it quarters in a public building. Because everybody can participate in its activities, enjoy its exhibits, and understand its objectives, the local historical museum is perhaps the most thoroughly democratic of cultural institutions. Old and young, rich and poor alike can feel that the local museum belongs to them, for all are represented in the story it preserves. It reflects, perhaps more fully than any other single institution in American life, the ideals for which we are staking our all in the present world conflict.

It is significant that the local historical museums here in Minnesota have come into being in the past two decades, in other words, since the first World War. Perhaps that crisis awakened us to an appreciation of our past, a realization that we could not take for granted the values for which our forebears braved the rigors of frontier life. The museum collections laboriously built up in this spirit are a new responsibility in another time of crisis. Like our liberties, these records of our past are beyond price. Once gone, they cannot be replaced. There is no substitute for them. We cannot afford to push them aside, to neglect them for what may seem more pressing and more immediate needs. For these historical collections are the concrete, tangible reminders of the liberties for which we are at war.

A leaflet issued recently by the National Resources Planning Board in Washington reminds us that the nation's "cultural institutions play an important role in the maintenance of national morale." This suggests a contribution to ultimate victory for America that can be made by all who in the past have helped to conserve its history. By working for and insisting upon the continued maintenance of our historical museums, we can help to maintain national morale. For those who remain on the home front, there probably is no more important duty.

THE LOCAL HISTORICAL SOCIETY IN WARTIME

G. Hubert Smith

THE OBJECTS of local historical societies in Minnesota are the discovery, preservation, and dissemination of knowledge of the history of the community. The accomplishment of these ends has been sought by collecting, recording, and preserving historical facts and materials of many kinds and by making them available to the public in exhibits and files, by holding public meetings devoted to history, by answering requests for information, by publishing historical material in newspapers, periodicals, and books, by sponsoring the preservation of historic sites and the erection of historical markers, and by aiding the cause of history in many other ways. These tasks — and, be it noted, they are self-imposed tasks — are but the acts of groups of people, and merely listing things done does not measure the importance of local historical work. My purpose here is to define the role of the local historical society in our times, to examine what the society should be, to see what it should accomplish in a democracy at war. Let us leave aside for the moment the matter of the things that historical societies should do; let us ask why these things should be done and what is the result when they are done.

It is beneficial to any cause if upon occasion its principles be examined, its underlying motives and its ultimate effects analyzed. This is just as true in time of peace as of war, but in time of war the examination must be more searching, and the need for examination is more urgent. In our present crisis it is right that we should look into the reasons for and the results of the activities of public groups — not, thank heaven, for the evil purpose of some Gestapo, but to determine whether they illustrate democratic principles at work.

We would all agree, I suspect, that the aims of historical societies are worthy ones. Such aims, like those of schools, colleges, and universities, of libraries and museums of art and science are expressions of the highest intellectual achievements of mankind. A historically informed people is a mainstay of democracy in peacetime, and historical societies contribute heavily to shaping public opinion and directing public action. Their contribution is, in fact, matched only by that of professional teachers of history. But if the aims of historical societies and of teachers are important in time of peace, how much more important are they in time of war! A knowledge of past sacrifice, of the meaning of blood shed for the sacred causes of the past, is a stimulus and a help to democratic peoples in the waging of a war.

It is a help to know one's self in relation to those who have suffered oppression and made sacrifices for the sake of conscience and of justice, who have helped to found civilization, or who have rallied to the defense of country when its life has hung in the balance. Thus the work of local historical societies aids in waging a just war, in fighting for the right of democratic ways for ourselves and for others. It should be the motive of such societies to preserve and to permit a full knowledge of the truth, to keep the record of man's successes and of his failures in maintaining justice and in establishing human rights.

Upon the attainment of the ideals of history there are special limitations. We have mentioned keeping the record of man's successes and of his failures, and history is based upon that record. Whether the record is a diary, or a photograph, or a garment, or a tool makes no real difference here. History itself, just as the record upon which it is based, is of many kinds, but history is a sham and worthless if it cannot be proved by reference to an original document of some kind. We might well doubt a Valley Forge if we had no yellowing letters, no tattered maps, or blood-stained, ragged leggings. If, then, we need the history of such a struggle, so also do we need the documents upon which its story is based, and if the history is important, so is the record. We must assure the proper collection and preservation and the final use of the documents of the war in which we are now engaged, if the history that will be written is to be full and sound and useful. More records seem to be created in time of war than of peace, and the job of collecting and preserving them is greater than we may imagine — too great, in fact, to be undertaken without thoughtful, well-planned co-operation.

If you have any doubts about the size and scope of the problem that now faces us as volunteer or professional historians, consider for a moment the following brief summary, published by the Minnesota War Records Commission in 1918, of some of the problems that it faced in the first World War. We must know, it reads, how Minnesota "played her part among the free peoples of the world in the fight for world freedom; how she furnished thousands of her sons to the fighting forces of the nation and how these men conducted themselves and what they experienced in camp, at sea, and on the field of battle; how she stood for loyalty at home and suppressed the Hun within her gates; how she readjusted her whole course of life, giving abundantly of her means, her substance, her thought, her time, her strength, her prayers, sacrificing luxuries and making spare use of the necessities of life, and, forgetting all petty rivalries, united in efforts" to win the war, to help the men at the front, and to aid war sufferers.[1] With certain additions, this might serve as an outline of our present problem. The local historical society should collect and preserve and make available records of all the ways in which the people of its community alter their lives to meet war needs.

To accomplish this, the historical society in time of war must be even more vigilant and alert than in time of peace. It must continue its normal tasks undiminished — the tasks that help tell the story of past peace — lest we lose sight of the goal for which we strive. It must also, however, undertake new tasks arising out of the war, lest we forget the lessons so harshly being learned afresh. These tasks of collecting, preserving, and using records must be undertaken with courage and conviction by those who stay at home. It must be a special duty of those whose time is not wholly occupied with other war services to help our historical societies discharge their rightful obligation to the future of democracy.

The local historical society that does its share of collecting and using community war records will become an important civic force, helping to maintain morale and contributing to the cause of democracy in a world filled with bitter enemies of that system. Emerging from the present period of trial — and, it may be, of adversity — with a shining record of public service, such a society can look forward to a future bright with promise when the victory of democracy has been won. It will have done its share for that cause and it will likewise have established its rightful place in community and world affairs. The society that sees and meets the challenge of the present will lay the foundation for future and still greater accomplishments for the cause of history itself.

COLLECTING WAR RECORDS

Lewis Beeson

"WHAT IS the purpose of the local historical society?" asks a writer in the *Canadian Historical Review* for September, 1932. His answer

[1] *A Statewide Movement for the Collection and Preservation of Minnesota's War Records*, 3 (Minnesota War Records Commission, *Bulletins*, no. 1 — St. Paul, 1918).

is, "To preserve. That at least is the final object." There may be many other objectives, he declares, which are useful and helpful in themselves, "but their ultimate value will be determined solely by their contribution to the work of preservation. Before keeping, of course, there must be finding, and the tasks of scholarship lie in between."[1] Records of an event cannot be preserved until they are found. It is to the task of finding records in wartime to which my remarks relate — a task which may be, as Mr. Smith has remarked, "greater than we imagine" and one in which the state and local societies of Minnesota can co-operate.

How, then, can the local society best collect the war records of the community? Perhaps the first thing that will occur to the local historian is the collection of letters, diaries, and accounts of experiences written by the men of the community who are serving in the armed forces of the nation. Societies might compile lists and the service records of local men who have enlisted in the army, the navy, the marine corps, and the coast guard. The most numerous type of "war history" of the Civil, Spanish-American, and first World wars consisted of the rosters of the men who served in the armed forces, with an accompanying war narrative or memoir. This is the task which in the past has been of primary interest to local historians. It is still of great value. The desire to list and record the war services of men from the local community is understandable and commendable.

But the military contributions made by a community in the present war certainly will not represent the whole of its war activities. In modern warfare there is a civilian as well as military front, and the civilian front, as has been shown in Great Britain, may be as important as the military. Hence, the local historical society, if it wishes to fulfill properly its functions as the recording secretary of its community, should be as active in the collection of the records of civilian as of military organizations.

The collection of such records is not easy, for modern total war brings within its scope practically all the members of a community.

[1] Louis Blake Duff, "The Problems and Opportunities of Canadian Historical Societies," in *Canadian Historical Review*, 13:253.

New organizations, such as Bundles for Britain, Chinese War Relief, and Russian War Relief, will be formed, and new officials, like air-raid and blackout wardens and nurses aids, will be appointed. The records of their activities should be collected. Older organizations, such as the Red Cross, the Y.M.C.A., and others will experience an unparalleled expansion, with an extension of activities into every community. Existing civilian organizations, such as clubs, lodges, churches, chambers of commerce, and the like, will subordinate their peacetime programs to a wartime program. State and national governmental agencies will devote more and more of their energies to the war. The activities imposed upon these organizations by military needs should be of interest to the local historical society. When it is realized that civilian morale, civilian contributions to those who have suffered from military activity, civilian buying of government bonds, civilian restriction of purchasing, and civilian production of agricultural products and war materials are as important in the war effort as is the military organization, many other opportunities for the collecting of the records of war activities will be perceived.

The immensity of the war effort will produce a great mass of records in even the smallest community. The Minnesota Victory Aides, for instance, recently announced by Governor Stassen, will extend to each block and half township. One small phase of the local historical society's task will be the collection of such records of this organization as are available.

The task of collecting the war records for a county is a formidable one, but it is one in which much can be done by a few interested people. War records are divisible into two groups: the correspondence, minutes, membership rolls, financial accounts, and the like, of organizations, which are needed in the transaction of their business and which cannot be obtained until that business is completed; and material which can be collected currently. The first class includes the archives of state and federal agencies which are not available for collection by the local society, because they will be preserved in state or federal archives. Yet, should there be a member of a local society who is a camera enthusiast, it might be possible for him to obtain for the local society microfilm copies of much archival material of governmental and national organizations, such as the United Service Organizations. Incidentally, the preservation of other kinds of material through the use of films should not be overlooked. In the second class fall publicity releases, leaflets, pamphlets, posters, badges, instructions to workers, forms of all kinds, such as pledge cards, and many other classes of material. These records can and should be collected currently, for many of them will be lost if they are not collected as they are produced.

By beginning its collecting activities at once, the local society can make contacts that will result later in the acquisition of much valuable material. Every organization has records that it cannot release immediately, but if the officials of an organization know the wants of the local historical society and are kept acquainted with them, it is not improbable that all its records can be obtained when it closes its activities. Thus each war organization in the community should be made aware of the local historical society's desire to obtain its records when it is through with them. It is possible to interest a key person in each organization and to enlist his services in collecting material for the local historical society. Certainly a key person should be seen periodically by someone representing the society and reminded of its desire to preserve material.

The local newspapers will aid in determining which are the important organizations and who are the important people in each. Essential to keeping track of the war activities in the community is the newspaper itself. Furthermore, it is the most important single war record, and its files should be preserved. Read the newspapers with care to determine which are the strategic war organizations. By this I mean that certain organizations will have liaison functions. They will know what other organizations in the community are doing and who is leading their activities. The organizations with general functions are the important ones from the standpoint of collecting. Their officials can help the local society in its collecting activities; they will know what organizations and which people are important.

At present it seems that the Victory Aides will be among the important key persons in the whole defense set-up, for among their duties are learning the general facts of the defense program and activities in the locality, the state, and the nation, calling at all homes within their areas, listing and reporting all families having members in the armed forces, encouraging participation in the war program, and the like.

My purpose has been to indicate some of the possibilities for collecting war records that await the local historical society. The task is an enormous one. It is one that should be started now. It is one in which no one society can hope to obtain completeness. It is one in which much mutual benefit will result from co-operation among the societies of the state. The Minnesota Historical Society alone cannot adequately collect the multitudinous records of war activity that will be produced throughout Minnesota. In that undertaking the state and county historical societies must co-operate.

Bemidji: A Pioneer Community of the 1890's[1]

Harold T. Hagg

MORE THAN a century before the beginnings of permanent settlement at Lake Bemidji a fur-trading post was built on its shores. About 1785 it seems to have been located on the east side of the lake, then known as Lac Traverse. In 1832, however, when Henry R. Schoolcraft in search of the source of the Mississippi reached Lac Traverse, he found on the west shore, north of the entrance of the Mississippi, a "small, deserted long building." This was a minor trading station of the American Fur Company and was occupied in winter by a clerk of William Aitkin of Sandy Lake.[2] Although abandoned many years before the coming of settlers, the post indicated the importance of the site of the future community. Today a marker on the lake shore recalls the period when the region about the present Bemidji was part of the vast fur country of the Northwest.

The age of settlement did not begin until late in the nineteenth century. In 1890, Beltrami County, in which Lake Bemidji is located, was little more than a wilderness. The entire county, then much larger than it is now, had only 312 white inhabitants. Because of its location in the northern part of the state and the attendant isolation, the region was one of the last frontier areas in Minnesota. The first white settlers at Lake Bemidji were G. E. Carson and his brother M. E. Carson, who went there from Detroit Lakes in the spring of 1888. On the neck of land between Lake Bemidji and Lake Irving the brothers built a log trading house which for several years was

---

[1] A paper read before the luncheon session of the ninety-third annual meeting of the Minnesota Historical Society, at the Women's City Club of St. Paul on January 12, 1942. Ed.
[2] Grace Lee Nute, "Posts in the Minnesota Fur-trading Area, 1660–1855," ante, 11:369; Henry R. Schoolcraft, *Summary Narrative of an Expedition to the Sources of the Mississippi River,* 231 (Philadelphia, 1855); James Allen, *Expedition to Northwest Indians,* 31, 43 (23 Congress, 1 session, *House Executive Documents,* no. 323 — serial 257).

the only store in the region. Near by lived Chief Bemidji and his small band of Chippewa Indians. To meet the needs of Indians, hunters, loggers, timber cruisers, and scattered settlers, the Carsons carried on a diversified business. They sold a variety of merchandise, operated a blacksmith shop, shipped game, fish, furs, wild rice, and berries, and engaged in other lines of business as demands arose. Supplies for the trading house were hauled over the sixty miles of road running eastward from Fosston, which the railroad reached in 1888.[3]

With this enterprise as the nucleus and the trail from Fosston as the route of migration, settlement about the lake shores grew slowly. In the early 1890's Freeman Doud and Thomas Joy settled there, and they were followed in 1893 by Robert Carr, Willis Nye, and Alfonzo Godbout. These men, all of whom were native-born Americans, came from western Minnesota counties. Joy bought a tract of railroad land, but the others filed claims. In the meantime hunting and fishing parties visited the region, and their members gave descriptions of the country that helped advertise it and attract settlers.[4]

In 1894 the trickle of migration became a steady stream. More than forty families, about half of them Scandinavians, settled in the township during the year. Most of the newcomers came from the prairies of the Dakotas and western Minnesota. During the summer G. M. Carson, father of the Carson brothers, built a hotel, the "Bemidji House." Late in the year a post office was established in Carsons' store, with M. E. Carson as postmaster. In 1895 John Steidl built the first sawmill. From it came the lumber for the first frame building in the settlement—a hotel erected by J. F. Remore on what is now the northeast corner of Third Street and Beltrami Avenue. Soon the Carson brothers built a new store, also a frame structure, on the southwest corner of the same intersection. Another general merchandise store was opened by J. W. White. More settlers

[3] William W. Folwell, *A History of Minnesota*, 3:139, 251 (St. Paul, 1926); *United States Census, 1890, Population*, 195; *Hubbard County Enterprise* (Park Rapids), March 29, 1895. See also a report of an interview with G. E. Carson, in which he describes his first years in Bemidji, in the *St. Paul Dispatch*, June 8, 1926.

[4] *Thirteen Towns* (Fosston), February 2, 1894; *Enterprise*, March 29, 1895; Minnesota, *Fourth Decennial Census, 1895*, p. 77.

came, including a colony of Germans from Douglas and Otter Tail counties.[5]

Since village, township, and county organization were lacking, pioneer co-operation for common objects was essential. Roads were opened, bridges were built, and a schoolhouse was erected by the settlers themselves. Homestead claims, the arrival of land seekers, new business enterprises, and railroad rumors were topics of interest. Farmers were also teamsters, loggers, trappers, and day laborers. Anticipations of growth and development compensated for the hardships and limitations of frontier existence. Thus did life and work in the little pioneer community repeat the pattern of countless earlier American frontiers.

Social interests helped to relieve the tedium and monotony of everyday living. Occasional religious services were conducted by visiting ministers. Among them was the Reverend J. A. Gilfillan, the well-known Episcopal missionary to the Chippewa. Holidays were occasions for social gatherings and celebrations. The first community Christmas party, which took place in 1893, "was largely attended and much enjoyed," according to a contemporary account. "Each one received a present and the tree was splendidly decorated and well-filled." Independence Day was also awaited eagerly. On July 4, 1894, Bemidji "had a grand old fashion celebration," wrote a Park Rapids newspaper correspondent. "The national salute was fired at sun rise, picnicing was the order of the day," and it "ended with a grand ball at the Bemidji House." A year later patriotic enthusiasm found an outlet in a more varied program, which included a lake excursion and a baseball game between teams representing Bemidji and Moose. Early in 1896 a dramatic club was organized. It presented plays and entertainments and on at least one occasion journeyed to Park Rapids and gave a performance there.[6]

By April, 1896, the population of the settlement had increased to

[5] *Enterprise,* December 14, 1894, January 4, March 29, 1895. See also the reminiscences of Mrs. Nels Willett, who went to Beltrami County in 1895, in the *Bemidji Daily Pioneer,* November 26, 1927.

[6] *Thirteen Towns,* December 29, 1893; *Enterprise,* July 13, 1894, February 15, July 12, 1895, February 21, March 13, 1896. Moose was a post office west of Bemidji, within the present area of what is now Moose Creek Township in Clearwater County.

about two hundred. Business enterprises included two general stores, two hotels, a hardware store, a meat market, three or four blacksmith shops, a drugstore, a restaurant, a saloon, and several livery stables. There was one resident physician, Dr. J. P. Omich, proprietor of the Bemidji drugstore. Those requiring the services of a lawyer usually engaged one from Fosston or Park Rapids. In August, 1896, the pioneer church of Bemidji was organized by the Presbyterians. The Reverend Joseph Zoll, who became its pastor, was the first resident minister. Another sign of growth was the establishment of two weekly newspapers. The *Bemidji Pioneer* began publication in March, 1896, and the *Beltrami Eagle* a month later. The editors, typical frontier newspapermen, were enthusiastic boosters of Bemidji, and their newspapers radiated a spirit of optimism and confidence in its future. During the summer the settlement was incorporated as the village of Bemidji. Another spelling which often appeared in the early years was "Bermidji." According to some authorities the village was named in honor of Chief Bemidji. Recent investigation reveals, however, that both the settlement and the chief probably took their names from Lake Bemidji, which was known by a contraction of the Indian name "Bemidjigumag."[7]

A new factor in the development of the community was introduced by the organization of the Bemidji Townsite and Improvement Company. The company acquired title to about ninety acres of land on the west side of the lake and platted a townsite. In March, 1896, the plat was filed and the sale of lots began. The president of the company was Tams Bixby, a prominent figure in the Republican party, who was then secretary to Governor David M. Clough. A. C. Clausen, the secretary of the company, was chief grain inspector of Minnesota.[8] With influential officials and adequate finan-

[7] *Pioneer*, April 30, 1896, October 20, 1898, August 1, 1936; Warren Upham, *Minnesota Geographic Names*, 36 (*Minnesota Historical Collections*, vol. 17); J. A. Gilfillan, "Minnesota Geographical Names Derived from the Chippewa Language," in Geological and Natural History Survey of Minnesota, *Annual Report*, 1886, p. 460. For a record of the incorporation of the Presbyterian church, see the "Miscellaneous Records" of Beltrami County, vol. 1, p. 251, in the county archives preserved in the courthouse at Bemidji.

[8] *St. Paul Dispatch*, December 26, 1895; *Pioneer*, May 7, 1896; Clarence B. Douglas, ed., *Tams Bixby, 1855–1922*, 61–64 (n.p., n.d.).

cial resources, the company was an effective booster of Bemidji and it played an important part in the settlement's growth.

Until the coming of the railroads, the settlers were dependent on wagon roads for travel and transportation. The cost and difficulty of wagon freighting made it imperative to develop a route to the nearest railroad town. When the railroad reached a town that was still closer, another road was built to that point to take advantage of the shorter distance. The experience of the Bemidji region in developing roads was similar to that of earlier pioneer communities in opening routes to market. At first all supplies for the new settlement came over the sixty-mile trail from Fosston. Then in 1894 a road was opened to Park Rapids, situated about fifty miles south of Bemidji. This road afforded a closer outlet to the railroad and a relatively direct route from Minneapolis and St. Paul. But these advantages were partially offset by the poor condition of the road, and, although Park Rapids became the principal source of supplies, Bemidji merchants continued to obtain a considerable proportion of their goods from Fosston until 1897. In that year Walker began to compete for the business of forwarding supplies to Bemidji. Goods were shipped by steamboat to Steamboat Landing, south of Cass Lake, and then by wagon over the twenty-five miles of road to Bemidji. From 1894 until the railroad reached Bemidji in 1898, however, most of the goods came from Park Rapids.[9]

Over the routes described, freight wagons hauled supplies, and stagecoaches carried travelers and mail. "It is no uncommon occurrence for twenty or twenty-five loaded freight wagons to string into Bemidji from Park Rapids in one afternoon," reads a report in the *Bemidji Pioneer* for April 21, 1898. They contained "freight for railroad contractors, freight for storekeepers, and freight for immigrants." This traffic was an important element in the pioneer economy, giving employment to teamsters, blacksmiths, liverymen, and wagon repairers. Along the roads were "stopping places" where men

[9] Arthur J. Larsen, "Roads and the Settlement of Minnesota," *ante*, 21:240; *Enterprise*, February 2, March 9, July 27, December 14, 1894, March 15, 1895; *Pioneer*, May 14, June 25, 1896; *Beltrami Eagle*, May 21, June 4, August 20, 27, October 22, 1897; *Cass County Pioneer* (Walker), July 22, August 5, 1897.

and teams could be accommodated overnight on the two-day trips to Park Rapids and Fosston. In 1896 a semiweekly stage carried passengers and mail to and from Park Rapids. The stage left Bemidji at 6:30 A. M., "arriving at destination same day." Later three round trips were made each week, unless impassable roads prevented travel. Sometimes the wretched condition of the roads interrupted service for a week or longer. On one occasion high water forced the driver to abandon his stage at the Schoolcraft River and to take the mail the rest of the way by boat. In 1898 a stage left Bemidji three times each week for Fosston. The trip required a day and a half, with passengers spending the night at Bagley.[10]

With the growth of population came a need for county organization. Although Beltrami County was established in 1866, it was attached to Becker County for record and judicial purposes after 1871. In 1894, a board of three Beltrami County commissioners was appointed by the governor. The authority of this board was limited, however, and there were recurring difficulties with Becker County officials. Furthermore the trip to the Becker County seat at Detroit Lakes was long and inconvenient. The impatience characteristic of pioneers who were obliged to deal with a distant government that seemed to neglect their interests now developed among the citizens of Beltrami County. In 1896, therefore, a movement to organize the county was started. But the interests of the settlers, who desired roads, schools, and a more conveniently located county government, clashed with those of the pine-land owners, for whom organization would mean increased taxation. Only after a prolonged struggle in the legislature was an act organizing the county for all purposes passed in April, 1897. Restrictions were placed, however, on the amounts of indebtedness the county could incur and on the taxes it could levy. These limitations were irritating and unwelcome to the people of the county and were attributed by them to the influence of the pine-land owners.[11]

[10] *Pioneer*, April 30, May 14, 1896, June 30, 1898; *Eagle*, April 9, 23, July 23, 1897.
[11] William Anderson and Bryce E. Lehman, *An Outline of County Government in Minnesota*, 145 (Minneapolis, 1927); *St. Paul Pioneer Press*, March 20, 1897; *Pioneer*, April 15, 1897, October 20, 1898; *Eagle*, April 9, 1897.

Interest then centered on the location of the county seat. Bemidji and several other settlements were eager to obtain it. At a meeting of the board of county commissioners in June, 1897, representatives of Bemidji, Popple, Peterson Lake, and Buena Vista appeared in behalf of their respective communities. The board then voted to establish the county seat at Bemidji, the largest settlement in the county. This increased the prestige and importance of the village and added another factor to aid its growth. The townsite company donated a block of land for a courthouse, but the county board purchased a building for the purpose. Perhaps the motive for this step was to make a change in the location of the county seat more difficult.[12]

"Land-seekers are arriving daily," reported the *Eagle* in May, 1897. Like the earlier settlers most of them came from the prairie regions of the Dakotas and western Minnesota. Drawn by the opportunity to acquire free homesteads of a hundred and sixty acres, the newcomers erected rude log cabins and filed their claims at the Crookston land office. Until the land could be improved, however, subsistence rather than commercial farming prevailed. Timber for fuel and building purposes was plentiful, and to the foodstuffs grown on the farms fish and game could readily be added. But the farmers needed some cash income, and to obtain it they took advantage of available opportunities for part-time work. Some labored in logging camps, while others found employment in railroad construction. In the late summer many went to the Red River Valley to work in the harvest fields.[13]

In the village, activity was brisk during the summer and fall months of 1897. Lots were offered for sale by the townsite company at prices ranging from fifty to two hundred and fifty dollars. The first addition to the original townsite was platted and the lots were placed on sale at prices beginning at twenty-five dollars. To meet

[12] *Eagle,* August 20, 1897; *Pioneer,* October 20, 1898. See also the "Official Records" of the board of county commissioners for 1897, vol. 2, p. 52, 53, in the county archives at Bemidji.

[13] *Eagle,* May 28, June 4, August 13, 1897. Material on homesteading was drawn also from a series of typewritten interviews with old settlers, made available through the courtesy of Mr. H. Z. Mitchell of Bemidji.

the needs of the growing population, more houses and business buildings were erected, new streets were cleared, and a new bridge was built across the Mississippi. New business and professional opportunities were created and work became more specialized. The first bank was established. Another physician, Dr. D. B. Newman, and a lawyer, W. F. Street, became residents. Several new stores were opened, among them two dealing in general merchandise, one, in furniture, and another offering "a fine line of millinery" with "dressmaking done at reasonable rates." [14]

Late in June, 1897, the *Eagle* reported that "tourists have begun to arrive and already several parties are camped on the lake shore, boating, bathing, and fishing in our beautiful lake." Every summer since 1893, the recreational opportunities of the Bemidji region had attracted tourists from North Dakota and western Minnesota. The early tourist industry, though small, played a not unimportant role in developing the community. It made the village better known, and it brought visitors who patronized local business places. It also added another note to town boosting; a bright future for Bemidji as a vacation center was confidently predicted. [15]

Residents as well as visitors enjoyed play and sport. Boating was very popular. Sailboats appeared on the lake as early as 1894; four years later a steamboat accommodating two hundred passengers was launched. Like most communities, Bemidji was infected with the cycling craze of the 1890's. In 1897 a rifle club was organized and shoots were held regularly. Baseball games attracted enthusiastic spectators. Occasionally contests ended with both teams claiming victory. Typical was one played in August, 1897, between Bemidji and the Great Northern surveyors. The game was "very spirited," reported the *Eagle,* "and as the results were not very satisfactory another game will be played next Sunday." The principal winter sport was skating. [16]

[14] *Eagle,* April 23, October 15, 29, 1897.
[15] *Eagle,* June 25, July 9, 23, 1897; *Thirteen Towns,* July 21, 1893; *Enterprise,* July 13, 1894; *Crookston Daily Tribune,* August 6, 1895; *Pioneer,* December 1, 1898.
[16] *Enterprise,* July 27, 1894; *Eagle,* May 7, August 27, 1897; *Pioneer,* June 16, 1898; interview with Mr. Earl Geil of Bemidji.

Lodges and other organizations also served to occupy leisure time. The Modern Woodmen, organized locally in 1897, were soon followed by several other fraternal societies. The ladies' aid society of the Presbyterian church was probably the earliest women's organization. In 1897 a group of women founded the Up-to-Date Club. The program presented at a meeting held in October included the reading of selections from Pope, Emerson, Burns, and other authors. Civil government and Whittier were assigned as topics for the next meeting, and "the physical culture hour was a delight to all." [17]

During 1898 free land attracted another tide of incoming farmers. "There were more than 300 homesteads taken in Beltrami County last month," reported the *Pioneer* in April. "If anyone doubts the reality of Bemidji and Beltrami County he has to put in but one day at this end of the stage line." The growth of settlement increased the importance of Bemidji as a center of trade for the surrounding area. New business enterprises were established and more professional men arrived. During the summer the Baptists and the Methodists organized congregations and began holding regular services. A new school building — a two-story brick structure — was completed. By the fall of 1898 the population of the village had increased to about five hundred. [18]

Located on the Mississippi River and Lakes Bemidji and Irving, with the pine timber of southern Beltrami and northern Hubbard counties tributary to it, Bemidji was clearly destined to become an important logging and sawmilling center. The first sawmill, built in 1895 by John Steidl, had a daily capacity of twelve thousand feet, which was later increased to twenty-five thousand feet. Farmers hauled or drove logs to the sawmill, often receiving lumber in exchange. A smaller sawmill was located at the junction of the Mississippi and Schoolcraft rivers, about two miles southwest of Bemidji. In 1898 another sawmill was built in Bemidji. [19] But the develop-

[17] *Eagle,* April 23, September 3, 24, October 1, 1897.
[18] *Pioneer,* April 21, June 16, September 29, 1898.
[19] *Enterprise,* November 22, 1895; *Pioneer,* April 30, 1896, July 14, 1898; *Eagle,* April 9, 1897; interview with Mr. Geil.

ment of the lumber industry on a large scale awaited the coming of railroads. Until logs could be shipped to sawmills elsewhere or lumber to outside markets, logging and sawmilling operations were limited to meeting local needs.

In 1893 the Great Northern Railroad surveyed a route through Bemidji. But the hope of the settlers that actual construction would soon follow was disappointed. The prospects became even more discouraging in 1896, when a new survey placed the line two miles south of the village. Fortunately, however, another change was made and the route was again located through Bemidji. The Great Northern then began construction on an extension from Deer River westward to Fosston by way of Bemidji. During the summer of 1898, the approach of the railroad was perhaps a more absorbing topic of interest to the residents of the village than the Spanish-American War. On August 13 the first carload of freight was delivered in Bemidji. The first passenger train arrived on August 29, with James J. Hill, the Empire Builder, and other officials of the railroad on board. A contemporary newspaper records that "As the train crossed the Mississippi bridge, the occupants all took a platform view of the two lakes, and then the train stopped at the foot of Beltrami Avenue and took a good long look at the future Broadway of northern Minnesota. After that they moved westward at the rate of ten miles an hour." In the meantime construction of the Brainerd and Northern line northward from Walker was begun, and in December it was completed to Bemidji.[20]

With the building of the railroads, Bemidji's pioneer period ended. Stagecoaches and freight wagons no longer carried travelers and supplies over the rough roads from Park Rapids and Fosston. During the two years from 1898 to 1900 the population increased more than fourfold, a result mainly of the swift development of the lumber industry. Minnesota lumbering was shifting northward, and Bemidji, with railroad facilities available, rapidly became an important logging center. At first most of the logs were shipped to Brain-

[20] *Thirteen Towns,* December 29, 1893; *Cass County Pioneer,* October 4, 1896; *Pioneer,* May 5, August 18, September 1, December 8, 1898.

erd; soon, however, large sawmills were built in Bemidji. But the rise of the exciting and picturesque lumber industry should not be permitted to obscure the significance of the preceding decade of pioneer beginnings. Institutional foundations, the beginnings of agriculture and the tourist industry, the courage and optimism of the early settlers, and the location of the county seat constitute the heritage modern Bemidji received from the pioneer community of the 1890's.

The Minnesota Historical Society in 1941

Arthur J. Larsen

TWENTY-FOUR YEARS have passed since the Minnesota Historical Society moved into its present home. In 1918, as in the present, we were engaged in a bitter war, fighting for historic ideals, for the preservation of the democracy upon which this nation is founded — the democracy which, in the final analysis, is personified in institutions like the Minnesota Historical Society. Within the quarter century that has elapsed since those earlier war days, the society has experienced a rebirth. In that period it has developed into one of the great historical agencies of America.

The society's position for meeting the challenge of a wartime world is not unfavorable. The membership lists indicate that it is in a healthy condition, although it is not growing as rapidly as we think it should. During the year a total of 102 new members were enrolled and one member was reinstated. Forty-six members were lost by death, however, and 56 were dropped for nonpayment of dues. At the close of the year, the society had a grand total of 1,609 members of all kinds, a net gain of one over the figure for last year. It is an active and interested membership, and it has demonstrated its friendly appreciation of the society in numerous and unexpected ways.

During the triennium just past, there were several changes in the personnel of the society's executive council. Three valued members of the council elected in 1939 were lost through death — Mrs. E. B. Young of St. Paul, Mr. Nathaniel P. Langford of St. Paul, and the beloved pioneer of Olmsted County, Mr. Burt W. Eaton of Rochester. In their places, Miss Laura Furness of St. Paul, Mr. L. A. Rossman of Grand Rapids, and the secretary-superintendent were elected.

A number of well-attended meetings were held during the year. The annual meeting, on January 20, commemorated the centennial of the founding of the chapel from which St. Paul took its name. The luncheon session, which was attended by more than four hundred persons, featured addresses by Archbishop John Gregory Murray and Mrs. Grace Flandrau, who described various aspects of the development of the capital city. A morning session was devoted to local history problems, and in the afternoon informal groups continued the discussion. At the evening meeting a brilliant account of the musical Hutchinson family in Minnesota was presented by Professor Philip D. Jordan of Miami University at Oxford, Ohio. It was excellently illustrated by typical songs of the mid-nineteenth century, performed by students from Hamline University. The Minnesota Historical Society joined with the Hennepin County Historical Society in April to present Dean Theodore C. Blegen in an illustrated lecture on the upper Mississippi. The meeting, held in the auditorium of the Historical Building, was attended by more than two hundred people. In July the society made its usual annual summer tour, which, after a morning session in the Nerstrand Woods in Rice County, culminated in the observance, in conjunction with the Nicollet County Historical Society, of the ninetieth anniversary of the signing of the treaty of Traverse des Sioux. Luncheon and dinner meetings were held at St. Peter, and in midafternoon Governor Harold E. Stassen addressed an audience of more than five hundred persons on the treaty grounds at Traverse des Sioux State Park. About a hundred people made the entire trip. The final meeting of the year was held in the Historical Building on October 13, in connection with the fall meeting of the executive council. Before an audience of about two hundred, Mr. Dewey Albinson of Minneapolis spoke on "Indian Life and Customs at Grand Portage," and motion pictures of the Grand Portage country, filmed by Mr. Elmer Albinson, were shown.

The principal contact that the society has with the people of the state is through its publications. The year was conspicuous for the success with which the challenge of the reading public was met. The twenty-second volume of the society's quarterly magazine, *Minnesota History,* a book of 448 pages, exclusive of the index, was published during the year. The volume contains fifteen major articles or documents, thirty reviews of books of interest to Minnesotans, and 137 pages of notes about items of historical interest. Forty authors contributed to make this a highly successful volume. One reader comments on the "high quality of professional historical work" and the "sense of friendly and local humane interests" which he finds in the magazine; and the editor of a national historical periodical compliments the society in these words: "I feel that you are setting a very high standard in state historical magazines, and there are some who feel there is no superior. The articles are well written and edited and the local news carry considerable sparkle."

In June, as the result of the friendly interest of a member of the society, the scholarly yet popular *Voyageur's Highway,* of which Dr. Grace Lee Nute is the author, was published. The book was priced to meet a popular demand, it was attractively printed and bound, and abundantly illustrated. Its success was immediate, and the first printing of four thousand copies was exhausted within sixty days of its publication. More than half of a second printing of three thousand copies also has been sold. A reviewer described the book as "an example of what can be done when an able professional historian turns her hand to popularization."

For years the society has felt the need for a fund devoted to the publication of special studies on Minnesota history. With the appearance of the *Voyageur's Highway,* the special publications fund of the Minnesota Historical Society was inaugurated. The fund is small, but it is a nucleus upon which to build. Gifts or bequests, large or small, will be welcomed as an aid to augmenting the publication fund.

The society now has in press a volume of documents relating to the history of early missionary activities in the Northwest, for which Dr. Nute has prepared an introduction and annotations. This is the first volume in a series dedicated to the memory of Clarence W. Alvord, who is often regarded as the outstanding American historian of the first quarter of this century. Professor Alvord had many Minnesota connections. He served for a time as a member of the history faculty of the University of Minnesota, and he was an active member of the executive council of this society. Upon his death the

Mississippi Valley Historical Association created the Alvord Memorial Commission to raise funds for the publication of volumes of documentary materials relating to the history of the Mississippi Valley and adjoining areas. Representatives of the Minnesota Historical Society have been associated with this commission from the beginning, with Dr. Solon J. Buck, Dr. Lester B. Shippee, and, more recently, Dr. Nute serving as chairman of the body. When the commission decided to inaugurate its publication program by issuing the missionary documents, the society was asked to prepare the volume for publication, arrange for printing, and see it through the press, and the Alvord Memorial Commission agreed to pay all printing costs. In return for its services, the society will be able to grant its members a substantial discount on the book. The manuscript for this volume is now in the hands of the printer, and publication has been promised for early spring. The book is a fitting tribute to a distinguished American historian, and the society is proud to have a part in initiating this series.

Throughout the year, the society has continued to supply the newspapers of the state with news stories of Minnesota historical interest. Twelve issues of the monthly *Minnesota Historical News* were distributed to over six hundred newspapers. A publication that the society formerly issued periodically, the quarterly *Checklist of Minnesota Public Documents,* has been discontinued. Since most of the information contained therein is included in other lists, it seemed wise to conserve the slender resources of the society for more urgent needs. Accordingly, the last issue, which carried the listing through 1940, was published in March.

For a generation before Minnesota Territory was organized, Fort Snelling stood guard over a frontier subject to threat of attack by enemies, red and white. In the shelter of its gray walls the Minnesota of today was cradled. It is but fitting that the society should recognize the significance of this pioneer military establishment in the development of the Northwest. When, in 1939, a movement was begun for the preservation of the old Round Tower as a historical museum, the Minnesota Historical Society heartily endorsed the project. The work was completed in 1941, and the museum was opened in the spring. Under the terms of an agreement between the commanding officer at the fort and the society, the Minnesota Historical Society has accepted ownership of the furniture and equipment and responsibility for the exhibits. The Round Tower has become a second museum for the society and a historical shrine for the people of the state.

Attendance figures for the society itself reveal a growing appreciation of its resources, for their use by the public during 1941 reached proportions never before equalled. More than 40,000 visitors to the museum were recorded. In recent years, the figures of museum attendance have been characterized by steadily increasing numbers of school classes and groups. In 1941 a total of 508 such school groups with a membership of 15,034 teachers and children visited the museum — almost 3,000 more than in any previous year. It is evident that the society is being used as an educational aid for thousands of school children who are enabled to visualize Minnesota life and customs of the past in terms of the actual objects that Minnesotans used in their daily lives. In the library 6,307 readers used almost 30,000 books and other printed items. The newspaper department served the needs of 3,393 persons, who used 8,106 bound volumes of newspapers and more than 70,000 current, unbound issues. The figures for these departments are about normal. An unprecedented demand for public service occurred in the manuscript division, as 3,165 persons descended upon it. The figure represents an increase of almost 1,000 over the total recorded in 1940, and it is almost ten times as great as that for 1931. To a large extent, the enormous increase is explained by the need for affidavits and certificates of age, residence, and citizenship for purposes of employment in national defense industries, for draft registration, for old-age assistance, and for general employment and travel demands. In many instances the sole sources of such evidence are the manuscript census schedules, which are in the custody of the society.

Significant work in collecting materials relating to Minnesota history was done in 1941. The manuscript division reports the addition to its holdings of 209 collections of papers, many of which are of great importance. They are divided into two large groups, originals and filmslides, with the filmslides in general slightly more significant than the additions to original collections. Among the important Minnesota collections which were filmed during the past year should be mentioned fur trade papers of Richard Chute and David Olmsted in the Ewing collection at Fort Wayne, Indiana; the entire Joseph N. Nicollet collection in the Library of Congress; the diary of a member of the Cass expedition of 1820, in private hands at Detroit; and the Flandrau Papers in the Indian office archives in Washington. Among important collections of original papers acquired during the year should be included the Civil War letters of Knute Nelson, the Henry Teigen collection, the papers of Charles L. Bartholomew, a Minneapolis cartoonist who was known as "Bart," the William Dean and Nathaniel P. Langford collections, and the papers of T. B. Sheldon and Company of Minneapolis, and important additions to the Lynn Haines and Sibley papers. Among records of organizations acquired are the papers of the Business Women's Holding Company of Minneapolis and an official list of Granges in Minnesota. Important products of the research of graduate students received in the manuscript division include a study of the Czechs in Minnesota and a history of agriculture in the state to 1885.

The library's search for items of historical interest resulted in the addition of 1,887 books and 678 pamphlets, about sixty-one per cent of which were received as gifts. In 1929, a far-seeing member of the society — Herschel V. Jones — established a trust fund the income from which was to be used for the acquisition of rare books, pamphlets, and papers, and for photographic reproductions of such materials. This has often proved a godsend to the society, and its usefulness has been demonstrated again this year. The filmslide copies of materials mentioned in the accessions of the manuscript division were obtained through the use of this fund, and it enabled the library to add to its collections such items as David W. Cartwright's *Natural History of Western Wild Animals,* published in 1875, M. Bell Irvine's *Report on the Red River Expedition of 1870,* a rare atlas of Ramsey County, an unusual book relating to the outlawed James brothers, and a report of the Minneapolis, Sault Ste.

Marie and Atlantic Railway Company for 1885, hitherto not represented in the society's library. Several years ago, a number of organizations began donating to the society books of more than ordinary interest, or funds for their purchase. From chapters of the Daughters of the American Revolution, the United Daughters of the Confederacy, the Colonial Dames, and other groups, important books have again been made available to the reading public. The society gratefully acknowledges the kindness of these friends.

Several hundred gifts representing many more than that number of publications poured into the newspaper department during the year. Of outstanding importance were such gifts as a file of the *Milan Standard,* covering the first three years of that paper's history, a valuable collection of Kenyon and Nerstrand newspapers, and a great mass of newspapers presented by Northwest Publications of St. Paul.

Gifts received for the society's museum have numbered 684. Their importance is great. Among them should be mentioned the interesting collection of American smoothbore muskets and rifles dating from 1834 to the present, received from Major Austin Corpe of Fort Snelling, which has been placed on display in the Fort Snelling Round Tower Museum. A large number of costumes and accessories, unusual pioneer household tools, reminders of the past wars in which the nation has engaged, and a striking collection of ecclesiastical and academic robes and honorary degree hoods that belonged to Bishop Henry B. Whipple are but a few of the gifts. The latter collection was presented by Whipple's granddaughters, Mrs. J. W. Burt and Mrs. B. W. Scandrett of St. Paul. Another interesting costume was used by a Lutheran clergyman; it consists of a coat, vest, and ruff, and was presented by Dean Blegen. Items reminiscent of the earliest days of Minnesota are represented in a gift received from members of the family of Colonel Josiah Snelling. It includes a silver watch, a silver mourning ring worn by Mrs. Snelling, and Snelling's commission as a lieutenant in the United States Army dated in 1808. The fur trade and Indian collections were enriched by the addition of such articles as an Assomption fur trade sash and an unusual painted elkhide robe. By far the most extensive gift of the year was the tremendous collection of pictures from the library of the *St. Paul Daily News*. It includes some seventy-five thousand pictures and about twenty thousand mats. Sorting and arranging them has taken most of the time of three people during the past nine months.

The staff of the society has diligently continued to make its facilities available to the public. The newspaper department has kept up with its current work and has assimilated all the major gift collections. The library, despite loss of time through illnesses and leaves of absence, has kept its work creditably up to date. In the museum much time has been spent on indexing pictures and other additions to the collections. Nevertheless, forty-eight special exhibits were arranged. One new miniature group, depicting a Lake Minnetonka summer scene in the 1880's, has been completed and installed. Special loan exhibits were made available for several business houses, and during the summer and fall the society co-operated with the Minneapolis Institute of Arts and the St. Paul Gallery and School of Art in presenting special exhibits of Minnesota art at these institutions. The manuscript division, which has experienced unprecedented expansion of its services to the public, has by strenuous effort and earnest application of its staff pushed its work of cataloguing and inventorying collections. It was even able to catalogue a collection of six hundred photostats of French maps, a task that required much time as well as a considerable knowledge of French, both old and modern.

Since 1919 the society has been custodian of the noncurrent state archives. An amendment to the Archives Law by the 1941 legislature widely extended the authority of the society over state and local archives and greatly increased its responsibilities. The amended law establishes standards for making and caring for public records, and it makes legal provision 'for copying, by photographic processes, records which are in danger of destruction through usage. It is of importance in this connection that the society has the duty of recommending the kind of photographic device that is to be used. Another noteworthy feature of the law is the provision for the regulated destruction of noncurrent, useless records under the supervision of the Minnesota Historical Society. Although the law adds to the work of the society, the new responsibility is accepted gladly, for it makes possible the regulation of permanent state and local records, a task which in future years will assume great importance.

Another law passed in 1941 which affects the society is that creating a Historic Sites and Markers Commission. Under its provisions, a commission composed of the director of state parks, the commissioner of highways, and the superintendent of the Minnesota Historical Society, or their representatives, is entrusted with supervising the erection of markers on historic sites in Minnesota.

The Historical Records Survey, under the direction of Mr. Jacob Hodnefield, has continued its record of substantial achievement. Thirteen inventories of county archives were published during the year, and progress was made on others. The results of the surveys in forty of Minnesota's eighty-seven counties have now been published.

During 1941 the WPA projects under the supervision of the society were reorganized. The work of the Historical Records Survey project was to continue as it had for the past several years, but arrangements were made for setting up two new projects, each of which was to assume specific tasks. A Historical and Archaeological Research Survey Project was organized to carry on research work in specialized fields under the co-sponsorship of the society, the department of state parks, the highway department, and the department of anthropology in the University of Minnesota. Its work was closely correlated with that of the Historic Sites and Markers Commission. Toward the close of the year, plans were made for the establishment, as a part of the Minnesota Art Project, of a state-wide museum assistance project under which not only the Minnesota Historical Society, but local societies throughout the state, would be able to do work not allowed under old WPA projects. The latter project has not yet gotten under way. Should the war bring about a cancellation of its plans, there is still a framework for a logically planned program of relief work to put into operation if the need for it arises.

Despite the pressure of work in an unusually busy year, members of the staff have actively engaged in research and other professional activities. They gave fifty-three addresses before groups whose membership was diverse and numerous. They prepared for publication in the society's quarterly and other journals numerous articles and reviews of books. They served on important committees of scholarly organizations, and two staff members taught history courses in Hamline University and the University of Minnesota. A number of changes in personnel have occurred during the year. The great burden of work in the manuscript division necessitated the addition of an extra worker to care for requests for census information. Miss Beatrice Edgar was assigned to that task, and Miss Phyllis Sweeley was employed as manuscript assistant. Mrs. Louise Blad, assistant in the museum, resigned her position in February, and Miss Henrietta Berge, who had been employed as stenographer in the library, was promoted to the position in the museum. Miss Rhoda Christensen was employed to take the place of Miss Berge. In the catalogue department, Miss June Day was granted a leave of absence for graduate work at the university. Miss Harriett Palin was employed temporarily to perform her work, but illness forced her to resign at the end of the year. In the general office, Mrs. Gladys Upham, office stenographer for the past several years, resigned on October 1, and her place was taken by Mrs. Florence K. Trelogan. Finally, it is with great regret that I announce that Miss Mary E. Palmes, who so faithfully has served as chief clerk for more than a quarter of a century, resigned her position on January 1. Members of both the executive council and the staff have been privileged to enjoy her friendship and the society as a whole has derived great benefit from her services through the years.

The legislature in its 1941 session appropriated $32,520 for salaries for each year of the biennium, and $13,000 for supplies. The total appropriations do not compare unfavorably with those for the previous biennium. The appropriations for materials and supplies, however, were reduced by $1,000 per year, and those for salaries were increased by $1,020 per year. Rising prices make the appropriation for supplies scarcely adequate to cover the society's minimum needs.

At the end of the calendar year, the society is faced with the problem of adjusting itself to the changed conditions of wartime. In a world at war, its work has assumed a new gravity, and it is facing new problems. It is in institutions like the Minnesota Historical Society that we find reflected the development of American culture. Such institutions personify America and, through the re-creation of the past, give life and meaning to American civilization. Especially in a wartime world the Minnesota Historical Society and kindred organizations must take the lead in conserving the cultural resources of our civilization. In doing so, the society can also aid actively in the wartime functions of the nation, for a knowledge of history, which, in time of peace is a useful tool, in time of war becomes a powerful weapon.

The 1942 Annual Meeting of the Minnesota Historical Society

Mary W. Berthel

THE NINETY-THIRD annual meeting of the Minnesota Historical Society on January 12 opened at 9:30 A. M. with the twenty-second annual conference on local history work in Minnesota, which was attended by about fifty people. Judge Julius Haycraft, vice-president of the society, who acted as chairman, recalled that he had presided also at the conference twelve years ago, in 1930, when there were only twenty local historical societies in the state. Now, he was happy to report, there are about sixty-five. He then introduced the first speaker, Mr. Harold W. Lathrop, director of Minnesota State Parks, who spoke on "The Historic Sites and Markers Commission of Minnesota." In explaining the need for such a commission, which was created by the legislature in 1941, Mr. Lathrop said that "the practice of commemorating historical events and marking historic sites had grown up and had remained a very haphazard process in Minnesota"; for there had been no general program, and no central organization to unify and direct activities. The result was "much confusion, some errors, some wasted effort, and even a certain amount of actual harm." It was not intended, he said, that the commission should replace quasi-public and private organizations that have been active in marking historic sites, but rather, that it should correlate, unify, and supervise their efforts, and give them aid. To indicate the nature of the commission's work, he reviewed briefly some of the actions taken since its organization in June, 1941, and outlined its policies and procedure.

Judge Haycraft commended the legislature for its action creating the commission and mentioned, as an example for the need of the guidance of such a body, a monument marking the site of old Fort Britt, which was originally placed a mile south of the actual site of the fort. Judge Haycraft himself dug it up and had it put in its proper place. The next speaker on the program, Miss Bertha L. Heilbron, assistant editor of *Minnesota History,* described and compared local historical collections in the state which she has visited during the past few years, and pointed out the importance of local historical museums in helping to maintain national morale in the present crisis. Miss Heilbron's paper, under the title "Local Historical Museums and the War Program," is printed in this issue of *Minnesota History.*

After mentioning some museums that are not so well kept as those just described, the chairman introduced Edward Blomfield, executive secretary of the Hennepin County Historical Society, who discussed "A Publication Program for the Local Historical Society." Mr. Blomfield related some of the experiences of the Hennepin County society in its attempts to obtain publicity, and stressed the importance of the newspaper in a publication program for a county historical society. The Hennepin County society's first publication, which described the organization of the society, its purpose, and the collecting of articles for its museum, was written for the Minneapolis Centennial in 1939. "Thus," said Mr. Blomfield, "in taking advantage of an important event in the history of Minneapolis, it helped us to become better known." In the speaker's opinion, "the best method of acquainting the public with the activities of a local society" is "the bulletin," which can be made "a medium not only to impart information to its members, but also to influence the community of which it becomes a part." He mentioned the various types of materials that have been included in *Hennepin County History: A Quarterly Bulletin,* which was first issued by his society in April, 1941, and pointed out other materials that might be used appropriately in such a publication.

The role of the local historical society in a democracy at war was the subject discussed by the next speaker, Mr. G. Hubert Smith, supervisor of the museum unit of the Minnesota Art Project, whose paper also appears in the present issue of this magazine. Following Mr. Smith's paper, the chairman opened the meeting to discussion, calling first upon Mr. Willoughby M. Babcock, curator of the state

society's museum. Mr. Babcock agreed with Mr. Smith's assertion
that local historical activities should be increased in wartime, and
suggested that a large part of the work of collecting day-by-day
evidences of war activities could be done by county historical societies, which might perhaps work out special committees consisting of
their entire memberships. The discussion was continued by Dr.
Lewis Beeson, head of the newspaper department of the society. Mr.
Beeson, whose remarks are printed in earlier pages of this issue of
Minnesota History, pointed out specific records of war activities
that should be collected by local historical societies and made some
valuable suggestions as to the means of securing these records. In
the audience was Mr. S. S. Beach, president of the McLeod County
Historical Society, who remarked upon the importance of preserving copies of local newspapers; he had found, he said, nothing of
such great value about the past of his community as what he had
learned from the files of local papers.

The recent formation of a Minnesota committee for the conservation of cultural resources, with Dean Theodore C. Blegen as chairman, was announced by Dr. Arthur J. Larsen, superintendent of the
state society. He pointed out that the pressure of war activities produces many changes in American life, and stressed the need for care
lest the tangible reminders of the past be destroyed. He mentioned
the drive for the collection and conservation of wastepaper and of
iron, and he cautioned against including in collections of such discarded material papers or objects of historical value. After brief
remarks by Mr. Henry N. Benson of St. Peter and Mr. Victor E.
Lawson of Willmar, members of the state society's executive council,
the conference was brought to a close.

About a hundred and thirty members and friends of the society
attended the luncheon session, which was held at the Women's City
Club in St. Paul. The chairman of the meeting was the president of
the society, Mr. Ira C. Oehler, who expressed his satisfaction that
the audience was so representative of the society's membership. Mr.
Oehler first introduced Colonel Frank W. Matson, who presented
to the society, on behalf of the grand lodge of Masons in Minnesota,
copies of photographs of all the men who have been grand masters

in the state. These photographs are a part of the material that is being collected for the centennial of the organization of the grand lodge, which will occur in a few years. In accepting the photographs for the historical society, Mr. Oehler commended to other groups in the state the example set by the grand lodge of Masons. He then called upon Mr. Harold T. Hagg, professor of history at the Bemidji State Teachers College, whose paper on "Bemidji: The Story of a Frontier Minnesota Community" traced the early settlement and development of one of the last frontier areas of the state. This interesting presentation of a bit of regional history may be found elsewhere in the present issue of this magazine.

In introducing Dr. Grace Lee Nute, curator of manuscripts of the historical society, Mr. Oehler spoke of her latest book, *The Voyageur's Highway,* which, he noted, has done much to popularize history in Minnesota. It was on that subject — "Popularizing Minnesota History" — that Dr. Nute spoke. It had been her experience, she told the audience, that practically everyone is interested in local history; but, she continued, "everything depends upon the way it is presented." She went on to suggest a few of the regions in Minnesota that are waiting to have their stories told by someone who can tell them "simply and skillfully and entertainingly" — in such a way as to make the past of these regions live for the reader. The route of Highway 61, from its entrance to the state at La Crescent to the Canadian boundary near old Grand Portage, the Minnesota Valley, the Red River Valley, the iron ranges, Lake Minnetonka, the Root and Sauk river valleys, and the valley of the St. Croix were some of the regions that she would like to see treated historically as units. And in connection with each of these regions she gave her listeners glimpses of some of the fascinating people and events that had been part of its past. After thanking Dr. Nute, Mr. Oehler spoke of the advantage of placing historical records that are worthy of preservation — records such as the photographs presented by Colonel Matson — in a safe, fireproof building like that of the historical society.

The afternoon session, which was held in the auditorium of the Historical Building, was called to order at 3:00 P. M. by Mr. Oehler, who presided. About sixty-five people were in the audience. Annual reports were read by the treasurer of the society, Julian B. Baird of St. Paul, and by the secretary and superintendent, Mr. Larsen, and the following thirty members of the society were elected to serve as members of the executive council during the triennium 1942–45: Dr. John M. Armstrong, Julian B. Baird, Henry N. Benson, Theodore C. Blegen, William H. Bovey, Kenneth G. Brill, Ralph Budd, the Reverend William Busch, Homer P. Clark, the Reverend James Connolly, William W. Cutler, Bert Fesler, Grace Flandrau, Guy Stanton Ford, Laura Furness, Edward C. Gale, Julius E. Haycraft, Louis W. Hill, Jr., Jefferson Jones, August C. Krey, Arthur J. Larsen, Victor E. Lawson, Albert J. Lobb, Andrew J. Newgren, Ira C. Oehler, L. A. Rossman, Lester B. Shippee, Charles Stees, Royal S. Stone, and Dr. Harry B. Zimmermann. Later in the afternoon the council met in the superintendent's office and elected the following officers: Lester B. Shippee, president; Julius E. Haycraft and Kenneth G. Brill, vice-presidents; Julian B. Baird, treasurer; and Arthur J. Larsen, secretary.

At the close of the business meeting, Mr. Richard R. Sackett, director of the Minnesota State-wide Archaeological and Historical Research Survey Project, spoke to the audience on "The Lac qui Parle Mission." After sketching briefly the colorful career of Joseph Renville, the trader who established Fort Renville at Lac qui Parle, and describing the work of the missionaries Williamson, Huggins, Riggs, Pond, and others who served there with the Sioux, Mr. Sackett traced the history of the efforts — in particular the efforts of the Chippewa County Historical Society — to preserve the site of the mission and to restore the chapel. The speaker commended the splendid work accomplished by the Chippewa County society in preserving for the people of the state a site so important historically.

Nearly five hundred people assembled in the auditorium of the Minnesota Museum of Natural History on the campus of the University of Minnesota at 8:00 P.M. for the program of the evening session. At this session, which was arranged under the sponsorship of the department of history of the university, the newly elected president of the society, Dr. Shippee, presided. Because his absence from the city made it impossible for the university's president, Dr.

Walter C. Coffey, to attend the meeting, he wrote a letter of greeting to the historical society, which was read by the chairman. Mr. Shippee then introduced Dr. Blegen, dean of the graduate school of the university, who addressed the audience on "The Minnesota Historical Society and the University of Minnesota." This address, which dealt with the tradition of close co-operation between the university and the historical society — a co-operation based upon an identity of ideals — is published in full in the first pages of this issue of *Minnesota History*. With the showing of "Minnesota Document," a motion picture of episodes in Minnesota history from 1863 to the present, which was produced at the University of Minnesota by the visual education service, the annual meeting was brought to a close.

Some Sources for Northwest History

RAILROAD ARCHIVES

Richard C. Overton

BENEATH TWO MAPS entitled "The Revolution in Rail Transportation, 1860–1890" in his *Political and Social Growth of the United States, 1852–1933,* A. M. Schlesinger declares: "The history of the time might almost be written in terms of railways." In the social and economic sense this statement is particularly true in regard to the Northwest. Although it was possible to establish a lumber industry in this region on the basis of river and lake transportation, the large-scale cultivation of grain, the development of mining, and the growth of the dairy business awaited the coming of the railroad.[1] A comparison of maps showing the railways on the one hand and the density of population on the other during the latter part of the nineteenth century reveals the striking correlation between railroad construction and the development of the Northwest.[2] In those days civilization followed the rails; it was perhaps inevitable that the railroads then, and for a long time thereafter, determined the economic and social life of the region.

This phenomenon, familiar to all students of the Northwest, has been often and ably described in historical writing. Frederick Jackson Turner, for example, sketched its broad outlines and general implications in the *International Monthly* for December, 1901.[3] Frederick Merk discussed and analyzed certain economic and political phases of the situation in his illuminating *Economic History of Wisconsin during the Civil War Decade* (1916). "The Colonization Work of the Northern Pacific Railroad," written for the *Mis-*

---

[1] See, for example, William J. Wilgus, *Railway Interrelations of the United States and Canada,* 122 (New Haven, 1937). Schlesinger's book appeared in 1934.

[2] Such maps for 1840–80, inclusive, drawn on the same scale, may be found in the writer's *Burlington West,* 12, 24, 190, 310, 394 (Cambridge, 1941).

[3] Turner's article is reprinted in his volume on *The Frontier in American History,* 126–156 (New York, 1920). See especially p. 143–153.

sissippi Valley Historical Review of December, 1926, by James B. Hedges, drew attention to the significant role played by one company in the direct settlement of the Northwest, and incidentally suggested the wealth of source material that might be available to the historian. In 1939 the same author presented, in *Building the Canadian West,* his full-length study of the Canadian Pacific's colonization work north of the border. Approaching the subject from a fresh angle, William J. Wilgus emphasized the international significance of the northwestern roads in an informative chapter of the *Railway Interrelations of the United States and Canada,* published in 1937. A valuable and detailed corollary to the two latter authors was provided in 1939 by Leonard B. Irwin's *Pacific Railways and Nationalism in the Canadian-American Northwest, 1845–1873.* Furthermore, colorful sidelights have been thrown on the subject by many a biography, including such well-known works as Walter Vaughan's *Life and Work of Sir William Van Horne* (1920), Hedges' *Henry Villard and the Railways of the Northwest* (1930), and Henrietta M. Larson's *Jay Cooke: Private Banker* (1936). These are but a very few of the studies concerned with the northwestern roads, yet they suggest the richness of the subject, the possible diversity of treatment, and the unexploited wealth of source material that is available.

Public sources for the writing of railroad history, such as newspapers, trade publications, local and federal government documents, and the like, are familiar to investigators in the field. It is the specific purpose of this paper to consider the primary records that are in the possession of the railroad companies themselves.

The heart and core of railroad archives are the corporate records which are usually under the jurisdiction of the secretary. These include charters, minutes of directors' and stockholders' meetings, annual and special reports, land-grant records (if any), contracts, corporate leases and deeds, and other material of a more or less permanent character. Surveys, maps, topographical data, records of construction, and in general all material pertaining to buildings, roadbed, bridges, ties, and rail are located in the engineering department. A record of the original physical properties, modified and kept up to date by subsequent inventories, together with information concerning the cost and value of facilities, are also in this department, which in turn is usually a part of the operating department. Since the operating department is also in charge of transportation, maintenance, and labor relations, and is thus the largest department of any railroad, its records are correspondingly voluminous. They cover, for example, such matters as train operations, upkeep, reclamation, equipment (including motive power), tests and research, shops, labor contracts, safety, and so forth.

The traffic department keeps records of traffic, rates, revenues, and service, and usually includes within its jurisdiction the agricultural and industrial development bureaus. The latter carry on, under modern conditions, whatever colonization may have been undertaken in earlier days; in their files are records of agricultural and technological demonstrations and of current community development. In many organizations all publicity and advertising originates in the passenger traffic division of the traffic department, although in some cases public relations are segregated and handled directly by the executive department. In any case, these publicity agencies generally have extensive information, including maps and photographs, concerning the history and current operations of the road. This material, however, may not be strictly primary in nature, having been derived from corporate, operating, or traffic source records.

The history of corporate financing is centered in the treasury department, although the law department, which participates in preparing contracts, mortgages, and equipment trusts, has nearly as much material on the same subject. The law department likewise has records of all cases in which the company has participated, both in the courts and before administrative agencies. This material covers a wide range of subjects, including construction, abandonment, unification, operation, finance, claims, and so forth. A land and tax department, in some companies organized within the law department, keeps right-of-way records and handles current real-estate and tax matters. It works in close collaboration with the agricultural and industrial development bureaus.

Vital statistics and service records concerning employees are located in the employment, personnel, or relief departments, while health records are kept in the medical department. Statistics for the entire operation of the railroad, as well as income and balance sheet records and accounts, are in the accounting department; records of purchases of company material are usually located in a separate department of purchases and stores. For matters of general policy there are the records of the executive department.

It should be pointed out, however, that various departments may contain supplementary records on the same subject. Therefore, even within the relatively restricted range of company archives, it may be necessary to look in several places for material concerning various phases of the same subject.

In addition to its permanent records, each department has, of course, voluminous files of correspondence. These, under section 20 of the Interstate Commerce Act, must be preserved for a varying number of years according to their contents.[4] Frequently, however, correspondence that may have some continuing value to the company is kept longer than the required period and may be stored with the permanent records. Inquiry would probably reveal that most companies have somewhere more than one basement or old freight house choked with what may be potentially significant historical material. On the other hand, many records of undoubted value from the historian's standpoint have been destroyed, pursuant to law, because of their lack of value for current railroad purposes.

Direct access to railroad archives depends primarily upon the judgment of the officers of each particular road. Most company archives contain material that is sufficiently technical in nature to require a trained man for its proper investigation, and it is not always easy for a company to ascertain an investigator's capabilities. Probably the best approach for the historian is to submit some evidence of his ability and to make his request as specific as possible.

In closing, a word of caution to the would-be writer of railroad

[4] Association of American Railroads, *Regulations to Govern Destruction of Records of Steam Roads Prescribed by the Interstate Commerce Commission* (Washington, 1938).

history may be ventured. Most historical writing tends to follow a chronological pattern, but generally speaking the distinctions between different phases of railroading and between the railroad history of different regions are clearer, both in fact and in available material, than are those between the events of specific years or decades. Consequently, there is much to be said for organizing a railroad study primarily along analytical or geographical lines, although within such limits the various homogeneous subdivisions may and probably should be treated chronologically.

When it comes to choosing a specific topic for investigation in such a broad and colorful field as railroad history, the greatest temptation is the common one of undertaking too much. The history of railroads is often of a controversial nature, thus requiring the conscientious historian to examine a wide range of sources, both public and private, before he can arrive at a sound conclusion on even relatively minor points. It is, therefore, obviously desirable at the outset to fix as definite limits as possible to any given study and to keep in mind its relation to other aspects of the general subject. Otherwise the green and tempting field of railroad research may turn into a dark and impenetrable morass.

Reviews of Books

Hennepin's Description of Louisiana: A Critical Essay. By JEAN DELANG-
LEZ, S.J., Ph.D., assistant professor of history, Loyola University,
Chicago. (Chicago, Institute of Jesuit History, 1941. viii, 164 p.
$2.70.)

Several years ago the Minnesota society of the Colonial Dames of
America published a popular translation by Miss Marion E. Cross of
Hennepin's *Description of Louisiana.* In an introduction to this translation Dr. Grace Lee Nute of the Minnesota Historical Society gave the
reader a glimpse of the intrigues and rivalries which permeated court
and even ecclesiastical circles in Hennepin's time. Now comes a book
on Hennepin of a different kind, written by Professor Jean Delanglez,
assistant professor of history in Loyola University, Chicago, and published under the auspices of the Institute of Jesuit History. Professor
Delanglez entitles his work "A Critical Essay." It might well be entitled
"A Very Critical Essay." It leaves the impression that the author is not
entirely free from the ancient prejudices, not to say animosities, of the
Jesuits toward the Franciscan order, to which Hennepin belonged. The
spirit of the book may be judged by the author's quotation from Tonty,
La Salle's faithful companion, that "Hennepin was insupportable to the
late M. de la Salle and to all of M. de la Salle's men. He sent him to the
Sioux to get rid of him."

Nevertheless, it must be acknowledged that the author has marshaled
a rather impressive accumulation of evidence to prove his main thesis —
that Hennepin was guilty both of wholesale plagiarism in his *Description of Louisiana,* published at Paris in 1683, and of claiming falsely in
his later *New Discovery* (1697) that he preceded La Salle down the
lower Mississippi. Professor Delanglez sets out to prove by "deadly
parallel" and other internal evidence that approximately the first two-
thirds of the *Description of Louisiana,* narrating the events of La Salle's
expedition to the time when Hennepin left La Salle at Fort Crévecœur
for the journey up the Mississippi, were taken bodily from the *Relation
des descouvertes et des voyages du sieur de la Salle,* compiled by the
Abbé Claude Bernou from the letters and notes of La Salle in 1682
and only discovered in recent years in the Archives du Service Hydro-

graphique in Paris. As if this were not enough, the author also endeavors to show that the remainder of Hennepin's *Description of Louisiana,* describing in detail the voyage up the Mississippi "on his own" as a narrator, is so crude in style, so confused and at times contradictory, that it is very evident that the narration is not by the same person who wrote the first two-thirds of the work.

The author further, and perhaps outside the main argument, discusses the sources of Hennepin's map, his nomenclature of the Great Lakes, and his names of the various Sioux tribes, all of which seems to confirm in the author's mind the general conclusion that Hennepin is not entirely trustworthy in his details. One outstanding fact, however, Professor Delanglez is unable to question or refute. Hennepin did actually make the voyage up the Mississippi. So far as is known, he kept no journal and few, if any, notes. His account of the journey must have been chiefly, if not entirely, from memory, colored, it may be, by a more or less harmless egotism. If Hennepin's narration differs in detail from La Salle's, one may well ask, where did La Salle get his account of Hennepin's journey as given in Bernou's *Relation?* La Salle was not of the party, nor is it known that he ever met Hennepin again after they parted company at Fort Crévecœur in the spring of 1680. He must have gotten his account either from one or the other of Hennepin's two companions, both of whom were more or less illiterate, or possibly in part from Du Lhut; and how accurate may that be?

In conclusion, this reviewer ventures to remark that, while the effect of Professor Delanglez' studies may be rather damaging to Hennepin's already somewhat tarnished reputation as a narrator of personal experiences, nevertheless many of us who live in the sight and sound of the Falls of St. Anthony and in the county bearing Hennepin's name have to confess to at least a secret sympathy with and admiration for the colorful and intrepid missionary-priest, Father Hennepin.

EDWARD C. GALE

The Crisis of 1830–1842 in Canadian-American Relations. By ALBERT B. COREY. (New Haven, Yale University Press, for the Carnegie Endowment for International Peace, Division of Economics and History, 1941. xi, 203 p. Maps. $3.50.)

To most Americans in the 1830's the eventful acquisition of British North America by annexation or conquest was a current assumption.

"Everywhere to the north," writes Professor Corey, "there spread the shadow if not the substance of the British lion, clearly not a welcome beast while the eagle was still sprouting feathers and growing talons." A flurry of rebellion in the two Canadas in 1837 was viewed consequently as the harbinger of a second American Revolution. In general, Americans then chose the role of neutrality, content to let the ripe fruit fall. But not so the frontiersmen of our northern border from New Hampshire to Michigan; inactive and restive because of poor crops and the current depression, they promoted filibustering expeditions to assist the supposedly oppressed Canadians.

Neither the United States nor Great Britain had the least desire for war, but the hotheads and jingoes on both sides of the Canadian-American boundary did much to bring it near. Border incidents, like the destruction of the "Caroline" in 1837, a renewal of filibustering, the "Arostook War" of 1839, and the trial of McLeod in 1841, raised questions of national prestige and honor that pitted the two great Anglo-Saxon nations squarely against one another. That Great Britain in 1838 sent the liberal-minded and conciliatory Earl of Durham to Canada to diagnose colonial ills was doubly fortunate. He wrote an admirable prescription for self-government in Canada and he made friendly contacts with Washington that did much to lessen the tension in Anglo-American affairs. General Winfield Scott, often using persuasion in lieu of power, also did his part to preserve peace along the troubled border. Happily the accession of new administrations in the United States and Britain in 1841 paved the way for direct negotiations between Secretary of State Daniel Webster and Lord Ashburton which led to the famous treaty of 1842.

In this reviewer's opinion Professor Corey has produced a scholarly and well-documented study that makes a notable contribution to the series of volumes devoted to the *Relations of Canada and the United States.* After passing lightly over the rather uneventful years from 1830 to 1837, he deals lucidly and objectively with the successive crises between 1837 and 1842. A logical and cohesive central theme is provided by the antecedents and consequences of the rebellions of 1837–38 in Canadian-American relations. The reader is filled with dismay upon learning how near the two nations came to an undesired war, and this situation enhances, in Professor Corey's estimation, the achievement of the Webster-Ashburton settlement. The latter was reached by broad and discerning statesmanship rather than by aggressive bargaining, and it cleared the ground for later understandings.

Three good maps, one of which shows the line from Lake Superior to the Lake of the Woods, illustrate the boundary adjustments of 1842. Minnesotans will observe with interest that Ashburton gave up the British claim to the Arrowhead region "as of little importance to either party" and thereby relinquished the Vermilion and part of the Mesabi Range. That Webster suspected the presence of mineral wealth was revealed in the message that he prepared for President Tyler to transmit to the Senate.

CLARENCE W. RIFE

Everyday Things in American Life, 1776–1876. By WILLIAM CHAUNCY LANGDON. (New York, Charles Scribner's Sons, 1941. xv, 398 p. Illustrations. $3.00.)

The recent emphasis on the significance of the homely aspects of life for a full understanding of history has brought forth books and articles on subjects hitherto held inconsequential by most historians. In *Everyday Things in American Life, 1776–1876,* Mr. Langdon takes his readers from Maine to South Carolina, through the Ohio Valley to New Orleans and the Lake Superior region by means of an evolving system of transport popular at the time discussed. Seven of the sixteen chapters are devoted chiefly to ways of travel — the eastern river craft, from logs and rafts to the South Carolina cotton-laden flatboats, the horse-trail corduroy road, the turnpike, and early river commerce sometimes aided by canals.

Newspapers, food, house furnishings, and clothing, as well as industrial and agricultural machines and county and state fairs are given attention. The reader is indeed provided with a miscellany, the parts of which sometimes seem to lack connection but which are made vivid by excellent and frequent illustrations. The last chapter describes the Centennial Exhibition of 1876.

This volume is the second on *Everyday Things;* the first covers similar material to 1776. The language, although usually simple, sometimes bogs down the reader with loosely knit clauses. The book is obviously designed for young readers. Certainly there are no new facts presented for the historian and the sources used are chiefly secondary.

BESSIE LOUISE PIERCE

The Keelboat Age on Western Waters. By LELAND D. BALDWIN. (University of Pittsburgh Press, 1941. xiv, 268 p. Illustrations. $3.00.)

It was the absence of navigable waterways that kept the English colonists so long confined to the Atlantic plains. Once the mountain barrier was crossed, the great inland waterway system of the Mississippi River and its tributaries aided materially in the rapid expansion of the American nation in the half century that followed the Revolution. In *The Keelboat Age on Western Waters,* Dr. Baldwin tells the part the rivers played in that expansion in the days before steamboats. The story deals chiefly with the Ohio and the Mississippi below the mouth of the Ohio, for the upper Mississippi and Missouri valleys were more dependent for their development upon steamboats than upon boats propelled by the brawn of man.

Dr. Baldwin describes in detail the different kinds of vessels used on western waters before the day of the river steamboat. Beginning with the round, hide-covered bullboat and the birchbark canoe, he traces the evolution of boats propelled by muscular power through successive stages until the graceful keelboat and the barge, the aristocrats of the pre-steamboat age, emerged. He describes the men who operated the boats, the Davy Crocketts and the Mike Finks and their compatriots, who were "half-horse, half-alligator"; he tells of the frontier merchants, like James Wilkinson, who opened trade with the Spaniards at New Orleans in the decades following the Revolution; and he discusses the casual immigrant boatman who knew only that he wanted to go west with his goods and his family, and chose the broad Ohio as his highway.

The rivers were wild beasts to tame, and the author demonstrates the grave difficulties, both natural and human, that had to be overcome. Shifting channels and uncharted snags, and the even greater terror of scalp-hungry red men and money-mad white pirates, were braved by the restless rivermen. The writer describes the difficulties of finding markets, and the troubles of the crew, whether professional boatmen or just farmer boys who sought adventure on the great river, in finding a way back to the frontier from whence they came. Sometimes they took passage from New Orleans to the eastern seaboard on ocean-going boats, and went home along the trails that they or their fathers had opened over the mountains; more often, they made the return journey on foot over the Natchez Trace. Only a small number of boats attempted the journey home again, for the current made it an arduous task. To take advantage of eddies and crosscurrents, the author reports, a boat might cross from one side of the Mississippi to the other as many as 390 times between New Orleans and St. Louis. By pushing mightily with great sweeps and poles, or mounting rapids with lines pulled by the crew on the shore, or warping the boat upstream by means of a winch and a cable, dreary progress might be made. The quickest trip between New Orleans and Cincinnati on record, according to the author, was made in 1811, when a barge covered the fifteen hundred miles in seventy-eight days.

"The triumph of the steamboat," says Dr. Baldwin, "meant the death of the Mississippi barge" (p. 193). Yet, the "keels," he points out, merely retreated to the upper tributaries, where they continued to serve river communities, and, when seasons of drought dropped river levels to a point where steamboats could not navigate, barges and keelboats quickly came out of cover to take on the task of marketing the produce of the frontier.

This is an interesting book, based upon extensive research. The format is excellent, and the decorations by Harvey B. Cushman are striking. For endpapers, a "Map of the Western Waters before 1800" is used, and the book is excellently illustrated with reproductions in aquatone of contemporary sketches, paintings, and excerpts from early publications relating to river traffic. The University of Pittsburgh Press is to be congratulated on the handsome book it has produced.

ARTHUR J. LARSEN

James Hall, Literary Pioneer of the Ohio Valley. By JOHN T. FLANAGAN. (Minneapolis, The University of Minnesota Press, 1941. vii, 218 p. Frontispiece. $2.50.)

The beginnings of literature in a new region have a value out of proportion to their purely literary worth. They are not easily separable from the beginnings of social culture and the shaping of the regional mind. So a literary pioneer is a pioneer in more than literature, and he ought not to be forgotten.

These values are clearly apparent in the career of James Hall, who performed vital functions as editor, historian, and storyteller in the early period of settlement of the lower Ohio Valley. It has been customary for historians to acknowledge obligation to Hall for his detailed accounts of western commerce and his descriptions of western life. With the publication of Dr. Flanagan's book, the first careful study of Hall as a man of letters, it will be possible for students of literature to think of him in new and meaningful terms.

For a frontier historian and writer Hall had a fortunate variety of experience. A youth of travel and military life, a trip down the Ohio with the full tide of westward migration in 1820, a dozen years in Illinois when the foundations of the state's political and social life were being laid, and a final thirty-odd years in Cincinnati, the cultural capital of the whole western country — his life paralleled some of the large movements of his time. As editor, lawyer, judge, banker, he exemplified the versatility of frontiersmen, and he came close to many of the currents in the life of the West.

That his writings do not draw deeply and directly upon that breadth of experience Mr. Flanagan explains by saying that Hall was a frustrated realist. This is a suggestive statement and it enables Mr. Flanagan to trace his literary relation in two directions — toward Cooper and Scott, and toward Eggleston, Kirkland, Garland, and Mark Twain. It becomes evident that he contributed but little to a realistic western literature.

An interesting chapter discusses Hall's "Characteristic Ideas." In this careful analysis, James Hall comes off with a somewhat higher score. He was a man broadly aware of the needs of his time, long-sighted in his views, an ardent Westerner, and yet a consistent nationalist. The fact that he established a magazine in Illinois when the state had but fifty thousand people, many of them illiterate, that he founded an Illinois historical society, helped to found the first college in the state, and edited the first western annual indicates the breadth of his interests.

Though he never gets very close to the man himself, Mr. Flanagan persuades one that his estimate of Hall is balanced and judicious. He makes no undue claims for his subject, but praises him for vigor, honesty, a forward-looking mind, and an influence surpassing that of many more gifted men. The book fills a vacancy and should find repeated use.

WALTER HAVIGHURST

Burlington West: A Colonization History of the Burlington Railroad. By RICHARD C. OVERTON. (Cambridge, Harvard University Press, 1941. xviii, 583 p. Illustrations, maps. $4.50.)

This book is not a general history of the Chicago, Burlington and Quincy Railroad. Rather, as the subtitle indicates, it is a history of the colonization work which the railroad undertook in order to people its federal land grants and the adjacent territory in southwestern Iowa and eastern Nebraska with traffic-producing settlers. Accordingly, the author's attention is concentrated on a thirty-year period from 1852 to 1882, during which the Burlington's grants, totaling about 2,700,000 acres, were sought and won, advertised, and, for the most part, sold to actual settlers.

The details of the story were buried in the voluminous records of the Burlington's land department, which in 1936 were deposited in the Baker Library of the Harvard school of business administration. Printed and manuscript materials still in the possession of the railroad company, as well as an abundance of local newspapers and some private correspondence, have also contributed to the production of a well-rounded and carefully documented account.

In two welcome introductory chapters Mr. Overton summarizes the origins of the Burlington system. While developing his main theme in the body of the volume, he incidentally traces the constituent parts of the system through organization, reorganization, and combination. He tells in cursory fashion of the building of the main line, which reached the Mississippi River opposite Burlington, Iowa, in 1855, the Missouri in 1869, and finally, a connection with the Union Pacific near Kearney, Nebraska, in 1872.

The senatorial debate which ended in the land grant of 1856 to the Burlington and Missouri River Railroad and three other proposed Iowa lines is summarized with some care, though one is vouchsafed no glance behind the scenes. Less attention is given to the more generous act of 1864, by which the Burlington was offered twenty alternate sections for each mile of the projected Nebraska extension. One may read in detail, however, of the work of the railroad's land department, which took stock of its holdings, fixed prices, launched a far-reaching advertising campaign, and in 1870 made its first important sales. The successive heads of the land department were interested, indeed, in the direct revenue from sales, but were eager above all to lay a basis for the permanent success of the railroad by attracting to its territory settlers of a superior sort. They were successful on both counts, to the advantage, Mr. Overton urges, of the railroad, the settlers, the states of Iowa and Nebraska, and the country at large. Enough evidence is presented to suggest that the Burlington had a sounder colonization record than some of its rivals.

But it is made clear that the railroad's land policy, however enlightened, was one of enlightened self-interest.

Although the Burlington in 1886 reached a long finger northward to St. Paul, this extension was constructed without benefit of a land grant. Accordingly, Minnesota receives scant attention, even as a competitor for settlers. One learns in passing that 123 Minnesotans purchased land in Nebraska from the Burlington between 1873 and 1876. James J. Hill's acquisition of control of the Burlington system in 1901 is barely mentioned, but one may not complain, given the limitation which the author imposed upon the scope of his study.

Mr. Overton's sympathies never run away with him, but it is clear that they lie with the officials of the railroad, which he now serves in an executive capacity. The only serious villains are the Iowa county governments, which by devious means gained prior possession of land that the Burlington claimed as a part of its grant. One wishes that an occasional sentence had been deleted. For example, it is not easy to believe that social life at Burlington, Iowa, in 1859 "was practically non-existent" (p. 112). Such incidental slips detract little, however, from the value of an exceedingly useful and interesting book. The volume is a handsome one, well illustrated with maps, photographs, and reproductions of colonization propaganda. It is abundantly supplied with statistical tables and graphs.

FRANK H. HECK

Wisconsin: A Guide to the Badger State. Compiled by Workers of the Writers' Program of the Work Projects Administration in the State of Wisconsin. (New York, Duell, Sloan and Pearce, 1941. 651 p. Illustrations. $2.75.)

The Wisconsin volume follows with few variations the national pattern of the *American Guide Series* devised and adopted by the WPA writers' program. A first section sketches in the general background by means of essays on the natural setting, Indians, history, immigrants, industry and transportation, labor, agriculture, the co-operative movement, recreation, education, religion, newspapers and radio, literature, and the arts. A second division treats the nine largest cities of the state — Green Bay, Kenosha, La Crosse, Madison, Milwaukee, Oshkosh, Racine, Sheboygan, and Superior. Then there are thirty-five tours along the main highways of "America's Dairyland." Excellent illustrations and a chronology, bibliography, maps, and index complete the volume.

The Wisconsin Library Association has done the citizens of the state real service in sponsoring the *Guide*. It becomes at once a standard book of reference and a delightful traveling companion. When confronted with any question concerning Wisconsin's past or present, one turns here first, usually to be rewarded with accurate, concise, and pleasantly written information. Motoring with the book gives new meaning to the Wisconsin countryside. Who would have suspected that little Sauk City was once known over Europe as the "Freethinkers Heaven"? Does "clean, shady, and spacious" Delavan in any way betray its glorious past as a circus town? West of Burlington, how many travelers would notice the marker on the site of Voree, that curious Mormon colony ruled by the strange "Prophet" Strang?

Volumes in the *American Guide Series* have been greeted with extravagant praise or savage criticism, often depending upon whether those commenting were friendly or unfriendly to New Deal plans for work relief. Since this has been the real basis for judging them, I may as well say that I am inclined to think that preparation of these guidebooks was not a task well adapted to the work relief program; I suspect that in most states they were brought out by a dozen or so nonrelief professional writers assisted by stenographic and clerical help from the relief rolls. The policy-making national staff of the project was naturally friendly to the Democratic administration and may even have had some left-wing sympathies, but I do not find undue prejudice in the *Guides,* certainly no more than should be expected from relief workers grateful for their jobs but not too enthusiastic toward laissez faire.

But, no matter how this volume may have been produced, it is obviously of high merit. I wish that it might have been possible to make it even more of a gazetteer with some information on all communities. There are a few flaws (What book does not have them?) such as labeling a view of Milwaukee harbor as Kenosha. But the *Guide's* accuracy is high because it is honestly written; its emphasis on social and cultural history is sound; and it is surprisingly easy to read. State Supervisor John J. Lyons and his staff deserve much praise for their work.

EDWARD P. ALEXANDER

The Minnesota Arrowhead Country. Compiled by Workers of the Writers' Program of the Work Projects Administration in the State of Minnesota. (Chicago, Albert Whitman & Company, 1941. xxi, 231 p. Illustrations. $2.50.)

Each year thousands of people go to the Minnesota Arrowhead country, a vacation land varied in resources and rich in historic interest. The purpose of this guide, as expressed by Margaret Culkin Banning in her foreword, is to enable these visitors to "enrich their experience."

Part 1 includes a sketch of the history of the region and reviews of various present-day aspects. The historical survey, based apparently on standard secondary authorities, is better than the description of the Arrowhead today. The latter is a compilation of materials on agriculture, industry, population, and social and cultural activities, with considerable repetition of some topics. The statement that there are "elaborate schools" on the iron ranges appears several times; Grand Portage is described twice. The compilers collected a mass of industrial and commercial data, but instead of weaving it into a well-organized account, they consigned it to an appendix. The first section concludes with a few pages on Lake Superior — exploration, shipping, and commercial fishing. In Part 2 are interesting and informative descriptions of the Chippewa and Superior national forests. Information and routes for fifteen canoe trips are included.

Part 3 contains almost fifty individual accounts of cities, towns, and villages. In each case, the origins and development of the community are sketched, and its economy, transportation facilities, public buildings, tourist accommodations, and recreational attractions are described. The articles appear to be based on information obtained from chambers of commerce and other civic organizations and tend to reflect community pride. In general, the material on contemporary phases is satisfactory; that on the past is disappointing. Colorful aspects often are emphasized at the expense of accuracy, and instead of a fused and careful narrative, a patchwork of facts and anecdotes is the rule.

Four automobile tours, with itineraries and other information, are included in Part 4. Points of interest along the routes are described. Part 5 contains industrial and commercial data, a glossary, a chronology, and a bibliography. The glossary and the chronology are not free from inaccuracies. The statement that the "Webster-Ashburton Treaty fixed the present International Boundary between the United States and Canada" (p. 202) is inexact. Beltrami County was not organized in 1896 but in 1897, and Bemidji became the county seat in 1897, not in 1896 (p. 208). Some of the statements in the chronology are in the past tense; others are in the present tense. The index is adequate. The numerous well-chosen illustrations are a pleasing feature of the format, which in other respects is not particularly attractive. A few small maps are included.

The most valuable parts of the guide are the tours and canoe trips suggested and the information given on tourist facilities and recreational opportunities. These features make the book almost indispensable for the Arrowhead visitor.

HAROLD T. HAGG

The Bohemian Flats. Compiled by the workers of the Writers' Program of the Work Projects Administration in the State of Minnesota, and sponsored by the Hennepin County Historical Society. (Minneapolis, University of Minnesota Press, 1941. 52 p. Illustrations. $1.50.)

For a great many years travelers across the Washington Avenue Bridge in southeast Minneapolis caught glimpses of a curious village edging the west bank of the Mississippi River. To spectators on the bridge the settlement looked chaotic indeed, with driftwood and tar paper shacks, lean-tos or porches attached to the more prosperous houses, picket fences running at crazy angles, irregular garden plots. Paint was generally absent, but there were splotches of color on sheds and roofs, and in summer embroidered window curtains and gay flowerpots caught the eye. For this was the Bohemian Flats, for seventy years the home of Slovaks and Czechs, of Danes and Irish and Germans, a hamlet below the river cliffs where peasants from the old country tried to preserve the life they knew.

The story of this exotic community has been charmingly told in *The Bohemian Flats,* a thin little book produced by the writers' program of the Minnesota WPA. Life began on the flats about 1870 with the arrival of Danes and Slovaks. Life continues there even today, although the construction of the barge terminal and coal docks has expelled all but a persistent handful of settlers. In the intervening years the newcomers to America labored in flour and lumber mills, extracted fish and deadheads from the Mississippi, baked *koláče* and potato dumplings, feasted and worshipped as their fathers had taught them to do. Despite the polyglot group, there was little friction, though one suspects that life on the levee was less idyllic than the writers of this book would have one believe.

The Bohemian Flats is a distinct contribution to local history. Competently written and attractively produced, it stimulates interest in the color of the past and reminds us that the development of industry and commerce is sometimes possible only by sacrificing the picturesque nonconformity of our ancestors. Readers should be grateful for this preservation of the story of a quaint community which prospered quietly below a modern city until the revival of water traffic crushed it. But there are other interesting Minnesota hamlets whose history should likewise be written. St. Paul's Swede Hollow and the Mexican settlement adjoining the Holman airport demand similar chronicles.

JOHN T. FLANAGAN

Minnesota Historical Society Notes

IN ORDER to meet the wartime need for conserving paper, a new type face has been selected for *Minnesota History*. Ever since the society's magazine made its first appearance in 1915, some form of Caslon type has been used in its pages. The new face is Granjon, which is more condensed than Caslon. By using Granjon, it is believed that, without sacrificing anything of readability, from a sixth to a fifth more matter can be presented on a page of this magazine than heretofore. Thus, an article that formerly would have occupied twelve pages, will be only ten pages long; an issue of a hundred pages can be reduced to slightly over eighty pages; a volume that once ran to five hundred pages will now come to only a little more than four hundred. When these differences are pictured in terms of an edition of twenty-five hundred, it will be seen that the saving in paper is considerable. And this will be accomplished without reducing the number of articles and sections presented, or their length in words. With the change in type, some slight differences in format have been inaugurated, among them the shifting of the author's name from the end to the beginning of an article. Furthermore, authors' addresses are no longer given in connection with articles and reviews. That information will be included, however, in a separate division of the present section, which, in this and future issues, will be devoted to notes about contributors.

Since the activities of the society in 1941, including the last quarter of the year, are surveyed in the superintendent's report, which appears elsewhere in this issue of *Minnesota History,* only a few supplementary items are mentioned in the present section.

One sustaining member — Miss Helen Bunn of White Bear Lake — and the following twelve annual members joined the society in the quarter ending on December 31: C. A. Carlson of St. Paul, Glenn Catlin of Pipestone, Dr. J. Frank Corbett of Minneapolis, the Rev. Melvin L. Frank of St. Paul, Remley J. Glass of Mason City, Iowa, Brigadier General C. B. Hodges of Baton Rouge, Louisiana, Edward Lafot of Lakefield, Clarence A. Lund of Willmar, Henry Mead of Aitkin, H. A. Perkins of Faribault, Dr. Walter R. Ramsey of St. Paul, and Lew P. Reeve of Austin.

Four active members of the society died during the three months from September 1 to December 31: James A. Melone of Rochester on September 25, Mrs. Alice P. Goodrich of Boston on November 5, William I. Price of Duluth on November 11, and Mrs. John Washburn of Minneapolis on December 12.

A thousand readers, the largest number ever recorded in a single quarter, used the resources of the society's manuscript division during the last three months of 1941. Of this number, 760 were looking for proof of age, citizenship, or residence in the manuscript census records. During the same period, between six and seven thousand people viewed the exhibits in the society's museum. Included were 1,688 visitors who came in classes or other groups.

Some two hundred oil paintings, water colors, lithographs, etchings, and the like from the society's picture collection have been photographed by the department of fine arts in the University of Minnesota. Another evidence of a growing appreciation of the value as art of some of the society's pictures was the display of eight of its paintings and lithographs by the St. Paul Gallery and School of Art early in December.

A number of special exhibits will be arranged in the society's museum in the next few months. Two displays of photographs that have been planned for April will serve as reminders of America's entrance into the first World War. Another exhibit of military interest will deal with "The End of the Civil War." Displays of "Spring Costumes and Millinery," of "Music of Long Ago," and of Sioux and Chippewa books also have been planned for April. The eighty-fourth anniversary of Minnesota's admission to the Union, which occurs on May 11, will be commemorated in an exhibit entitled "Minnesota Becomes a State." Other exhibits for May will deal with "Ships and Victory, 1918," American troops abroad in 1917–18, "Historic Flags," and "Lumber Camp Life." "Activities on the Home Front" and the "Training of Fliers" in the first World War are among the titles of exhibits planned for June. There will be others showing summer costumes, fans, and hairdressing of the past.

"Methods Used in Minnesota in Organizing County Historical Societies" were described by the superintendent before a meeting that resulted in the organization of the Iowa Association of Local Historical Societies at Des Moines on October 11. Mr. Larsen also presented talks and addresses on the "Minnesota Historical Society as a Laboratory for the Social Studies" at Hamline University on October 22, on "The Local Historical Society and Its Work" before the Olmsted County Historical Society at Rochester on October 29, on "The Fur Trade of the Upper Mississippi Valley" before the La Crosse County Historical Society at La Crosse on November 7, on "Joseph R. Brown, Pioneer Minnesotan" before the Sibley County Historical Society at Henderson on November 14, on "A Workshop for the Historian" before a meeting of Phi Alpha Theta, an honorary history fraternity, at the University of Minnesota on December 4, and on "Minnesota in the Defense of America" before the Minneapolis chapter of the Sons of the American Revolution on December 11. Miss Nute spoke on "Pioneer Women" before meetings of the mothers' section of the Faculty Women's Club of the University of Minnesota on November 19 and of the Washington County Historical Society at Mahtomedi on December 2, and she described "Canoeing in the North Woods" before the Hamline Christian Association at Hamline University on November 30. "Minnesota in the Defense of America" was the subject of a talk presented by Mr. Beeson before a men's club of the Olivet Congregational Church in St. Paul on October 27, and Mr. Babcock gave an illustrated talk on Lincoln for students in an English class of Mechanic Arts High School meeting in the society's building on November 7.

CONTRIBUTORS

FOR NEARLY two decades preceding 1939, Dean Theodore C. Blegen of the university's graduate school, who discusses herein "The Minnesota Historical Society and the University of Minnesota," served the society first as assistant superintendent and then as superintendent. During much of that period he was also a member of the history faculty in the university. He is thoroughly familiar with the resources of both institutions, having drawn upon them in his teaching activities as well as in his work as a writer and an editor. His most important historical publications relate to two fields — the history of Minnesota and Norwegian immigration to America. Recently he edited for this magazine an important documentary source on the early history of the state, the "Narrative of Samuel W. Pond." In his present article he not only reviews the growth of the collections of the two great cultural institutions that he knows so well, but he makes clear the importance of giving them special care in wartime.

Three other writers contribute to the section on "Conserving Minnesota's History in Wartime." Miss Bertha L. Heilbron, the assistant editor of this magazine, has visited and described in its pages many of the local historical museums mentioned in her discussion of "Local Historical Museums and the War Program." Mr. G. Hubert Smith, who evaluates the place of "The Local Historical Society in Wartime," was supervisor in the museum assistance unit of the Minnesota Art Project under the WPA until his recent enlistment in the United States Army Medical Corps. He is now stationed at Camp Grant, Illinois. Dr. Lewis Beeson, curator of newspapers on the society's staff, gives some practical suggestions to those who will undertake the job of "Collecting War Records" in the present conflict.

An interest in the backgrounds of the Minnesota city in which he resides prompted Mr. Harold T. Hagg to make a study of "Bemidji: A Pioneer Community of the Nineties." Mr. Hagg is a member of the history faculty of the Bemidji State Teachers College. He also contributes to this issue of *Minnesota History* a review of a recently published guide to the area of northeastern Minnesota.

The superintendent of the society, Dr. Arthur J. Larsen, presents herein his report on the activities and accomplishments of "The Minnesota Historical Society in 1941." He edited for the society's *Narratives and Documents* series a volume of the Civil War letters of Jane Grey Swisshelm, and he has contributed articles and book reviews to this magazine. He is represented also in this number by a review of a book dealing with a frontier form of transportation. Mrs. Mary W. Berthel, who reports on "The 1942 Annual Meeting of the Minnesota Historical Society," is editorial assistant on the society's staff. She is engaged in making a detailed study of geographic names in the state, and in December, 1940, she published an article on "Place Names of the Mille Lacs Region."

Contributing to the section devoted to "Sources for Northwest History" is Mr. Richard C. Overton, who has taken advantage of his position as executive assistant of the Chicago, Burlington and Quincy Railroad Company at Chicago to give readers of this periodical a clear picture of the nature and arrangement of "Railroad Archives." Mr. Overton drew upon the archives of his own company in the preparation of his recent historical study entitled *Burlington West,* which is reviewed in the present issue of *Minnesota History.*

In addition to Dr. Larsen and Mr. Hagg, seven writers are represented in the section devoted to book reviews. Mr. Edward C. Gale is a Minneapolis lawyer who served as president of the society from 1936 to 1939 and has long been a member of its executive council. His deep interest in the Belgian friar who discovered the Falls of St. Anthony led Mr. Gale to visit the explorer's birthplace at Ath in Belgium some years ago, an adventure that he described in an article entitled "On the Hennepin Trail" published in this magazine for March, 1930. Dr. Clarence W. Rife, who frequently contributes reviews to these pages, is professor of history in Hamline University, St. Paul. Professor Bessie Louise Pierce of the history faculty in the University of Chicago gives much attention to social history in her definitive *History of Chicago,* two volumes of which have appeared. Dr. Edward P. Alexander took up his duties as superintendent of the State Historical Society of Wisconsin in the fall of 1941. He had previously served as director of the New York State Historical Association. Dr. Frank H. Heck, assistant professor of history in Miami University at Oxford, Ohio, is the author of a recent volume on *The Civil War Veteran in Minnesota Life and Politics,* which will be reviewed in this magazine in the near future. Like Dr. Heck, Professor Walter Havighurst is on the faculty of Miami University, where he is associate professor of English. He contributed to the *Rivers of America* series a volume on the *Upper Mississippi* (1937). The book that he reviews herein, though it deals with the Ohio Valley, is the work of Professor John T. Flanagan of the department of English in the University of Minnesota, who has reviewed for this number a book dealing with a Minnesota locality. As the author of a series of articles on the experiences in Minnesota of well-known literary figures, Dr. Flanagan is familiar to readers of this magazine.

ACCESSIONS

A letter written from Prairie du Chien on September 10, 1819, in which Colonel Henry Leavenworth informs John C. Calhoun that "a Post has been established at the St. Peter's River, agreeably to an order from your department of the 8th of February last," is among twenty-six letters and reports in the National Archives recently copied for the society on filmslides. The papers relate to events and expeditions in the Minnesota country in the years from 1818 to 1822. A number contain material on Captain Matthew J. Magee's expedition from Council Bluffs on the Missouri River to the new fort at the mouth of the Minnesota River in 1820, when he undertook to determine the best route for a road between these points. Others relate to Governor Lewis Cass's expedition to the headwaters of the Mississippi in 1820. Included are letters and reports prepared by Henry R. Schoolcraft, Charles Trowbridge, and other members of the expedition.

A diary kept in 1846–47 by Dr. Hiram W. Catlin while he was serving as assistant surgeon of the Second Indiana Volunteer Infantry in the Mexican War is the gift of his grandson, Dr. John J. Catlin of Buffalo. The diary includes a vivid description of the battle of Buena Vista. After the war Dr. Catlin removed to Minnesota, settling in St. Peter in 1855 and practicing his profession there.

A biographical sketch of James Taylor, the father of James Wickes Taylor, a St. Paul lawyer who became American consul at Winnipeg, is a recent addition to the latter's papers (see *ante,* 17:464). The sketch, which bears the title "The Taylors in Penn Yan, New York," was written and presented by Mr. James Taylor Dunn of Olean, New York.

Fifteen letters written in the early 1860's by John Faith, a journalist who was active in the Minnesota Valley in this period, have been received from Miss Louise Stegner of Omaha, Nebraska. Among the subjects that Faith discusses are the policies of the newspapers with which he was connected — the *St. Peter Tribune,* the *Shakopee Argus,* and the *Le Sueur Gazette.* He writes vividly of the battles of New Ulm in 1862, describes the Nicollet County Fair of 1860, and notes the showing at St. Peter in 1861 of a panorama of the Arctic. He praises the Minnesota climate for its healthfulness, remarking that at St. Peter "there is no ague, and I have only known of one natural death since I came here, and very little sickness of any kind." Faith's correspondent seems to have been a violent abolitionist, and the letters contain frequent mentions of the slavery issue.

A diary kept by Captain William L. Silvis of Company I, Eighth Minnesota Volunteer Infantry, while engaged in the Sioux War as a member of the Sully expedition of 1864, has been copied on filmslides for the society through the courtesy of Mrs. B. C. Trevett of St. Paul. The journal includes descriptions of the country through which the expedition passed, names and locations of camps, records of distances marched each day, and accounts of skirmishes with the Indians.

Daily weather records for 1886 and 1892 and expense accounts are among the entries in three memorandum books kept from 1881 to 1892 at St. Paul and Owatonna by Henry R. Moore and recently presented by his grandson, Mr. Mark D. Moore of St. Paul. Included in the gift are some military land warrants and other papers accumulated by Moore, who had been a merchant at Janesville and Beloit, Wisconsin. There is also a description of the St. Paul winter carnival of 1888.

Some letters relating to the payment of annuities to the Sioux in 1896 are included among thirty-three items recently added to the papers of the Reverend William C. Pope, a pioneer Episcopal clergyman of St. Paul, by his daughter, Mrs. Edward H. Eckel of Tulsa, Oklahoma. The earliest item in the collection is a report on Pope's scholarship while attending college in 1858. Included also are the constitution, minutes of meetings, and signatures of members of the Minnesota branch of the American Church Temperance Society, of which Pope was secretary; a record book in which are listed the names of people who contributed information for a history of the Episcopal church in St. Paul; and answers to a questionnaire about the advantages of church hospitals.

A copy of the *Dairy Maids' Carnival* of Duluth for November 11, 1887, a publication hitherto unrepresented in the society's files, has been received from the University of Wisconsin Library. Other rare Minnesota newspapers added to the society's collection during the last three months of 1941 include issues of the *Hastings New Era* for October 8, 1875, and November 28, 1882, and the *Hastings Democrat* for September 30, 1886, from Mr. Lee A. Sauer of St. Paul; and the *Sibley County Independent* of Henderson for October 26, 1883, from Mr. G. A. Buck of Henderson.

The years from 1906 to 1920, when vaudeville was in its prime, are covered in a file of programs of the most important St. Paul theater offering that form of entertainment, the Orpheum, recently presented by Mr. Lou Golden of St. Paul. The programs, which should be of special interest to students of social and theatrical history, are bound in fourteen volumes.

The adventures of a Piegan chief are pictured on a painted elkskin robe presented by Major L. I. Cooke of San Diego, through the courtesy of Mr. Ira C. Oehler of St. Paul. It is accompanied by a description of the episodes depicted. The robe was presented to Major Cooke's father, Captain L. W. Cooke, in 1893, when the latter was serving as agent to the Blackfoot Indians. A beaded belt that was probably made by Crow

Indians is the gift of Dr. J. C. Ferguson of St. Paul. He has also presented a toy bank representing a Boston bulldog.

Among recent additions to the society's collection of domestic utensils and household articles are a hand-woven linen sheet from Mr. Willard E. Perkins of Northfield, a fluting iron from Mr. Robert R. Reed of Minneapolis, a pewter spoon mold with a spoon that was cast in it and a sampler of 1805 from Mr. Albert C. Noyes of St. Paul, a calfskin trunk more than a century old from Mrs. Ida Mooney of St. Paul, a zither dating from 1850 from Miss Katherine A. Tschida of St. Paul, and a copper kettle from Mr. A. R. Johnson of St. Paul. Mr. Edward Lafot of Lakefield has presented a milk pail used in 1850 and two copper pails used in Sweden in 1870, and a small hand lamp of a type in which gasoline was burned.

A cradle used in his family is the gift of Dean Theodore C. Blegen of the University of Minnesota. He has also presented a Lutheran clergyman's coat, vest, and ruff worn by his father, the Reverend J. H. Blegen.

A sewing kit carried by Josiah Parvin while serving with the American forces in the War of 1812 has been added to the society's military collection by Mrs. Frank O. Kuehn of St. Paul. The Civil War is represented by a pair of surgeon's scissors found on the battlefield at Bull Run and presented by Mr. Milton Thompson of Minneapolis. A uniform and cap worn by a veteran of the Spanish-American War has been received from Mr. Hugo V. Koch of St. Paul, and a suitcase carried by a chaplain in the first World War, the Reverend E. C. Clemans, has been presented by the Reverend William E. Thompson of St. Paul. A uniform, ditty bag, knitted cap, and other items used by Seth A. Brown while serving with the United States Navy are the gifts of his mother, Mrs. Barbara Lindstrom of Mason City, Iowa.

A substantial addition to the costume collection, including gowns, suits, wraps, a silk automobile coat, and other items dating from the late 1880's to the early years of the present century, has been received from the estate of the late Mrs. Mary Johns of Hastings, through the courtesy of Mr. Lee A. Sauer of St. Paul. Miss Vera Cole of Minneapolis has presented a woman's and a man's bathing suit of about 1905, beach slippers, men's vests and collars, some ice skates, a miniature iron kettle, a doll, a toy house, and other items. Two elaborate fans and a comb are the gifts of Miss Maud M. Case of St. Peter.

A lithograph of an "Indian Wigwam in Lower Canada," based upon a painting made by Cornelius Krieghoff about 1847, is the gift of Mrs. E. C. Lindley of New York. Miss Reba L. Wakefield of St. Paul has presented 213 photographs of Mississippi River and St. Paul scenes. A crayon portrait of Dr. William H. Leonard, a pioneer Minneapolis physician, is the gift of his daughter, Miss Gertrude J. Leonard of Los Angeles; and a copy of an oil portrait of Charles D. Gilfillan, who settled in St. Paul in 1854 and later became prominent in the Minnesota Valley, has been presented by Charles O. Gilfillan of Redwood Falls.

Genealogies received during the last quarter of 1941 include: Ronald T. Abercrombie, *The Abercrombies of Baltimore* (Baltimore, 1940. 35 p.); Herbert Barry, *Samuel Barry, Born in Boston, 1761, and His Descendants* (1941. 48 p.); Raymond M. Bell, *The Bell Family of Mifflin County, Pennsylvania* (Washington, Pennsylvania, 1941. 77 p.); Lyle L. Benedict, *The Story of the Benedicts, a Genealogy of the Benedict Family for the Descendants of Ira and Seely Benedict of the Seventh Generation in America* (Belmont, Wisconsin, 1939. 31 p.); Walter L. Brown, *Ancestors of Florence Julia Brown, and Some of Their Descendants* (Albion, New York, 1940. 341 p.); Gertrude B. Wilgus, *Sketch of the Life of Gershom Clark of Weathersfield, Vermont, 1753–1813* (Weathersfield, 1941. 35 p.); John L. Crawford, *Whence We Came* (Corbin, Kentucky, 1941. 47 p.); Laura E. Crews, *My Kinsfolk, A Story and Genealogy of the Crews, Sampson, Wilber and Waddel Families* (Enid, Oklahoma, 1941. 169 p.); George B. Sedgeley, *Dow, The Ancestry and Posterity of Joshua Dow of Avon, Maine* (Rutland, Vermont, 1938. 27 p.); Frank M. Ferrin, *Captain Jonathan Farren of Amesbury, Massachusetts, and Some of His Descendants* (Cambridge, Massachusetts, 1941. 222 p.); Lister O. Weiss, *Homeland in Canaan, a History and Genealogy of the Fetzer Family* (Akron, Ohio, 1941. 43 p.); Austin W. Smith, *The George-Lacy Genealogy* (Cookeville, Tennessee, 1940. 77 p.); John H. Hauberg, *History and Memoirs of the Haubergs' Homestead since the Indians Left, 1851–1941* (Davenport, Iowa, 1941. 63 p.); William E. Johnson, *John Johnson and Other Johnsons* (McDonough, New York, 1940. 117 p.); Melvin E. Jones, *Ancestral Lines, Revised and Enlarged* (Trenton, New Jersey, 1941. 535 p.); Robert H. McIntire, *Descendants of Micum McIntire* (Rutland, Vermont, 1940. 158 p.); Ira D. Mallery, *American Lineage of the Mallery Family of Wayne County, Pa.* (Windsor, New York, 1940.

36 p.); Lester D. Mapes, *A Tentative Correction of the Mapes Family Line* (New York, 1941. 21 p.); Edward K. Meador, *The Meadors and the Meadows* (Boston, 1941. 57 p.); Doris M. Schneider, *Genealogy of the Descendants of Andrew (Müller) Miller of Millers Mills, N. Y.* (Winnetka, Illinois, 1940. 41 p.); Austin W. Smith, *Mitchell-Mc Glocklin and Allied Families* (Cookeville, Tennessee, 1940. 85 p.); Virginia C. Stumbough, *The Mulhollands, History, Genealogy, Letters* (Peoria, Illinois, 1941. 32 p.); Ray C. Thomas, *Histories of the Families of Archibald Parker, Lettie Parker and of Joseph Thomas* (Gary, Indiana, 1940. 24 p.); Henry Parsons, *The House of Cornet Joseph Parsons together with the Houses of a Line of His Descendants and Their Allied Families, 1655–1941* (Kennebunk, Maine, 1941. 52 p.); Walter G. Davis, *The Ancestry of James Patten, 1747?–1817 of Arundel (Kennebunkport) Maine* (Portland, Maine, 1941. 113 p.); Walter P. Quist, *Quist Family Album* (Stillwater, Minnesota, 1941. 8 p.); Albert Rathbone, *Supplement to the Pamphlet Printed in 1937 regarding Ancestors and Descendants of Samuel Rathbone and Lydia Sparhawk, His Wife* (1941. 102 p.); Jennie M. Holley, *Arthur Scovell and His Descendants in America, 1660–1900* (Rutland, Vermont, 1941. 285 p.); Austin W. Smith, *The Smith-Jarratt Genealogy* (Cookeville, Tennessee, 1941. 204 p.); Robert A. Swink, *Genealogy, the Swink Family of Missouri* (Pasadena, California, 1940. 77 p.); George B. Sedgeley, *The Wellcome Family of Freeman, Maine, Israel Riggs Bray, 1808–1890, Henry Solomon Wellcome, 1853–1936* (Phillips, Maine, 1939. 26 p.); Lucius E. Allen, *Eleven Generations of the Wellman-Allen Line in America* (Guntersville, Alabama, 1940. 38 p.); Georgia C. Washburn, *Witter Genealogy, Descendants of William Witter of Swampscott, Massachusetts, 1639–1659* (New York, 1929. 394 p.); and volumes 6 and 7 of *Colonial and Revolutionary Lineages of America* (New York, 1940).

Twelve states are represented in the local histories and source materials of value to genealogists added to the library in recent months. Books from the New England states include: *Records of the Congregational Church in Suffield, Connecticut, 1710–1836* (Hartford, Connecticut, 1941. 224 p.); volume 3 of *Vital Records of New Bedford, Massachusetts* (Boston, 1941. 191 p.); *Vital Records of Otis, Massachusetts* (Boston, 1941. 159 p.); John H. Bartlett, *The Story of Sunapee* [New Hampshire] (Washington, D. C., 1941. 196 p.); Ozias

C. Pitkin, *History of Marshfield, Vermont* (1941. 308 p.); M. Elizabeth Minard, *History of Westminster* [Vermont] (Westminster, 1941. 174 p.); and William Teg, *Hiram* (Cornish, Maine, 1941. 107 p.). The last volume is a history of a township in Oxford County, Maine. Typewritten copies, made by Grace Limeburner, of gravestone inscriptions from cemeteries at Penobscot and Sedgwick, Maine, with notes relating to some of the families whose names appear in the records, also have been added to the Maine local history section.

New York state is represented by *New Rochelle Tombstone Inscriptions,* published by the local chapter of the Daughters of the American Revolution (New Rochelle, 1941. 165 p.). A detailed history of *Harford Township, Susquehanna County, Pennsylvania, 1790–1940* has been published by the Harford Sesqui-centennial Committee (Harford, 1940. 480 p.); and another Pennsylvania book, *Annals of Old Wilkinsburg and Vicinity,* has been compiled by a local "Group for Historical Research" (Wilkinsburg, 1940. 549 p.). Of particular interest to Minnesotans is a section in the latter volume on Jane Grey Swisshelm, who is described as "The Queer Woman Crusader of Wilkinsburg."

Additions to the material on other states include volume 2 of *Maryland Genealogies and Historical Recorder* by Annie W. Burns (Washington, D. C., 1941. 101 p.); volume 7 of the *Calendar of New Jersey Wills,* covering the years from 1786 to 1790 (Trenton, New Jersey, 1941. 337 p.); *The Book of the Society of Colonial Wars in the State of New Jersey* (1933. 339 p.); *Crown of Life, History of Christ Church, New Bern, North Carolina, 1715–1940* (New Bern, 1940. 245 p.); and a history of a North Dakota county, *Along the Trails of Yesterday: A Story of McIntosh County,* by Nina F. Wishek (Ashley, North Dakota, 1941. 437 p.).

A variety of materials on Virginia has been received recently. Books on churches include Henry I. Brock's *Colonial Churches in Virginia* (Richmond, 1930. 94 p.), and B. Duvall Chambers' *Old Chapel and the Parish in Clarke County, Virginia* (Washington, D. C., 1932. 291 p.). Valuable records of Augusta and Rockingham counties are made available in Peter C. Kaylor's *Abstract of Land Grant Surveys, 1761– 1791* (Dayton, Virginia, 1938. 150 p.). *Index to Marriage Notices in the Religious Herald, Richmond, Virginia, 1828–1938* (Richmond, 1941. 2 vols.) is a publication of the Historical Records Survey. Other Virginia books include volume 2 of Annie W. Burns, *Virginia Genealogies and*

County Records (Washington, D. C., 1941.　124 p.); Blanche A. Chapman, *Wills and Administrations of Elizabeth City County, Virginia and Other Genealogical and Historical Items, 1610–1800* (Smithfield, Virginia, 1941.　302 p.); Beverly Fleet, *Charles City County Court Orders, 1661–1664* (Richmond, 1941.　116 p.); and Clayton Torrence, *Genealogy of Members, Sons of the Revolution in the State of Virginia* (Richmond, 1939.　530 p.).　　　　　　　　　　　　　　　　　L. F.

News and Comment

HISTORY, writes Robert L. Schuyler in the *British Columbia Historical Quarterly* for October, "belongs to all subjects; it is a way of studying any of them. . . . History is commonly thought of nowadays as related most closely to the social sciences, but really it has no greater natural affinity with them than with art, religion, physical science, or what you will." In his discussion of "History in a Changing World," Professor Schuyler takes issue with the modern tendency to use history "to explain the present." He contends that "present-mindedness is and always has been the great source of anachronism, the great distorter of the past, the great enemy of historical-mindedness."

A course in the work of historical societies is being offered in Columbia University beginning in February. It consists of fifteen lectures by Alexander J. Wall, director of the New York Historical Society, who will cover such topics as the cataloguing of manuscripts, maps, and broadsides, the preservation of library and museum items, the use of photographic equipment, the planning and equipping of buildings for historical societies, and the administration of large and small institutions.

A session of the fifty-sixth annual meeting of the American Historical Association, which was held in Chicago from December 29 to 31, was devoted to Frederick Jackson Turner, with Dean Theodore C. Blegen of the University of Minnesota as chairman. "An Appraisal of Frederick Jackson Turner as a Historian" was presented by Avery Craven, and "Turner's Frontier Hypothesis in the Light of Modern Criticism" was discussed by George W. Pierson. Of special interest also were sessions on "The Study of Local History" and on "Records of Emergencies." The discussion in the latter case was led by Dr. Solon J. Buck of the National Archives.

The help given "to the making of the West and through this to the general process of American development . . . by missionaries and teachers of whatever denomination, are factors which may not be ignored in any attempt to philosophize on the ultimate reasons which made this nation what it is." This conclusion is reached by Gilbert J. Garraghan in a paper on "Non-economic Factors in the Frontier Movement" appearing in *Mid-America* for October. He demonstrates that while Frederick J. Turner originally "accounted for American development by a single factor and that a geographic-economic one, he later repeatedly declared that non-economic factors also had to be reckoned with in explaining the phenomenon in question."

The fifth and latest volume issued in the *Appleton-Century Historical Essays* series has appeared under the title *Democracy in the Middle West, 1840–1940* (New York, 1941). It embraces four essays edited by Jeannette P. Nichols and James G. Randall, who reveal in their preface that these papers were presented before the annual meeting of the Mississippi Valley Historical Association at Memphis in 1939. Three of the essays "were part of a carefully planned symposium on 'The Changing Function of the Middle West in American Democracy'." In this volume they appear as "Regionalism and Democracy in the Middle West, 1840–1865" by Henry C. Hubbart, "Contradictory Trends in Middle Western Democracy, 1865–1900" by Jeannette P. Nichols, and "Our Own Middle West, 1900–1940" by John D. Hicks. The fourth paper, presented by William O. Lynch as his presidential address, deals with "The Advance into the Middle West."

"In the main, I think the social historian may count the historical motion picture as a valuable ally in the diffusion of popular education regarding the everyday life of the past," writes Charles W. Jefferys in an article on "History in Motion Pictures" which appears in the December issue of the *Canadian Historical Review*. He expresses the hope that in the future some of the "conscientious study, the research devoted to the reconstruction of the visual details may extend into the domain of the scenario." A survey of recent motion pictures based upon Canadian history leads Mr. Jefferys to conclude that the "costumes are more authentic than the motives or forces that move the actors who wear them; the outward trappings are studied more profoundly than the underlying psychology." He hopes for a time when the "real protagonist of the drama of history, the period itself, and its life forces, shall be more clearly revealed." Among the pictures considered by Mr. Jefferys are "Northwest Passage," in which the chief character is Robert Rogers, and "Hudson's Bay," which centers about the story of Radisson.

Evidence that natives of Canada as well as of the United States are developing an interest in local history is to be found in an article on

"Local History Projects for County Libraries" by Ethel Canfield, appearing in the November issue of the *Ontario Library Review*. "There is an ever increasing demand from teachers and students for local history," reports this Canadian librarian, "and libraries should endeavor to meet that demand." She suggests that the local libraries collect not only books, but letters, diaries, newspapers, photographs, church and school records, and many other types of materials, for, she writes, "the search for local history knows no bounds."

"Too many family papers are dumped in the basement or the garret to be forgotten. Too many bundles of non-current business records are destroyed because an owner or manager needs the space and thinks they are of no further value." Thus writes Charles M. Gates of the department of history in the University of Washington in the December issue of the *Washington Alumnus*. Under the title "The University Library Hunts," Professor Gates describes the activities of the curator of the university's collection of Northwest Americana in assembling the manuscript sources for Washington's history. It will be recalled that in 1934–35 Dr. Gates served as acting curator of manuscripts on the staff of the Minnesota Historical Society.

A useful *Glossary of Mississippi Valley French, 1673–1850* has been prepared by John Francis McDermott and published by Washington University as number 12 of its *Language and Literature Studies* (St. Louis, 1941). "Although the French used by educated people in the Mississippi Valley was as good as that spoken in any other place, the conditions of the new life obviously called for an extension of the vocabulary," writes Professor McDermott in his introduction. "The many races and nationalities in the great territory — Canadian, Indian, Spanish, Negro, West Indian, Louisiana French, and the French of France — all contributed to Mississippi Valley French," he continues. "The new fauna and flora, as well as new occupations, made necessary additional words and extended the meaning of old ones." Professor McDermott states that his glossary "is intended for the use of students of any phase of French culture in the Mississippi Valley." Certainly, students of history will welcome this convenient tool, and those who are interested in the fur trade of the upper valley will find it particularly useful.

In a discussion of "Pénicaut and His Chronicle of Early Louisiana," which appears in the October number of *Mid-America*, Elizabeth Mc

Cann gives special attention to the chronology of this record of the French in the Mississippi Valley. Mention is made of certain explorers who saw and knew the Minnesota country. Hennepin, for example, is said to have "popularized the fact that Louisiana could be reached by sea and by the Mississippi." Confusion of dates in Penicault's account of Le Sueur's expedition to the upper Mississippi also is mentioned. Miss McCann confines her discussion to the region south of the mouth of the Arkansas, but she notes that "actually, the travels of the chronicler were more extensive than the geographical limits set herein, for he accompanied a mining expedition up the Mississippi as far as the present state of Minnesota."

Those who have followed the recent exploitation of long-neglected physical historical remains in the United States will welcome the first major contribution from the St. Augustine Historical Program. This is *The Defenses of Spanish Florida, 1565 to 1763,* issued by the Carnegie Institution of Washington as number 511 of its *Publications* (1941. 192 p.). The volume is the work of Verne E. Chatelain, formerly of the staff of the Minnesota Historical Society, and more recently in charge of the Florida undertaking. The study, beautifully planned and executed, deals with the colonization of Spanish Florida and the evolution of its defense system. Students may now look forward to other reports, particularly of field work, the interest and importance of which are suggested by a photograph and two diagrams in the present volume of archaeological work on the Cubo redoubt. Mr. Chatelain's study will be doubly valuable when it is supplemented by the physical data of the old defense system of St. Augustine itself.   G. Hubert Smith

A mass of detailed information, relating at times to the tribes of the Northwest, is presented by George D. Harmon in his volume on *Sixty Years of Indian Affairs, Political, Economic, and Diplomatic, 1789–1850* (Chapel Hill, North Carolina, 1941). In Chapter 11, the author touches upon relations with the Sioux in the early decades of the nineteenth century, outlining briefly the stories of Pike's treaty of 1805 and of the negotiations at Prairie du Chien in 1825 that resulted in the defining of a Sioux-Chippewa boundary. The treaties of 1837 and 1851 with both Sioux and Chippewa are dealt with in Chapter 20. Among the Minnesota characters who figure in the book are Taliaferro, Ramsey, Sibley, and Joseph R. Brown.

A bibliographical tool that will be welcomed by students of Northwest history is a *List of the Agricultural Periodicals of the United States and Canada Published during the Century, July 1810 to July 1910*, recently issued by the United States department of agriculture as *Miscellaneous Publication* no. 398 (Washington, 1941. 190 p.). The list was compiled by the late Stephen Conrad Stuntz, who began work on the project as early as 1902 while he was in charge of the classification of agriculture for the Library of Congress; it has been edited for publication by Emma B. Hawks, assistant librarian in the department of agriculture. A number of little-known Minnesota items are included on the list.

A general discussion of "Farm Journals, Their Editors, and Their Public, 1830–1860" is contributed by A. L. Demaree to the October issue of *Agricultural History*. Of special interest to Midwestern readers is an article in the same issue dealing with "Artesian-well Irrigation: Its History in Brown County, South Dakota, 1889–1900" and written by Marc M. Cleworth.

Brief histories of nearly seventy-five varieties of spring wheat grown in Minnesota, Montana, and the Dakotas are included in a *Dictionary of Spring Wheat Varieties* published by the Northwest Crop Improvement Association (Minneapolis, 1941. 92 p.). The account of each variety is accompanied by a photograph. The booklet presents also some information on stem rust epidemics that have occurred in the Northwest.

The daily life and ordinary experiences of the "deputy surveyors who followed the pointing of the compass back and forth across the land and blazed their trails through the forest, or erected on the open prairie mounds of sod to mark their lines" are described by Dwight L. Agnew in an article on "The Government Land Surveyor as a Pioneer," which appears in the *Mississippi Valley Historical Review* for December. Many of the examples of surveying activities used by the writer are localized in the Middle West, chiefly in Iowa and Wisconsin. The importance of the surveyors' "hard and hazardous work," writes Mr. Agnew, lies in the fact that it resulted in a "system of records by which every settler who bought land from the government might claim and accurately identify his plot of ground," thus giving him "a feeling of security in the possession of his land."

The Minneapolis area receives some consideration in Glenn E. Mc Laughlin's study of the *Growth of American Manufacturing Areas: A Comparative Analysis with Special Emphasis on Trends in the Pittsburgh District,* recently published by the bureau of business research of the University of Pittsburgh (1941. 358 p.). The relation between population growth and industrial expansion is brought out.

An interesting chapter in the history of communication in America is suggested in an article on "Business and the Telephone, 1878, as Illustrated by Early Directories," which appears in the *Bulletin* of the Business Historical Society for December. It was in 1878 that exchange systems were installed for the first time in a number of American cities, making the telephone a "practical instrument for the businessman." The speed with which businessmen adopted the new device is illustrated by the fact that "only four months after the telephone exchange had been installed in the young city of Chicago, the large number of telephones made necessary a systematic arrangement of the names of the subscribers" in a printed directory. A page from the classified section of this early Chicago telephone directory is reproduced with the article. Minnesotans will be specially interested in an article, in the November number of the *Bulletin,* dealing with "James J. Hill's Philosophy of Railroad Management." The author, William J. Cunningham, has been James J. Hill professor of transportation in the Harvard graduate school of business administration since the establishment of the chair in 1916. Shortly after his appointment, Professor Cunningham interviewed Hill at Jekyl Island, Georgia, and the report of this interview, in which the Empire Builder "expounded his philosophy of transportation and expressed his ideas about the things that should be emphasized," is herewith presented.

The October number of *Hardware Trade* commemorates "50 years of hardware progress in the great Northwest" and presents numerous articles and sketches relating to changes in this industry in the past half century. Two articles deal with the early history of the Minnesota Hardware Association; one tells of the founders of the organization, and the other reviews the story of its organization in 1897. There are descriptions of some of the wares featured in early hardware stores, such as stoves and ranges, bicycles, washing machines, and iceboxes. Many of the smaller items included in the hardware merchants' stock are pictured in a section labeled "Hardware Museum." The reminiscences of a number of hardware merchants and salesmen are included. Among them are some recollections of Mr. Paul Allen of Jamestown, North Dakota, who recalls that "Dakota Settlers Bought Housekeeping Needs in 'One Package'." In the 1880's and 1890's, according to Mr. Allen, most of the merchandise was purchased through wholesale dealers in the Twin Cities, and "it would take at least a week to get an order." Brief accounts of the wholesale firms that supplied merchants throughout the Northwest from St. Paul, Minneapolis, and Duluth also are included in the issue.

An unusual immigration document is reproduced in the *Mennonite Quarterly Review* for October under the title "A Passenger List of Mennonite Immigrants from Russia in 1878." In it are given the names, the home communities, and the destinations of steerage passengers who sailed from Bremen for New York on the steamship "Strassburg" on June 18, 1878. About a fourth of the passengers listed were bound for the Mennonite settlement at Mountain Lake in Cottonwood County, Minnesota. The original list is in the library of Goshen College.

Ole Bull's first American tour, which was made in the years from 1843 to 1845 and extended as far westward as St. Louis, is the subject of an article by Mortimer Smith entitled "Ole Bull Conquers the New World" in the *American Scandinavian Review* for December. This is a chapter from a forthcoming biography of the Norwegian violinist, by an author who had access to a mass of unpublished letters and papers. Since the volume will contain accounts of Bull's "utopian colony for his Norwegian countrymen in the forests of northwestern Pennsylvania" and of concert tours into the Northwest, including Minnesota, it should appeal to many Minnesota readers.

Several chapters of Carl Mangard's *Svenska öden i Amerika: En resa fran Atlanten till stilla havet* relate to Minnesota scenes and personalities (Uppsala, 1939. 261 p.). The author is a Swedish journalist who reported the tercentenary celebration of 1938 for the press of his homeland. His American travels included a visit with relatives in Le Sueur. One chapter deals with the "Swedish Model Farm" of Charles E. Swenson at Chisago City, and another is entitled "Among the Farmers in Minnesota."   J. H.

Those who have read *Five Fur Traders of the Northwest,* which was edited by Dr. Charles M. Gates and published in 1933, will be interested in knowing that Dr. Gates continues to be active in the publication of historical source materials. Last year he edited the *Messages of the Governors of the Territory* of Washington, which consists of official documents of interest primarily to research workers (see *ante*, 22:330). Dr. Gates's latest work is of greater general interest. *Readings in Pacific Northwest History — Washington, 1790–1895* (Seattle, 1941. 345 p.) includes many selections from the writings of explorers, fur traders, missionaries, government officials, army officers, travelers, early settlers, farmers, and businessmen, as well as from legislative enactments and official reports. Excerpts from over sixty contemporary records provide a well-rounded selection on the development of Washington for approximately a hundred years after Quimper's exploration in 1790. Dr. Gates has provided each excerpt with a brief introduction. This selection of *Readings* gives students of Washington history easy access to a horde of interesting and valuable materials on the background of that state.

L. B.

The final volume of the *American Guide Series,* that dealing with Oklahoma, appeared in November. The series consists of fifty-one books, one for each state in the Union and others for the District of Columbia, Puerto Rico, and Alaska.

Professor John T. Flanagan of the University of Minnesota is the author of an article on "James Hall and the Antiquarian and Historical Society of Illinois," which appears in the December issue of the *Journal* of the Illinois State Historical Society. Hall was the leading spirit, according to Dr. Flanagan, in a group of men who late in 1827 "gathered at the statehouse in Vandalia for the purpose of organizing a society to encourage interest in Illinois history," and he was the first president of the resulting organization. A review of Dr. Flanagan's recent biography of Hall will be found in another section of this magazine.

A convenient sketch of "Historical Michilimackinac" forms the first of three sections in a booklet entitled *Mackinac under Three Flags,* published by G. H. Wickman to serve as a "Tourist Guide and History of Mackinac Island and the Straits Country" (95 p.). Points of interest on the island and its attractions as a summer resort are the subjects of the other sections. The illustrations are, perhaps, the most interesting feature of the booklet, for they include both exterior and interior views of the restored buildings of old Fort Mackinac, a photograph of Mackinac in 1868, pictures of exhibits in the local museum, and portraits of some of the more important characters connected with the island's history.

The first issue of the *Wisconsin Historical News,* a clipsheet for newspapers containing news items about historical activities in Minnesota's neighbor to the east, was published by the State Historical Society of Wisconsin in January. It is edited by Dr. Edward P. Alexander, the newly appointed superintendent of the Wisconsin society.

A meeting held at Des Moines on October 11, 1941, resulted in the organization of the Iowa Association of Local Historical Societies, which has the support both of the State Historical Society of Iowa and of the State Department of History and Archives. Another result of the meeting is the publication by the State Historical Society of Iowa, as number 16 of its *Bulletin of Information Series,* of a booklet on the *Organization, Purposes and Activities of Local Historical Societies in Iowa,* compiled by Ethyl E. Martin (1941. 38 p.). Here is a useful guide for workers in the field of local history, and particularly for leaders of local historical societies. Included are statements about the importance of local historical societies, their organization, membership, purposes, activities, property, and housing, their relations with public libraries and the state organizations, and their publications. The constitution and bylaws of one county society and the articles of incorporation of another are presented by way of illustration. According to a foreword, "some very timely suggestions" included in the booklet were derived from an address on "Methods Used by Minnesota in Organizing County Historical Societies," presented at the Des Moines meeting by Dr. Arthur J. Larsen, superintendent of the Minnesota Historical Society.

An interesting example of publication by a local historical society is the *Ringgold County Bulletin,* a quarterly issued by the Ringgold County Historical Society at Mount Ayr, Iowa. In format the *Bulletin* resembles a newspaper; it is made up in four sheets of six columns each. It is sold for ten cents a copy or twenty-five cents a year, and subscribers include former residents of the county living in many parts of the Union. The *Bulletin* is printed in the office of the *Mount Ayr Record-News,* which keeps standing and contributes the type for items from its own columns that have local historical interest.

Sketches of eleven *Pioneers in Iowa Horticulture* prepared by Kent Pellett appear in a little book published by the Iowa State Horticultural

Society in commemoration of its seventy-fifth anniversary (Des Moines, 1941. 68 p.). An opening chapter deals with the "Sour Apple Trees" introduced into the Iowa country by such frontier figures as Louis Tesson and Antoine Le Claire, who planted orchards in the early decades of the nineteenth century. Henderson Luelling, "Iowa's first commercial nurseryman," who settled at Salem in 1836, is the subject of the first biographical sketch in the volume. It is evident from several of the accounts that these Iowa horticulturists influenced the development of fruit culture in Minnesota as well as in their own state. The author notes, for example, that Suel Foster, who helped to found the Iowa Agricultural College in 1857, "was enthusiastically heralding the Wealthy" apple in 1874. He planted some trees sent to him from Minnesota by Peter Gideon, and, writes Mr. Pellett, Foster "did more than Gideon to spread its [the Wealthy apple's] fame. He said he had sent the Wealthy into every state." Apple varieties imported from Russia in the 1880's by Professor J. L. Budd of the Iowa Agricultural College met with greater success in Minnesota than in Iowa, according to the writer of this volume.

An important leader of a farmers' organization in Iowa is the subject of a biography of *Milo Reno, Farmers Union Pioneer,* recently published as a "memorial volume" by the Iowa Farmers Union (Iowa City, 1941. 207 p.). As a background for the story of Reno's career, an account is presented of the beginnings of the Farmers Union, which had its origin in Texas in 1902. Reno's "Rise to Leadership" after joining the organization in Iowa in 1918 is described in one chapter, and others deal with his "Grass Roots Philosophy" and with special phases of his activity as a leader of the Farmers Union.

Frontier life in northern Iowa in the 1870's is depicted vividly by Arthur Pickford in a little book of reminiscent sketches entitled *Westward to Iowa* (1940. 97 p.). In the earlier chapters the author describes conditions in the English manufacturing district where he was born and tells of his family's emigration to America in 1866. After ten years in Wisconsin and Illinois, the writer's father decided to turn to farming in Iowa, and much of the narrative has its geographical setting in that state. Included are brief chapters on "Country Schools," social life, religion on the frontier, roads, blizzards, methods of communication, "Wood and Water" supplies, and the development of creameries.

An account of life in "An Early Norse Settlement in Iowa" is contributed by Andrew Estrem of Red Wing to the October number of the *Iowa Journal of History and Politics*. Roads, farm buildings, farm machinery, fences, the language used by the immigrant settlers, churches, schools, clothing, and holiday celebrations are among the subjects touched upon. The settlement is not named, but it is located on the border between Howard and Chickasaw counties.

Under the title *Along the Trails of Yesterday: A Story of McIntosh County*, Nina Farley Wishek presents the history of the North Dakota community to which she went as a pioneer settler in 1887 (1941. 437 p.). Some of the writer's best chapters deal with the social life of the pioneers who settled on the Dakota prairies of the eighties. She deals not only with the Americans who were establishing new homes in the West, but with the Russian and German settlers of the vicinity, telling what they wore and ate, how they built and furnished their houses, and describing the farming methods they used and some of the folk customs they brought with them from their homelands. There are interesting chapters also on "Old Trails and Stage Lines," on the building of railroads, and on the frontier schools.

"Milestones in the Progress of the Hudson's Bay Company," from its founding in 1665 to the present, are enumerated and explained by Clifford Wilson in the *Beaver* for December. A number of the incidents described center about the Red River settlements, which originated in an attempt to solve the "problem of feeding the fur brigades" traveling into the interior of Canada. The Red River country figures also in an article on "Ballantyne the Brave" by C. Parnell, in the same issue of the *Beaver*. It tells of the experiences of R. M. Ballantyne, who entered the service of the Hudson's Bay Company a century ago, and who came to know not only Fort Garry and York Factory, but the border lake country between Canada and Minnesota.

The acquisition by the Thunder Bay Historical Society of a manuscript "Journal of Transactions and Occurrences at Fort William, Lake Superior, 1823–24," is announced in the *Daily Times-Journal* of Fort William for November 15. Many interesting entries from the journal, which covers the period from October 18, 1823, to September 15, 1824, are quoted in connection with the announcement. They indicate that the volume reflects vividly the life of the trader and the daily events in the Hudson's Bay Company post at Fort William. Among the entries quoted is one that tells of a trip to Grand Portage and another that describes the traders' celebration of New Year's Day. The journal is now included in the museum of the Thunder Bay Historical Society, which was opened in the basement of the public library of Fort William on January 10. A special guest at the opening was Judge William E. Scott of Two Harbors, who represented both the Minnesota Historical Society and the North Shore Historical Assembly. Some of the exhibits and collections in the museum are described in the *Times-Journal* for January 12.

A useful and concise article on the "Origin of Canadian Railroads," in which George R. Belton undertakes to explain "why, when, where and how the railroads of western Canada came to be constructed," appears in the *Winnipeg Free Press* for November 15. Special attention is given to the railroads in the vicinity of Winnipeg. Among these is the Midland road constructed by James J. Hill in the 1890's.

General Minnesota Items

Records of such historical importance as those of the general land office and the office of Indian affairs are listed in the Minnesota Historical Records Survey's most recent addition to its *Inventory of Federal Archives in the States,* a volume devoted to the department of the interior (1941. 190 p.). Included are the archives of Indian agencies at Cass Lake, Grand Portage, Leech Lake, Nett Lake, White Earth, Pipestone, and Red Lake. A publication of timely interest issued by the Historical Records Survey is an *Inventory of Records of World War Emergency Activities* in Minnesota (1941. 85 p.). It includes a list of "World War Activity Agencies" that were operating in the state in 1917 and 1918. The survey has added four more volumes to its *Inventory of the County Archives of Minnesota.* They present lists of local records preserved in the courthouses of Beltrami County at Bemidji (no. 4 — 176 p.), of Houston County at Caledonia (no. 28 — 155 p.), of Redwood County at Redwood Falls (no. 64 — 139 p.), and of Yellow Medicine County at Granite Falls (no. 87 — 150 p.).

"Minnesota Document," a motion picture produced by the visual education service of the University of Minnesota, had its first showing at Northrop Auditorium on the university campus on November 12. The production of the film in the University of Minnesota was made possible by a grant from the Rockefeller Foundation. The scenario has been described as a "story of change and growth in the Northwest from Civil War times until today," picturing westward expansion and the "days when the Empires of Timber, Wheat, Iron, and Railroads were being built" and contrasting them with the "present complex diversified aspects of a great modern commonwealth." Members of the Minnesota Historical Society were given an opportunity to see the film at the evening session of the society's annual meeting on January 12.

A second group of water colors of Minnesota and western Indian scenes by Peter Rindisbacher is now on display in the Round Tower Museum at Fort Snelling. An earlier group is described *ante*, 22:434. The pictures now on view depict an "Indian Taking Scalp," the "Chippewa Mode of Traveling in the Spring and Summer," a "Chippeway Scalp Dance," a "Drunken Frolick amongst the Chippeways and Assineboins," a group of "Bison Attacked by the Dog Trains," and "The Murder of David Tully and Family by the Sissatoons, a Sioux Tribe." The artist probably witnessed the tragedy depicted in the latter picture. Both Tully and Rindisbacher were Swiss settlers from the Red River colony near the present city of Winnipeg, and both left that place to go to Fort Snelling in 1823. Tully and his family were attacked near Lake Traverse, and two young sons who were taken captive later were found and brought to the fort. The Rindisbacher pictures are being displayed in Minnesota through the courtesy of the United States Military Academy at West Point, which owns eighteen original water colors by this frontier artist.

Two account books containing records of transactions with Winnebago and Chippewa outfits at Sauk Rapids, Leech Lake, Rainy Lake, and other points in northern Minnesota are described in the *White Bear Press* for October 31. Among the items quoted is one which reads, "Invoice of sundries furnished Winnebagos whilst removing Summer 1844." Such names as Henry M. Rice, Alexis Bailly, Alexander Ramsey, and Henry H. Sibley appear frequently. The editor of the *Press* obtained the volumes from Mr. G. H. Eachus of Mahtomedi.

Tams Bixby, a native of Virginia who gained distinction both in Minnesota and in Indian Territory, is the subject of a biographical sketch by Robert L. Williams in the *Chronicles of Oklahoma* for September.

Bixby's activities as a newspaper publisher at Red Wing and as secretary of three Republican governors in the 1880's and 1890's are recalled. Emphasis is placed, however, on his activities in the Southwest, especially as a member of the commission to the Five Civilized Tribes of Indian Territory.

The fiftieth anniversary of the founding of Concordia College at Moorhead is commemorated in the issue for October 9 of the school paper, the *Concordian*. The school was opened in 1891 in a building previously used by the Bishop Whipple School, an Episcopal institution. Articles appearing in the anniversary issue deal with this building and others erected later on the Concordia campus, with the college presidents, with the history of college athletics, and with student and faculty activities. An entire section of the *Moorhead Daily News* for October 10 is devoted to articles about Concordia College and its history. Among them is a review of its founding and growth by Professor H. C. Nordlie.

An entire chapter of Louis Adamic's latest book, *Two-way Passage* (New York, 1941), is devoted to a discussion of the St. Paul Festival of Nations. Under the title "Unity within Diversity in St. Paul," Mr. Adamic retells the story of the local International Institute and describes the elaborate folk festival that it staged in 1939. A similar festival will be presented in May, 1942.

A pictorial record of *100 Years of Medicine in Minnesota* has been published by the Minnesota State Medical Association (St. Paul, 1941. 26 p.). Medical progress had its beginning in Minnesota, according to an introductory statement, when Dr. Christopher Carli "arrived at the site of what is now Stillwater on May 24, 1841, and became the first civilian medical practitioner to settle permanently in the territory." A portrait of Dr. Carli appears on the cover of the pamphlet. Pictures of an early drug store, a pioneer doctor's office, and the first hospital in Minneapolis, and portraits of early doctors are among the more interesting illustrations.

"The Minnesota City Medicine Made" is the title of a chapter in Frank J. Jirka's volume on *American Doctors of Destiny,* in which he presents "historical narratives of the lives of great American physicians and surgeons whose service to the nation and to the world has transcended the scope of their profession" (Chicago, 1940). The "Minnesota city" of this volume is, of course, Rochester, and the doctors of the chapter are William W. Mayo and his sons. The development of the Mayo Clinic and Foundation as well as the careers of the doctors are briefly sketched. The author's complaint that "a comprehensive history of the Doctors Mayo and their Clinic has never been written" is no longer valid, for the need for such a work was filled in 1941 with the publication of Miss Clapesattle's *The Doctors Mayo*, which is reviewed *ante*, 22: 404–408.

Sketches of "Certain Homeopathic and Eclectic Pioneers" who practiced in Minnesota make up the three final installments of James Eckman's history of "Homeopathic and Eclectic Medicine in Minnesota" in the October, November, and December issues of *Minnesota Medicine*. Mr. Eckman's study is published as part of a general "History of Medicine in Minnesota" (see *ante*, 22: 334, 434).

The founding of the Minnesota Public Health Association in 1906 by Dr. H. Longstreet Taylor of St. Paul is recalled in the *St. Paul Pioneer Press* for November 2, which calls attention to the organization's thirty-fifth anniversary. It was known originally as the Minnesota Association for the Relief and Prevention of Tuberculosis, but in 1914 plans were made to broaden its activities and the name was changed.

Minnesota scenes form the background for many events in the life of Father John A. Ryan, an important Catholic leader in the field of social reform, whose autobiography has been published recently under the title *Social Doctrine in Action: A Personal History* (New York, 1941. 297 p.). Father Ryan was born on a Dakota County farm in 1869, was raised in a typical Irish Catholic community, and received his early education and training for the priesthood in the Catholic schools and seminaries of St. Paul. His simple farm home, he records, offered only meager "opportunities for culture in the form of books, magazines, and newspapers," but it is interesting to note that, in addition to religious treatises and a work on Ireland, he had access to a history of Dakota County. Among those who influenced substantially what Father Ryan describes as his "Early Social Education" were two prominent Minnesotans, Ignatius Donnelly and Archbishop Ireland. It was the latter who sent the author to the Catholic University of America and who gave him the opportunity, upon graduation, to teach moral theology in the St. Paul Seminary. The chapters dealing with his professorship there from 1902 to 1915 also tell of Father Ryan's activities in the "Field of

Organized Charity," including services as vice-president of the Associated Charities of St. Paul.

A volume containing the "official history and record" of the *Ninth National Eucharistic Congress, St. Paul and Minneapolis, June 23–26, 1941* has been published by the executive committee of the congress (St. Paul, 1941.   293 p.). A brief chapter on the history of "The Eucharist in the Archdiocese and Province of St. Paul" is contributed by Father Thomas J. Shanahan. Under this heading he tells of the priests who served the French posts of Fort Beauharnois and Fort St. Charles, of early Catholic missionaries at Grand Portage and Pembina, and of the building of the Chapel of St. Paul.

The gap between a New England community and the Minnesota frontier of the 1830's is bridged in a recent volume by Wilbur Stone Deming entitled *The Church on the Green: The First Two Centuries of the First Congregational Church at Washington, Connecticut* (Hartford, 1941.   235 p.). From this church Samuel and Gideon Pond went forth on their search for the mission field that they found among the Sioux of Minnesota in 1834, and to it Samuel returned to study for the ministry and to be ordained. The brothers' long period of service as missionaries to the Sioux and as preachers to congregations of pioneer Minnesotans is reviewed in a chapter entitled "The Church and the Indians."

The story of the hearthstone used in Dr. Thomas S. Williamson's house at Lac qui Parle while he served there as a missionary is reviewed by Mrs. A. N. Kohr in the *Montevideo American* for December 5. She reports that in 1886 Alfred Riggs, a son of Stephen R. Riggs, who occupied the house after Williamson left, visited Lac qui Parle and removed the stone to Santee, Nebraska, where he was connected with an Indian mission school. Recently the stone, which weighs some two thousand pounds, was returned to the site of the Minnesota mission, where it will be permanently preserved in the Lac qui Parle State Park.

A study of conditions in St. Paul and Minneapolis is the basis for a monograph on *Land Values as an Ecological Index* by Calvin F. Schmid, which has been published by the State College of Washington as volume 9, number 1, of its *Research Studies* (1941.   36 p.). The author discusses the "patterning of land values" in the two cities, their relationship to population growth and to automobile and pedestrian traffic, some of the racial elements in the population, prices per front foot of property in various sections, and a number of other topics. Considerable information on business and social history is included.   S.A.D.

Reports on two recent Minnesota studies, one of which is reviewed *ante,* 22:314, are included in a discussion of "Consumers' Cooperatives in the Middle West" appearing in the October number of the *Monthly Labor Review* of the United States department of labor. In the upper lakes region of Michigan, Minnesota, and Wisconsin, according to this survey, are "generally successful associations built up from most unpromising economic and social conditions." The fact is brought out that "in the economy of the whole region, the Finn has played an important part — as miner, lumberjack, and farmer — and he also has been the backbone of the cooperative movement there." The results of a study of "Cooperative Oil Associations in Minnesota," made by the agricultural experiment station of the University of Minnesota, also are considered.

In his pursuit of *Murder Out Yonder* (New York, 1941), Mr. Stewart H. Holbrook uncovered a bit of Minnesota folklore in the form of a ballad with the following catching refrain:

> Then tell the tale of a criminal,
> Kit was his promised bride.
> Another fate to answer;
> Another fatal ride.

Mr. Holbrook gives the entire ballad as well as an account of the famous murder which inspired it — that of Kitty Ging by her supposed sweetheart, Harry Hayward, in Minneapolis in 1884 — in his recent volume bearing the subtitle, "An Informal Study of Certain Classic Crimes in Back-country America." In the same volume is retold another Northwest incident, the battle of Cameron Dam, Wisconsin, which "was well into folklore . . . almost before the powder smoke along the Thornapple had blown away." In telling the latter story, Mr. Holbrook includes with the account of John Dietz's stand at the dam, some of the repercussions of the event in Minnesota, where Dietz became a symbol of the "Embattled Farmer" in both the foreign-language and third-party presses. The part played by Floyd Gibbons, young Minneapolis reporter who covered the battle, is likewise included.   SARAH A. DAVIDSON

Mr. Holbrook plays up a Minnesota catastrophe in still another recent book, a popular history of the lumber industry entitled *Tall Timber* (New York, 1941). In a chapter entitled "Death in the Woods," he retells the story of the forest fire of 1894, emphasizing the horrors that accompanied the destruction of Hinckley. In general the book records the westward movement of the lumber industry, with brief mention of the movement into Minnesota of the Maineites and later of Germans and Scandinavians, and a chapter on the "Second Migration" to the Pacific coast as the timber holdings of the Middle West were exhausted. A brief account of the career of Frederick Weyerhaeuser is included in the latter chapter. As a final section, the author presents a useful "Lumberjacks' Dictionary."

"Forest Invasion and Succession on the Basins of Two Catastrophically Drained Lakes in Northern Minnesota" is the title of an article by Etlar L. Nielsen and John B. Moyle appearing in the *American Midland Naturalist* for May, 1941. The lakes considered are Bass Lake in St. Louis County, which almost disappeared in 1925, and Sunken Lake in Itasca County, much of which was drained in 1915. The plant life that has grown up in the old lake basins is the object of study by the present authors.

The second of the "Conservation Pioneers of Minnesota" whose careers are described for the *Conservation Volunteer* by Evadene B. Swanson is "Andrews, Father of Forestry" (see *ante,* 22:337). The soldier, lawyer, and diplomat from St. Paul who studied forestry while serving as United States minister to Sweden is the subject of a sketch in the October number of the *Volunteer*. In the November issue, a section devoted to "Notes on Natural History" contains a review by G. N. Rysgaard of the provisions of some of Minnesota's early game laws.

Local Historical Societies

Co-operation between Canada and the United States has been extended into the historical field in northeastern Minnesota, where the .ocal historical societies of St. Louis, Lake, and Cook counties, which formerly constituted the North Shore Historical Assembly, have admitted to that organization the Thunder Bay Historical Society of Ontario. The assembly holds a joint meeting in a North Shore community each summer.

At a meeting of the Anoka County Historical Society held in Anoka on December 8, the following officers were elected: P. C. Heard, president, Mrs. Julia DeLong, vice-president, Lynn French, treasurer, Mrs.

L. J. Greenwald, corresponding secretary, and Theodore A. E. Nelson, secretary. A library formerly owned by the local high school and now in the possession of the society was described by Mrs. Fannie Lenfest.

The Carver County Historical Society held its annual meeting at Mayer on October 24. All officers were re-elected and a program of brief talks was presented. Mr. O. D. Sell, the society's president, reported that 1,745 objects had been classified and arranged in the society's museum, which was open for inspection. He also revealed that visitors during the past year included more than four hundred school children and people from eighteen states. The museum is open regularly on Wednesday and Friday afternoons, according to an announcement in the *Waconia Patriot* for December 25.

The Chippewa County Historical Society is one of the sponsors of a WPA project that has for its object the reconstruction of the Lac qui Parle mission church. The work of rebuilding the church began on October 13. The society has agreed to raise seven hundred and fifty dollars as its contribution toward the project. A committee, of which Mrs. A. N. Kohr of Montevideo is chairman, has charge of raising the money.

Judge Julius E. Haycraft of Fairmont was the speaker at the annual meeting of the Cottonwood County Historical Society at Windom on October 11. He related incidents in the early history of the county, giving special attention to the results of the census enumerations made in 1857 and 1860. Officers elected for the coming year include E. E. Gillam, president, Fred Earlewine, vice-president, and N. J. Bell, secretary.

All officers of the Dakota County Historical and Archaeological Society, of which Mr. Fred E. Lawshe of South St. Paul is president, were re-elected at a meeting held at Hastings on November 5. Mr. Lawshe presented a brief review of the county's history.

At the annual meeting of the Ignatius Donnelly Memorial Association, which was held in the Historical Building in St. Paul on November 21, Frank Muirhead of Hastings was named president, Victor E. Lawson of Willmar, vice-president, and Mrs. Annie Brown Morris of Minneapolis, secretary. The association has made temporary repairs on the Donnelly House at Nininger, and during the summer it kept the house open for visitors.

Measured by actual accomplishment, perhaps the most active local historical society in the state during the last quarter of 1941 was that in Hennepin County. Outstanding among its activities was the sponsorship of a little volume entitled *The Bohemian Flats,* compiled by workers of the writers' program of the WPA and published by the University of Minnesota Press. The book is reviewed in another section of this magazine. The society issued also, in October, the regular quarterly number of *Hennepin County History: A Quarterly Bulletin,* with notes on meetings, accessions, membership, museum displays, attendance, and other activities, and brief articles of local historical interest. Among the latter is an account of the "Creation of Hennepin County" by Dana W. Frear, and on "Early School Days in Hopkins" by R. J. Mayo. The annual meeting of the society, at which all officers were re-elected, was held in Minneapolis on October 7, and regular monthly meetings were held on November 5 and December 2. The November meeting was held at Bloomington, and Mr. F. Wilson Pond and others recalled events in the early history of the community. A "Hobby Show" with more than twenty exhibitors was the feature of the December meeting.

At its regular meeting on October 1, the Kandiyohi County board appropriated the sum of a thousand dollars for the Kandiyohi County Historical Society. The money is to be used for constructing a fireproof vault in the society's museum on the county fair grounds, thus assuring the safe preservation of archives and other valuable records in the custody of the organization. An editorial in the *Willmar Daily Tribune* for October 2 commends the action of the board in thus providing for the preservation of county and other local records. The writer asserts that the "safe-keeping of county records is only one small part of the mission of the county historical society," which should also make an effort to collect and make available school, church, township, and other records of local value.

Mr. Oscar Beckman was named president of the Lake County Historical Society at its annual meeting, held at Two Harbors on November 5. Other officers for the coming year include Dr. J. A. Jumer, vice-president, and William E. Scott, secretary-treasurer.

About a hundred people attended the quarterly meeting of the McLeod County Historical Society held at Glencoe on October 27. The program, which was arranged by Mrs. Isabelle Zrust, president of the local chapter of the society, included papers and talks on the early history of Glencoe by Miss Mae Hankenson; on the experiences of a pioneer, G. K. Gilbert, by his granddaughter, Miss Clara Gilbert; and on an early Glencoe merchant and banker, Captain M. Theony, by his daughter, Mrs. Minnie Austin. A special display of pioneer objects was arranged in connection with the meeting. Meetings of the Hutchinson chapter of the McLeod County society were held on October 21, November 18, and December 16. At the November meeting, Mr. S. S. Beach was named president of the chapter, Dr. S. E. Bennion, vice-president, and Mrs. Grover Finney, secretary-treasurer. Sketches of frontier life in McLeod County, contributed by Mrs. Sophie P. White, secretary of the county society, have been appearing under the heading "Pioneer Pictures" in the *Hutchinson Leader*. The influence of settlers from New England, who built the town of Hutchinson around a public square, thus using as a model the villages they had known in the East, is brought out in the sketch published on October 17. In the issue for November 7, Mrs. White tells a story of Charles P. Kittredge, an early settler from Maine. When he moved into his own log cabin in Hutchinson, his relatives in the East, picturing a pretentious residence, sent him a silver door plate engraved with his name for his new house. A pioneer Christmas celebrated by the German settlers of Acoma Township is described in the issue for December 19.

At the annual meeting of the Marshall County Historical Society, which was held at Warren on December 12, plans were discussed for a summer meeting in 1942 "with all communities of the county participating in showing the make-up of America." All officers of the society, including Judge Nels M. Engen, its president, were re-elected.

The sum of eight hundred dollars for the work of the Olmsted County Historical Society was appropriated by the county board at a meeting held on October 10. The society's president, Mrs. Bunn T. Willson of Rochester, headed a delegation that appeared before the board to explain the organization's needs and aims. Among other communities represented were Stewartville, Byron, Chatfield, and High Forest. At the society's annual meeting, which was held in Rochester on October 28, Dr. Arthur J. Larsen of the state historical society presented an address on "The Local Historical Society and the Community." Officers of the society read reports which revealed that the organization now has a hundred and seventy-five members and that more than three thousand objects have been assembled for its museum collection.

Pioneer residents of Fergus Falls and life there in the 1880's were described by Judge W. H. Goetzinger of Elbow Lake in an address presented before the annual meeting of the Otter Tail County Historical Society, which was held at Fergus Falls on November 8. He emphasized the importance of historical museums like that of the Otter Tail County society, wherein the records of the past can be preserved and displayed. Another speaker, the Reverend William Van Dyken, described the society as a "link between the past and present." Reminiscent talks were given by two pioneer Otter Tail County women, Mrs. R. Bogstad of Eugene, Oregon, and Mrs. M. H. Wellman, an early teacher. Officers elected at the meeting include Judge Anton Thompson, president, M. J. Daly, first vice-president, Elmer E. Adams, treasurer, and E. T. Barnard, secretary. More than thirty thousand visitors who registered have viewed the Otter Tail County society's museum exhibits, according to the "Historical Society Notes" prepared by Mr. Barnard for the *Fergus Falls Daily Journal* of December 5. Gifts recently added to the society's collections are described in this and other issues of the *Journal.*

The possibility that the Pipestone County Historical Society may soon obtain quarters for a museum is announced in the *Pipestone Leader* for November 25. Mr. H. A. Petschow, the society's president, suggests that the home of a pioneer family might be purchased and remodeled for use as a museum. In the issue of the *Leader* for December 9, the suggestion is made that a proposed addition to the courthouse include a room for the historical society.

Dr. Paul Hagen was named president of the Polk County Historical Society at its annual meeting, which was held at Crookston on December 14. Other officers elected are E. A. Estenson, vice-president, Mrs. Bert Levins, secretary, and John Saugstad, treasurer.

"Personal Recollections of Judge Thomas E. Buckham and Anna Mallory Buckham" was the title of a paper read by Mrs. Charles Batchelder before the annual meeting of the Rice County Historical Society in Faribault on November 4. Her paper appears in installments in the *Faribault Daily News* for November 5, 6, and 7. All officers of the society were re-elected at the meeting. They are Carl L. Weicht, president,

Mrs. Howard Bratton, vice-president, Miss Mabel Pierce, corresponding secretary, Miss Amy Babcock, secretary, and Donald Scott, treasurer.

Plans are under way for the publication of a history of Roseau County, with the Roseau County Historical Society acting as sponsor in co-operation with the county board and the Minnesota writers' project. Material for the book will be assembled under the supervision of Mr. Earl Chapin, editor of the *Warroad Pioneer*. Since only meager materials on the history of this northernmost section of Minnesota are in print, the forthcoming volume should prove particularly useful.

The career of Joseph R. Brown was reviewed by Dr. Arthur J. Larsen, superintendent of the Minnesota Historical Society, at the annual meeting of the Sibley County Historical Society in Henderson on November 14. Election of officers resulted in the naming of A. L. Poehler as president, Einar A. Rogstad, secretary, and G. A. Buck, treasurer. Some early legal documents presented to the society for its museum collection are described in the *Henderson Independent* for December 19.

Programs for meetings to be held in the fall and winter by the Lake Pepin Valley Historical Society were outlined at a meeting held in Lake City on October 14. Most of the programs will center about events in the history of Lake City. Officers elected at the meeting include R. C. Bartlett, president, Francis H. Kemp, vice-president, and Emil Bohmbach, secretary-treasurer.

At its quarterly meeting, which was held in Waseca on October 6, the Waseca County Historical Society announced its plan "to honor the memory of each departed member with a book to be placed in the county library." Other matters discussed were the publication of a volume dealing with the history of the county, and heating arrangements for the society's log cabin museum.

At the annual meeting of the Washington County Historical Society, which was held at Stillwater on October 6, E. L. Roney was named president, Miss Mary Bailey of St. Paul Park, first vice-president, Mrs. Rollin G. Johnson of Forest Lake, second vice-president, Mrs. George Goggin of Stillwater, secretary, and Miss Ruth Grandstrand of Marine, treasurer. Among the new accessions displayed at the meeting were some seventy-five photographs of houses and stores in pioneer Stillwater, made by an early itinerant photographer who identified the pictures but, unfortunately, failed to date them. Dr. Grace Lee Nute, curator of manuscripts for the Minnesota Historical Society, was the speaker at a meeting held at Mahtomedi on December 2. She took as her subject the contributions of pioneer women to the development of Minnesota.

LOCAL HISTORY ITEMS

Some "Personal Memories of Early Life in What is Now Hazelton Township," Aitkin County, are presented by Alice K. Hazelton in an article appearing in three installments in the *Aitkin Republican* for October 30 and November 6 and 13. Mrs. Hazelton tells of going to Aitkin County and settling on a homestead after her marriage at Excelsior in 1885. Many of the early settlers in the vicinity are named and many phases of frontier life are described.

Some information about the early history of Blackduck in Beltrami County is included in the fortieth anniversary edition of the *Blackduck American,* issued on December 11. An account of the village's first year is reprinted from the first number of the *American,* published on December 11, 1901.

A voyage by sailboat from Norway to Quebec and thence overland by railroad and wagon to Brown County, Minnesota, is recalled by Ole K. Broste in a reminiscent narrative which he dictated to Petra M. Lien and which has been issued in multigraphed form (12 p.). The Broste family was one of several Norwegian families who immigrated in a group in 1868 and who settled in Linden Township, Brown County. The log cabins and sod huts in which they lived and the hardships with which they were forced to contend are vividly described by Mr. Broste. The grasshopper plagues and the blizzards of the 1870's are among the events recalled.

Winter sports in Hastings in the 1880's are recalled in an article accompanying two views of a toboggan slide built on West Second Street in 1886, appearing in the *Hastings Gazette* for December 5. According to this account, Hastings boasted "well patronized toboggan clubs" which made trips to St. Paul, and the "clubs of the capital city came to Hastings by train with brass bands, and they formed parades up and down the streets." A photograph of the sawmill owned by R. C. Libbey at Hastings in 1874 is reproduced with a descriptive note in the *Gazette* for November 21.

A "History of Winnebago" compiled from various printed sources by Mrs. Cecil Robertson appears in the *Winnebago City Enterprise* for October 2. This account of a Faribault County community was read before a meeting of the Round Table Study Club of Winnebago.

A history of the Trinity Lutheran Church of Blue Earth is included in a booklet issued on September 21, 1941, to commemorate its fiftieth anniversary. The congregation was organized in 1891 as the Blue Earth City Scandinavian Evangelical Lutheran Church. The account includes sketches of pastors who have served the congregation, descriptions of church buildings, and reviews of the activities of various church organizations.

The fact that the "Wheels of Industry in Albert Lea Started 85 Years Ago" is brought out by Lester W. Spicer in a feature article appearing in the *Evening Tribune* of Albert Lea for October 11. Logging operations inaugurated by George S. Ruble in the fall of 1856 marked the beginning of industrial development at Albert Lea, according to Mr. Spicer. The dam that Ruble built across the Shell Rock River and early mills and bridges are described in the article. The history of the Hayward Creamery, a co-operative plant established in 1885, is reviewed by Charles Nelson in the *Tribune* for October 28.

Under the title "Gordonville Village Before & After," a reminiscent narrative by Livy E. Joppa appears in installments in the *Glenville Progress* from October 23 to December 11. In the issue for November 13, the author tells of the fruit trees and bushes transported from Pennsylvania by Thomas J. Gordon, one of the earliest settlers in the vicinity; an early Fourth of July celebration is the subject of the sketch appearing on November 20; and a co-operative creamery established in 1889 is described in the final installment.

The village of Hader in Goodhue County is the subject of an interesting sketch in the *Wanamingo Progress* for October 30, which calls attention to the fact that the original plat of the town, dated August 22, 1857, is owned by Mr. S. O. Haugen of Wanamingo. The present account reveals that Hader was an important station on the stagecoach line between Faribault and Red Wing in the 1850's, that the first Goodhue County fair was held there, and that it rivaled Red Wing in the contest for the county seat. In 1920 a co-operative cheese factory was established at Hader, and its story is reviewed in the *Bulletin* of the Goodhue County Rural Electrification Association for October. The latter article is reprinted in the *Zumbrota News* for October 24.

Installments of a "History of Houston County" by H. P. Krog have been appearing in the weekly issues of the *Hokah Chief* since October 30. An editorial note informs the reader that the narrative is based upon "notes and sketches found among papers of the late Edward Wheeler, well known La Crescent citizen of fifty years and more ago." The beginnings of settlement in southeastern Minnesota are described in the opening installments, and many of the men who went there before 1856 are named. A list of "interesting events chronologically arranged," beginning with 1854, appears in the issue for December 4.

The background of Scandinavian settlement in Kandiyohi County that resulted in the founding of Bethel Lutheran Church at Willmar in 1891 is brought out by Victor E. Lawson in a review of "Bethel's Past," published in the *Willmar Daily Tribune* for October 8. The article appears with an account of the celebration by this Swedish congregation of its fiftieth anniversary.

The course of one of the Red River trails through what is now Gennessee Township in Kandiyohi County is traced in a brief article in the *Atwater Herald* for October 3. It includes a quotation from an early description of a Red River train.

Articles about the early history of Koochiching County and its pioneer citizens continue to appear in the *International Falls Press* under the heading "Down the Years with Our Pioneers" (see *ante,* 22:346). Particularly valuable are the historical sketches of villages, townsites, and ghost towns in the county, most of which were founded within the present century. Included, for example, are accounts of Hannaford, Mizpah, Little Fork, and Big Falls, in the issues for October 2, and November 6, 13, and 15, and a list of ghost towns in the number for December 4. Noteworthy also is a brief review of the history of Fort Frances, the city on the Canadian side of the Rainy River, in the issue for October 16. Interesting accounts of dams in the Rainy River country and of the Women's Civic League of International Falls are published on October 23 and 30. The articles appear also in the Saturday issues of the *International Falls Daily Journal.*

Some recollections of Barney Arnesen, who has lived in the Lake of the Woods country since 1894, are reported in the column entitled "Over the Editor's Desk" in the *Warroad Pioneer* for December 25. He names a number of traders who were operating in the area in the 1890's and locates their trading stores, and he tells the story of an Indian pow-wow that he witnessed in 1899.

The "only industrial development that ever took place in the Northwest Angle country of Minnesota" is the subject of an article in the *St. Paul Pioneer Press* for October 26. It deals with the exploitation of felspar mines in the area, beginning in 1928, when a mill which ground the product for market was erected at Warroad. Transportation of the felspar by barge over the Lake of the Woods proved impractical, and production ceased in 1937. The dismantling of the mill at Warroad is announced in the present article.

The fiftieth anniversary of the founding of a business that developed into the present firm of George A. Hormel and Company is the occasion for the publication, in the November number of *Squeal: The Hormel News-Magazine,* of a detailed history of an important industry at Austin. Year-by-year improvements in the packing plant that Mr. George A. Hormel opened in a remodeled creamery in the fall of 1891 are described in this elaborately illustrated issue. Included also are sketches of the founder of the firm and of members of his family who later entered the business in southern Minnesota. The student of business history will find much to arrest his attention here, for among the illustrations are reproductions of pages from early account books, of price lists issued by the firm, of early newspaper advertisements, and the like; and similar types of materials have been used in the preparation of the narrative. Notable also are the many photographs which illustrate the growth of the packing plant and the development of its products.

The Hormel company and its place in the history of Austin receive attention also in the golden anniversary edition of the *Austin Daily Herald,* published on November 8. A wealth of information about the history of Austin and of Mower County is presented in this issue. It contains, for example, an account of the organization of the village of Austin in 1868, with a detailed record of the year-by-year activities of the council, based upon its minutes for a period of twenty years. Industrial development is stressed, with reviews of the growth of railroads since their first operation in the region in 1867, and accounts of such local business firms as a printing shop, a sawmill, motion picture houses, and the *Herald* itself. The stories of the founding of the township and the origin and growth of the city are recounted in detail, and the history of the community's public utilities is reviewed. The Opera House that was the city's "social and cultural center" in the 1890's is the subject of an article by Don V. Daigneau. There are numerous articles dealing with the history of the county and of its smaller settlements. The many interesting illustrations add to the value of the edition.

R. W. Terry is the author of a brief review of the history of Murray County which appears in the *Murray County Herald* of Slayton for October 2. The narrative was prepared for a volume in preparation under the auspices of the Minnesota Editorial Association.

Members of the Woman's Missionary Society of the Union Presbyterian Church of St. Peter celebrated the organization's sixty-fifth anniversary on November 14. The history of the society was reviewed by Mrs. E. C. Carlton, and some recollections of early members were presented by Mrs. H. L. Beecher. Some information about the beginnings of the organization in 1876 is presented in the *St. Peter Herald* for November 12.

The store at West Newton which still remains as it was in 1898 when its owner, Alexander Harkin, decided to return to his native Scotland is described as a "Historian's Paradise" in the rotogravure section of the *St. Paul Pioneer Press* for December 7. A brief account of the West Newton store accompanies a series of interesting photographs showing the exterior, the pigeonholes in which mail was distributed, the wood-burning stove behind which are shelves filled with drugs and spices, and other merchandise characteristic of this pioneer store.

A former postmaster of Ada, Mr. Jason Weatherhead, reviews the "History of Ada and County Postal Service" in the *Norman County Index* of Ada for December 18. He traces the beginnings of regular mail service in the vicinity back to 1874, when a post office known as Macdonaldville was established in a farmhouse on the Wild Rice River. Postmasters who have served at Ada since an office was established there in 1876 are named, other post offices in the county are listed with the names of the first postmasters, and "post offices that were in operation in Norman county at various times but are now discontinued" are given with the years during which they were open.

Some "Hunting Stories of Long Years Ago," gleaned from the files of the *Fergus Falls Journal,* are combined in an article appearing in the issue of that paper for October 6. Among the stories included are those of a morning's hunt that netted fifty-three ducks in 1873, of two hunters who bagged eighty prairie chickens in a single day in 1880, and of the men who brought in forty-two wild geese in 1888.

"Fisher's Landing, Minnesota," is described by Alfred Torrison as a "town which has been made and then destroyed in the course of railway extension," in the *North Dakota Historical Quarterly* for October. The importance of the settlement on the Red River during the era of steamboat transportation as well as in the period of railroad building is brought out. Some rather startling errors occur in the text; the "Anson Northup," the pioneer steamboat on the Red River, for example, is designated as the "Anse Northrup."

The seventy-eighth anniversary of the Pilgrim Baptist Church of St. Paul, which is said to have been founded by a "little band of Negro slaves who escaped from their masters in Civil War days," is the occasion for the publication of an article about its history in the *St. Paul Pioneer Press* for November 9. Among the illustrations is a portrait of the Reverend Robert T. Hickman, who founded the church.

The memory of Frank Hibbing, who discovered iron in the vicinity of the community that bears his name and who platted the original townsite, was honored on October 21, when the Frank Hibbing Memorial Park was dedicated and a bronze statue of Hibbing was unveiled. In the *Hibbing Daily Tribune* for October 20, Mrs. David Graham retells the story of Hibbing's discovery of ore in 1892 and of the founding of the community. Pictures of the Hibbing monument appear in the *Tribune* for October 20 and 22.

Miss Gertrude B. Gove is the author of a *History of Technical High School* in St. Cloud, which has been published as a pamphlet (16 p.). As a background for the development of high-school education in the Stearns County city, Miss Gove traces the story of education in the community back to 1858, when the "first tax-supported school held in the pioneer village" opened its doors. She mentions also a school conducted by a Benedictine father, a private school organized by Miss Amelia Talcott, a seminary established in 1860, and a high school planned in 1862 by Jane Grey Swisshelm. The steps by which the city attained a high-school room, a three-year course, and finally a fully organized high school are carefully traced.

With a joint history of the townships of "Long Prairie and Round Prairie," O. B. DeLaurier has concluded the series of detailed histories of Todd County townships that have been appearing in the *Long Prairie Leader* for some years past. The final section opens in the issue for October 23 with reviews of the geology, archaeology, Indian inhabitants, and exploration of the district under consideration.

"Newspaper History of City Dates Back 86 Years" reads the headline of an article in the *Winona Republican-Herald* for December 6. It not only tells of the founding of the city's papers, but describes the activities of pioneer journalists, such as W. J. Whipple and Daniel Sinclair. Various types of presses that have been used in Winona newspaper offices since 1892 are described in other articles appearing in the same issue of the *Republican-Herald*.

MINNESOTA HISTORY

VOLUME 23 • PUBLISHED IN JUNE 1942 • NUMBER 2

The Middle Western Farm Novel

John T. Flanagan

THE MIDDLE WESTERN farm novel, like the American farm novel in general, has been slow to develop. And this delay is the more inexplicable when one realizes that the Middle West has been and is largely rural and agrarian. But American novelists have been strangely loath to use farm backgrounds and themes in their stories. For most of its existence the United States has been a predominantly agricultural country, yet it was not until the rise of industrialism that writers began to choose rural settings for their novels. One can call the roll of the major American novelists of the nineteenth century: Irving, Cooper, Hawthorne, Melville, Twain, Howells, James; not one ventured to give with any completeness the agricultural background from which the infant nation derived its strength. The Revolution, the frontier, legends of Dutch and Puritans, the forest, the Mississippi River, the ocean, the activities of cosmopolitans and expatriates — all these seemed more vivid, more consequential, than the labor and struggles and mores of the farmer. Even Edward Eggleston, the first novelist to exploit the backwoods and its natives, devoted himself to circuit riders, land speculators, and rural pedagogues rather than to farmers. As late as 1900 only a handful of genuine farm novels had appeared.[1]

Moreover, those writers who did see in the farmer a suitable protagonist rarely viewed him realistically. Agriculture in the pages of

[1] A selective bibliography of Middle Western farm novels appears in the "Notes and Documents" section, *post*, p. 156–158.

the average nineteenth-century novel had a curious musical-comedy air about it. Tillers of the soil were romantic creatures, singularly far removed from actualities like manure and chilblains; barn dances and sewing bees and husking frolics were the order of the day, and almost every evening milkmaids sang around the old oaken bucket to welcome the returning laborers. Thus Bayard Taylor in his valuable and interesting novel, *The Story of Kennett* (1866), managed to give falsely romantic impressions of rural life in the Brandywine Valley. Helen Hunt Jackson in her famous *Ramona* (1884) mingled with her poignant picture of a persecuted race scenes which presented the grain farmer as a heroic figure. And Opie Read in *The Jucklins* (1895) began his tale with convincing sketches of life in the North Carolina plantation country, but soon plunged the reader into a melodramatic courtship.[2]

Toward the end of the nineteenth century, however, a few novels appeared which not only presented the farmer in sharp focus but also treated him with a salient and intimate realism refreshingly different from earlier glorification. And it is significant that the best of these productions came from the Middle West.[3] In 1883 E. W. Howe published his *Story of a Country Town,* a book which sketched the wheat farmers of the Kansas plains with bitter clarity and which revealed the drabness and futility of their life no less sharply than the morbid, hysterical religion in which they sought relief. The book deals as much with the village virus as with the life of the farmer, yet its characters are essentially rural, and Howe depicted their bare, cankered existence with memorable fidelity.

Four years later Joseph Kirkland published *Zury: The Meanest Man in Spring County,* a chronicle of central Illinois admittedly modeled on Hardy's Wessex tales. Kirkland had been reared on the Michigan frontier, where he was early exposed to the crudity of speech and roughness of manners indigenous to primitive commu-

---

[2] A brief general treatment of the subject which omits significant novels is Caroline B. Sherman's article on the "Development of American Rural Fiction," in *Agricultural History,* 12:67–76 (January, 1938).

[3] In *Seth's Brother's Wife* (New York, 1886), Harold Frederic wrote an incisive picture of farm life in upper New York state.

nities. Later he removed to Illinois and engaged in coal mining ventures near Danville, an enterprise cut short by the Civil War. He served honorably as infantry officer and aide-de-camp until the battle of Antietam, then left the army to devote himself to law and journalism. But his experiences in field and camp had sharpened his observational powers, and his novel is too teeming with details of life and speech to deserve the obscurity into which it has fallen. Zury, the parsimonious, avaricious, cunning farmer who builds up a fortune, is a brilliant portrait done with humor and insight. By indefatigable industry and the exercise of native shrewdness Zury makes himself the dominant figure in the county, feared but respected. To build his chronicle, Kirkland drew copiously from his knowledge of frontier farming and moreover transcribed the dialect of his characters with such phonetic exactness that he found it necessary to help his readers by supplying a glossary. *Zury* remains one of the most important fictional treatments of the American farmer.[4]

Finally in the 1890's came the work of Hamlin Garland, the most publicized if not the most gifted of farm chroniclers. In such volumes as *Main Travelled Roads* (1891), *Prairie Folks* (1893), *Rose of Dutcher's Coolly* (1895), and *Jason Edwards* (1897), Garland convincingly demonstrated his doctrine of veritism, the creed that a man should write accurately and truthfully about what he knows. Not for nothing was he called the first dirt farmer in American literature. For Garland had been brought up in a small valley in southwestern Wisconsin, where erosion washed the soil and cut deep gullies in the hillsides. He had followed his family into Iowa, constantly seeking more fertile land, and he had pre-empted a claim in Dakota Territory and had lived in a soddy while he wrestled with the prairie loam. Garland knew farmers who lived "under the lion's paw" in mortal fear of mortgage sharks; he had seen his own family struggling against debt and climate. The scenes he drew were unprecedented in the pages of American fiction.

After the turn of the century Garland shifted over to romantic

[4] For an account of Kirkland's life and work, see John T. Flanagan, "Joseph Kirkland, Pioneer Realist," in *American Literature*, 11:273–284 (November, 1939).

fiction until *A Son of the Middle Border* (1917) brought him back to the realism of his youth, but his earlier books revealed the sharpness of his perceptions. A half century has passed since his gaunt farm wives and work-harried farmers first appeared in fiction, but they have not been forgotten. No one before Garland drew with such bitter truth the hopeless struggles of the coulee dwellers or the efforts of men on the Dakota prairies to raise wheat in the face of wind and drought. His books have influenced every subsequent novelist of the farm.

In one sense, however, Garland's picture was distorted. His eviscerated farmers had only one objective: to escape from the farm. They were either fugitives from a way of life they could not dominate, or they hated their environment with a vindictive if futile bitterness. Conditions were such that only flight promised relief. Yet even in the days of railroad rate wars, Populist protests, and anti-imperialist juntos there were farmers who had faith in the land and who wrested a living from it despite the obstacles of climate, depressed markets, and predatory bankers. Such figures do not appear in *Main Travelled Roads*. It remained for later writers to present a more balanced picture of the farm.

In the first years of the present century, despite the rise of literary naturalism, attempts were made to continue the early romantic treatment of rural themes. Arthur Stringer in such books as *The Prairie Wife* (1915) and its sequels used the vivid colors and broad canvas of the Canadian Northwest. More particularly Willa Cather in her Nebraska novels, *O Pioneers!* (1913) and *My Ántonia* (1918), glorified farming and the farm wife. She not only touched on the racial stratification of the Middle West, but she drew characters who believed in the land and who were able to realize their convictions by persistence, industry, and a little good fortune. Thus Alexandra Bergson, by buying when land values are depreciating and by gambling on the perennial demand for wheat, succeeds magnificently. And Ántonia Shimerda develops into the perfect farm woman, energetic, calm, fecund. The farm novel in Miss Cather's hands reached a lucidity and a beauty of style which it did not have previously and which it has rarely attained since.[5] But unfortunately her characters are more than a little romanticized and as a consequence somewhat unconvincing. Her feminine protagonists especially have the cards conveniently stacked in their favor.

The farm novel is such a commonplace today that there are few corners of the Middle West untouched by the storyteller, but the romantic tradition has been greatly modified. At times the writer has combined history with fiction. Thus Louis Bromfield's *The Farm* (1933) deals with several generations of an Ohio family and shows how as the country gradually became settled, and as industry developed, the ancestral farm shrank in size and decreased in importance. In the century since the arrival of Colonel MacDougal in 1815 many changes took place, not the least of which — as the author asserts in his preface — was the decay of integrity and idealism. Almost a complementary study is Harold Sinclair's *American Years* (1938), which traces the evolution of a typical Illinois town from a crossroads community to which professional men of various kinds eventually gravitated. On the other hand, Sterling North's *Plowing on Sunday* (1934) depicts a southern Wisconsin community in which the characters are complacent in their isolation from national and world affairs but happy because of their success in breeding prize stock and in growing bonanza crops. In all these stories the backgrounds are real, the occupations and customs are accurately described, and the characters are neither caricatures nor rebels against the farm.

The 1920's brought a spate of farm novels of the Middle West, most of them competent and many of them interesting. Mr. and Mrs. Haldeman-Julius produced in *Dust* (1921) a dreary picture of the destitution of the Kansas plains. G. D. Eaton's *Backfurrow* (1925) applied the same treatment to the interior of Michigan. John T. Frederick in *Druida* (1923) utilized the Red River Valley as a salient background for his interpretation of wheat farmers and the vapidities of a provincial normal school. Somewhat more dramatic is Cornelia Cannon's *Red Rust* (1928), which deals with life in

[5] Among the few farm novels of genuine literary distinction, Ellen Glasgow's study of rural Virginia, *Barren Ground* (New York, 1925), is conspicuous.

northern Minnesota and the attempt of a gifted farm youth to develop a rust-resisting wheat. Interwoven with this theme is the struggle of a group of Swedish immigrants not only to hew homesteads out of the wilderness but also to maintain their own cultural ideals. The characters are insufficiently vitalized, but the setting is honest and rich. The most skillful of these novels is Martha Ostenso's *Wild Geese* (1925), a story set among the Finns and Icelanders of northwestern Minnesota and southern Manitoba in which the dominant figure, Caleb Gare, is a combination of domestic tyrant and Yankee slave driver. The story is extremely vivid. One sees school board meetings, families stuffing themselves at dreary meals, toilers in stubble and woods. And Miss Ostenso has filled her book with a dramatic narrative which only a garish melodrama weakens. Although *Wild Geese* is still one of the most satisfying of American farm novels, when the author returned to the subject in subsequent books she was less effective. *The Mad Carews* (1927), for example, fails because of a lack of concentration on the rural background and the absence of such striking characters as Caleb Gare and his rebellious daughter Judith.

About the time that Miss Ostenso turned her attention to the Red River Valley, Herbert Quick was producing his novels of frontier Iowa, *Vandemark's Folly* (1922), *The Hawkeye* (1923), and *The Invisible Woman* (1924). These books are inconsistent and often too highly colored, yet they contain remarkable pictures of the immigrant farmers who developed the prairie state. Young Jake Vandemark, "a buttermilk-eyed, tow-headed Dutch boy with a face covered with down like a month-old gosling," is an interesting and useful protagonist.[6] He helps to expel a claim jumper by the tried process of tarring and feathering, he serves in the Civil War and is wounded at Shiloh, he survives a prairie fire and a blizzard, and by dint of shrewd trading and hard work he builds up a prosperous stock farm. Into this novel and its sequels Quick poured a flood of detail, which is emphasized by his colloquial but idiomatic style. In *The Hawkeye* desperadoes and rustlers play a needlessly large role,

[6] Quick, *Vandemark's Folly*, 212 (Indianapolis, 1922).

but the narrative remains authentic. Later Iowa writers like Ruth Suckow, Phil Stong, and Paul Corey have brought the story down to date, but Herbert Quick's books are invaluable documents in the social history of the state. Whether he writes of the corruption of county government, the rise of the Grangers, the crudities of rustic education, or necessary processes such as threshing and cornhusking and plowing, his scenes are vivid and real. And nowhere will one find a more beautiful description of the Iowa prairie as it was in the 1870's than in the pages of *The Hawkeye*.[7]

Nevertheless, O. E. Rölvaag's *Giants in the Earth* (1927) is the one Middle Western novel of the period which, while accurate and graphic in particulars, succeeds in transcending its milieu and develops into an epic chapter of man's struggle against the elements. Written originally in Norwegian and then translated into English, it tells the saga of Per Hansa and Beret, immigrants to the Dakota prairies, who discover that the climate and *Weltansicht* of the West require a fortitude, a perseverance, an adaptation of habit and method which they had scarcely dreamed of. Per Hansa is on the road to successful adjustment when he meets his fate in a blizzard. With intelligence and Norwegian tenacity he had learned to break and till the prairie mold, to endure the northern winters, and even to enjoy little intervals of companionship with other voyagers from the homeland. But to Beret the immense loneliness of the new land, the lack of trees, the howling winds, the vast emptiness of the sky were all but insupportable. Beret represents a whole group of pioneer mothers and wives who found the independence of the West an inequitable substitute for the spiritual security of their homes. Their bodies endured silently, but their souls and sometimes their minds seemed lost.

Published on the eve of the depression, *Giants in the Earth* is written with such skill and covers such an enormous canvas that it dwarfs other attempts to treat the same theme. Per Hansa and Beret are both individuals and types, heroic when judged by human stand-

[7] Quick, *The Hawkeye*, 152 (Indianapolis, 1923). Readers interested in regionalism and local color should also observe Quick's reiterated plea for the use of Iowa material for literary purposes, in the same work, p. 476.

ards, pygmies when seen against the infinite space of the West. Rölvaag builds up the background with consummate art in a style
which, even in translation, shows brilliance. In other ways, too, *Giants
in the Earth* is significant. It put an end to the jejunely romantic
treatments of the farm by serious novelists, and it likewise halted the
depiction of the farmer as a creature happy only if and when he
escaped from his environment. There are moments of triumph and
moments of defeat in the novel, exactly as there are in life, and sometimes the emotions are mixed. But above all, Rölvaag's Norwegian
immigrants are convincing. The land they have chosen will yield
them a living, but ultimate prosperity will entail, as it always must,
both poverty and pain.

In the last ten years the farm novel, no longer a novelty, has become a firmly established subspecies of American fiction, but it still
seems largely indigenous to the Middle West.[8] Besides becoming
popular, it has also assumed various forms. Occasionally it becomes
a modified success story; more frequently it shows the farmer battling the twin evils of financial depression and drought. But unlike
the Joad family, the farmers commonly stay with the land; they do
not emulate the wandering hen. Possibly conditions abroad offer
small inducement for migration; more probably the farmers feel
that the one thing permanent in an age of social convulsions is the
land, and that the land must produce as it always has produced the
staples of human existence.

One of the most successful recent exponents of the rural Middle
Westerner is Ruth Suckow. In such books as *Country People* (1924),
Iowa Interiors (1926), and *The Folks* (1934), she has portrayed
the Iowa farmer, the renter, the old folks who retire and move into
the county seat to spend their declining years, the hired girl, and the
distant relative who has made a success in the city and who returns
home to flaunt his prosperity and his sophistication. In her calm and

[8] Among interesting farm novels of the 1930's with a locale outside the Middle West
one might mention Gladys Hasty Carroll's stories of Maine, — *As the Earth Turns*
(1933), for example, — and particularly Marjorie Kinnan Rawlings' perceptive and
finely wrought tales of the Florida scrub, *South Moon Under* (1933) and *The Yearling*
(1938). In her charming autobiography, *Cross Creek* (1942), Miss Rawlings continues
her vivid pictures of the southern backwoods.

occasionally dull style she paints a complete picture, revealing not only the daily routine, but the complacency and the imperviousness of her people to outside ideas. Her characters do not read and rarely travel, unless like so many good Iowans they end their days in southern California. Their life is completely domestic and rural. Thus, although Miss Suckow's books lack conscious satire, in their presentation of a drab and spiritless existence they draw up an indictment of provinciality almost as scathing as Sinclair Lewis' in his more outspoken *Main Street.*

But Ruth Suckow is by no means the only articulate Iowan in the field of the novel. Paul Corey has recently published a trilogy dealing with the widow Mantz and her four children and their persistent struggle to free their farm from debt. *Three Miles Square* (1939) narrates the successful fight of the oldest son, Andrew Mantz. With intelligent tenacity he improves the farm, makes necessary improvements, increases the stock, and wins the respect of his neighbors. Although members of the Mantz family are the protagonists, Corey, by means of what might be called a lateral technique, introduces various other characters through whom the reader perceives the central figures. Covering the half-dozen years before America entered the first World War, *Three Miles Square* gives an interesting panoramic view of the Iowa countryside at a time when the farmer was becoming excited over Henry Ford's new method of locomotion and when it was necessary to join a meat ring to be assured of fresh meat during the summer. In *The Road Returns* (1940), Corey follows the fortunes of the Mantz children, emphasizing in various ways the desire of each to escape from the farm, one through professional training in architecture, one through an aptitude for machinery, and one through a college education and a white-collar job. The significance of *County Seat* (1941) lies chiefly in the fact that the depression has convinced the youngest boy, Otto, that his place is not behind a desk but on the seat of a plow. Corey's style is simple and accurate, his realism earthy, and if neither his plot nor his characterization is brilliant, the reader nevertheless feels the honesty and forthrightness of the treatment. As a reviewer in the *New York*

Times remarked of *County Seat,* "The novel achieves distinction through virtue of its accent on mediocrity."[9]

Phil Stong has also used the Iowa background, the best-known of his several stories probably being *State Fair* (1932). His decision to present with enthusiasm so characteristic a Middle Western institution as a state fair and to choose for his hero a prize-winning hog was gratifyingly successful, and his book is obviously free from the obsessions and neuroses which warp many a farm novel. The same spirit is detectable in Paul Engle's *Always the Land* (1941), which expresses faith in human beings and in modern scientific farming. Engle, better known as a poet than as a novelist, delineates a family interested in breeding fine horses and sketches with vigor and deftness the place of the county fair in the farmer's life.

Other Middle Western states have likewise produced farm novels of competence. Herbert Krause's *Wind without Rain* (1939) treats of a German community in western Minnesota and of a family resembling somewhat the Gares of *Wild Geese,* bred to hard work, deprived of relaxations and independence, tyrannized over by an obdurate father. The result too is similar: the children rebel. Krause's book is somber and overwritten, but many of the scenes are remarkably effective. The author himself grew up in Otter Tail County in a locality blind to the impingement of the outside world, so that the mores and social life of the foreign settlers lingered with a corrosive effect. The hatred of the younger generation for the farm, Krause clearly attributes to the deprivations endured in youth.

Since Hamlin Garland introduced the Dakota prairies to fiction, several writers have chosen that locale. Rose Wilder Lane in two novels has striven to present the combined rancher-farmer battling to make a living on marginal land. In *Let the Hurricane Roar* (1933) and *Free Land* (1938), she reveals sympathetically the struggle to exist on semiarid soil in a country harried by wind and drought and cyclonic storms. *Free Land* centers on the attempt of a young couple to homestead north of Yankton. They only half succeed. As David Beaton remarks to his father, "I've been on this

[9] Rose Feld, in the *New York Times Book Review,* September 7, 1941, p. 7.

claim five years come August, and today it's not worth a hoot in Hades. I started with as good as fifteen hundred dollars and I put five years work on top of that and sunk it. I couldn't sell out today, every jot and tittle I own, and pay over half what I owe. But it's a good country. I'll be right here, father, when this farm's worth something." [10] The significant thing is that Beaton remains. Various afflictions have not crushed him. *Free Land,* superficial and badly written as it is, is almost a history of the work facing every pioneer Westerner: breaking the land, building a soddy, digging a well, caring for horses and a cow (and occasionally for oxen), reaping and harrowing and threshing. The characters are incompletely realized, but the background is authentic.

In another story of Dakota, Horace Kramer's *Marginal Land* (1939), the protagonist is equally certain that life can succeed despite adversity and ill fortune. Stephen Randall, facing death in Chicago from consumption, returns to his father's ranch and begins anew as a stockman. For a time he is tempted to convert his ranch into a wheat field, but successive droughts persuade him that nature never intended marginal land to grow grain. The story ends with Randall a prosperous breeder of stock selling horses to the Allies. *Marginal Land* is not merely a chronicle of slow achievement. There are ample details of western life: battles against drought and blizzards and prairie fires, the replacement of sod houses with frame dwellings, attempts to raise flax and beans and raspberries, visits to the market town, social gatherings such as a Fourth of July celebration or a barn dance. In most of this activity, Randall is central. But his physical struggle is the complement of his spiritual struggle against the environment, a struggle complicated by his Chicago-bred wife's utter refusal to co-operate or indeed to live with him in his ranch home. In this novel the author with considerable less effect dealt with the same theme which Rölvaag handled so brilliantly in *Giants in the Earth.* The motives in settling on the prairies are different, but the problems are similar.

An equally interesting treatment of the cattle country is Mari

[10] Rose Wilder Lane, *Free Land,* 330 (New York, 1938).

Sandoz' *Slogum House* (1937), a strongly flavored novel of the Nebraska range in which the attention focuses on stock raising rather than on agriculture. The Slogum family is vicious and is led by a memorable fury, Gulla Slogum, victor in many a cattle feud by unscrupulous methods. Miss Sandoz' intention in this rather unrestrained story was apparently to give a dramatic account of the range before law and order were completely established. Her intimate knowledge of irrigation, dry-land farming, riparian rights, and cattle raising sometimes swamps the story. But one does not forget the predatory matriarch who lets nothing balk her.[11]

Thus, within the last fifty years and especially within this century, the farm has become a recognized precinct of American fiction. Curiously enough, it was not until the census statisticians began to denominate the country as more urban than rural that novelists began to write persuasively and interestingly about the farm. People revolted physically against a rural life only to recreate it artistically. But today agriculture and the farmer are common themes for our artists. It is peculiarly fitting that the Mississippi Valley, the great productive center of the nation, should have produced the most satisfying rural novels. Ellen Glasgow has written beautifully of agrarian Virginia, Erskine Caldwell achieved a *succès à scandale* with his picture of Georgia in *Tobacco Road* (1932), and John Steinbeck's *Grapes of Wrath* (1939) is essentially an agricultural novel with the scene shifting from Oklahoma to California, yet in bulk our best farm novels from the beginning to the present have come from the Middle West.

What might be said of the quality of these novels? The fact that one remembers only characters like Alexandra Bergson and Beret and Gulla Slogum suggests one generalization: our farm novelists on the whole have not succeeded in individualizing their people. Fresh characterization is the crying need not only of drama but of fiction. Yet very few of the novels already discussed contain portraits instinct with life. Two or three names and faces stand out; the rest

[11] In *Old Jules* (Boston, 1935), which is excluded from discussion here because it is not strictly fiction, Miss Sandoz has sketched life in the Niobrara Valley in western Nebraska with remarkable power.

are puppets on whom certain narrative strands are hung. Their mediocrity quickly consigns them to oblivion. Secondly, the reader observes that most of the novelists bring to their field only the meagerest technical equipment. The style is usually competent, seldom either salient or rich. It is accurate, simple, direct, but often stereotyped and impoverished. In similar fashion the technique of the narrative is bare and unoriginal, and many of the plots lack intensity. Good storytellers are rare among these novelists of rural life. Only exceptional writers like Rölvaag and Miss Cather escape this arraignment. Finally, one is convinced that as a result of the slow evolution of farm novels, the authors have learned to present their backgrounds with fidelity and completeness. There is no longer vagueness, uncertainty; instead one sometimes feels that the pendulum has reversed too far and that there is a superfluity of detail. The spareness of Miss Cather's later books might well instruct less competent artists.

Eventually a great farm novel is bound to appear (unless one is willing to accept *Giants in the Earth* as the desideratum), a novel as tremendous as *Moby Dick,* as lucid and poignant as *The Rise of Silas Lapham,* as human and real and galvanic as *Huckleberry Finn.* For man, despite refinements and adjustments, remains a creature of earth, and no human being is closer to the elements, to nature, than the farmer. And when that book appears it will be the natural and logical culmination of a long series of rural fictions.

With Cass in the Northwest in 1820

Edited by Ralph H. Brown

On November 18, 1819, Governor Lewis Cass of Michigan Territory placed before John C. Calhoun, secretary of war, his long-considered plans for an exploration of the interior Northwest. "It has occurred to me," he said in preface, "that a tour through that country, with a view to examine the production of its animal, vegetable, and mineral kingdoms, to explore its facilities for water communication, to delineate its natural objects, and to ascertain its present and future probable value, would not be uninteresting in itself, nor useless to the Government." [1]

This would seem to constitute a full program for a summer's expedition, but several "political objects," more definitely Cassian, also are listed. These include a personal inspection of the Indian tribes, the extinction of Indian land titles at many strategic sites, an examination of the copper deposit on the Ontonagon River, an inquiry into the attitude of the Indians at Chicago respecting the removal of the Six Nations to that area, a survey of the state of the British fur trade in the more remote districts, and instructions to the Indians of the views of the United States relative to their intercourse with the British at Malden and elsewhere.

Believing that the border Indians, especially the Chippewa, should be ruled with a firm hand, Cass proposed to announce to them in unmistakable terms that their visits to British posts "must be discontinued." The time had come, he said in effect, to exhibit to the Northwestern Indians the power and beneficence of the federal government. "I think it very important," writes Cass, who was experienced in Indian affairs, "to carry the flag of the United States into

[1] Lewis Cass to John C. Calhoun, November 18, 1819, in *American State Papers, Indian Affairs*, 2:318. The exploration of the headwaters of the Mississippi was not officially referred to, although the Cass journalists included this in their lists of objectives. The examination of the copper deposit at Ontonagon is listed as a "political objective," presumably because of the government's interest in copper for use in building ships.

126

those remote regions, where it has never been borne by any person in a public station." If economy must be thought of, one canoe, piloted by French boatmen, would be adequate, but if the government wished some display of power, an additional canoe, "manned with active soldiers, and commanded by an intelligent officer," was highly to be recommended. Allegiance of the aborigines could also be maintained or won over by the distribution of presents. For this, funds would be required, but not in staggering amounts. In fact, it was estimated that the whole tour could be financed for less than fifteen hundred dollars, to be diverted from the usual sum appropriated for Indian expenditures.

As Calhoun read toward the end of the letter, the full scope of the expedition was gradually revealed. Would it not be desirable to assign to the party an officer from the corps of engineers, one capable of taking astronomical positions and of constructing a correct map? Furthermore, "some person acquainted with zoology, botany, and mineralogy" would contribute greatly to the geographical objectives of the party. Cass closed his long letter by saying that he would like an early reply, "as it will be necessary to prepare a canoe during the winter . . . should you think it proper to approve the plan."[2]

For several weeks, Cass awaited an answer, or at least an intimation of the secretary's attitude. In the hope of speeding a decision, Cass requested that William Woodbridge, Michigan's territorial delegate in Washington, act in his behalf. As early as mid-December a correspondent urged that if Calhoun approved of the expedition "it would be peculiarly desirable to Gov. Cass to be advised of such fact as early as possible. The materials of which the Bark canoes of the Lake Country are made, can be procured only by sending a great distance to Indians remote from Detroit, and the apprehension is lest they should not be purchased in time for the next season."[3] When

<hr>

[2] Cass to Calhoun, November 18, 1819, in *American State Papers, Indian Affairs,* 2:319.

[3] From an unsigned letter to Calhoun, dated December 13, 1819, and probably written by William Woodbridge, in the Department of War, Letters Received, National Archives, Washington. The Minnesota Historical Society has microfilm copies of all letters and other items from the National Archives cited herein. See also, Cass to Calhoun, November 18, 1819, in *American State Papers, Indian Affairs,* 2:319.

Cass learned that his "political objects" had not found favor with the secretary of war, he again sought Woodbridge's intervention. "I am peculiarly solicitous," he informed the delegate, "that directions be given for the extinction of the land titles at the places stated in my letter to Mr. Calhoun. These were 1. In the vicinity of the Straits of St. Marys, 2. At the bed of copper ore on Lake Superior, 3. At Prairie du Chien, 4. At Green Bay, 5. Upon the water communication between the two latter places. . . . I consider it very necessary that the country upon each side of the Fox and Ouisconsin Rivers should belong to the United States. At present we are mere trespassers." [4]

The proposed tour was officially sanctioned on January 14, 1820, Calhoun expressing personal approval, even enthusiasm, for its geographical objectives. He suggested in addition that "Should your *reconnaissance* extend to the western extremity of Lake Superior, you will ascertain the practicability of a communication between the Bad or Burntwood [*Brule*] river and the Copper or St. Croix and the facility they present for a communication with our post on the St. Peter's [*Minnesota*]. The Montreal rivers will also claim your attention, with a view to establishing through them a communication between Green Bay and the west end of Lake Superior." However, Cass was not to engage in treaty making except as prescribed in a letter of April 5 by which he was authorized to negotiate for a military site, not exceeding ten miles square, at the Sault de Ste. Marie. Finally, the expedition was approved, provided it could "be made out of the sum allotted to your superintendency of Indian affairs, adding thereto one thousand dollars for that special purpose." [5]

The personnel of the expedition was to include, according to Calhoun's original plan, "some officers of the topographical engineers"

[4] Cass to Woodbridge, January 29, 1820, Woodbridge Papers, Burton Historical Collection, Detroit Public Library.

[5] Calhoun to Cass, January 14, April 5, 1820, in *American State Papers, Indian Affairs*, 2:319, 320. The post to which Calhoun refers is Fort St. Anthony, now Fort Snelling, which was established at the junction of the Minnesota and Mississippi rivers in the summer of 1819. The Cass expedition cost exactly $6,318.02; Dr. M. M. Quaife suggests that the "results accomplished were in inverse proportion to this insignificant item." See "From Detroit to the Mississippi in 1820," in *Burton Historical Collection Leaflet*, 6:60 (March, 1930).

and "a person acquainted with zoology, and botany, and mineralogy." Many likely candidates were approached by both Cass and Calhoun before the staff was finally complete. Economy dictated that members should receive no more than a dollar and a half a day, a stipend which many competent scientists considered to be inadequate. For example, Cass first proposed Andrew G. Whitney, "a respectable and intelligent lawyer of this place," as observer in zoology and mineralogy. The secretary of war gave his approval to this nominee, although Whitney, whose knowledge touched broadly upon many fields, questioned his own fitness. "I shall endeavour to pick up a little knowledge," he wrote, perhaps with undue modesty, in January, "more than I now have of Botany, Mineralogy, etc., to make my observations more useful"; but later he said, "If I should not go, it will be no loss. My going still depends on the quantum of pay." Whitney finally did not join the party, but aided it nevertheless by buying some of the equipment and interviewing candidates while he was traveling in the East. Many condemned the government's penny-wise policy; a professor of mathematics, for example, urged that by all means the party should include a "first rate astronomer, geologist, and mineralogist," and should be equipped with at least two astronomical theodolites.[6]

Calhoun made two principal appointments: Captain David B. Douglass and Henry R. Schoolcraft. Douglass, then on the West Point faculty, was appointed primarily to fill the post of topographer. He was informed that "The astronomical and topographical observations will of course be made by you, and the departments of zoology and botany will require as much of your attention as you may be able to bestow upon them." Douglass finally accepted the assignment following a lengthy period of consideration during which he wrote to an acquaintance of his concern that acceptance "would have laid me constructively under the obligation to resign even though the expedition (of which at the time I was not so well informed)

[6] Calhoun to Cass, January 14, April 5, 1820, in *American State Papers, Indian Affairs,* 2:320; A. G. Whitney to Woodbridge, January 28, March 7, 1820, Woodbridge Papers; Cass to David B. Douglass, March 17, 1820, Cass Papers, Burton Historical Collection.

failed to hold out advantages sufficient to justify such a step." [7] Calhoun introduced Schoolcraft to Cass as "a gentleman of science and observation, and particularly skilled in mineralogy [who] has applied to me to be permitted to accompany you on your exploring tour. . . . I have directed him to report to you for that duty, under the belief that he will be highly useful to you, as well as serviceable to the Government and to the promotion of science." [8]

Perhaps Calhoun knew something of Schoolcraft's literary ambitions, which had already been displayed in the publication of one book and the writing of a number of magazines distributed in manuscript form. Calhoun doubtless surmised that the expedition would gain some publicity as a result of the appointment. In this instance, Schoolcraft proved to be more than prompt, for the *Detroit Gazette* of February 9, 1821, announced that "We are happy to learn that an account of this interesting tour may be expected from the pen of this gentleman, for it is believed that few persons are more competent to the task. His view of the Lead Mines in Missouri, has shewn that in all the essential requisites of an observer and an author, he will ere long claim a distinguished station among the literary men of our country. . . . We learn that Mr. Schoolcraft's book will be printed in Albany, N. Y. and that it will be completed in March or April." [9]

The wide coverage and popularity of the Schoolcraft narrative may have forestalled the completion of a geographical work by Douglass. Even after Schoolcraft's book had been on the market for some weeks, Douglass was writing from West Point saying, "The Sec'y of War has just communicated his approbation to a plan lately furnished by me upon an understanding with Gov'r Cass and

[7] Douglass to Woodbridge, February 10, 1820, Woodbridge Papers; Cass to Douglass, March 17, 1820, Cass Papers.

[8] Calhoun to Cass, February 25, 1820, in *American State Papers, Indian Affairs,* 2:320.

[9] Schoolcraft's *Narrative Journal of Travels through the Northwestern Regions of the United States . . . to the Sources of the Mississippi River* was published at Albany in 1821. Two years after his expedition of 1832, which resulted in the discovery of Lake Itasca, Schoolcraft issued a new journal, and in 1855 his *Summary Narrative,* which combines accounts of both expeditions, appeared at Philadelphia. The Minnesota Historical Society has a photostatic copy of the file of the *Detroit Gazette* that is owned by the Burton Historical Collection.

Mr. Schoolcraft for the publication of the geographical and other scientific results of our last summer's expedition." The projected volume was to be of wide scope, apparently, for, wrote Douglass, "Agreeably to this plan, besides a map, a memoir Geographical, Descriptive and peradventure Philosophical on the country generally embraced by our observations will fall to my share in the execution of it." Cass wrote approvingly of the prospective Douglass report, saying "The progress of our geographical knowledge has not kept pace with the extension of our Territory, nor with the enterprize of our traders. But I trust that the accurate observations of Capt. Douglass will render a resort to the old French maps for information respecting our own Country entirely unnecessary." [10] Possibly Douglass was glad to be freed from the necessity of completing so stupendous a task. Had Cass lived to see all the printed matter which originated in his tour, however, he would probably have been satisfied. Newton H. Winchell attributes to this source fifteen scientific papers by members of the party or by others to whom botanical and geological collections had been sent.[11]

Cass appointed the other men who assembled in Detroit late in May for the great adventure. He informed Calhoun that he planned to take Dr. Alexander Wolcott, "Indian Agent at Chicago with the expedition: I do this," Cass explained, "because he is a scientific man and a skilful Physician, and we are therefore not under the necessity of engaging a person for the latter object. The information to be derived from the tour will be useful to him in his future communications with the Indians." [12] James D. Doty, official journalist, prepared at least two reports. Extracts from one, written in the form of a let-

[10] Douglass to Augustus B. Woodward, August 14, 1821, Woodward Papers, Burton Historical Collection; Cass to Calhoun, September 27, 1820, Department of War, Letters Received, National Archives.

[11] See N. H. Winchell, in *The Geology of Minnesota*, 1:32 n. (Geological and Natural History Survey of Minnesota, *Final Report* — Minneapolis, 1884). Among the authors of papers listed are Samuel L. Mitchill, John Torrey, D. H. Barnes, and Isaac Lea. A letter that accompanied a keg of minerals sent to Dr. Daniel Drake of Cincinnati indicates that Schoolcraft carefully selected and labeled the specimens. See Cass to Drake, March 11, 1821, Cass Papers, Chicago Historical Society.

[12] Cass to Calhoun, March 23, 1821, Department of War, Letters Received, National Archives.

ter to Governor Cass, were first published by Jedidiah Morse, who also made a tour of the upper Great Lakes country during the summer of 1820 under the authority of Calhoun. A more complete version of this report was later edited by Lyman C. Draper and published under the title of "Northern Wisconsin in 1820." The other Doty report, primarily a narrative, was edited by Reuben G. Thwaites and may be known briefly as the "Official Journal." This report ends abruptly, for no assigned reason, with the arrival of the party at Prairie du Chien on the return journey. An anonymous account which bears many resemblances to these reports appeared in five installments in the *Detroit Gazette*. The inference that the newspaper story derives from Doty is inescapable. Cass's own report to Calhoun was not intended for publication, though in it he promised later to submit a more complete statement which apparently never was written.[18]

Cass was also responsible for the appointment of Charles Christopher Trowbridge, whose journal of the expedition is herewith reproduced in full. This youth of twenty had been a resident of Detroit for only a year before the organization of the Cass party. When asked by his employer, Major Thomas Rowland, if he would like to accompany the expedition, the young man replied with emphasis that "he would rather black boots than miss it." Following the tour, Trowbridge returned to Detroit where, in 1826, he married Catherine Whipple Sibley, eldest daughter of Judge Solomon Sibley, a family connection which may have led to later visits to the Minnesota area. At least there is some indirect evidence that Trowbridge visited his brother-in-law, Henry H. Sibley, at Mendota in 1843. Bishop Jackson Kemper, who traveled by boat to Fort Snelling in the summer of

[18] Extracts from Doty's letter are included in Jedidiah Morse, *Report to the Secretary of War of the United States on Indian Affairs*, 55; Appendix, 31–41 (New Haven, 1822). For Doty's "Northern Wisconsin in 1820" and his "Official Journal," see *Wisconsin Historical Collections*, 7:195–206, 13:163–219. The anonymous account is in the *Detroit Gazette* for November 24, and December 8 and 29, 1820, and January 12 and 19, 1821; news items announcing the departure and return of the expedition appear in the issues for May 26 and September 15, 1820. Cass's original report of thirteen pages, in the form of a letter to Calhoun, dated October 21, 1820, is among the papers of the office of Indian affairs, in the National Archives; it is published in Schoolcraft's *Summary Narrative*, 280–284.

1843, referred to "C. C. Trowbridge, an assessor on board," and stated his relationship to Sibley.[14]

Trowbridge was serving a kind of apprenticeship in his 1820 journey, for on that occasion he began a study of French-Canadian and Indian dialects which fitted him for a post in the Michigan superintendency of Indian affairs. While thus employed, he prepared several documents relating to Indian traditions and cultures, two of which have been published recently. Some of his valuable records were loaned to Francis Parkman during the preparation of that famous author's *Conspiracy of Pontiac*. In 1864 Trowbridge deposited many of his manuscripts in public institutions in Detroit. He evidently enjoyed writing, but, unlike Schoolcraft, was not eager to publish. Exemplifying the essential modesty of this scholar who wrote much but published little is his brief list of titles.[15]

It appears probable that Trowbridge's journal of the Cass expedition was written in Detroit from more copious notes recorded in the field. This surmise derives in part from the consistent legibility of the handwriting and the similarity of the ink used throughout. The volume does not seem to have suffered the vicissitudes which might be expected during a lengthy canoe voyage. Furthermore, in 1868, on the one occasion when Trowbridge is known to have quoted from his notes, the statement differs in wording and length from the corresponding portion of the journal.[16] The narrative contains

[14] James V. Campbell, "Biographical Sketch of Charles C. Trowbridge," in *Michigan Pioneer Collections*, 6:478–491; Grace Lee Nute, ed., "Bishop Jackson Kemper's Visit to Minnesota in 1843," *ante*, 7:269n. Additional biographical information has been derived from M. M. Quaife's "Manuscript Briefs," in the Burton Historical Collection.

[15] Trowbridge's *Meearmeear Traditions* and his *Shawnee Traditions* have been published recently by the Museum of Anthropology of the University of Michigan as numbers 7 and 9 of its *Occasional Contributions* (Ann Arbor, 1938, 1939). The former volume has been edited by Vernon Kinietz; the latter, by Mr. Kinietz in collaboration with Erminie W. Voegelin. Perhaps the most comprehensive publication issued by Trowbridge during his lifetime is his "Detroit, Past and Present," in *Michigan Pioneer Collections*, 1:371–385. He is the author also of a letter on "Gen. Cass at St. Marie in 1820" and of a "Note on Eleazer Williams," in *Wisconsin Historical Collections*, 5:413–416, 7:413; and of a letter on the life of Robert Stuart, a "History of the Episcopal Church in Michigan," a letter of September 5, 1878, on the history of Allegan, and accounts of "The First Saw-mill in Detroit," and of "Detroit in 1819," in *Michigan Pioneer Collections*, 3:53–56, 213–221, 4:173–176, 410, 471–479.

[16] Compare Trowbridge's letter in the *Wisconsin Historical Collections*, 5:413–416, with his entry for June 16. In the letter, Trowbridge states that "my journal of the events is now before me."

some additions and corrections, minor changes which could have
been entered over a lengthy period, for Trowbridge lived to a ven-
erable age, in fact, he outlived all other members of the expedition.
The journal remains essentially the writing of a youth who had
grown to manhood in Albany and then was plunged into the raw
Northwest frontier in 1820. Through a hundred and fifty pages, the
youthful traveler hews closely to his self-appointed task of recorder
of facts, incidents, and personal observations. His record, at least,
helpfully supplements and clarifies the accounts of the Cass expedition previously published.

The pocket-size journal, written in an admirable hand, is now
owned by Mrs. Thomas B. Byrd of Boyce, Virginia, a member of
the Trowbridge family. Through her courtesy and the co-operation
of Mr. Frank B. Hubachek of Chicago, Dr. Grace Lee Nute of the
Minnesota Historical Society, Dr. Randolph G. Adams of the William L. Clements Library in the University of Michigan, and Mr.
Edward R. Wright, Mr. Cleveland Thurber, and Mr. Ferris D.
Stone of Detroit, the journal was made available to the present
writer. Dr. Milo M. Quaife, secretary of the Burton Historical Collection in the Detroit Public Library, has furnished by interview and
letter much valuable material necessary to the annotation of the narrative. Extracts from a typewritten copy of the journal made many
years ago by Clarence M. Burton for the Burton Historical Collection have been quoted in one of its publications.[17]

[17] M. M. Quaife, "From Detroit to the Mississippi in 1820," in *Burton Historical
Collection Leaflet*, 6:49–64 (March, 1930). A film copy of the original journal is owned
by the Minnesota Historical Society, which received it from the writer. It is accompanied
by a copy of an unsigned booklet of rough sketch maps and notations made in pencil,
which was found by Mr. Vernon Kinietz among the Trowbridge Papers, in the Burton
Historical Collection. Internal evidences suggest that the booklet, which is the same
size as the journal, contains field sketches made by Trowbridge as a method of keeping
notes. The copying of the Trowbridge journal on filmslides and a trip which included
among its purposes the inspection of the manuscript by the present writer were financed
in part by funds granted by the graduate school of the University of Minnesota.

THE JOURNAL OF CHARLES C. TROWBRIDGE,
MAY 24–SEPTEMBER 13, 1820[18]

THE EXPEDITION fitted out by Gover[n]ment, under the direction of his Excellency Lewis Cass, Governor of the Territory of Michigan, for the purpose of exploring the country north and west of Lake Superior, and the practicable communications between that Lake, and the Mississip[p]i River, left the City of Detroit, on the twenty fourth day of May 1820 at 4 p.m, in three bark canoes. These canoes were about five fathoms in length and one fathom in breadth, and being sufficiently strong to withstand the violence of the waves, were capable of carrying about two tons burthen, besides the men and their personal baggage. The Governors suite was composed of eight, viz, Capt. David B. Douglass of the Corps of Engineers, Henry R Schoolcraft Esq a mineralogist, Alexander Woolcott, Physician, Lieut A[e]neas Mackay, of the corps of artillery, Robert A Forsyth Esq private Secretary, James Duane Doty Esq, journalist, A[lexander] R Chase and myself in the capacity of assistants to Cap[t] Douglass. We had twelve french voyageurs well acquainted with this mode of travelling, Eleven Soldiers, most of them frenchmen, selected by the Governor on account of their capacity to endure fatigue, Nine Indians of the Ottawa and Chippeway nations, and Two Interpreters, making our party to consist in all of forty three persons, a number sufficiently strong to repel any attacks which we might expect from the savages among whom we intended to travel.[19]

[18] The original form of the Trowbridge manuscript has been closely followed. The diarist's paragraphing, spelling, and capitalization are reproduced throughout, and his punctuation has been followed except in cases where he used dashes or colons at the ends of sentences. In the interest of clearness, such punctuation marks have been replaced by periods. Words or passages that Trowbridge crossed out have been omitted unless they contain significant information not otherwise included, in which case they are enclosed in brackets and followed by footnotes explaining that the author intended to omit them.

[19] Of this group, only Cass and Schoolcraft again engaged in exploration. Upon returning from the expedition, Douglass became professor of mathematics at West Point and later was president of Kenyon College. Doty was destined to serve as governor of two territories, Wisconsin and Utah. For sketches of these men, as well as of Cass and Schoolcraft, see the *Dictionary of American Biography*, 3:562–564, 5:390, 405, 16:456. Forsyth, who had the rank of major in 1820, continued his military career. Lieutenant Mackay, who had command of the soldiers of the expedition, also remained in the army and served with distinction in the Mexican War. Dr. Wolcott was Indian agent at Chicago until his death in 1829. Alexander Ralston Chase, a brother of Salmon P. Chase, became a merchant in southern Ohio. The interpreters were James Ryley and Joseph Parks. The entourage, according to Schoolcraft's *Narrative Journal*, 78, included "ten Canadian voyageurs, — seven U. S. soldiers, — ten Indians of the Ottaway and Shawnee tribes, an interpreter and a guide, making thirty-seven persons exclusive of myself."

We were escorted to Grosse Pointé, a distance of ten miles above Detroit, and at the head of Detroit River, by the citizens, in carriages and on horseback,[20] and here we were obliged to remain in consequence of violent adverse winds until Friday the 26th at noon, when we ventured to cross Lake St Clair, although the wind had not yet entirely subsided; indeed the waves ran so high that our canoes were sometimes almost filled with water, but by keeping a man at work constantly to throw out, we succeeded in making Lautons Island, about four miles from the mouth of the River S[t] Clair, by nine in the evening: On this island are some handsome farms, cultivated by scotch peasants, by whom we were treated with much hospitality, in part owing perhaps to our wearing Plaided cloaks, which the good old Lady said, gave us a very friendly appearance.[21]

There are a great many mouths to this River but only one ship channel, though there is a resemblance between them: I beli[e]ve there is no difficulty however in finding the correct one.

Saturday 27[th] May. This morning at 7 we left our friends of the island, not without many prayers for our safety and much caution for our health, & we proceeded up the river, occasionally assisted by a breese, at the rate of four miles an hour, against a current which for most of the distance is extremely rapid. At 5 oclock p.m. we arrived at Fort Gratiot and landed amidst the roar of cannon, which contrasted with the animated songs of our frenchman had a pleasing effect. The River S[t] Clair is forty miles in length, generally half a mile in width, and extremely regular in its course. The lands are rich and its banks are rendered beautifully picturesque by the many handsome settlements,

[20] The ceremonies attending the departure of the expedition are described as follows in the *Detroit Gazette* for May 26, 1820: "The canoes (three in number) are propelled by twenty-six men with paddles, of whom ten are Indians of the Chippewa nation, ten *voyageurs,* or Frenchmen accustomed to the Indian trade, and six U. S. soldiers. A handsome U. S. flag is placed in the stern of each canoe. . . . The departure of the expedition afforded a pleasing, and, to the strangers of this place, a novel spectacle. The canoes were propelled against a strong wind and current with astonishing rapidity; the *voyageurs* regulating the strokes of their paddles by one of their animated row-songs, and the Indians encouraging each other by shouts of exultation. On leaving the shore considerable exertion was made by the voyageurs and Indians in order to take the lead, and a handsome boat race was witnessed, in which the Indians displayed their superior skill, and soon left the other canoes far behind."

[21] The island doubtless was Laughton's Island, which was also known as Stromness. In a letter to the writer, dated November 19, 1941, Dr. M. M. Quaife of the Burton Historical Collection, Detroit, expressed the opinion that the Scotch settlers referred to were some of the refugees from Lord Selkirk's Baldoon settlement, which lay immediately across the channel from the island.

chiefly made by french people, who if they can have nothing more will build good houses and cultivate fine gardens. There are two principal islands in this River besides Lautons, vis, Hursons & Elk islands; the former is the largest, affords fine farms and is thickly settled.[22]

Fort Gratiot is situated on a handsome eminence, commanding the entrance to Lake Huron as well as the Lake itself for some distance, and also the country for miles around. There is at present a very small force stationed here, and that is to be removed before our return, to the upper posts, as there is at present no necessity for their remaining to guard the Country, and above they may be usefully employed in constructing fortifications, &c.

Two Rivers of considerable sise empty their waters into River St Clair, Belle Riviere or Handsome River, and Black River.

Sunday 28th May. At eight a. m. We parted with our friends Majr [Alexander] Cummings and Lieut Hunt.[23]

We found the appearance of the Lake and its borders to day much as they had been represented to us, the timber heavy, the soil apparently strong, though the land is generally Low, and we landed and encamped on a Sandy Beach near Long Point, having made to day 33 miles, according to our Voyageurs' estimation.

Monday 29th May. Embarked at 6 oclock a.m. and proceeded on with much ease and pleasantness for 30 miles when a violent wind arose and we were obliged much against our wish to put ashore on a very rocky point, where with the greatest difficulty we succeeded in getting our canoes ashore uninjured; in fact the construction of these vessels, so frail yet so generally and so wisely used for the purposes of navigation on the Rivers of this Country, is such, that without the most extreme caution, the traveller is every hour in danger of losing his canoe, baggage and perhaps his life; for the Bark of which they are constructed is not more than 1/16 of an inch in thickness, and this is stretched over and then sewed to Beams or knees which are not more than ⅜ to ½ inch

---

[22] The first-named is probably Harsen's Island. Dr. Quaife, in his letter of November 19, 1941, infers that Elk Island is Isle aux Cerfs.

[23] At this point in the journal Trowbridge crossed out six and a half lines; they are illegible in the film copy. The officers referred to were stationed at Fort Gratiot, in command of sixty men. "The present Fort," says Schoolcraft, in his *Narrative Journal*, 81, "is understood to have been built about the close of the late war, (1814)." He notes that "at a very early period the *Coureurs du Bois*, had erected a Fort at this spot at their own expense. — This was afterwards occupied by the French Government, under the name of *Fort St. Joseph*, and finally abandoned and burnt by the commandant, La Hontan, on the 27th August, 1688."

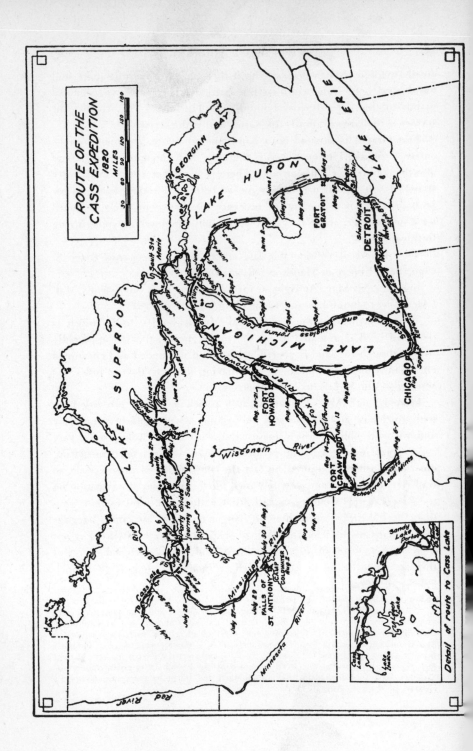

ROUTE OF THE
CASS EXPEDITION
1820

MILES
0   30   60   90   120   150   180

thick; between these knees (which are placed very close to each other) and the bark, are thin pieces of cedar wood, of the thickness of a quarter of an inch and length of ten to twelve feet, and arranged in such a manner as to join the edges, whereby the bark on the outside is prevented from yielding to trifling pressures.

But the greatest strength of a canoe of this kind is in the gunwale (which is made of strong tough wood and well bound with watape) and the stiffening poles which are laid in the bottom of the vessel to support the lading, and prevent it from breaking in the waves. So that a canoe is equally strong and safe, whether laden or empty, provided it is not too heavily laden.[24] This afternoon we met five canoes loaded with Indians who were on their way to their hunting grounds. They looked comfortable & happy, and no doubt each one of them who is possessed of a canoe, a gun, a dog and (last because they respect them least) a wife, feels himself a man of as much consequence as the greatest Potentate in Europe.

On this Rocky point we were obliged to remain, very much to our mortification, until Thursday the 1st day of June, when although the wind had not subsided altogether, we were so disgusted with our confined situation that we were glad to put to sea and try our fortune.

Thursday 1st June. But we only proceeded to the next point, three miles distant when we were obliged to land again and stay until 3 in the afternoon. Here however we found something to amuse ourselves with, as the squirrels were plenty, & the land open and dry. In hunting to day one of our indian Hunters shot a very large Bear but did not succeed in getting him.

From this point the distance is eight miles to Black River, a stream of 20 yards in width and in certain seasons is said to abound in fish. From this River to Point[e] au[x] Barque[s] or Vessel Point (so called from the resemblance of the Rocks at the point to a vessel) the distance is 15 miles, and for the whole distance the coast is extremely rocky and dangerous, but particularly so at the point, from which a reef of sharp rocks extends about two miles into the Lake, or rather Bay. This is the southern or south eastern point of Saganau Bay. We had a fair wind

[24] This description adds a few essential details to that in Schoolcraft's *Narrative Journal*, 66–70 and plate. Compare also with earlier descriptions in Alexander Mackenzie, *Voyages from Montreal . . . in the Years 1789 and 1793*, xxiv–xxvi (London, 1801), and Douglas S. Robertson, ed., *An Englishman in America, 1785, Being the Diary of Joseph Hadfield*, 108 (Toronto, 1933). Watape is a thong made from the pliant boughs and roots of spruce.

this afternoon which partly compensated us for our misfortune of the morning, and at Sundown we landed in the Bay of Saganau three miles from P^t au Barque, having made 23 miles.[25]

Friday June 2nd. At 5 oclock this morning we left our encampment, and proceeded up Saganau Bay for Point au Chene [*Oak Point*]. About 6 miles from P^t au Barque is La Riviere au Tourte or Pigeon River, which is navigable for Boats a few miles and takes its rise in a small Lake near P^t au Chene, called Me-ke-nau-ko-kau-ning or Turtle Lake, which is 5 miles in circumference.

From Point au Chene (which is 15 miles distant from P^t au Barque) the distance to the crossing island is 12 miles. The course from the point to the island is N.67.w. — it is called by the Voyageurs Mackinaw island,[26] and by the indians Shau-wanagunk, is four miles in circumference, well timbered, and has proved very interesting in the mineralogical way, as Mr Schoolcraft procured some elegant specimens of chalcedony and flint here. There are two small islands near this between which the water is very shallow.

After remaining on the island a short time to rest the men, we steered for the northern point of the Bay, which is called Cranberry point and is distant from the island 20 miles.[27] This is a low Sandy point, destitute in a great measure of herbage & affording in other respects little appearance of vegetation.

From this point we continued on ten miles, when we arrived at La Riviere au Sable or Sandy River, where we encamped.

This river is thirty yards wide at its mouth and though its entrance is obstructed by a sand bar, it is very deep above; it is navigable for 6 miles with boats of considerable sise, and to the head waters which are about 60 miles from the Lake, with canoes; its waters abound in fish particularly sturgeon, of which an abundance was presented to us by the natives, who reside here at all seasons of the year in considerable numbers. In consequence of a fair wind for this afternoon, we made to day 62 miles.

Saturday June 3rd. On inquiry I learn that Saganau Bay at its mouth

[25] Probably the site of present-day Port Austin, Huron County. Pointe aux Barques derived its name, according to Doty, in *Wisconsin Historical Collections*, 13:170, from the fancied resemblance of the rocks to the stern of a vessel.

[26] The larger of the Charity Islands, in modern nomenclature.

[27] Cranberry Point is identifiable as Tawas Point, east of Tawas City. The mouth of the Au Sable River, where the party encamped, is about fifteen canoe miles from Tawas Point.

is about 55 miles wide, but seldom crossed there on account of the danger should a wind rise from any direction.[28]

To day we embarked at 6 a m. from Sandy River to Thunder Bay the distance is 30 miles and the shore is extremely uninteresting. The Bay is 14 miles wide at the mouth and 16 m. deep. We crossed it in one hour and forty minutes with a fair wind.

In a direction N.E. from the northern point of Thunder Bay, and about two miles distant from the shore lay three islands called Thunder Bay Islands. From Saganau to Thunder Bay the shore is sandy. After waiting the arrival of one of the canoes which had remained behind through fear, we continued our journey, and at night landed on a point 12 miles distant from Thunder Bay, called Sho-she-ko-kau-ning or Flat Stone Point. On this point Mr. Schoolcraft collected an abundance of specimens, chiefly organic remains and many of them of animals now extinct. The land from Saganau to this place appears sandy and barren, but we are told that it falls into a low swampy country. Opposite to flatstone point and about 2 miles from the shore lays middle Island, so called, as is supposed from its being equidistant from P^t au Barque & Michilimackinac.[29]

Sunday June 4th This morning we embarked at 6 but before we had proceeded two miles, a violent storm arose accompanied by thunder and lightning, and we were in consequence of it obliged to stay 2 hours when we again put out and continued on the water until sunset, when we landed on a point called by the indians Ke-no-sha-kah-ning, or Portage Point. Here we were much troubled with the musqu[i]toes, now very numerous, and succeeded in getting little sleep on account of their invasions, for although we were all provided with Bars or Nets, yet we did not trouble ourselves to pitch them. The evening was somewhat cold, and we found our Buffaloe skins and Blankets very comfortable.

Monday 5th June. We left Portage Point at 8 a m. and in Two hours our canoes arrived at She-bah-tah-wah-gog or Presqu' Isle, we having been obliged to walk on account of the wind, which blew extremely hard. Here we remained until the wind subsided, which was not until 5 p.m. when having carried our goods &c across the portage, a distance of only 120 yards, while around, it is about 2 miles, we con-

---

[28] This distance is correct if Saginaw Bay is measured from Au Sable to Pointe aux Barques. It is fifteen miles from Point Lookout to Oak Point.

[29] Trowbridge's supposition about Middle Island, still so named, is correct. Flat Stone Point is northwest of the present city of Alpena.

tinued our course, with the intention to travel all night, but an adverse wind arose, and at 11 at night we were glad to get ashore,[30] satisfied with having made 20 miles from Presqu' Isle.

Tuesday 6th June At 20 minutes before 5 we put out tho' the wind had not ceased, and by unremitted exertion we were at 2 o'clock, at the foot of Bois Blanc Isle, or White wood Island. This Island is 18 miles in length, but as the land is not thought valuable there have as yet been no settlements made upon it.[31]

We continued up the west shore of Bois Blanc and before dark arrived at Mackinac, having made to day against a strong wind 60 miles.

The Island of Michilimackinac is about nine miles in circumference. The town, harbor, and the forts, Mackinac & Holmes, present to the traveller a view at once picturesque and sublime. Fort Mackinac is situated on the cliffs which completely surrounded the island and render it inaccessible to an enemy, is about 120 feet above the water and completely overlooks and guards the town and harbor. Fort Holmes, not only commands fort Mackinac but the whole island, and is built on a circular eminence 150 feet higher than Fort M. The situation of this fortress is so peculiar, that with a garrison of 200 men it would be tenable against any number; and it was in consequence of a strategem in getting possession of this that the whole island fell into the hands of the British troops during the late war. The Town contains 100 buildings, including a Court house and jail; The houses are generally constructed of bark. The population is chiefly french, who are mostly very poor.[32]

The island is situated about 4 miles from the main shore, and 2 m. from B. Blanc; near it (8 miles distant,) lay the St Martin Islands, on which large and apparently inexhaustible beds of gypsum have been found. At this place is stationed the Head Quarters of the American Fur Company: this company is very extensive and their establishments are

---

[30] Near the present town of Rogers.

[31] Bois Blanc Island is about twelve miles long. The journalist's distances are often only rough approximations and there appears to be no consistency in the errors.

[32] Mackinac Island and its environs are treated more fully in Schoolcraft's *Narrative Journal*, 110–124. Schoolcraft distinguishes between the "modern town of Michilimackinac" on the island and the ancient town "which was located on the extreme point of the Peninsula of Michigan," the present site of Mackinac City. Following the capture of Mackinac by the British in 1812, they erected a fort, which they called Fort George, on the highest point. The Americans changed its name to Fort Holmes when they regained possession of the island after the War of 1812. Fort Mackinac, which was established by the British in 1780, and was held alternately by the British and the Americans until 1815, was south of Fort Holmes on lower ground. For brief accounts of these forts, see Edwin O. Wood, *Historic Mackinac*, 1:534–537 (New York, 1918).

spread over all the country between the Mississipi & the great lakes. They have about 300 men in their employment, who come to Mackinac in the spring with the fur collected during the winter, where they stay from one to three months, when they receive another assortment of goods and proceed to their wintering grounds. Here during the winter they live like savages, enduring every privation and hardship for the sake of lucre. The capital employed is 300,000, but I am informed that they never have use for the whole amount.

Tuesday June 13th. Having procured two additional canoes of the burthen of three tons, and left one of ours which we found too weak for safety, and having repacked our provisions which had been sent from Detroit by a schooner, from Barrels into Kegs, we left Mackinac at 10 o'clock, with a fair wind for the Sau[l]t de St Marie   Nine miles from Mackinac, in the course from the island to the mouth of St Marys River lays Goose[berry] Island, memorable on account of battles fought there in the old wars.[33] The main shore on our passage across the bend, to the River, was too distant to afford us much matter for the satisfaction of our curiosity, and at night we landed five miles from the mouth (or rather one of the mouths) of the St Marys and opposite to Drummonds Island, on which is a military post of the British Gov^t, and also a small village. The islands in the mouth of this river are almost innumerable, and their elevated situation and beautiful foliage, contrasted with the clear and extended expanse of water, afford to the contemplative traveller a source of infinite gratification. From Mackinack to the Detour, or turn i.e. the mouth of the River the distance is 45 miles.[34]

Wednesday 14th June. At 5, we embarked and proceeded to ascend the river for twenty miles, where our guide through ignorance or from some other cause, led us through the wrong channel, and we had much difficulty in ascending the numerous rapids which opposed our progress; in one of these we injured our canoes so much that it became necessary to land and repair them. This is done with much facility by the Voyageurs, who are always supplied with the necessary articles of Bark, Watape and gum, for that purpose; indeed we find it necessary to gum

---

[33] An engagement of the War of 1812 occurred on Gooseberry or Brant Island, one of the cluster in the Cheneaux group.

[34] The post on Drummond's Island was Fort St. Joseph, which was erected in 1795. Since it was abandoned and burned by the British in 1814, only the ruins were visible to the exploratory party of 1820. See a note by R. G. Thwaites, in *Wisconsin Historical Collections*, 13:178 n.; and Wood, *Historic Mackinac*, 2:629. The "Detour" is indicated as the "Detour Passage" on modern pilot charts.

our canoes every night after landing, which however, and fortunately too, is a work of little labor. We found the ascent of the river upon the whole quite interesting, and though no inhabitants were to be seen, the scenery possessed sufficient variety. The general width of the River is ¾ of a mile, though in some places it is twice that width.

At 6 in the afternoon we landed at the Saut, and the appearance of our little sq[u]adron spread an universal astonishment among the natives who had assembled to witness our arrival. Our show was rendered much more imposing by an escort of 25 men under the command of Lieut [John S.] Pierce, who had accompanied us from Mackinac to render assistance in case of any hostility on the part of the indians, who, we had been informed were not altogether so friendly in their disposition as we could have wished.[35]

Immediately after our arrival we were welcomed to the Saut by M[r] George Johns[t]on, a son of Co[l] [John] Johns[t]on, and invited to his fathers house, where during our stay we were treated with the greatest hospitality. Co[l] Johnson has resided at the Saut for a great number of years. He married a native, a daughter of one of the influencial chiefs, by whom he has a large family of children.[36]

Mrs Johnson though not very comely in her person, being quite as dark complexioned as the natives generally, is yet extremely easy and polite in her manners; and the young gentlemen and ladies are highly accomplished, one of them having received her education, and in fact passed the early part of her life in Europe.

Thursday 15th June. To day we walked up to the head of the falls and descended in a canoe. They are extremely rapid and dangerous on the American side of the river, tho' barges sometimes descend them with the usual lading. The length is about ½ mile, and in that distance the fall is 22 feet and 10 inches. The rocks over which the water falls is a red sand stone.

Below the falls, i.e. at the foot of them, we saw a number of indians in the act of taking white fish. These delicious fish are caught here in very great quantities and in fact constitute the principal food of the indians who are generally about 50 families in number, as well as that of

[35] Lieutenant Pierce was a brother of President Franklin Pierce. The augmented party, now numbering sixty-six men, was taken in a twelve-oared barge to Sault Ste. Marie.

[36] John Johnston, who settled at the Sault in 1793 and married an Indian woman, was in Europe in the summer of 1820. His eldest daughter, Jane, who had been educated in Ireland, later became Schoolcraft's first wife.

the whites, who are agreeably to the census lately taken 80 in number, men, women and children.[37] They take them in scoop-nets, with which they fish from canoes and the rocks. The fish caught at this place are acknowledged superior to any of the kind caught in the Lakes, possessing more richness of flavor, and being of much greater weight.

Friday June 16th. A treaty for the cession of a small quantity of Land at this place for the purpose of the establishment of a military post had been contemplated, and accordingly on this morning the Indians were assembled in council at the Marquee of the Governor, and their sentiments were required with respect to the Cession! There were not many old chiefs at the Council, and the young men of influence, were very vehement in their protestations against a cession. The Governor informed them that we were perfectly sensible of our rights to the land by the Treaty of Greenville, and a copy of that treaty was produced and explained to them, but they would listen to no terms, and were apparently determined to prevent any innovation of their rights.[38] They were informed that a military post would certainly be established there, and that although they had once received a compensation for their lands, yet if they chose to improve the present opportunity another would be granted them, but if they suffered the present one to pass by, another never would offer. This forcible reasoning had no effect on their minds, and the council broke up, when the Chiefs returned to their camp. Immediately after they had retired the Governor observed the British flag flying at their lodges, and with that bravery and just sense of honour

[37] Various estimates or actual counts of the Indian population are available. Many censuses were made by Indian agents. Typical is the exhaustive census of the Indians of the Northwest made by Nicholas Boilvin and enclosed with a letter from Cass to Calhoun, December 31, 1818, in Department of War, Letters Received, National Archives. Boilvin was United States agent for the Winnebago, with headquarters at Prairie du Chien. Reuben G. Thwaites, "Notes on Early Lead Mining in the Fever (or Galena) River Region," in *Wisconsin Historical Collections,* 13:285.

[38] The treaty of Greenville, Ohio, was concluded on August 3, 1795, between Anthony Wayne and chiefs representing the Delaware, Shawnee, Wyandot, and Miami Confederacy. It established a definite boundary within the Northwest Territory between Indian lands and those open to white settlement. Lands westward and northward of the treaty line were conceded to the Indians, except Detroit and other specified French settlements. The United States claimed a tract of land at the Sault by virtue of an earlier grant made to this country by France and confirmed by the treaty of Greenville, and reconfirmed by the treaty of Spring Wells or Detroit on September 8, 1815, and by the treaty of Fort Harrison on June 4, 1816. See the *Dictionary of American History,* 2:425 (New York, 1940); Schoolcraft, *Narrative Journal,* 136 n.; and William W. Folwell, *A History of Minnesota,* 1:103 n. (St. Paul, 1921). It is perhaps understandable that the two hundred Chippewa at the Sault would not be amenable to observing the terms of a treaty entered into a quarter of a century earlier by confederate nations inhabiting the Ohio country.

which characterizes a great man, he walked up without an attendant (for he would suffer none to accompany him) and entering the encampment amongst that ferocious band of savages threw the flag to the ground.

So much bravery terrified the Indians, and the Governor called to his Interpreter through whom he told them that if they attempted to raise the flag again he would order his men to fire on them without reserve. He concluded however to send the flag to his own encampment there to keep it until his departure.

In less than ten minutes from this time every woman and child with all their baggage was on the opposite side or crossing the River. The indians prepared themselves, expecting an attack from us, and we being under the same apprehensions from them, loaded our arms, doubled our guards, and made every preparation to sell our lives as dearly as possible. During this part of the scene our attention and admiration were particularly attracted by the conduct of one of our indians, a young man of a very uncommonly prepossessing appearance and dignified deportment for a native, who, when the other indians of our party strongly protested against taking arms in opposition to their bretheren, came to the Governor, & demanded a gun with ammunition &c. saying that the conduct of the others should be no rule for his conduct, and that as he had joined the Governors party with the expectation of sharing the difficulties and dangers with them, he would now, however repugnant to his feelings, offer his services against his relatives and acquaintances, in the same manner, as if they were his enemies, for from what he had observed he considered their conduct highly reprehensible. The Brave fellow had no cause to exert his good courage, for a new council was held at the house of Mr Johnson, from which the young and boisterous chiefs were excluded, and in consideration of certain goods paid them on the spot, they ceded to the United States a tract of Land Sixteen Square miles commencing at the head of the falls, running down the line of demarkation to the little Rapids, thence back from the river so as to make the above quantity of land.[39]

The young chiefs afterwards apologised to the Governor for their rude conduct, and humbly solicited his pardon.

[39] This incident has been recounted in a dozen places, especially in biographies of Lewis Cass, wherein the actual course of events has often been confused by the imaginations of the several authors. The most complete summary heretofore available is in *Wisconsin Historical Collections*, 5:413–416, in which a letter by Trowbridge, who was living at the time of its publication, is quoted. See *ante*, p. 133.

We have to acknowledge ourselves much indebted for this session, to Mr Geo Johnson, without whose kind offices nothing would have been effected.

Saturday 17th June. In consequence of our too great quantity of lading, of which we were not aware at the time of our departure from Mackinac, where we received on board our stock of provisions, we were obliged to procure an additional canoe at this place, after purchasing which we procured two french guides and proceeded to take our goods &c to the head of the falls. This is a work of considerable labor, as the difficulty and danger of ascent is so great, that only about one third of an ordinary load can be carried at a time. With much exertion we had by four p.m. succeeded in getting all our lading above the falls, and we continued our course up the River to Point aux Pins or Pine Point, so called from the growth of pine timber here which is somewhat unusual in this country. From this point which is 6 miles distant from the falls, & 12 m. from the lake, the Voyageur has an extensive view of that vast inland sea, on which perhaps he is destined to encounter almost insurmountable difficulties. At this place we passed the night very comfortably and on the morning of

Sunday June 18th, we prepared to take a serious departure (for we had hardly considered it so as yet,) from civilized Beings. The natural reflection that it would be the melancholy lot of some of us never to return, here strongly suggested itself to our minds, and our spirits were enlivened only by the animated boat songs of our Canadians. In three hours we were at the head of this beautiful river which connects the waters of Lakes Huron & Superior. The whole length is 63 miles; its banks afford very fine timber and a rich alluvial soil well adapted to the purposes of husbandry. This river is the great and in fact the only key to the upper country, and the importance of a military post at the Saut of St Marys must strike forcibly on the minds of all persons, acquainted with the advantage of a security to our Traders in the indian country, as well as to the white inhabitants at that place.

We continued to row all day against very unfavorable winds, and at 12 at night, exhausted with fatigue and hunger we Landed at Shell Drake River 24 miles from the head of the St Marys, having made only 42 miles to day.

Here we found two lodges of Indians of the Chippeway nation, who resided on the head waters of the Mississipi River; and who were now on there way to Mackinac, for the purpose of soliciting the interposition of the U. S. Indian Agent at that place in their quarrels with their neighbors the Sioux, with whom they are perpetually at war. They appeared to be in a miserably poor condition, and when we gave them a plug of tobacco each, they were transported with joy. They told us that it would take them a great while to earn sufficient or rather to collect a sufficient quantity of furs for the purchase of so much as we had presented them gratuitiously.

Shell Drake River is thirty yards wide at its mouth and very deep, though the entrance is much obstructed by an extensive Sand bar.

We are becoming quite accustomed to our mode of travelling and sleeping, and it has been resolved that if our appetites continue to increase as they have done, we shall on our return surprise our friends.

[*To be continued*]

The Minnesota War History Committee

Lewis Beeson

AT THE SUGGESTION of the Minnesota Historical Society, Governor Stassen has established the Minnesota War History Committee to advise and consult with all agencies and individuals engaged in war activities "in the making and preparation of records in order to assure the collection of adequate records pertaining to Minnesota's participation in the war; to insure the preservation of such records; and, to collect and co-ordinate for the Division of Civilian Defense, information pertaining to war agencies and organizations."[1] The committee is responsible to the state defense co-ordinator and to the chief of staff of the Minnesota Office of Civilian Defense. Information collected by the committee is available only to these two officials and to persons authorized by them to use it. Records collected by the committee are to be housed in quarters provided by the Minnesota Historical Society.

The establishment by Governor Stassen of the War History Committee as a state war agency constitutes a recognition by those responsible for the marshaling of Minnesota's resources for war of the importance of record collecting. The agency charged with this specific task now will be able to assemble much material which otherwise could not be obtained or which will not be available later. The War History Committee expects not only to collect and preserve the records of the war, so that after it is won the history of Minnesota's part in the victory may be written, but to assemble information of current value to other Minnesota war agencies.

Dr. Arthur J. Larsen, superintendent of the Minnesota Historical Society, is chairman of the committee. The Minnesota Office of Military Defense is represented by Major General Ellard A. Walsh, adjutant general of Minnesota. Mr. C. A. Zwiener, chief of staff of the Office of Civilian Defense, Mr. H. C. Schmid, chairman of the

[1] Office of Civilian Defense, "General Orders," no. 13, May 18, 1942.

Human Resources and Skills Advisory Committee, Mr. Herbert J. Miller, chairman of the Industrial Resources and Production Advisory Committee, Dr. Theodore C. Blegen, dean of the graduate school in the University of Minnesota, and Mrs. Lionel R. Upham, president of the Minnesota Federation of Women's Clubs, also are members of the committee. The present writer is its executive secretary and the director of its work.

A state-wide organization is to be established through the appointment of a local representative by each of the 107 chairmen of county and municipal civilian defense councils in Minnesota. The primary responsibility of the local representatives will be the collecting of records originating within the county or municipality — materials which the state committee otherwise might not obtain. Their secondary task will be the collection and preservation of war records for the county or municipality. The local representatives are expected to advise and consult with the heads of other local state war agencies and private organizations about the proper preservation of their records, to impress upon individuals in the community the desirability of preserving business or family records which bear upon the war, and to enlist the aid and services of other people in collecting and preserving records.[2]

The War History Committee believes that it is as important to organize the material it collects, in order to make it available for use, as it is to collect it. This is no mean objective in view of the immensity of the work of collection.

Certain conditions now exist which make the assembling of war records for a state different from and more difficult than in past wars. There is no need to elaborate upon the great scope of the present war, and upon the fact that we are engaged not only in an unparalleled military effort, but in an unprecedented civilian effort. The first World War involved civilian participation and organization, with accompanying disruption and change in civilian life undreamed of during the Civil or Spanish-American wars. In this respect the last and the present wars are similar. Nevertheless, the

[2] Office of Civilian Defense, "Circular," no. 9, May 19, 1942.

problem of collecting the records of the present conflict for a single state is more complex than it was in 1917–18.

The present war effort is more centralized nationally than it was in the first World War with respect both to the federal governmental organization and to the manner in which nongovernmental civilian activities are organized. The federal government is relying less upon education and a voluntary program, and more upon centralized direction than in the last war. The United States Food Administration in 1917–18 succeeded in sending food abroad to the nation's allies through the voluntary co-operation of the people, who were induced to save food by an intense campaign of education. The fast pace of the present conflict did not allow time for similar methods with respect either to food shipped to Britain or to the rationing of such commodities as sugar.

The greater centralization nationally of both federal governmental and private organizations makes more difficult the collecting of such materials as mimeographed instructions, bulletins, and other records not intended for public release. They may, however, be obtained by alert collectors who have access to regional offices of federal agencies. Both the federal government and national private organizations have developed the concept of archives since 1918; consequently records are less available to state collecting agencies than formerly. Records of the United States Employment Service, the Red Cross, the Boy Scouts, and alien registration were among those collected by the Minnesota War Records Commission in the last war. The commission was able to collect such material because it began its activity as an agency of the Minnesota Commission of Public Safety, which had unprecedented authority to direct the war effort within the state. The Office of Civilian Defense, which now performs this function, does not have comparable powers, nor is it likely to receive them. Eventually records of Minnesota significance originating in federal or private organizations — records similar to some collected by the War Records Commission of the last war — may be microfilmed for the files of the War History Committee.

Organization on a national scale now extends into fields untouched in the last war. This is true in almost every type of activity. Within fields closely allied to the activities of the Minnesota Historical Society, for instance, there have been established the Committee on the Control of Social Data and the Committee for the Preservation of Cultural Resources, to name but two. Particularly numerous are organizations devoted to furthering the war effort, such as the United Service Organizations, fund raising organizations, like the Russian War Relief, and organizations whose purpose it is to influence opinion. Almost all national organizations have war programs that reach out into Minnesota.

The manipulation of public opinion today is based upon methods and techniques developed from those in use a generation ago. Public opinion and public response to the appeal of a program in Minnesota is influenced and obtained not only through local sources but through national ones. New mediums, such as the radio, have come into use since the last World War.

The immediate task of the War History Committee is to acquaint Minnesota state departments, local governmental units, and private organizations engaged in war activities with the desirability of preserving office records in such form that they may become available for use by historians after they are no longer current. The work of collecting printed material issuing from federal, state, and private organizations will be started at once. In order to avoid unnecessary duplication, the committee will consult with other depositories in the state, such as the Minnesota Historical Society, the University of Minnesota Library, and the public libraries of St. Paul and Minneapolis, about the material they are assembling and preserving. The War History Committee will attempt, insofar as it can, merely to supplement in its collections what other depositories are not obtaining. The committee will be on the alert for records of many kinds — archives of governmental and private agencies, private letters, diaries, account books, ration cards, newspapers, books, pamphlets, leaflets, handbills, posters, photographs, motion pictures, radio transcriptions, phonograph records, musical scores, badges, buttons. In addition, the committee will undertake to accumulate such items as lists of organizations and their officers, newspaper and periodical files, bibliographies, and specialized lists of publications that may be of value to the Office of Civilian Defense and the agencies under its direction.

The records on which written history is based always have been diverse in character. The foregoing list demonstrates that the records of modern total war are especially diverse. The historian of the present era will be forced to use materials as complex, as varied, and as widespread as the war itself. Thus, the collector of the records of Minnesota at war must take account not only of materials originating in the state, but in the nation as a whole, not only of written or printed records, but of photographs, motion pictures, radio transcriptions, and the like. Such material, all of which requires special handling, must be collected and preserved along with the manuscript and printed records that have made up the archives of past wars.

Notes and Documents

A RINDISBACHER WATER COLOR

Grace Lee Nute

SEVERAL DESCRIPTIONS of Peter Rindisbacher's paintings, reproductions of some of them, and biographical data on the artist have appeared from time to time in this magazine. Within the past year many water colors of the Minnesota country by this Swiss artist have been on special display in the Round Tower Museum at Fort Snelling through the courtesy of the United States Military Academy at West Point, which owns eighteen originals.[1] Therefore, it is pleasant to add that an original water color by Rindisbacher is now owned in Minnesota. It has been acquired by a St. Paul man, Mr. Ernest R. Reiff. As the accompanying reproduction shows, it depicts one of the artist's favorite scenes, a buffalo hunt on the Dakota prairies.

In 1821 Rindisbacher, a lad of fifteen, migrated with his family to Lord Selkirk's colony in the Red River Valley between Pembina and the junction of that river with the Assiniboine. Thus he grew to manhood surrounded by Indians and half-breeds. How carefully he studied them and the countryside is obvious to anyone who examines the details of his paintings for data on Cree, Chippewa, and Assiniboin dress, habits, weapons, animals, and dwellings. Hence his paintings have more than art value. They are replete with information for the historian, the anthropologist, and the geographer.

Rindisbacher may well have attended some of the seniannual buffalo hunts of Red River half-breeds on the prairies, for at least six of his known paintings relate to buffaloes. Moreover, at least three of them, including that owned by Mr. Reiff, almost certainly show

[1] For accounts of the artist and his work, see Grace Lee Nute, "Peter Rindisbacher, Artist," and "Rindisbacher's Minnesota Water Colors," and Alice E. Smith, "Peter Rindisbacher: A Communication," *ante*, 14:283–287, 20:54–57, 173–175. Notes on the exhibits of Rindisbacher paintings in the Round Tower Museum appear *ante*, 22:434, 23:94.

A Buffalo Hunt

[From an original water color by Peter Rindisbacher, in the possession of Mr. Ernest Reiff of St. Paul.]

Missouri River scenery in the background. The half-breeds customarily went to that region on their expeditions. Mr. Reiff, who is well acquainted with the area at the junction of the Cheyenne and Missouri rivers — still largely unchanged from Rindisbacher's day — feels certain that it is that region which serves as background in his picture. The painting itself, however, probably dates from the St. Louis period in Rindisbacher's life, after he left the Red River Valley, for it is larger than his early paintings, being eighteen by thirty inches, and more finished in nearly all respects. He doubtless worked from an early sketch and may even have revisited the prairies by going up the Missouri by boat.

It has long been known that Rindisbacher, like so many artists of his day, used one theme for several pictures. Probably one such picture was painted and achieved considerable fame. Then patrons requested similar items for their own collections. However that may be, it is certain that Rindisbacher painted three pictures on the subject of a buffalo hunt by Indians in what seems to be the Missouri River country. One appears in reproduction as the frontispiece of volume 1 of Thomas L. McKenny and James Hall's *History of the Indian Tribes of North America* (Philadelphia, 1855). A second is to be found in an original water color at West Point, which was recently on display with others in the Round Tower. The third is Mr. Reiff's. All vary only in small details, such as clouds, flowers, the length of an Indian rider's headpiece, the exact location and size of buffalo herds, and the like. Probably a skilled artist could detect data that would indicate the order in which the three were painted.

According to statements by the previous owner of Mr. Reiff's water color, Miss Alyes N. Agnew of Washington, D. C., it has been in the hands of her family since it was presented by Rindisbacher to her great-grandfather, Benjamin West Tingley of Philadelphia, while on a visit to St. Louis. As the artist died in St. Louis in 1834, it is obvious that the painting was produced before that year. Tingley's parents did not err in naming him for a great colonial artist. He became a famous collector of his day, as did so many of his Quaker business associates and banking partners. It is not strange, therefore, that a struggling young artist on the extreme frontier about 1830 presented him with one of his choicer pieces. Though dealers and critics refer to it as a water color, it is obvious that Rindisbacher had his own unique formula for mixing his pigments. The result often leads the uninitiated to believe that what he is beholding is a lithograph. Careful examination, however, reveals brush marks and a pigment that can be washed off with comparative ease. The original frame and glass are still on the picture, if family tradition is correct. At least the frame is very old and the glass has the imperfections and interesting tints of an early period.

A display of this picture in the Round Tower is planned for the near future, after all eighteen of the West Point water colors by Rindisbacher have been exhibited.

A BIBLIOGRAPHY OF MIDDLE WESTERN
FARM NOVELS

Compiled by John T. Flanagan

The following list of Middle Western farm novels written during the last six decades makes no pretense to be complete. It does include, however, most of the work of the better-known authors who have essayed to write rural fiction, and as such it may have value for the interested reader. The locale of these stories may be defined roughly as that part of the United States west of the Allegheny Mountains, north of the Ohio River, and east of the Rockies.

ALDRICH, BESS STREETER, *A Lantern in Her Hand*. New York and London, 1928.
———, *Song of Years*. New York and London, 1939.
ALLISON, JOY, *Billow Prairie*. Boston and Chicago, 1892.
BEERS, LORNA DOONE, *Prairie Fires*. New York, 1925.
———, *A Humble Lear*. New York, 1929.
———, *The Mad Stone*. New York, 1932.
BOYLES, KATE and VIRGIL D., *The Homesteaders*. Chicago, 1909.
BROMFIELD, LOUIS, *The Farm*. New York, 1933.
CANNON, CORNELIA, *Red Rust*. Boston, 1928.

CATHER, WILLA, *O Pioneers!* Boston and New York, 1913.

——, *My Ántonia.* Boston and New York, 1918.

COOK, FANNIE, *Boot-heel Doctor.* New York, 1941.

COREY, PAUL, *Three Miles Square.* Indianapolis, 1939.

——, *The Road Returns.* Indianapolis, 1940.

——, *County Seat.* Indianapolis, 1941.

EATON, G. D., *Backfurrow.* New York and London, 1925.

ENGLE, PAUL, *Always the Land.* New York, 1941.

FERBER, EDNA, *So Big.* Garden City, 1924.

FREDERICK, JOHN T., *Druida.* New York, 1923.

——, *Green Bush.* New York, 1925.

GARLAND, HAMLIN, *Main Traveled Roads.* Boston, 1891.

——, *Prairie Folks.* Chicago, 1893.

——, *Rose of Dutcher's Coolly.* Chicago, 1895.

——, *Jason Edwards.* New York, 1897.

——, *Moccasin Ranch.* New York and London, 1909.

GROVE, PHILIP FREDERICK, *Our Daily Bread.* New York, 1928.

HALDEMAN-JULIUS, MR. and MRS. E., *Dust.* New York, 1921.

HOWE, E. W., *The Story of a Country Town.* Boston and New York, 1883.

KIRKLAND, JOSEPH, *Zury: The Meanest Man in Spring County.* Boston and New York, 1887.

KRAMER, HORACE, *Marginal Land.* Philadelphia, 1939.

KRAUSE, HERBERT, *Wind without Rain.* Indianapolis, 1939.

LANE, ROSE WILDER, *Let the Hurricane Roar.* New York and Toronto, 1933.

——, *Free Land.* New York and Toronto, 1938.

MACLEOD, LEROY, *The Years of Peace.* New York, 1932.

——, *The Crowded Hill.* New York and London, 1934.

MUNGER, DELL H., *The Wind before the Dawn.* Garden City, 1912.

NORTH, STERLING, *Plowing on Sunday.* New York, 1934.

OSTENSO, MARTHA, *Wild Geese.* New York, 1925.

——, *The Mad Carews.* New York, 1927.

——, *The Stone Field.* New York, 1937.

——, *The Mandrake Root.* New York, 1938.

QUICK, HERBERT, *The Fairview Idea*. Indianapolis, 1919.

——, *Vandemark's Folly*. Indianapolis, 1922.

——, *The Hawkeye*. Indianapolis, 1923.

——, *The Invisible Woman*. Indianapolis, 1924.

READ, OPIE, *A Yankee from the West*. Chicago and New York, 1898.

RÖLVAAG, O. E., *Giants in the Earth*. New York and London, 1927.

——, *Peder Victorious*. New York and London, 1929.

SANDOZ, MARI, *Slogum House*. Boston, 1937.

SINCLAIR, HAROLD, *American Years*. New York, 1938.

STONG, PHIL, *State Fair*. New York, 1932.

STRINGER, ARTHUR, *The Prairie Wife*. Indianapolis, 1915.

——, *The Prairie Mother*. Indianapolis, 1920.

SUCKOW, RUTH, *Country People*. New York, 1924.

——, *The Odyssey of a Nice Girl*. New York, 1925.

——, *Iowa Interiors*. New York, 1926.

——, *The Folks*. New York, 1934.

WESCOTT, GLENWAY, *The Grandmothers*. New York and London, 1927.

WILSON, MARGARET, *The Able McLaughlins*. New York and London, 1923.

Reviews of Books

Songs of Yesterday: A Song Anthology of American Life. By Philip D.
Jordan and Lillian Kessler. (Garden City, New York, Double-
day, Doran & Co., Inc., 1941. 391 p. Illustrations. $3.00.)

Here are reproduced, in all the lacy elegance of the original designs,
the words and music of nearly a hundred songs from the hit parades of
yesterday. These are the songs that nineteenth-century Americans sang
around the parlor organ at home, with convivial cronies in the town tav-
ern, on the westward trail, in frontier cabins, at all sorts of sociables.
There are songs about street vendors, homesick immigrants, and restless
goldseekers, about the turnpike gate and the reaper on the plains, about
soldiers in blue and in gray. They are not great music, not even enduring folk songs; most of them are quite unknown nowadays except to
historians, antiquarians, and the oldsters whose memories reach back to
the days when they were sung. But there are some gay, jaunty tunes
among them, singable still.

It is happily evident from the preface and the bits of text accompanying the songs that the compilers had a heap of fun collecting these old-
time favorites. They straddled their hobby and rode it hard, tracking
down stray lyrics and melodies in far places and odd. They have arranged their chosen numbers in some twenty sections, each introduced
with a brief description of the particular aspect of the social scene it illustrates and the whole prefaced with an excellent historical sketch.

The section titles are such as these: "Oh I Should Like To Marry —
Songs of Courtship and Marriage," "Back-of-Beyond — The West,"
"The Crystalline Tear — Songs of Sentiment," "Ho, the Car Emancipa-
tion," and "Songs of the Stars and the Bars." Among the songs of fash-
ion are the daring "If Your Foot Is Pretty, Show It" and "The Jenny
Lind Mania," which pokes fun at the final phase of a national love affair.
The songs of the countinghouse include the whimsical "Have You Struck
Ile?" and on the other side "Out of Work," with a plaintive chorus that
might be much less than a century old:

> Must I starve in this great city,
> Where there's food enough for all?

Most of the songs in the group headed "Traveling Troupes of Family Singers" and many in other sections too were composed or introduced by the widely popular Hutchinson family — just as hit songs of today are introduced by one of the "big name bands." As the compilers tell us, the repertories of such family quartets "contained little of the operatic, less of the classical, and none of the mystical. Rather, they emphasized the melodramatic, the comic, and the sentimental; songs that were robust, told a story, or pointed a moral." And for re-creating the temper of the time, it is worth many a chapter of generalized description just to read through the songs the people packed the concert hall to hear — just to know, for example, that they paid well for the pleasure of blubbering and sniveling while the singers enacted the tragedy of insanity according to the words of "The Maniac," or dramatized the sad state of little Sissie in "Father's a Drunkard, and Mother Is Dead," a tear-jerking companion piece to the better-known "Father, Dear Father, Come Home with Me Now," or mimed the anguish of the despairing mother in "The Snow Storm":

> "O God!" she cried, in accents wild,
> "If I must perish, save my child."

But entertainment alone was not enough, of course; the puritan-pioneer must have moral uplift and self-improvement too. Each of the reform movements in that heyday of crusades had its own songs, and many of them appeared on the concert programs. The Hutchinsons were once called a "band of young apostles teaching love and truth," and with some reason. Their programs rang with the perfectionism and millennialism of the day, with "eloquent denunciations of the drunken sot . . . earnest pleas for peace, woman suffrage, and emancipation of the Negro." Indeed, this song anthology in passing quite cries aloud the possibilities of the Hutchinsons as subjects for a period portrait in words. Written with full attention to the background, their biography would make a fascinating piece of American social history.

HELEN CLAPESATTLE

The French in the Mississippi Valley, 1740–1750 (Illinois Studies in the Social Sciences, vol. 26, no. 3). By NORMAN WARD CALDWELL. (Urbana, The University of Illinois Press, 1941. 113 p. Map. $2.00.)

In this book Norman Ward Caldwell has made a cross section of the political and economic history of the Mississippi Valley when the struggle between France and England was about to reach its climax. He has presented, first of all, an able summary of the political and financial structure of New France and has illustrated well the current practices. In the next chapter is an analysis of population, with some discussion of food, health, morals, agriculture, and mining. To the fur trade, of course, an entire chapter is devoted; the system is described in some detail as well as the state of the trade in the mid-century. General Indian relations is the subject of the fourth chapter, and the Indians and the Ohio question that of the fifth and last chapter.

The five conclusions to which Mr. Caldwell comes may not all be new, but they are firmly grounded and indisputable. The political scheme for the colonies was "utterly unfit for the conditions of frontier life." In this period the French at last came to realize the need of strengthening Canada and Louisiana against the more populous English colonies. The extension of the fur trade by the French to the Northwest more than balanced the establishment by the English of their trade on the lower lakes and the upper Ohio. The French superiority in managing the Indians is repeatedly demonstrated. The importance of the colonies to France in its struggle with England is at last fully realized.

Mr. Caldwell's monograph, based largely on manuscript sources, is thoroughly documented and supported by an adequate bibliography. If the title seems to promise a broader view of the French life in the Mississippi Valley, the reader will soon discover that the author is interested in political, not cultural, history, and as such his book is a valuable contribution.

JOHN FRANCIS McDERMOTT

Our Landed Heritage: The Public Domain, 1776–1936. By ROY M. ROBBINS. (Princeton, Princeton University Press, 1942. x, 450 p. Maps, illustrations. $5.00.)

Several surveys dealing with the operation of the federal land policy have appeared since the publication in the 1880's of Thomas Donaldson's work, *The Public Domain.* The study of Roy M. Robbins entitled *Our Landed Heritage* is the latest of these.

In organizing his materials, the author follows the traditional pattern of most scholars, including Donaldson, who have written general works upon this subject. Thus he undertakes to outline the stages of development of the national land system, and he is chiefly concerned with describing the enacted laws, administrative orders, and machinery designed to insure effective federal operation. In his analysis of the New Deal's agrarian program in relation to the policies of conservationists, like the first Roosevelt and other early twentieth-century liberals, Dr. Robbins makes a real contribution, although some of his conclusions in this respect may be challenged. Moreover, the author's attractive literary style and his happy selections of illustrations and maps will doubtless appeal to the average college or university history student, as well as to the general reader.

Tested by the highest standards, however, *Our Landed Heritage* falls short of the goal that must be reached if ever a definitive work on the American land system is to be written. In this regard the author's use of newspapers and periodicals is significant, since, for the most part he limits himself to those of national circulation and neglects especially the many frontier sheets so essential to a complete story. This shortcoming admittedly is one for which the present author is only partly responsible. The real blame rests upon the shoulders of the entire historical profession, which, though unquestionably recognizing the serious difficulties in dealing adequately with a subject so tremendous in scope, has nevertheless failed thus far to formulate and to carry out a co-operative plan for producing monographs, by states or possibly by even smaller sections, thoroughly covering the materials relating thereto. Such studies would deal effectively with local newspapers and other sources and would go far toward filling the gaps now existing with reference to the organization and activities of hundreds of local land and surveying offices, and the personal histories of numerous receivers, registers, and surveyors whose careers in many respects are the keys to an understanding of the general problem. Until such a series of monographs is written, no definitive synthesis, it is submitted, can be possible.

The inadequacies of the surveys already produced, including the present one, are particularly evident in the tendency to assert incomplete and often inaccurate conclusions. This weakness is all the more serious because, despite the seeming nationwide uniformity in the application of the land laws, there was actually a disconcerting lack of uniformity. When Dr. Robbins says (p. 237) that pre-emption was extended to unsurveyed lands by the act of June 2, 1862, he overlooks the fact that in some regions, like Minnesota, such a condition had existed for several years prior to that time. Other instances of hasty generalization might be cited. Illustrative also of the insufficiency of analysis is the failure to evaluate properly the importance of the public land sales under the pre-emption system, which before 1860 were largely responsible for the frontier upheaval culminating in the West's endorsement of Lincoln.

VERNE E. CHATELAIN

Uncle Sam's Stepchildren: The Reformation of United States Indian Policy, 1865–1887. By LORING BENSON PRIEST. (New Brunswick, Rutgers University Press, 1942.   x, 310 p. $3.75.)

In *Uncle Sam's Stepchildren* Professor Priest deals with two post-Civil War decades in the history of the United States Indian policy, a subject which heretofore has received inadequate treatment at the hands of the historian.

Based upon such important sources as the Indian office records, the Dawes and Schurz papers, and the correspondence of the board of Indian commissioners, this careful study traces the United States Indian policy from the earliest efforts at reformation on the part of eastern philanthropists to the passage of the Dawes Severalty Act in 1887. Phases of the Indian problem covered in the study include the treaty, annuity, and reservation systems, the problem of Indian education, the development of Indian land policies, and severalty legislation.

The author skillfully traces the influences of such groups as the Indian Rights Association and the Lake Mohonk conferences in combating frauds in the management of Indian affairs and in effecting reforms. He shows how the repudiation of the policy of segregation was brought about by the combined opposition to the reservation system by eastern philanthropists and western settlers. Dr. Priest appraises the Dawes Act both in the light of its contemporary effects and in that of the present Indian policy of the United States, and concludes that the tragic effects of this first attempt to solve the Indian problem permanently were due to the misapplication of the law by its administrators rather than to any evil intent on the part of the legislators who sponsored it.

Though the book is designed primarily for the general reader with a casual interest in Indian affairs, the author has carefully documented it in order to make it useful to the specialist in the field. It is well balanced, impartial in its discussion of controversial issues, and accurate in its details. Dr. Priest has made an important contribution to the history of federal Indian policy.

MARTHA LAYMAN

Native American: The Book of My Youth. By RAY STANNARD BAKER. (New York, Charles Scribner's Sons, 1941. viii, 336 p. $3.00.)

In 1875 Joseph Stannard Baker arrived at St. Croix Falls to take charge of the Caleb Cushing lands in the valley and bring order out of a quarter of a century of negligence and mismanagement. This Baker, the father of the author of *Native American,* is easily the central figure in this autobiography. A prodigious storyteller, a fascinating companion on Sunday afternoon excursions, as well as an exacting disciplinarian, he was a hero in the eyes of his six sons. He gloried in the work and adventure of the new, hard surroundings. On long drives through the northern wilderness, he would note with pleasure the advent of each new settler and predict that some day the country would develop into a rich and prosperous community.

Life in the St. Croix Valley was pretty primitive in those first years. Remnants of the Chippewa tribe still lingered in their old resorts on the numerous lakes and streams. In the spring the river drive brought to the village the boisterous woodsmen, picturesque in their rough speech and in their heavy red woolen jackets. Homeseekers, most of them Scandinavian immigrants, drove northward with their ox teams. The one-room district school presented dubious opportunities for education, but on the Minnesota side of the river, Taylor's Falls had established a high school, the first in the region, offering courses in Latin and algebra, and "unlimited horseplay and fist-fighting, with a pallid principal vainly trying to keep order."

But life, though simple, was full of a joyous expectancy of great things ahead. This same enthusiasm and colossal faith existed at the Michigan Agricultural College, where young Baker continued his education. The whole institution was permeated with the conviction that science was the supreme key to human endeavor. To substantiate it, the instructors cited Pasteur's creed that "science and peace will finally triumph over ignorance and war."

During intervals between terms, or on his occasional days of freedom, Baker began the practice of slipping away for solitary overnight trips on foot through the woodlands. His delights in this sort of excursion he later shared with the world in his *Friendly Road, Adventures in Contentment,* and other books written under the pseudonym of David Grayson.

Chicago, too, appeared to him at first as another field for big adventure when he sought a newspaper position there. But experiences on the wrong side of the bread line and contacts with the chronically poor and oppressed brought changes. He deepened his sympathy with the individual and his problems. There came, too, a dawning realization that, while the lessons of perseverance and fortitude learned on the frontier were still applicable, conditions were irrevocably changed. The frontier itself was gone forever.

These new convictions took form in terse newspaper stories of the bitter conditions that existed in Chicago during the winter preceding the World's Fair. These studies were the preliminary to the "exposure" or "muckraking" articles that made the name of Ray Stannard Baker famous in the early years of the twentieth century.

At this point *Native American* ends. The strength of the narrative lies in its simplicity and honesty. The author is genuinely proud of his typically American origin and training. In his lifetime there have been telescoped all the stages in the history of the nation's development. For a future volume he promises a record of his further discoveries and explorations in an area wider than four Midwestern states.

ALICE E. SMITH

The Civil War Veteran in Minnesota Life and Politics. By FRANK H. HECK. (Oxford, Ohio, The Mississippi Valley Press, 1941. 295 p. Maps. $3.50.)

The author's original purpose was to investigate the part which the Grand Army of the Republic played in the politics of this state, but he found it necessary to include other veterans' groups and to study the social influence of the G.A.R. In the small-town community of the reviewer's youth the terms "Civil War veteran" and "G.A.R." were synonymous; indeed, the latter epithet, being shorter, was preferred. Professor Heck has found that about half of the "Old Boys" belonged to no veterans' clubs at all, and that other Civil War organizations played an important role. He has also found that much of the importance of the G.A.R. was its place as a social organization.

Shortly after the soldiers returned from the Civil War, a number of veterans' organizations were formed. The G.A.R. became the largest and most important of these groups. It was, perhaps, inevitable that politicians should try to use them. Theoretically, the G.A.R. was nonpartisan; actually, many, if not most, of its members appear to have supported the

Republican party. As Professor Heck points out, however, it was not as simple as that. The G.A.R. did not present a solid block of support for the Republican party. Other things being equal, the "Old Boys" probably voted "right." But there were Democrats in the G.A.R., and when all candidates were old soldiers, other things counted. It was to the interest of the Republican politicians to insinuate that the G.A.R. always voted "right," but Professor Heck shows that this did not always occur.

Pensions and veterans' preference were the things in which the old soldiers were interested, and they tended to support the candidates who gave their desires the most effective aid. Since both parties usually vied for the old soldier vote, the candidate's particular fitness for the office, his wounds and war record, or an especially effective waving of the "bloody shirt" might swing the tide.

Professor Heck has told an interesting story. He has used a mass of material and gives a good picture of the workings of grass-root politics. He concludes that the G.A.R. was not an appendage of the Republican party, or vice versa.

RODNEY C. LOEHR

Minnesota Historical Society Notes

IN VIEW OF the tire shortage and the general curtailment of automobile travel, the society's 1942 summer tour and convention will be confined to a single day and will be held in the neighborhood of the Twin Cities. Plans have been made for a Flag Day program at Fort Snelling at 2:00 P. M. on Sunday, June 14, conducted jointly by the society and the commissioned and enlisted personnel of the fort. It will open with the military ceremony of the presentation of the color to the 710th Military Police Battalion by Major General F. E. Uhl, commanding general of the Seventh Corps Area. If the weather permits, these exercises will take place at the marquee on the polo field of the fort. The field house of the garrison will be used for the program of talks and addresses that will follow the opening ceremony. Professor Lester B. Shippee of the University of Minnesota, president of the society, will preside; Colonel Harry J. Keeley, commanding officer of Fort Snelling, will welcome the visitors; and General Uhl will present a brief address. The chief speaker of the afternoon will be Brigadier General Harold E. Wood of the Minnesota State Guard, who will discuss "The Shape of Things to Come." Music by the Fort Snelling Military Band and the singing of the national anthem will bring the program to a close. Arrangements for the Fort Snelling program were made by the society's curator of manuscripts, Dr. Grace Lee Nute. The exercises are open to the public, and everyone interested is invited to be present.

An abstract of an article on the "Medical Books of Dr. Charles N. Hewitt" by Thomas E. Keys, published in the issue of this magazine for December, 1940, appears in the issue for November 12, 1941, of the *Proceedings* of the staff meetings of the Mayo Clinic.

The number of readers using the resources of the society's manuscript division continues to increase at a rapid rate, with nearly two thousand recorded for the first three months of 1942. The manuscript census records drew to the division no fewer than 1,788 people who were seeking proof of age and residence in order to obtain birth certificates, citizenship papers, old age assistance, and the like. In addition to these, 191 readers who were engaged in historical research were served during the quarter.

Three new workers were employed recently to assist with the census work in the manuscript division — Miss Dorothy Deutsch, Miss Mary Dunkl, and Miss Caryl Johnson. Miss Beatrice Edgar, who formerly had charge of this work, resigned on March 15.

Miss Nute is the author of an article on the "Migration of the Blue Geese at Lake Traverse in Early Spring" which appears in the April issue of the *Conservation Volunteer*.

The following eleven annual members joined the society in the first quarter of 1942: Dr. Anna Amrud of Montevideo, Bergit I. Anderson of Minneapolis, Charles B. Cheney of Minneapolis, William M. Cummings of Newport, Mrs. John W. G. Dunn of Marine, James Eckman of Rochester, Alice B. Grannis of Winona, Dr. M. K. Knauff of St. Paul, Eben E. Lawson of Willmar, Harry C. Libby of St. Paul, and Mrs. Mary Weaver of Anoka.

The superintendent spoke on "The Local Historical Society and Its Work" before a meeting that resulted in the organization of the Wright County Historical Society at Cokato on February 20. He also participated in an interview, with Dean Blegen of the University of Minnesota graduate school, on the work of the committee on the conservation of cultural resources over radio station WLB on February 28. Talks on "Life in Fur Trade Posts" and on the history of northern Minnesota were given by Miss Nute before meetings of the Minnesota Archaeological Society in Minneapolis on February 13 and the Plymouth Masonic Lodge of Minneapolis on February 23, and she wrote a paper on Minnesota folk customs for presentation before the Michigan Academy of Arts and Sciences at Ann Arbor on March 13. The International Relations Club of Wilson High School, St. Paul, heard talks on "Immigration and the Westward Push for Settlement" by Mr. Babcock on February 2, and on "Immigration in Minnesota" by Miss Jerabek on February 16.

CONTRIBUTORS

Somewhat wider in scope and more general in its appeal than earlier contributions to this magazine by the same author is Dr. John T. Flanagan's article on "The Middle Western Farm Novel." In previous articles, Dr. Flanagan, who is assistant professor of English in the University of Minnesota, has recorded the Minnesota experiences of authors of distinction. The most recently published of this series, appearing in the issue for June, 1941, deals with Hamlin Garland. Dr. Flanagan's latest book, a biography of *James Hall, Literary Pioneer of the Ohio Valley,* which was published late last year by the University of Minnesota Press, is reviewed *ante,* p. 62.

Studies in the field of historical geography led to the discovery by Professor Ralph H. Brown of the journal of Charles C. Trowbridge, published herewith under the title "With Cass in the Northwest in 1820." The introduction and notes that accompany the journal are the work of Dr. Brown, who is associate professor of geography in the University of Minnesota. Among his professional activities is his service as secretary of the Association of American Geographers. In the *Annals* of this organization for September, 1941, Professor Brown published an article on "The American Geographies of Jedidiah Morse." Recently he participated in a program of lectures on "War Comes to America," presented at the University of Minnesota under the sponsorship of its defense committee. His lecture, on "The Role of Latin America," is published in abbreviated form in the *Minnesota Alumni Weekly* for March 28.

The work and objectives of the newly organized Minnesota War History Committee are explained by Dr. Lewis Beeson, its executive secretary and director, who is curator of newspapers on the society's staff. The society's curator of manuscripts, Dr. Grace Lee Nute, contributes to the "Notes and Documents" section a brief account of "A Rindisbacher Water Color." Her interest in the frontier artist, Peter Rindisbacher, goes back to 1933, when she wrote a general account of his career and his work for this magazine, and she later presented a description of a collection of pictures by the same artist in the United States Military Academy at West Point (see *ante,* 20: 54–57). In the same section, Dr. Flanagan supplements his article with "A Bibliography of Middle Western Farm Novels."

The author of a recent best seller, the biography of *The Doctors Mayo,* heads the list of book reviewers in the present issue. Miss Helen Clapesattle is chief editor on the staff of the University of Minnesota Press. Her book is reviewed *ante,* 22: 404–408. Professor John Francis McDermott is a member of the English faculty in Washington University at St. Louis. Readers will recall his article on "An Upper Mississippi River Excursion of 1845" in the issue of this magazine for March, 1941. Mr. Verne E. Chatelain of Washington, D. C., is director of the St. Augustine Historical Program. He has made a special study of public lands in

Minnesota and he deals with one phase of this subject in an article published in the issue of this magazine for September, 1941. Miss Alice E. Smith, curator of manuscripts on the staff of the State Historical Society of Wisconsin, has an intimate knowledge of the section of the St. Croix Valley in which much of the autobiography that she reviews herein is localized. Miss Martha Layman is a member of the history faculty in the State Teachers College at Valley City, North Dakota. Dr. Rodney C. Loehr of the department of history in the University of Minnesota edited the volume of *Minnesota Farmers' Diaries* that was published by this society in 1939.

ACCESSIONS

Diaries kept by Joseph N. Nicollet during his western expeditions of the late 1830's, sketch maps, and other items have been copied on filmslides for the society from the originals in the Library of Congress. Nicollet made a detailed exploration of the Mississippi headwaters and the Itasca basin in the summer of 1836 and he spent the winter that followed at Fort Snelling. His diaries contain valuable records of his expedition above the Falls of St. Anthony and of other journeys in the vicinity of the fort, as well as of trips into the Missouri River Valley from 1838 to 1840. Parts of Dakota, Iowa, and Minnesota, including the sites of Fort Snelling, Little Crow's village, and what became St. Paul, are depicted on the sketch maps, which were doubtless used by the explorer in the preparation of his definitive map of the Northwest. The materials photographed occupy four reels of films.

A large collection of Civil War correspondence, comprising 149 letters written by Thomas Montgomery of Cleveland and St. Peter, has been copied on filmslides for the society through the courtesy of his son, Mr. Charles Montgomery of St. Paul. As a member of the Seventh Minnesota Volunteer Infantry, Montgomery participated in the Sibley expedition against the Sioux in 1862, and he helped to guard the condemned Indians before their execution at Mankato. Later in the South he served as captain of two Negro regiments — the Sixty-fifth and Sixty-seventh United States Colored infantries. Letters written during this period contain frequent discussions of Negro problems, such as education and civil rights, and they mention a proposed Negro colony in the St. Peter land district. They also give interesting sidelights on life with the Union forces in the Civil War, telling of such matters as the soldier's food, recreation, religion, and surroundings. There are frequent mentions of the Masonic Order, to which Montgomery belonged. Before he was mustered out of the service in 1867, he had attained the rank of major.

The papers of George B. Wright, who platted the city of Fergus Falls in 1870 and was prominently identified with land speculation in central Minnesota in the decades that followed, have been presented by his grandson, Mr. Thomas C. Wright of Fergus Falls. Included in the collection are 214 land deeds and 344 township plats. Among the latter are plats of the Hennepin County townships of Plymouth, Greenwood, Corcoran, and Maple Grove in 1870, on which property owners of the time are indicated. Two record books of the Grant and Dakota Railway Company for the years from 1879 to 1884, kept by Wright's nephew and business associate, Charles D. Wright, who was treasurer of the company, also are included in the gift.

An inventory of bills filed among the papers of Ignatius Donnelly in the Donnelly House at Nininger has been presented by Miss Elsa Krauch, hostess at this historic residence during the summer months.

Of timely interest is a letter, presented by Major L. I. Cooke of San Diego, which was written on August 2, 1900, by Emilio Aguinaldo, leader of the Filipino insurgents in their rebellion against the American occupation of the Philippines. In it, he advocates continued resistance on the part of the Filipinos, writing that "If we allow ourselves to be lured by sweet words and seductive promises . . . it may be considered a prelude to our enslavement." Major Cooke's gift includes copies of two of Aguinaldo's orders and a series of censored telegrams of 1899. The latter were submitted to the American military authorities in the Philippines by the *Manila American,* which asked to be reimbursed for charges paid on words struck out by the censor. Major Cooke also has presented a collection of seventy-seven photographs of Indian and military scenes.

A copy of a term paper entitled "Dassel, Past and Present: A Survey of Recent Changes in an Agricultural Community," prepared for a course in history in the University of Minnesota, has been presented by the author, Miss Doris Pearson of Dassel.

An unusual and interesting addition to the society's collection of Minnesota music is a song about the frontier territory composed by Robert

Pike for a Fourth of July celebration at Minnesota City in 1852, both the words and the music of which were recently recalled and written out by Mrs. Della Hancock Carpenter of Williston, North Dakota. In an accompanying letter, Mrs. Carpenter relates that her father, whose family settled at Wabasha in the spring of 1852, "often sang this song to us. After his death in 1901 I began to wonder about its origin, and wrote to a sister of my father's." The latter revealed the story of the song's origin and recalled that it "was sung by a quartet with the audience joining in the chorus." The music collection has been enriched also by seven pieces of sheet music by Minnesota composers of more recent date, the gift of Mr. Howard R. Woolsey of St. Paul. Represented in this group, which dates from 1893 to 1919, are such local composers as W. W. Chapple, George Bittrich, and J. Tracy Young. Included are several World War songs and an item entitled "Ramsey Park March." Others who have in their possession manuscript or published music by Minnesotans or relating to the state are urged to follow the examples set by Mrs. Carpenter and Mr. Woolsey by placing such items with the society for permanent preservation.

Issues of *Rivington's New-York Gazetteer, or, the Connecticut, Hudson's River, New-Jersey, and Quebec Advertiser* for November 4, 1773, and September 28, 1775, are the gifts of Judge Royal A. Stone of St. Paul. These rare newspapers, which are among the earliest in the society's collections, were published at New York by a Tory printer, James Rivington, while the city was occupied by the British.

Much of the collection of logging tools and lumberjack equipment formerly displayed in a log bunkhouse at the State Fair under the auspices of the state division of forestry has been turned over to the society by the State Fair board. The collection consists of more than a hundred items, including peavies, canthooks, axes, stamp hammers, blacksmiths' tools and equipment, logging chains, loading hooks, and bunkhouse equipment. This material supplements admirably the society's earlier collection of lumber camp equipment. Included in the State Fair board's gift are ninety-two photographs of Minnesota lumbering scenes.

A number of military items, including a powderhorn, a shot flask, and grenades of two different types, are the gifts of Mr. Albert L. Noyes of St. Paul. He has also presented a silver castor and twenty-eight photographs of St. Paul scenes and views of a Northern Pacific Railroad celebration.

Recent additions to the numismatic collection include a Continental currency note for five dollars issued in 1778, from Mr. Beverley Fleet of Richmond, Virginia, and a North Carolina treasury note for ten dollars, bearing the date 1863, from Mr. Lloyd Wilson of Mankato. A German bank note for a hundred marks, dating from 1910, has been received from Mr. Walter Fohernkamm of St. Paul, and another for a hundred thousand marks, issued during the inflation of 1923, is the gift of Mr. Walter Lunzman of St. Paul.

The St. Paul winter carnivals of the late 1880's are pictured in sixty photographs of the Nushka Club, a St. Paul winter sports organization, contained in two albums presented by Dr. John M. Armstrong of St. Paul. A third album included in the gift is made up of pictures of the activities of the Minnesota Boat Club in 1890. Dr. Armstrong also has presented a coverlet of wool and linen dating from 1800, and a beautiful child's dress of fine linen and lace worn in 1880 by Kate C. Spalding, later Mrs. A. H. Cathcart.

A number of additions to the toy collection, including a steamboat, a train, and an oxcart in miniature, and two humming tops, one of which dates from 1846, are among the items recently presented by Mrs. R. P. Warner of St. Paul. Her gift includes also several early household items from Sweden, such as a spinning wheel and a coffee grinder, the latter dating from 1761; two pairs of handmade leather shoes; and a number of items of ethnological interest. Several cardcases and needle cases, a coat of red wool trimmed with black fur, and a doll's hat of felt are the gifts of Mrs. Charles B. Wright of Minneapolis.

The state flowers of every state in the Union have been embroidered with facsimiles of their governors' signatures on the squares of a patch quilt presented by Mrs. O. E. Peterson of Forest Lake. Represented also by squares are the Hawaiian Islands and Canada.

Portraits in crayon of nine former state auditors have been received from the state auditor's office, and a photograph of a tenth, W. W. Braden, is the gift of the Honorable Julius A. Schmahl of St. Paul.

Valuable source material is included in the volumes dealing with local history received since the first of the year. Wills, pension records, and names of Virginia residents from the 1810 census records are published in volumes 3 to 5 of *Virginia Genealogies and County Records* compiled by Annie W. Burns (Washington, 1941–42). Similar material assembled by the same compiler is found in volumes 3 and 4 of *Maryland Genealogies and Historical Recorder* (Washington, 1941–42) and in *Kentucky Genealogical and Historical Recorder* (Washington, 1942). Two kinds of court records are represented in *Petitions for Guardians from the Minutes of the Salem County, New Jersey, Orphans' Court* by H. Stanley Craig (Merchantville, New Jersey. 134 p.), and in *Charles City County Court Orders, 1664–1665*, compiled by Beverley Fleet (Richmond, Virginia, 1942. 116 p.). Elmer I. Shepard has included vital records of various places in his *Berkshire Geneological Notes* (Williamstown, Massachusetts, 1940–41. 3 volumes). These include *Marriages in Pownal, Vermont to 1850, The "Register" of Dr. William H. Tyler and Additions to Williamstown Vital Records to 1850.* A number of families of the Mohawk Valley are represented in *Marriage and Birth Records as Recorded by Rev. James Dempster, 1778–1803* (St. Johnsville, New York, 1935. 31 p.) and many Maryland names are in *Marriage Records of Prince Georges Co. Maryland 1777–1836* compiled by Sylvia G. Greene (Mount Ranier, Maryland, 1941. 129 p.).

A record of Revolutionary soldiers, made particularly valuable by the inclusion of much family data, is the *Roster of Revolutionary Soldiers in Georgia* by Ettie T. McCall (Atlanta, Georgia, 1941. 294 p.). Soldiers of Maryland, Virginia, and North and South Carolina who settled in Georgia, many of them on land grants received in payment for service, are included.

Other local histories recently received are: Francis J. Audet, *Contrecoeur: Famille, Seigneurie, Paroisse, Village* (Montreal, 1940. 276 p.); Leon C. Hills, *History and Genealogy of the Mayflower Planters and First Comers to Ye Olde Colonie (Cape Cod Series,* vol. 2 — Washington, D. C., 1941. 284 p.); Gladys M. Sinclair, *Bayonne Biographies* (Hudson County, New Jersey, 1941. 211 p.) and *Bayonne Old and New* (New York, 1940. 251 p.); *Somerset County 250 Years* (Somerville, New Jersey, 1938. 192 p.); Morgan H. Seacord, *Biographical Sketches and Index of the Huguenot Settlers of New Rochelle, 1687–1776* (New Rochelle, New York, 1941. 54 p.); Frederic S. Klein, *Lancaster County, 1841–1941* (Lancaster, Pennsylvania, 1941. 198 p.); and

Edwin H. Marshall, *History of Obion County* (Union City, Tennessee, 1941. 272 p.).

The first volume of the *American Genealogical Index* (Middletown, Connecticut, 1942), which covers 330 genealogies and local histories, 305 of which are available in the society's library, was received during the first quarter of 1942. In this volume surnames from Aaron to Anthony are indexed, with subentries for first and middle names. Other useful compilations recently acquired are volume 7 of the *Compendium of American Genealogy* by Frederick A. Virkus (Chicago, 1942. 1040 p.); volume 3 of *Pioneer Families of the Midwest* by Blanche L. Walden (Athens, Ohio, 1941. 160 p.); and *Southern Lineages: Records of Thirteen Families* by A. Evans Wynne (Atlanta, Georgia, 1940. 405 p.).

Records of Minnesota residents or of people who once lived in the state can be found in nearly half the genealogies received by the society during the winter quarter. The *Nicholas Adams Family Tree, 1799–1941* by Dorothy K. Adams (Milwaukee, 1941. 32 p.) is largely devoted to members of the Adams family in Mower County. A map of the part of Waseca County where the Cleland farm was located, is included in *The Clelands of 1941* by Spencer B. Cleland (St. Paul, 1941. 18 p.). *The Cory Family* by Harry H. Cory (Minneapolis, 1941. 117 p.) and the *Van de Mark or Van der Mark Ancestry* compiled by John W. Van Demark and others (Minneapolis, 1942. 394 p.) are Minnesota publications. Other genealogies in which Minnesotans are mentioned include: Olive B. Daniels, *The Bell Family, Descendants of John Bell of Beverly, Yorkshire, England and Shrigley, Melancthon, Ontario* (Madison, Wisconsin, 1939. 47 p.), and *The Greer, Elliot, Sabin, and Jerome Ancestry of Mary Elliot Greer Bell* (Madison, Wisconsin, 1940. 124 p.) with Daniels and Farrington charts; Edward C. Moran, Jr., *Bunker Genealogy, Ancestry and Descendants of Benjamin 3 (James 2, James 1) Bunker* (Rockland, Maine, 1942. 232 p.); Edward M. Chapman, *The Chapmans of Old Saybrook, Connecticut, a Family Chronicle* (New London, Connecticut, 1941. 74 p.); John S. Cleland, *Cleland: A Few Facts and Rumours about the Clelands* (Monmouth, Illinois, 1937. 15 p.); Truman Abbe, *Robert Colgate the Immigrant; a Genealogy of the New York Colgates* (New Haven, Connecticut, 1941. 464 p.); Amos E. Voorhies, *The Amos S. Earle Branch of the Ralph Earle Family in America* (Grants Pass, Oregon, 1940. 106 p.); Spencer Gordon, *Our*

Gordon Family, a Genealogical and Biographical Record (Washington, 1941. 50 p.); Henery S. Jacoby, *Supplement to the Jacoby Family Genealogy* (Lancaster, Pennsylvania, 1941. 56 p.); Lorand V. Johnson, *The Descendants of William and John Johnson, Colonial Friends of Virginia* (Cleveland, Ohio, 1940. 196 p.); Philip H. Shaub, *Kuhns, a Genealogy* (Jefferson, Iowa, 1941. 22 p.); Louie C. Mathewson, *A Mathewson Lineage Including the Descendants of John and Lois (Hicks) Mathewson* (Hanover, New Hampshire, 1941. 29 p.); Ella M. Milligan, *Christian Metzger, Founder of an American Family, 1682–1942* (Denver, Colorado, 1942. 477 p.); Doyle M. Craytor, *Descendants of David Pollock, 1755–1841* (Cincinnati, Ohio, 1941. 25 p.); volume 2 of Lester LeRoy Roush, *History of the Roush [Rausch] Family in America* (Parkersburg, West Virginia, 1942. 579 p.); Mary C. Schoppe, *The Schoppe Family Genealogy, 1782–1932* (1932. 201 p.); and Vincent D. Wyman, *Wyman Historic Genealogy, Lowell Genealogy Supplement, Phelps Ancestral Lines* (Coral Gables, Florida, 1941. 144 p.).

Among other genealogies received are: Claribel Albright, *Some Records of the Albright Family* (St. Joseph, Missouri, 1941. 135 p.); Adelaide B. Crandall, *Blanchards of Rhode Island* (Ann Arbor, Michigan, 1942. 263 p.); Barry H. Burgess, *Burgess Genealogy, Kings County, Nova Scotia, Branch of the Descendants of Thomas and Dorothy Burgess Who . . . Settled in Sandwich, Massachusetts* (New York, 1941. 75 p.); Maurice L. Carr, *The Story of John Karr* (Avon, Illinois, 1938. 32 p.); Doyle M. Craytor, *Descendants of Moritz Crater, 1703–1772* (Lakewood, Ohio, 1939. 51 p.); Alfred S. Dameron, *Historical and Genealogical Sketch of the Dameron Family of England and Virginia* (Newport, Kentucky, 1940); H. W. L. Dana, *The Dana Saga, Three Centuries of the Dana Family in Cambridge* (Cambridge, Massachusetts, 1941. 61 p.); Dora D. Farrington, *They Saw America Born; Adventures of an American Family (Davis) Pioneering from the Atlantic to the Pacific, 1638–1938* (Los Angeles, 1941. 188 p.); George B. Hyde, *Some Descendants of Jonathan Hyde in the Tenth Generation* (Ashland, Massachusetts, 1941. 7 p.); Louise Diman, *Leaves from a Family Tree, Being Random Records, Letters and Traditions of the Jones, Stimson and Clarke Families* (Providence, Rhode Island, 1941. 123 p.); John H. Schneider, *Genealogy of Peter Kregel of Grambow, Province of Pommern, Germany and His Descendants Who Came to America in 1857 and Settled in Wisconsin* (Winnetka, Illinois, 1941. 52 p.); Alexander

Du Bin, *Le Roy Family and Collateral Lines* (Philadelphia, 1941. 32 p.); Walter McElreath, *My Folks* (Atlanta, Georgia, 1941. 124 p.); Gérard Malchelosse, *Généalogie de la Famille Malchelosse* (Montreal, 1918. 31 p.), *La Famille Roupe* (Montreal, 1918. 8 p.), and *La Famille Wasbroad* (Montreal, 1937. 8 p.); Estelle M. Harrington, *Ida Amelia, a True Story Connected with the Messenger Family of Illinois* (St. Louis, 1940. 79 p.); Jesse R. Overturf, *History of the Overturfs* (Palo Alto, California, 1941. 33 p.); Myrtle H. Phillips, *Genealogy of Rev. Reuel Phillips, Sr., and His 14 Children and Descendants* (Los Angeles, 1941. 154 p.); N. Louise Lodge, *The Tribe of Jacob (Piatt)* (Springfield, Missouri, 1934. 170 p.); James R. Slonaker, *A History and Genealogy of the Slonaker Descendants in America since Early 1700* (Los Angeles, 1941. 732 p.); Hubert W. Hess, *The Staring Family* (St. Johnsville, New York, 1929. 28 p.); Isaac F. Swallow, *The Swallows and Gustons, A Family History from the Earliest Records in the American Colonies to the Present Generation* (Kansas City, Missouri, 1941. 60 p.); Thomas J. Thornhill, *Thornhill Genealogy* (Dallas, Texas, 1940. 149 p.); Dudley Hill, *Genealogy of the Toll Family* (Schenectady, New York, 1941. 47 p.); Peter U. Schmidt, *The Peter Unruh Genealogy, Beginning with Unrau Born about 1675* (Newton, Kansas, 1941. 128 p.); Louise C. Potts, *Biographical Sketches and Family Records of the Gabriel Weimer and David Weimer Families* (Rockvale, Tennessee, 1936. 270 p.); volume 5 of John R. Wilbor, *The Wildbores in America* (Baltimore, 1941. 304 p.); and John A. Woestemeyer, *Woestemeyer Family Genealogy* (St. Paul, 1940. 27 p.). L.M.F.

News and Comment

IN AN ARTICLE on "Historians and Archivists in the First World War," appearing in the *American Archivist* for January, Waldo G. Leland gives "some idea of the way in which a national voluntary organization of historians and archivists set about organizing and making available to the nation the services of their profession" in 1917. He reviews the work of the National Board for Historical Service over a period of two and a half years, and he asserts that its professional record demonstrates that the "highest ideals of conscientious scholarship were maintained throughout an honest effort to be of service to the country." The influence of this record upon post-war scholarship also is considered.

"We are confident that the study of our state and local history is a patriotic duty, and while bowing always to the war needs of our country, we shall try to make our Society even more influential." This statement appears in a section devoted to "Chats with the Editor" in the March issue of the *Wisconsin Magazine of History*. Only by understanding our past, writes the editor, "can we appreciate the country in which we live, the importance of the way of life which has fused into one great nation the varied emigrants who had fought tooth and nail in Europe, and the sacrifices made by our forebears and now demanded of us."

"The types of material required for use by the cultural historian . . . must throw light on mass behavior as well as on the behavior of individuals; they must reveal activities not ordinarily a matter of formal record; they must deal with the inarticulate as well as the articulate groups in society; they must make it possible to reach down into the home and community where the details of life are lived." Thus reads the introduction to a section on "Sources and Materials for the Study of Cultural History" appearing in a work on the *Cultural Approach to History,* which has been edited for the American Historical Association by Caroline F. Ware (New York, 1940. 359 p.). This section, which concludes the volume, contains suggestive chapters on the "Value of Local History" by Constance McLaughlin Green, on the "Use of Population Data" by Frank Lorimer, on "Folklore as a Neglected Source of

Social History" by B. A. Botkin, and on "Folk Music as a Source of Social History" by Charles Seeger.

Under the title "How Not to Write History," Margaret Leech tells, in *Harper's Magazine* for March, of the long years of historical research and collecting and organizing material that preceded the publication of her recent best-seller, *Reveille in Washington.* "Like an old-fashioned novelist, I had begun at the beginning," writes Miss Leech. "This is the hard way, the long way, and, I suspect, the wrong way to write history. I knew nothing about analyzing my material fully in advance, and did not anticipate that my chronological development would have to be interrupted to permit the discussion of special subjects." Some of her adventures in the use of original manuscripts in the National Archives and elsewhere and in the consultation of newspaper files are described by the writer. One day in the Library of Congress, Miss Leech reports, "I opened a dirty brown volume, about two-thirds the size of a modern newspaper, and found myself embarked on the happiest adventure of my research. . . . For good or ill, *Reveille in Washington* was made out of the newspapers. They gave me the flow of life, the shape of thought, the sense of participating in history as it was being made." One must take issue, however, with her contention that "most historians look down their noses at newspapers." Certainly in the local field, some of the most important raw material that professional historians utilize today comes from newspaper files.

A review of *Price Administration, Priorities, and Conservation of Supplies Affecting Agriculture in the United States, in 1917–18,* by Arthur G. Peterson, has been published by the United States department of agriculture as number 3 of its *Agricultural History Series* (16 p.). The author gives consideration to the country's experience in the first World War in conserving such supplies as farm machinery and equipment, fertilizers, leather products, and foods. He concludes that the "application of widespread price regulation and the use of priorities were new in this country and progress was necessarily slow" in 1917–18. "Today we have considerable knowledge from the first World War to guide us."

Parts of the 1940 *Yearbook of Agriculture* issued by the United States department of agriculture have been reprinted and bound as *Yearbook Separate* no. 1783, which bears the title *An Historical Survey of Ameri-*

can Agriculture: The Farmer's Changing World (1941. p. 103–326, 1184–1196). This convenient pamphlet will be found very useful as a text or reference book for American agricultural history. Special attention is called to two of the articles in the separate — "American Agriculture — The First 300 Years," by Everett E. Edwards, and "A Brief Chronology of American Agricultural History," compiled by Dorothy C. Goodwin under the direction of Paul H. Johnstone. Mr. Edwards, who is familiar to readers of this magazine, is the leading authority in the field of American agricultural history, and contributions from him are always welcome. His story covers the period from the beginning of settlement to the first World War and discusses such phases as land policy, migration, the frontier, sections, social organization, farm equipment, agricultural labor, crops, livestock, trade, markets, competition, transportation, the growth of cities, agricultural education, agricultural politics, and government policy. A select bibliography of more than two hundred items contains literature cited. The "Chronology" by Miss Goodwin and Mr. Johnstone covers the years from 1785 to 1939 and gives the dates of the principal events in the American agricultural story. Its brevity and typographical arrangement will appeal to the student and the reference librarian.   RODNEY C. LOEHR

"The Western Farmers and the Drivewell Patent Controversy" is the title of an article by Earl W. Hayter in the January issue of *Agricultural History*. A feature of the controversy was a decision of the Minnesota Supreme Court "favoring the 'drive-well' swindle," that is, upholding the claims of a patentee who sued for royalties. One result was Senator William Windom's "excoriating speech in Congress against the patent system in general and the drivewell patent in particular."

An address on "The Botany and History of Zizania Aquantica L. ('Wild Rice')," presented before the Washington Academy of Sciences by Charles E. Chambliss in January, 1940, is published in the *Annual Report* of the Smithsonian Institution for 1940. The importance of the cereal to explorers and traders in the Northwest as well as to the native red men is brought out by the writer. Radisson's comments on a "kinde of rice, much like oats" that served the Indians as "food for the most part of the winter" and remarks about the use of the grain that were published by Alexander Henry and David Thompson are quoted. The reactions to the plant of European scientists, like Peter Kalm, who visited

America at an early date also are cited. Indian methods of harvesting and preparing wild rice are described, and photographs are reproduced showing Minnesota Chippewa who are engaged in harvesting, parching, and hulling the grain.

"Some Traits of the Dakota Language" are discussed by Franz Boas of Columbia University in a recent volume on *Race, Language and Culture* (New York, 1940). "A few features of the language of the Dakota Indians which seem to have a wider linguistic interest" are selected for elaboration by the author. In a chapter dealing with "Romance Folk-lore among American Indians," Professor Boas declares that a "variety of French material has become part of Indian lore."

Carrie A. Lyford is the author of an interesting study of the *Quill and Beadwork of the Western Sioux,* which has been published by the education division of the United States office of Indian affairs as number 1 of an *Indian Handcrafts* series (1940. 116 p.). Among the subjects considered are the types of articles decorated by the Sioux, such as clothing and tipis; methods used in preparing and dressing skins; the techniques, materials, and stitches used in quill and in bead work; and the "development of Sioux designs." A list of "museums in which choice collections of Indian arts and crafts can be found" is included. Numerous illustrations and diagrams add to the value of the booklet.

An important collection of "Drawings by George Catlin," which the New-York Historical Society acquired from the artist in 1870, is described by M. Maxson Holloway in the society's *Quarterly Bulletin* for January. Although the collection consists of "220 original pencil and ink drawings of North American Indians," the writer has failed to find it "recorded in any published book or bibliography on Catlin." A special exhibit of Catlin's work was placed on display by the society in December and January. In addition to items from its own collection, twenty-one paintings owned by the American Museum of Natural History were displayed.

The publication in the relatively obscure *Canadian Antiquarian and Numismatic Journal* at Montreal of René Thomas Verchères de Boucherville's recollections passed almost unnoticed practically a century after the occurrence of the events he recounted. Thus few libraries have a copy of this entertaining and historically valuable French narrative of Verchères' trip in 1803 to Grand Portage, Rainy Lake, and Fort Dauphin, of his life at that fort during the ensuing winter, of his return trip to Boucherville in 1804, of his experiences as a merchant at Amherstburg, and of his observations of the War of 1812. These recollections, written in old age, have now been published as a volume of the *Lakeside Classics,* in an English translation edited by Milo M. Quaife and bearing the title *War on the Detroit: The Chronicles of Rene Thomas de Boucherville and the Capitulation by an Ohio Volunteer* (Chicago, 1940). The second half of the volume is devoted to a reprint of a rare account of part of the War of 1812 from an American's point of view, which in the original bore the title, *The Capitulation, or, A History of the Expedition Conducted by William Hull, Brigadier-General of the North-western Army* (Chillicothe, Ohio, 1812). Minnesota readers are indebted to Dr. Quaife and the Lakeside Press for bringing to light, through Verchères' narrative, a new account of travel along the international boundary waters west of Lake Superior. It includes one of the few extant descriptions of Grand Portage in its heyday. The post, writes Verchères, "had been built by the Northwest Company and consisted of palisades of tall cedar pickets with bastions at the four corners. Within the enclosure were several good buildings for the use of members of the Company, and towering over all was an immense flagstaff from which on Sundays and when heralding the arrival of the principal bourgeois, floated a large and very handsome flag."   G.L.N.

How the frontier housewife met the culinary problems of the log-cabin kitchen is the subject of an article by Della T. Lutes published under the title "Settlers' Grub" in the *American Mercury* for January. In winter "it behooved the frontier family to have on hand a supply of preserved foods — salted, smoked, dried or 'jerked,'" writes Mrs. Lutes. The covered wagon which characterized the "hazardous venture of emigration to the new home" for many of the settlers of the frontier West was usually loaded with supplies that would help to tide its occupants over the first winter in the wilderness. Mrs. Lutes is inclined to scoff at the "picture of luxuriant plenty" painted by some writers of frontier lore. "Roads were treacherous and sometimes a man's family could starve to death while he was away hunting for food," she writes. "Most historians," she continues, "touch upon the culinary experiments of first land-breaking days but lightly and with little heart. Besides, there are not too many authentic records. Men were too busy to keep the ledgers, account books and journals in which, through simple statements, they later revealed their own hard-found lives." Among the interesting suggestions made in this article are the "many things about cooking in the wilderness" that the Indian women taught the settler's wife.

Although much of Florence L. Dorsey's biography of Henry Shreve, published under the title *Master of the Mississippi* (Boston, 1941), deals with the lower river, there are occasional interesting references to traffic above St. Louis. A trip that Shreve made in 1810 to the Fever River country to trade with the Indians for lead is described in one of the early chapters. Shreve was an important figure in the development of steamboating on the lower river, but it was not until after his death in 1851 that traffic on the upper Mississippi reached its greatest importance. A final chapter is devoted largely to the story of river traffic just before the inauguration of railroads, with some attention to transportation between St. Louis and the Falls of St. Anthony. Among the subjects touched upon are the panoramas, from which "Mississippi travel received international advertisement," the "fashionable tour," and the railroad excursion of 1854.

There were "naturalists, conchologists and lieutenants, as well as draughtsmen, artists and topographers" among the "Artists of the Explorations Overland, 1840–1860" whose work illustrates some well-known travel narratives, writes Louise Rasmussen in the *Oregon Historical Quarterly* for March. Some of the artists discussed, such as Paul Kane and J. M. Stanley, left pictorial records of the frontier Middle West as well as of the Far West. The author notes that in addition to Stanley, the Pacific railroad survey of 1853 included among its numbers two other artists, George Gibbs and Gustavus Sohon.

"The oldest Hutterian community in this country, settled in 1874, is the Bon Homme Colony near Tabor, Bon Homme County, South Dakota," on the Missouri River, according to A. J. F. Zieglschmid, who contributes an article on the "Hutterians on the American Continent" to the February issue of the *American-German Review*. He describes in some detail the costumes of the Hutterians, who "believe in community of goods and thus have all property in common." Some interesting pictures of the South Dakota colony accompany the article. A "list of all the existing Hutterian colonies in America" is published as an appendix.

In an article entitled "Wagon Roads West," which appears in the January number of the *Annals of Iowa,* Alice V. Myers tells of the overland expeditions from Iowa and Minnesota to the Montana gold fields in the 1860's that were "but a part of that larger story of the frenzied search for gold throughout the western part of the United States." The author's chief concern is for the expeditions that left Sioux City in 1865 and 1866 under the leadership of James A. Sawyers. Miss Myers is interested also, however, in expeditions organized from 1862 to 1867 at St. Paul and other points in Minnesota, and she presents brief accounts of the activities of Thomas Holmes, James L. Fisk, and Captain P. B. Davy, who led groups of emigrants across the plains.

A charming picture of "The District School" in Grant Township, Boone County, Iowa, is presented by Dean Carl E. Seashore of the University of Iowa in the *Palimpsest* for March. The school, which was opened in 1873, served the Swedish settlement at Dayton, where the author's parents had established a home four years earlier. For eight years, Dr. Seashore relates, he attended this little rural school, where he learned English and acquired the elements of a primary education. He estimates that he "had attended the district school only about 600 days and had never seen a high school" when he "went to the Academy at Gustavus Adolphus College in 1884 and was admitted to an advanced class." After a year in the academy, Dr. Seashore "returned to teach District No. 1 and drew the munificent salary of thirty dollars a month."

George B. Hartman is the author of an exhaustive study of the "Iowa Sawmill Industry," which appears in the *Iowa Journal of History and Politics* for January. The author points out that the sawmill industry was of considerable importance in the "early settlement and subsequent development of Iowa" and that it drew upon a wide territory for its raw materials. The presence of logs from the St. Croix Valley in the Iowa mills is, for example, noted. Some attention is given also to the activities in Iowa of Frederick Weyerhaeuser, who was later prominent in the development of the Minnesota lumber industry.

A contribution to Midwestern social history of more than ordinary interest is Ayres Davies' article on "Wisconsin, Incubator of the American Circus," which appears in the *Wisconsin Magazine of History* for March. As early as the 1840's, Mr. Davies records, a circus family bought a farm "near Delavan and established winter quarters there. Here the budding circus blossomed and here began the growth of other Wisconsin tented shows." Much of the narrative centers, however, about Baraboo, the "birthplace of the Ringling Brothers' Circus in the 1880's." Members of the Ringling family, the author notes, "also resided at McGregor, Iowa; Prairie du Chien; Stillwater, Minnesota; and Rice Lake." "A Portrait of Wisconsin" is the title of a general interpretation of the history of the state contributed to the same issue by Louise Phelps Kellogg. She describes geographic feaures on the Mississippi and the St. Croix that Wisconsin shares with Minnesota, and touches upon the exploits of many explorers whose travels carried them into the areas of both states.

A poem written by Oliver Wendell Holmes in 1887 on the occasion of the dedication of a hospital named in his honor at Hudson is reprinted in the *Hudson Star-Observer* for January 22. The name for the hospital was selected by Dr. Irving D. Wiltrout, who greatly admired the American poet. Holmes's poem and an accompanying letter dated April 25, 1887, were read at the dedication ceremonies by Dr. Cyrus Northrop of the University of Minnesota.

Henry R. Schoolcraft's role as "A Vital Figure in Early American Education" is discussed by Chase S. Osborn and Stella B. Osborn in an article appearing in the February number of the *Quarterly Review* issued by the alumni of the University of Michigan. Special attention is given to Schoolcraft's efforts on behalf of the University of Michigan after its reorganization in 1837, when he became a member of the board of regents. In the following year he established the Michigan *Journal of Education*, which is said to have been the "first educational journal published in the United States."

The Oakes Collection: New Documents by Lahontan concerning Canada and Newfoundland, edited with an introduction by Gustave Lanctot (Ottawa, 1940), is a booklet of documents by and about Lahontan. They are presented in the original French with English translations, and are supplemented by maps, plans, illustrations, and a census table. While the collection has little of specific Minnesota interest, it cannot fail to be of use to students of the French regime in Minnesota, since all details of Lahontan's career have direct or indirect connections with the region's history.   G.L.N.

The first installment of a study of the "Canadian Halfbreed Rebellions of 1870 and 1885" by Sister Ursula Dunlevy appears in the January number of the *North Dakota Historical Quarterly*. Most of the material here presented relates to the background of the rebellions, going back to the rivalry of the Hudson's Bay and Northwest companies in the Red River Valley and the establishment of the Selkirk colony. Conditions in the settlements on the lower Red River and the relations of the colonists with settlers in the growing Minnesota communities are brought out. In the same issue of the *Quarterly* is an account of "Early Steamboating on the Red River" by Captain Fred A. Bill. The latter narrative has been reprinted from the *Burlington* [Iowa] *Post,* in which it appeared in 1928.

A radio address on the "Red River Cart," prepared and delivered by Olive Knox of Winnipeg, is published with some excellent early and modern pictures of carts in the March issue of the *Beaver*. The writer interviewed a number of old settlers in the Red River Valley who remembered the carts, and she consulted the narratives of explorers, immigrants, artists, and adventurers who traveled through the valley in the middle decades of the last century, when the cart trade was in its prime. Descriptions of cart trains, which were an important factor in the traffic between the Canadian Red River settlements and St. Paul, are quoted from the writings of Manton Marble, Charles Hallock, and others. Mrs. Knox reveals that she "was lured on the trail of the Red River cart by the sight of one that stands" in the museum of the Hudson's Bay Company at Winnipeg. It should be noted that another example of these primitive carts is preserved in the museum of the Minnesota Historical Society.

A surveyor who was operating in western Canada for the Canadian government in 1881, J. L. Morris, compares "Old Fort Garry in 1881 and 1939" in the *Canadian Geographical Journal* for January. In 1939, the writer remarks, he stood on the site of old Fort Garry and pictured "the Winnipeg of 1881, with Portage Avenue and Main Street gumbo-paved and nearly impassable, with the fort preventing Main Street from reaching the Assiniboine River, and the city's 8,000 population being more than sufficient for its limited housing accommodation." Among the interesting illustrations that accompany the article is one showing a party of frontier surveyors encamped for the night, with their "Red River carts and buffalo skinned teepee."

GENERAL MINNESOTA ITEMS

What is perhaps the most usable and informative brief "History of Minnesota" in print has been contributed by Arthur J. Larsen to the Minnesota Editorial Association's newly published *Who's Who in Minnesota* (1941. xx, 1239 p.). In fifteen pages of two columns each, the superintendent of the Minnesota Historical Society surveys the story of the state, discussing his subject under five headings — "Backgrounds" of geography and Indian life, "Exploration and Discovery," "The Pioneer State," "The Agricultural State," and "The Modern State." This is followed by a three-page sketch of the "Beginning of Government" in Minnesota by William Codman. The volume is arranged by counties, with a brief historical review of each county serving as an introduction for the biographical sketches. Among these county histories are some of real merit, for example, the accounts of Clay County by Ella A. Hawkinson, of Rice by Carl L. Weicht, and of Ramsey by Grace Lee Nute. Represented among the authors of the county sketches are numerous leaders and officers of local historical societies — Fred W. Johnson for Brown County, William E. Scott for Lake, Victor E. Lawson for Kandiyohi, Sophie P. White for McLeod, Horace W. Roberts for Blue Earth, Edward A. Blomfield for Hennepin, Otto E. Wieland for St. Louis, and many others. The county sketches vary greatly in length, and there seems to be no relationship between the amount of space allotted to an account and the size and importance in the state's history of the county under consideration. Nine pages, for example, are devoted to Stearns County, while Hennepin receives only five; five and a half pages are given to Brown, and only two and a half to Rice; five go to Chisago, and slightly over two to St. Louis. There seems to be no uniformity of style or method in the presentation of the material in the historical sketches. Some appear as consecutive narratives, others are broken up into sections in newspaper style, still others are little more than lists of "firsts." But perhaps the volume's most serious fault relates to its arrangement. Although this is by counties, no effort to follow an alphabetical order has been made. Furthermore, there is no table of contents to guide the reader. The only way the user can locate a county section or a biographical sketch is by turning to a thirty-three page index at the back. This is a real detriment to the volume's usefulness as a reference work.   B.L.H.

To the shelf of useful reference works issued by the Minnesota Historical Records Survey, a volume dealing with *Minnesota Judicial Districts* has been added recently (1942.   86 p.). An explanation of the state's judicial organization, which serves as an introduction, is followed by a section devoted to "Judicial Districts and Their Boundary Changes." There, each of the nineteen judicial districts into which the state is divided is dealt with separately. Other sections present lists of "Judicial Districts and Their County Alignment," showing changes made from 1849 to the present, and "Counties and Their Districts" at various dates. Newly issued volumes in the survey's *Inventory of the County Archives of Minnesota* make available comprehensive lists of local records preserved in the courthouses of Anoka County at Anoka (no. 2 — 135 p.), of Fillmore County at Preston (no. 23 — 156 p.), and of Mille Lacs County at Milaca (no. 48 — 191 p.). Inventories of archival materials in forty-three of the eighty-seven counties of Minnesota have now been published in this series.

Newspapers and local historical societies throughout the state are co-operating in the movement inaugurated by the National Resources Planning Board for the conservation of cultural resources. The *Waconia Patriot* of January 15, for example, cautions its readers against including records and letters of historical value with wastepaper collected for local war agencies. Give wastepaper to any organization that is collecting "this defense material in your home community," reads an announcement in the *Patriot*, "but save the old newspapers and old records that have historical value for your county museum."

The feature of the October issue of the *Minnesota Archaeologist* is an article on "Big Sandy Lake: An Important Indian Site in Minnesota" by Dr. Kenneth W. Miner. Emphasis is placed upon Indian life in the Sandy Lake area as it can be reconstructed from artifacts found in local excavations. Many objects, chiefly of Chippewa origin, recovered in the area are illustrated in connection with the article. Some attention is given also to the Northwest Company post on the lake. In the same issue appears a brief article by Richard R. Sackett on "An Unidentified Trading Post on the 'Portage La Savanna'." This portage was extensively used by traders traveling between the waters of the Mississippi and those of Lake Superior, for it connected small streams flowing into Sandy Lake and the St. Louis River. The site described by Mr. Sackett was discovered in the summer of 1932 by a state forester, Mr. Edward Lawson. Excavations on this site yielded a number of interesting "articles used in Indian trade a century or more ago." Mr. Sackett expresses the opinion that this was the site of a "stopping-off place, a camp, or overnight resting station for the trader or trapper traveling across the portage" rather than that of a large trading post.

Minnesota Indian scenes of the 1820's, painted in water color by Peter Rindisbacher and displayed in the Round Tower Museum at Fort Snelling during the spring months, are described in an illustrated article in the *St. Paul Pioneer Press* for March 1. A list of the six paintings in the display appears *ante*, p. 94.

A "historical review of the various land grants made by Congress to the state and the disposition of the proceeds from the sale of such lands" is presented in a booklet entitled *The Trust Funds of Minnesota: A Heritage to Protect*, recently published by Julius A. Schmahl, state treasurer (1942. 19 p.). Most states "sold their school and other public lands on a liberal basis and used the money derived from them for the immediate needs of the state," reads an introductory statement, but "Minnesota was the first state to conceive the plan of conserving these resources for the benefit of future generations." The influence of Governor Ramsey in bringing about the establishment of a permanent school fund is given recognition; and the contributions of William W. Braden, state auditor in the 1880's, who obtained the enactment of a law "permitting the leasing of state lands for iron mining purposes," are reviewed. The booklet contains useful sections on the Congressional land grants received by the state and on the investment of funds obtained from the sale and lease of such lands.

A detailed review of the "Milestones in the History of School of Mines and Metallurgy" of the University of Minnesota was presented by Professor Elting H. Comstock on January 13 before a meeting commemorating the fiftieth anniversary of the founding of the school. The address is published in full in *Minnesota Chats*, a university publication, for January 14. Professor Comstock notes the influence of Professor Christopher W. Hall in bringing about the first faculty resolution in favor of a school of mines in 1887. A legislative appropriation in 1891 was followed by the appointment of William R. Appleby as professor of mining and metallurgy, and in the next year four students were enrolled in his courses and "quarters were fitted up in Pillsbury Hall." Originally, according to this narrative, the mining courses were given in the college of engineering, and it was not until 1897 that separate colleges were established.

The American Institute of Swedish Arts, Literature and Science in Minneapolis is designated as a "Minnesota Center for Study of Swedish Culture" by A. A. Stomberg in the *American Swedish Monthly* for January. The institute's museum is housed in a structure built for use as a home about "forty years ago by Swan J. Turnblad, the successful owner and publisher of the Swedish-language weekly, *Svenska Amerikanska Posten*," and presented to the institute in 1929. Mr. Stomberg describes the elaborate house in some detail, presents accounts of special exhibits displayed therein, and reviews the institute's program of activities. The institute's *Bulletin* for January includes an article on "Scandinavian Libraries in the Twin Cities," in which the opinion is expressed that the Scandinavian collection of the Minnesota Historical Society is "undoubtedly the largest collection of books and other materials dealing with the history of the Scandinavians found anywhere in this country." Special attention is given to the library of the Swedish-American Historical Society. The large and important collection of Scandinaviana in the library of the University of Minnesota also is described and evaluated. In the same issue of the *Bulletin*, an account of "A Remarkable Community Museum" at Cokato, originally published *ante*, 21: 440–442, is reprinted "in slightly abbreviated form."

The "History of Medicine in Minnesota" that has been appearing for some time in *Minnesota Medicine* is continued in the first three issues for 1942 with the opening installments of a "History of the Minnesota State Medical Society" by Dr. Arthur S. Hamilton. He presents the records of a medical convention held in St. Paul in July, 1853, which, he asserts, "represents the first attempt to hold a medical meeting" in Minnesota Territory. The convention, writes Dr. Hamilton, passed a motion to "resolve itself into the Minnesota Medical Society," and several meetings were held in the years that followed. It was not until 1869, however, that a permanent organization, from which subsequent annual meetings have been dated, had its origin. Much of the material presented consists of quotations from contemporary newspapers and from the proceedings and records of the society.

Archbishop John Ireland of St. Paul is an important figure in Theodore Maynard's recent volume on the *Story of American Catholicism* (New York, 1941. 694 p.). It includes a brief reference to the Irish Colonization Society, which the Minnesota prelate helped to found, and to Ireland's effort to transform "fishermen from Connemara" into Minnesota farmers. Some attention is given to the scheme of Catholic education "tried at Faribault and Stillwater in Ireland's diocese" and to the "famous controversy within the Church" that it precipitated. Recollections of the archbishop's sisters, Mother Celestine and Mother Seraphine, and of his nephew, the Reverend James Howard, are presented by James C. Byrne in the "Notes and Comment" section of volume 32 of the United States Catholic Historical Society's *Historical Records and Studies* (New York, 1941).

The purchase by the federal government of 473 acres of land in the Nerstrand Woods of Rice County was announced in the *Faribault Daily News* for March 13. Plans are under way to exchange this remnant of the Big Woods area of southern Minnesota for certain state-owned lands in northern Minnesota that the federal government wishes to add to national forest areas. When this has been done, the Nerstrand Woods will become a state park. As funds become available, additional tracts will be added to the "present nucleus of what will stand as a memorial to the pioneers . . . who laid out the timber tracts and their descendants who have preserved the forest" in Rice County, according to the *Northfield News* for March 26. Articles reviewing both the history of the Nerstrand Woods and of the long struggle to preserve the area as a park are contributed by Carl L. Weicht to the *Faribault Journal* and the *Northfield Independent* of February 19. In the former paper he credits the preservation of the area to the fact that some 170 "farsighted Norwegian and German settlers had divided two sections of forest land into small woodlots to provide a permanent source of fuel for the surrounding farms." These pioneers and their descendants "practiced very acceptable forestry methods in clearing out the older trees and keeping a heavy stand of growing trees on the land," with the result that the "Nerstrand Woods best retains today the real character of the historic Big Woods."

"Just as State Parks preserve scenic portions of original Minnesota, so do State Memorial Parks, State Waysides and State Monuments preserve and perpetuate outstanding events in State history," writes Harold W. Lathrop in an article on "History in Our State Parks," appearing in the April issue of the *Conservation Volunteer*. This is the first of a series of articles covering the "field of historical conservation, as carried on by the Department of Conservation, through the Division of State Parks." In it several sites associated with the Sioux War of 1862 are described — Fort Ridgely State Memorial Park, Milford Monument, and Schwandt Monument.

The life of Emil J. Oberhoffer, who organized the Minneapolis Symphony Orchestra and served as its conductor for nineteen years, is the subject of a sketch in volume 12 of the *Encyclopedia of American Biography* (New York, 1941). Other Minnesotans whose careers are reviewed in this volume are Dr. Olaf M. Norlie of Minneapolis, psychologist, teacher, pastor, and editor; and three prominent businessmen, James A. Nowell of St. Paul, Frank M. Steiner of Minneapolis, and Frank L. Thompson, whose work as a railroad executive identified him with many parts of the state. Sketches of a number of important Minnesota business executives appear in volume 13 of this work. Included are Frederick G. Atkinson, George W. Stricker, and James L. Robinson of Minneapolis, and Francis J. Ottis of St. Paul. The life of President George H. Bridgman of Hamline University also is reviewed in this volume.

Under the heading "Picture Story of Minnesota," scenes from "Minnesota Document," a motion picture about the state (see *ante,* p. 93), are reproduced in the rotogravure section of the *Minneapolis Sunday Tribune and Star Journal* for January 11. The film was produced by the visual education service of the University of Minnesota.

Three Mendota houses that are closely identified with the early history of Minnesota are included in Lewis Barrington's recent book on *Historic Restorations of the Daughters of the American Revolution* (New York, 1941). Descriptive sketches of the Sibley, Faribault, and De Puis houses are presented, with brief accounts of their significance in the history of the state. Each sketch is accompanied by a photograph of the house described.

LOCAL HISTORICAL SOCIETIES

Some of the exhibits in the museum of the Blue Earth County Historical Society at Mankato are described in detail by May Fletcher in articles appearing in the *Mankato Free Press* for January 15 and 30, and February 16. That the museum is rich in materials brought from foreign lands by immigrant settlers of Blue Earth County is revealed in the third of these articles. A meeting of the society on January 28 resulted in the election of Mr. Horace Roberts as president, Mrs. Mary Sugden, vice-president, and Mr. E. Raymond Hughes, secretary-treasurer.

In a report to the city council of New Ulm on March 17, Mr. Fred W. Johnson, who is head of the local library board as well as president of the Brown County Historical Society, stressed the need for additional space in the building occupied jointly by the society's museum and the public library. He called attention to the fact that "New Ulm can boast of a library and museum which is second to" no other in a "city the size of New Ulm and far outshines those of larger cities," and he expressed appreciation for the funds provided "through public contributions" for the museum's excellent equipment. Mr. Johnson announced that there is "no more room available in the museum" for equipment, and that as a result much interesting material cannot be displayed. He asked the council to consider the problem of enlarging the museum building sometime in the future.

At a meeting of the Chippewa County Historical Society held at Montevideo on February 25, Mr. Victor Lawson of Willmar spoke on local historical work in Kandiyohi County, Mr. Norman Reitan presented a report on the work of reconstructing the mission chapel at Lac qui Parle, and Mr. Richard R. Sackett of the Minnesota Historical Records Survey commented on the excavations conducted on the mission site. Plans were discussed for the dedication of the chapel, which is nearing completion.

The sum of three hundred dollars was appropriated by the Clay County board of commissioners at its meeting on March 4 for the use of the Clay County Historical Society. The money is to be expended in completing the society's museum quarters on the campus of the Moorhead State Teachers College.

The museum of the Goodhue County Historical Society, which is located in the courthouse at Red Wing, is open daily from 9:00 to 11:00 A. M. and from 1:00 to 4:00 P. M., according to an announcement in the *Daily Republican Eagle* of Red Wing for March 3. The museum "is becoming increasingly popular with residents of both Red Wing and the surrounding communities," reads the announcement.

The fact that the work of the Hennepin County Historical Society is receiving recognition beyond the borders of the state is illustrated in the issue for March 22 of *Herodotus,* a multigraphed publication issued by the Rochester [New York] Museum of Arts and Sciences. It includes a letter from Mr. Edward A. Blomfield, executive secretary of the Hennepin County society, describing the work of his organization and pointing out its opportunities for service in wartime. Over six hundred visitors, icluding nine groups of school children, viewed the exhibits in the society's museum at St. Louis Park in the first three months of 1942. During the same period thirty-one new members joined the society. About seventy-five people attended a meeting of the organization at St. Louis Park on February 17 at which Judge Luther W. Youngdahl presented a talk on "America and Our Future."

A program built about the history of the "Early German Settlements" of McLeod County was presented before a meeting of the McLeod County Historical Society at Hutchinson on January 30. The beginnings of German settlement in Acoma Township were described by Mrs. Charles Heller and the "Westphalian Pioneers" of the Winsted area were recalled by Clement Otto. The latter's paper appears in full in the *Winsted Journal* for February 12.

Plans for the summer meeting of the Otter Tail County Historical Society are announced in the *Fergus Falls Daily Journal* for February 28. It will take the form of a picnic at Thompson Point on Prairie Lake near Pelican Rapids, and will be held on June 28.

The Polk County Historical Society completed the arrangement of its museum in the courthouse at Crookston early in February, when it was opened to the public. The museum is open each Monday, and Mrs. Bert Levins, secretary of the society, is in charge.

The Reverend Frederick F. Kramer, warden of the Seabury Divinity School for two decades, was honored at a meeting of the Rice County

Historical Society held at Faribault on March 17. As the feature of the program, Dr. Kramer read a detailed autobiography, which was subsequently published in installments in the *Faribault Daily News* from March 18 to 25. The later sections of the narrative contain much material about the Faribault school with which the author became identified in 1912.

At the annual meeting of the Waseca County Historical Society, which was held at Waseca on January 5, J. P. Coughlin was named president, Herman Peterson, vice-president, Arnold Runnerstrom, secretary, and Arthur Brisbane, treasurer. The society recently placed in its log cabin museum two bronze plaques, one inscribed with the names of the life members of the society and the other with the names of pioneer settlers of the county. The lists inscribed on both plaques appear in the *Waseca Herald* for January 1.

Life in the logging camps of the St. Croix Valley was described by Mr. S. A. Kolliner of Stillwater in a talk presented before a meeting of the Washington County Historical Society at Stillwater on February 3. Plans were discussed for a "permanent and authentic logging display" in the society's museum.

The Wright County Historical Society was organized at a meeting held at Cokato on February 20. An address on "The Local Historical Society and Its Work" was presented by Dr. Arthur J. Larsen of the state historical society.

LOCAL HISTORY ITEMS

"Ghost Towns of Brown County" are enumerated and discussed by LeRoy G. Davis in a series of articles appearing in recent issues of the *Sleepy Eye Herald-Dispatch*. Among the subjects of the detailed historical sketches of vanished towns and villages presented in this series are Iberia, which "became the market place and social center for a territory extending" from Lake Hanska to Sleepy Eye Lake, February 19; the village of Leavenworth, March 5; and Golden Gate, March 19 and 26. Most of the material presented by Mr. Davis is drawn from his personal recollections and from interviews with fellow pioneers. In each case he includes long lists of early residents and business enterprises.

The "registration of 12 students" on October 15, 1891, marked the opening of Concordia College in Moorhead, according to an article in the *Ulen Union* for January 22. One of the original students, Mr. W. P. Rognlie of Grand Forks, recalls in this account that many additional students enrolled for the winter term and that as a result "accommodations were not adequate." He relates that "even furniture dealers did not have [a] sufficient supply of chairs" and that "students took their chairs to the dining hall" for meals and later carried them back to their rooms.

Plans for the restoration of the little Catholic church at Grand Portage, which marked its centennial in 1938, are announced in the *Duluth News-Tribune* for January 25. Although the congregation had its origin in 1838, the present structure, built of logs and covered with siding, dates from 1863. A picture of the present church and two views of Grand Portage from paintings made by Eastman Johnson in the 1850's accompany the article about the history of the church.

A member of a party that established the settlement of Excelsior on Lake Minnetonka in 1853, Robert B. McGrath, is the author of the "Story of Excelsior in the Early Days," which appears in installments in the *Minnetonka Record* from January 15 to February 26. The group, which left St. Anthony in the spring of 1853, was under the leadership of John H. Stevens. The writer includes accounts of such events as the first Thanksgiving celebration in the new settlement, the opening of a district school, and the building of a stockade for defense against the Indians during the outbreak of 1862. McGrath's narrative was published originally in the *Record* for 1906, from which it is reprinted.

A pioneer Minneapolis lawyer, Franklin Clinton Griswold, is the central figure in a volume recently published by his son, Charles C. Griswold, under the title *As the River Flows* (1939.   104 p.). The story is that of a young New Englander who went west and settled in Minnesota on the eve of the Sioux Outbreak. Lengthy quotations from letters that Griswold wrote to members of his family in the East give color to the account of his participation in the frontier war. A journey of investigation up the Mississippi to St. Anthony, "now much resorted to by the pleasure seekers of the summer," and thence through the Minnesota Valley to Mankato preceded his decision to settle in Minnesota. He intended to "make a careful choice, to locate where I shall want my home for life, a pleasant, healthy and business place." The spot selected was a farm now in the heart of Minneapolis, at Minnehaha and Lake streets. The author, who was born there, adds many of his own recollections to the account of life in early Minneapolis. Much genealogical information is included in the volume, and there is a section on "Griswold Family Research in England."

A pictorial record of the Farmers and Mechanics Savings Bank of Minneapolis is presented in a booklet entitled *Minneapolis Album, 1874–1942* (20 p.). It outlines briefly the history of this local business from the day in 1874 when it was organized in "Thomas Lowry's law office on the second floor of the Academy of Music" to the recent opening of its new building.

Dale Kramer's exposition of the complicated story of "The Dunne Boys of Minneapolis," which appears in the March issue of *Harper's Magazine,* contains a mass of detailed information about the Minneapolis truck drivers' strikes of the 1930's and the organization of Local 544.

The history of a northern Minnesota creamery, the Cloverleaf Cooperative, which is marking its thirtieth anniversary this year, is reviewed in the *Baudette Region* for February 27. A group of pioneers living in what is now Lake of the Woods County organized the creamery in 1912, and two years later it began operations.

Forty years of teaching in the Martin County schools are recalled in an article about Miss Mamie Smith, who was connected with various local schools from 1880 to 1920, in a biographical sketch appearing in the *Sherburn Advance-Standard* for January 29. Miss Smith's family settled in Manyaska Township in 1870, and there ten years later she began teaching in the district school. "Some of her school terms were of two and three months and salary $20 per month." The names of many Martin County residents who were her pupils are mentioned, and some of the changes in teaching methods that took place during her long career are described. With two portraits of Miss Smith, the article is reprinted in the *Fairmont Daily Sentinel* for February 3.

A huge log jam "one-half mile to one mile wide and as thick as sixty feet in some places," which occurred in the vicinity of Little Falls in the early 1890's, is described by Val Kasparek in the *Little Falls Herald* for February 27. "Due to low water in the fore part of the driving season of 1893, the logs and timber did not float as rapidly," the writer relates, going on to explain that "when the water got higher the logs were floating down the many streams tributary to the Mississippi river and filled it beyond capacity of the 'sorting works' here in Little Falls." How the jam was broken is explained and some of the men who aided in the work are named.

A pioneer Fosston business firm, Mark's Drug Store, which was established in 1892 by P. M. Mark and his son H. F. Mark and is still operated by the latter, is the subject of a historical sketch in the *Thirteen Towns* of Fosston for March 6. The town as it appeared when the younger Mr. Mark arrived there in March, 1892, is described, and the changes in the nature and location of his business over half a century are recounted in the present narrative.

To commemorate the dedication of a new church building on February 15, the Reverend M. Caspar Johnshoy issued a booklet containing a *Brief History of Fron Evangelical Lutheran Congregation* at Starbuck (1942. 29 p.). The author traces the story of Lutheran activity in Pope County back to 1867, when the Lake Johanna Lutheran congregation was organized, but he notes that the Fron congregation had its origin in 1880 and built its first church in 1889.

The wrecking of the old Lafayette Emmett house in St. Paul, where Daniel D. Emmett is said to have composed "Dixie," was the occasion for the publication of a number of items about the history of the old house in the St. Paul papers in January and February. Among them is an editorial, bearing the heading "St. Paul Landmarks," in the *St. Paul Dispatch* for January 30. In response to those who belatedly urged the restoration of the structure, the writer of the editorial asserts that "this would serve little purpose unless there were some method of . . . providing for its maintenance." The suggestion is made that plans be drawn up in advance for the preservation of some of the city's other historic houses.

Dramatic entertainment in St. Paul in the 1890's, as recalled by Mr. Arthur White, "dean of St. Paul theatrical men," is the subject of three articles in Paul Light's column, "So What!," appearing in the *St. Paul Pioneer Press* for January 15, 16, and 19. Among the entertainments described are medicine shows that Mr. White saw on the St. Paul streets as a boy, the dime museum, the music hall, and the panorama of the battle of Gettysburg. Also noted are some of the performances staged by prominent actors of the day at the Grand, the People's, and the Metropolitan theaters.

"Carrying the Mail — Pioneer Style" in the vicinity of Duluth is the subject of a feature article by Orville Lomoe in the *Duluth News-Tribune* for January 4. The services of frontier carriers who transported mail by dog team in winter and in packsacks in summer are recalled by early residents of the region, whose narratives are quoted. The use of stage lines in the late 1860's also is noted.

Anecdotes about "Hibbing of the past and about the people who built that Hibbing" have been appearing since February 6 in the *Hibbing Daily Tribune* under the title "Old Colony Days." Most of the material presented consists of short items about events and personalities of the 1890's and the early years of the present century, with emphasis upon social life in the frontier community.

Minutes of the meetings of the "Sauk Centre Board of Trade, from its inception more than 60 years ago on August 15, 1881, to the last recorded meeting of April 15, 1901," are included in a volume recently discovered in Sauk Centre, according to an announcement in the *St. Cloud Daily Times* for March 13. Interesting items are quoted from this manuscript record of early business activity.

"St. Cloud has always been a good circus town, though because of its location many shows passed to the north into Dakota, or to the south, through southern Minnesota into Iowa," writes Dr. H. H. Conley in an article on the "Circus History of St. Cloud," which appears in the *St. Cloud Daily Times* for February 27. The writer lists many of the "big circus names" that are linked with the amusement history of St. Cloud, and he gives the dates when they played there.

A special edition of the *Blooming Prairie Times,* issued on February 12, marks the fiftieth anniversary of the local co-operative creamery by presenting a survey of its history and sketches of men who have contributed toward its progress. Plans were made originally by a group of farmers to establish a creamery at Newry, but Blooming Prairie was eventually chosen as a location because a cream station was operating there and it could be reached by railroad. A sketch of the history of this

Steele County industry, which was incorporated in March, 1892, appears also in the *Austin Daily Herald* for February 16.

The Central Cooperative Oil Association of Steele County is described as "a pioneer among cooperative oil organizations" in an article by Hugh H. Soper, who calls attention to its twentieth anniversary in the *Steele County Photo News* of Owatonna for January 15. The president of the association, Mr. A. P. Bartch, recalls that in Steele County "the movement grew out of the visit to the county of a Hereford cattle breeder from Lyon county" who left information about the "successful cooperative oil organization then existing in his own county."

Aspects of "Pioneer Life in Winona County" are described by William Codman in an article appearing in three installments in the *Winona Republican-Herald* for February 6, 13, and 20. Modes of transportation, amusements, Christmas celebrations, lighting methods, and food are among the subjects touched upon.

MINNESOTA HISTORY

VOLUME 23 • PUBLISHED IN SEPT. 1942 • NUMBER 3

A Hundred Years of North America[1]

Lawrence J. Burpee

"ANYONE at all inquisitive about the distribution of human beings in North America cannot fail to have been struck by the basic American stock of the Maritime Provinces and Ontario in Canada, the millions of French Canadians in New England and New York, the traces of the Canadian in the American Middle West and of the American on the Canadian prairies, and the persistent to-and-fro movement of both stocks along the Pacific coast from Mexico to the Bering Strait. Here is a continent where international boundaries have been disregarded by restless humans for almost two centuries."

This passage is taken from the foreword of a remarkable study entitled *The Mingling of the Canadian and American Peoples,* planned and for the most part written by the late Marcus Lee Hansen of the University of Illinois, completed by John Bartlet Brebner of Columbia University, and forming part of an ambitious series designed to illustrate the many-sided relations of Canada and the United States. The series is being prepared, under the direction of James T. Shotwell of Columbia University and the Carnegie Endowment for International Peace, by a group of scholarly men, some of whom are Canadians and the others, Americans. Among them are several, like Professor Shotwell and Professor Brebner, who were born in one

---

[1] An address presented before the fourteenth annual North Shore Historical Assembly, meeting at Fort William, Ontario, on August 1, 1942. One session of this joint meeting of the historical societies of St. Louis, Lake, and Cook counties, Minnesota, and of Thunder Bay, Ontario, commemorated the centennial of the Webster-Ashburton treaty. The speaker whose address is published herewith officially represented the Canadian government at the meeting. *Ed.*

country and are making their contribution to the life of the other.

The nature and purpose of the series and the relationship of the men who are preparing it to these two North American commonwealths are, it seems to me, profoundly significant. Where else the world over will you find two neighboring countries whose relations are so extraordinarily intimate that it should have been thought worth while to devote a score or more of substantial volumes to their examination?

But, while it is quite true that for the better part of two centuries the boundaries between what today are Canada and the United States have been disregarded by restless pioneers seeking homes for themselves and their families, the intimate relations that we recognize today have not always been intimate, have not always been even friendly or neighborly. Without going back more than a hundred years, one finds in the period since the signing of the Webster-Ashburton treaty a growth in neighborly relations between the peoples of these two countries that bears a good deal of resemblance to the growth of a tree.

As the years have gone by the history of the continent reveals variations in the annual growth of neighborliness. There have been setbacks. How could it be otherwise in a human world? We have known the drought of misunderstanding, the blight of national jealousies, the insect pest of ancient grievances. But, as the tree has become securely rooted in the North American soil and has sent stout trunk and branches up into the North American sky, it has been able to brush aside these enemies and afford the world an example of two neighboring nations united but free — one in their democratic way of life; one in their hatred of tyranny and their instinctive resistance to undue regulation; one in their contempt for sham and dishonesty in word or deed; one in their practical sympathy for suffering or distress; one in their insistence upon political, social, religious, and intellectual freedom; one in their enlightened ideas about education, sanitation, transportation, and even such minor matters as outdoor games; one in a good many of their likes and dislikes; one, perhaps above all, in that keen sense of humor that, fortunately, steps in from time to time and prevents men and nations from making themselves ridiculous. And, at the same time, each is free to carry on its own ideas of government without even the shadow of interference by the other.

A glimpse of international relations along the American-Canadian boundary something more than a hundred years ago is to be found in a delightful little book of travel, *The Shoe and Canoe,* by Dr. John J. Bigsby, secretary to the British section of the boundary commission under articles 6 and 7 of the treaty of Ghent. Bigsby, writing of what is now Fort Frances on the Rainy River, says: "Walking out, the morning after our arrival, with Mr. W. M'Gillivray, the Lieut.-Governor, I saw on the opposite side of the river some buildings, and a tall, shabby-looking man, angling near the falls. I asked my companion what all this meant. He replied, 'The two or three houses you see form a fur-trading post of John Jacob Astor, the great merchant of New York. The man is one of his agents. He is fishing for a dinner. If he catch nothing he will not dine. He and his party are contending with us for the Indian trade. We are starving them out, and have nearly succeeded.' "

A thousand miles or so to the east, at a time when memories of the War of 1812 still rankled in the minds of Americans and Canadians, the government of the United States spent a million dollars — a much larger sum then than now — on a massive stone fort. It stood near the northern end of Lake Champlain, and was known as Fort Montgomery. It was also, for sufficient reasons, called "Fort Blunder" by the people on both sides of the boundary. Here, very briefly, is the story. As long ago as 1772 or thereabouts two well-meaning and supposedly competent land surveyors, Thomas Valentine and John Collins, ran a line from the upper waters of the Connecticut to the upper St. Lawrence, touching briefly en route at almost the extreme northern point of Lake Champlain. The line they were supposed to be running was the forty-fifth degree of north latitude, and everyone might have been happy had not two professional busybodies named J. C. Tiarks and Ferdinand Hassler, many years afterward, resurveyed the line and found that the Valentine and Collins line was far from accurate, that in fact it wavered rather disreputably about the forty-fifth parallel and left an ominous gap of three-quarters of a mile at Lake Champlain. In that gap stood the all-too-solid mass of Fort Montgomery, unmistakably on Canadian soil. After years of negotiation, those astute statesmen Daniel Webster and Lord Ashburton solved the problem. They decided that, as something must be moved, and it was not practicable to move Fort Montgomery, the only thing to do was to move the boundary. So it was solemnly decreed that the inaccurate Valentine and Collins line should remain the boundary — to the great distress of all conscientious land surveyors, to whose profession it is a perpetual reproach.

Fort Montgomery offers one of many illustrations of the change in relations between the United States and Canada that time has brought about. Built, it would seem, ostensibly to protect peace-loving Americans from turbulent Canadian desperadoes, it became as the years went by more and more of an absurd anachronism, and also more and more of a financial white elephant. The authorities found it embarrassing to have to justify appropriations for the maintenance of a huge fortification that was supposed to protect a region where Canadians and Americans moved back and forth across a boundary line they had almost forgotten; where Canadians were living on the United States side and Americans on the Canadian side; where they intermarried, went to the same church, belonged to the same lodge, and did everything in fact but vote for the same political candidate. Finally, after poor old "Fort Blunder" had been used for various casual purposes shockingly out of keeping with its original calling, it was sold to the contractor who built the causeway and bridge across Lake Champlain. And so, when the time returns that one can again drive as far as from Port Arthur to Lake Champlain, some of you may go there and thus have the opportunity to reflect that you are probably driving over the grave of a portion of Fort Montgomery.

Echoes of the War of 1812 that were responsible for the making of such blunders as the building of Fort Montgomery took some years to finally sink into silence. An odd memory of my remote childhood is a game of hide-and-seek called "Yankee Lie Low." It was very popular in my part of Ontario, but the name had long lost any significance.

It was not, in fact, until many years later that it suddenly occurred to me that this game of ours was a belated echo of the old war. Once, perhaps, a fierce battle cry for men, it had been transformed, happily, into an amusing game for children.

Some years ago the members of an international tribunal were received by an eminent American statesman in Washington. Something had been said about the old controversy over the Maine-New Brunswick boundary. The statesman smiled. "I wonder," he said, "if you have heard the story of how Campobello became Canadian. It appears — and far be it from me to vouch for the correctness of the yarn — that Lord Ashburton and Mr. Webster were coming down the St. Croix in a British gunboat. They dined together on the boat. Mr. Webster, as you may have heard, enjoyed his glass of wine. Lord Ashburton was most hospitable. Finally they went on deck. Lord Ashburton — so the scandalous tale goes — had arranged with the captain of the gunboat to sail around a side of the island that could be navigated only at high tide. He now turned to Mr. Webster. 'How does this appeal to you, Mr. Webster, for the boundary line?' Mr. Webster by this time was seeing three or more Campobellos, and assured Lord Ashburton that it was quite all right with him."

The incident on Rainy River described by Dr. Bigsby — and there are of course many like it that could be told if one had time — suggests the tenseness of the attitude of Canadians and Americans to one another a century ago, and the fact that the boundary, however imaginary it might be, was then a very real boundary. How amazingly different that attitude is today!

A few days ago the members and staff of the International Joint Commission traveled over a number of the boundary lakes between Lake Superior and the Lake of the Woods looking into certain matters that come within their jurisdiction. The commission has been carrying out similar inspection trips at various points on the long boundary between Canada and the United States, or holding public hearings in cases involving sometimes Canadian, sometimes American, interests, for thirty years. The history of the commission is in a very real sense the history of Canadian-American relations as they are today. It consists of three members appointed by the President and three appointed by the King on the recommendation of the Canadian government. These six North Americans hear cases and then sit down together around a table to decide what is to be done about them. In thirty years they have never failed to reach a conclusion reasonably satisfactory to the people directly interested on either side of the boundary, and in nearly every case the decision has been unanimous.

I happen to have been the Canadian secretary of the commission since its establishment, and I have known all its members and have been present at all its hearings and executive meetings. I could not imagine any group of six Canadians or six Americans, acting as a national tribunal of any kind, giving more wholehearted, impartial service to their own people than the members of the International Joint Commission have given to the people of both countries.

Probably the most severe test to which we have been put, as a group of Americans and Canadians pledged to work together for the welfare of North America, came as long ago as 1915. We were then in the middle of the Lake of the Woods investigation, and had just completed a public hearing at International Falls. After a rather sketchy luncheon, we started down Rainy River in a motorboat. There were, if I remember aright, some twenty of us in the boat — commissioners, secretaries, lawyers, engineers, and reporters — and we were on our way to Warroad on the Lake of the Woods, where the next hearing was to be held.

We went by boat instead of by train so that the commission might have an opportunity to study physical conditions on the river. It was an unfortunate decision, as we managed to wreck the boat in the Manitou Rapids. After we had waded ashore, we found ourselves on a desolate clay bank, many miles from the nearest town. At that time there was not even a farm within reach. The only thing to do was to wait patiently until some sort of craft appeared on the river by which we could send for assistance. Unfortunately it was midnight before, by means of a bonfire, we managed to attract the attention of some Indians. Up to that time a census of available supplies had produced only half a cake of milk chocolate and half a flask of Bourbon whisky.

And what was that among so many! The Indians, however, supplied half a dozen smallish sturgeon, which we broiled on twigs over the bonfire and divided among the party. No fish of any kind was ever so thoroughly appreciated. We ate them with our fingers and without salt, and licked our fingers thereafter. Meanwhile one of the engineers had been sent off with the Indians to Emo, the nearest town. Through a variety of misadventures, relief boats could not be procured for several hours, and it was nearly four o'clock in the morning before we reached Emo. For something like twelve hours a score of men, roughly half of them American and half Canadian, had been shipwrecked on an inhospitable shore, under very uncomfortable conditions. The majority were well on in years, and all were subject to the human reaction to lack of food and drink and tobacco and anything even approximately soft to lean tired bodies against. Yet they managed to get through the long night without quarreling, thanks, perhaps, to that sense of humor which, as I have said, is one of the joint possessions of Americans and Canadians. It may be worth remembering that the owner of the flask of Bourbon was Jim Tawney of Winona, chairman of the United States section of the commission, and that he divided its contents with strict impartiality.

As a memorial of the occasion the Canadian secretary compiled a burlesque account of an imaginary investigation into the circumstances surrounding the wreck, and the United States chairman had it privately printed at Winona. It is now, I imagine, among the comparative rarities of Minnesotaiana.

The International Joint Commission — to return to more serious matters — has always made it a point to go to the people, instead of making them come to it. Hearings are held at some point that is most convenient to those mainly concerned. No man, however humble, is denied the opportunity of being heard before the commission and having his day in court, and the policy has always been to get at the essential facts without being hampered too much by strictly legal procedure. The commission has never hesitated to waive its own rules of procedure when that seemed desirable in the circumstances of a particular case.

I make no excuse for taking up so much of your time with this account of the International Joint Commission, because, it seems to me, no other Canadian or American, or jointly Canadian and American, organization or institution illustrates so strikingly the intimacy of the relations that have grown up between these two neighboring countries and their people.

Last year the commission held a public hearing in Hibbing, in the very heart of the Mesabi Range. While I looked into the vast hole in the ground out of which such incredible quantities of ore have been taken to feed the furnaces of Pittsburgh, and thought of the enormous contribution that this part of Minnesota has made to the wealth and industrial progress of the United States, I was reminded of a letter written by Lord Ashburton to Daniel Webster at the time the treaty of 1842 was being negotiated.

You will, of course, recall that there had been a good deal of discussion as to the line the boundary should follow from Lake Superior to the Lake of the Woods. The British commissioner under the treaty of Ghent had contended for a line from Fond du Lac, or, approximately, Duluth, as it would be today, by way of the St. Louis and Vermilion rivers to Rainy Lake. The American commissioner had asked for a line from the mouth of the Kaministikwia, or more or less where we are now, up that stream to Dog Lake and Sturgeon Lake, and by a variety of small waterways to Rainy Lake. Neither side would give way, apparently not so much because a compromise of their differences was impracticable as because the problem of routes was tangled up with the entirely different and, as we see it now, relatively insignificant question of which country should get St. George's (now Sugar) Island, in the waterway between Lake Huron and Lake Superior.

Now listen to Lord Ashburton: "The first point [*St. George's Island*] I am ready to give up to you, and you are no doubt aware that it is the only object of any real value in this controversy. The island of St. George is reported to contain 25,920 acres of very fertile land; but, the other things connected with these boundaries being satisfactorily arranged, a line shall be drawn so as to throw this island within the limits of the United States.

"In considering the second point, it really appears of little importance to either party how the line be determined through the wild country between Lake Superior and the Lake of the Woods; but it is important that some line should be fixed and known."

Oddly enough, while Canadian writers who are unfamiliar with all the facts have repeatedly abused Lord Ashburton for his settlement of the northeastern boundary and his supposed surrender of many square miles of what was thought to be Canadian soil, no one, so far as I can remember, has drawn attention to the very casual way in which he tossed aside an area that has already produced two thousand million tons of iron ore. Imperial wars have been fought for much less than this, while the area that was added to Maine by the Webster-Ashburton treaty was actually considerably smaller than that awarded to the United States by the king of the Netherlands in an earlier arbitration and turned down by the United States Senate.

So far as the boundary west of Lake Superior was concerned, Webster and Ashburton finally compromised on the old canoe route of the fur traders by way of the Grand Portage — or, more precisely, on the Pigeon River and the trader's route beyond the Grand Portage — reserving to the British the right to use the portage. That right, I suppose, may be set off against the loss of the iron ranges. Be that as it may, one notes here the Anglo-Saxon talent for compromise, afterward to be applied to the boundary beyond the Rockies.

I seem to have been drifting away from the thought I had in mind when I began this address, that is, the growth of good-neighborliness between Canadians and Americans. The point we have already reached, where there is the closest harmony of common interests, with at the same time complete independence of government, seems to me to offer an ideal example not only to other neighboring nations but to all nations. There is a passion today among many people — a natural reaction from the barbarous inhumanity of the present war — for a structural union of nations, with a single parliament, a single code of laws, and so forth. The same idea has been advocated, and to a limited extent tried out in Canada and elsewhere, in the field of religion. It is highly improbable that the great body of Christians throughout the world will ever consent to unite in a single church.

Agreement is easy on certain fundamental doctrines, but when it comes to the form in which worship shall be expressed, people must inevitably differ. You, perhaps, find satisfaction in one form of service; I, in another. You may find discomfort or annoyance in mine; and I in yours. And that is so in spite of the fact that there is much more tolerance now of the religious manners and customs of one's neighbors than there was a century ago.

And what is true of the average man's religious life is equally true of his political life. If he is any good, he will put love of his own country second only to love of his own kindred. Men have cheerfully given their lives for their native land; but one cannot easily imagine men sacrificing themselves for, let us say, a league of nations.

Some sort of union or confederacy of the democratic countries must come out of this war, but if it is to live and be worth while it must be flexible, not rigid, providing the most complete international co-operation consistent with national freedom. One hopes for a group of independent nations working together in as perfect harmony as human frailty will permit, not merely to make the world safe for democracy, but to build up a democracy worth saving.

The Shape of Things to Come[1]

Harold E. Wood

TWENTY-FIVE years ago today, in that first June of American participation in the first World War, Woodrow Wilson spoke in Washington. He said: "This flag which we honor and under which we serve
is the emblem of our unity, our power, our thought and purpose as a
nation. It has no other character than that which we give it from
generation to generation. The choices are ours. It floats in majestic
silence above the hosts that execute those choices, whether in peace
or in war. And yet, though silent, it speaks to us — speaks to us of the
past, of the men and women who went before us and of the records
they wrote upon it. We celebrate the day of its birth; and from its
birth until now it has witnessed a great history, has floated on high
the symbol of great events, of a great plan of life worked out by a
great people. We are about to carry it into battle, to lift it where it
will draw the fire of our enemies. We are about to bid thousands,
hundreds of thousands, it may be millions, of our men, the young,
the strong, the capable of the Nation, to go forth and die beneath it on
fields of blood far away." To what purpose? For answer, in 1942 as
in 1917, "We are accountable at the bar of history and must plead in
utter frankness what purpose it is we seek to serve." And if our answer
be right, as we are confident it is, "our flag shall wear a new luster
. . . and a new glory shall shine in the face of our people."

Today, in the most literal sense, throughout the world — from Iceland and Greenland and Alaska down to Trinidad, from England
and Ireland across the vast reaches of the Atlantic, the continental
stretches of the United States, and the even greater distances of the
Pacific, to Australia, and India, and the Near East — better than four
million of our soldiers, sailors, and marines join a hundred and
thirty million other Americans in celebration of this day. How fitting

[1] The principal address on a Flag Day program presented under the joint auspices
of the Minnesota Historical Society and the commissioned and enlisted personnel of
Fort Snelling on June 14, 1942, at Fort Snelling (see *post*, p. 267). *Ed.*

that we of the upper Mississippi Valley should meet on this historic ground! An hour since, crack units of a great citizen army passed in review. It was composed in part of the Third Infantry, the oldest regiment in the United States Army, which has a history dating back to 1784. For more than fifty years it has been identified with Minnesota and the Northwest. It boasts not only of service in Mexico, with the Army of the Potomac, in Cuba, in Alaska, in the Philippines, and in scores of skirmishes far afield, but of traditions of things endured and things accomplished, such as regiments hand down forever. As one watched, there came to mind the words of General Marshall at West Point the other day: "In physique, in natural ability, and in intelligence" our new army is the "finest in the world. In their eagerness to work, to endure and to carry through any mission, they are all that could be desired of soldiers."

Similar scenes were witnessed here at Fort Snelling in the first World War, when the men of the first and succeeding officers' training camps marched by; in 1898, when the Fifteenth Minnesota was quartered here; and in 1861, when the First Minnesota, later immortalized at Bull Run, and Antietam, and Fredericksburg, and Gettysburg, heard on another June 14 that it had been ordered to the East. Then as Dr. Folwell relates, "pandemonium reigned in camp." Eight days later the men of the First Minnesota went on board two waiting transports here at the water's edge.

Thus four generations of fighting men have left Fort Snelling in the flower of their manhood to honor their obligations, and the obligations of their forebears, to a government which opened up this abundant world of prairies, rivers, and woods, that therein we might multiply, and prosper, and enjoy a democratic way of life.

Into the happy hunting grounds of the Sioux and the Chippewa, this nascent empire of the voyageur, the trapper, and the fur trader, came Captain Jonathan Carver on an autumn day in 1766, stood on the bluff which rises at the junction of the Mississippi and the Minnesota rivers, and viewed the wonderful landscape which lay before him. Prophetically he wrote: "To what power or authority this new world will become dependent, after it has arisen from its present uncultivated state, time alone can discover. . . . But the seat of Empire, from time immemorial, has been gradually progressive towards the West."

Lieutenant Zebulon M. Pike, standing near the same confluence thirty-nine years later on September 23, 1805, saw the advantages "which would arise from a fort located at that point. From the high bluff . . . the course of both streams would be under the sweep of the guns. Sheer walls of stone rising from the Mississippi could prevent invasion; and the fur trading business could be regulated" from the Great Lakes to the plains of the Missouri, "as all boats entering or leaving the Indian country must use one or the other of the two rivers." Then and there he bought the site from the Sioux for presents valued at two hundred dollars, and sixty gallons of liquor.

Fourteen years passed. On August 24, 1819, about a hundred men of the Fifth United States Infantry disembarked, and log cabins and a stockade — "Cantonment New Hope" — were built opposite the towering height where a few years later rose the white stone walls of Fort Snelling, originally known as Fort St. Anthony. A year later Colonel Josiah Snelling took command. "As a soldier he was a true leader of men, loyal to his country and his superiors; as a pioneer he raised the flag of authority in a lawless wilderness, and as a builder he erected more than stone walls for he laid the foundations of civilization in the Northwest."

By 1823 Colonel Snelling had located and practically completed on the extreme point of land between the two rivers a new fort which for years was one of the strongest outposts on the western frontier. "Lying far from the seats of government, in a region of wandering traders and red men, the fort became the exponent of the government — the only symbol of governmental restriction in a region almost entirely without law." There it served to keep the "Indians friendly while the foundations of American life were being laid." The history of this fort, however, "was not made by the rifles and sabers of the soldiers." The Indian, the Indian agent, the trapper, and the trader are gone, but "the axe and the plow of the pioneer who worked in safety beneath its potential protection have left their history upon the landscape of the great Northwest." Like many other lonely posts, Fort Snelling fostered settlement and thus made a "permanent contribution . . . to the development of the surrounding region."

Here and at Mendota were the first American settlements in southern Minnesota. Here were women and children, with books, schooling, religious services, entertainment. Here the first cultural existence in the state began. Soldiers and civilians alike evinced "the self-confidence and the grim determination which are the products of frontier service."

The history of these people — their experience and that of all other Americans — has created for us the significance of our flag. When at Wake Island, on the beaches and in the jungles of Bataan, in the Coral Sea, and at Midway, we reaffirm our greatness, it is the tradition of the past — patriotism, and loyalty, and sacrifice, and high purpose for the future — which speaks. The builders of Fort Snelling were the pioneers on the frontiers of a new nation. We are the pioneers on the frontiers of a new world. All we seek is freedom, and a lasting peace. Our generation has trod this road before. Why did we fail to achieve our goal? We cannot fail again.

It avails nothing to say that we won the last war and lost the peace. In an immediate sense we did win. "What did we get out of it?" the skeptics ask our generation. We established for ourselves and for our children the right for twenty-five years to live as we chose to live. That is a great deal in itself. Had we lost, they would have known in the oppression of the conqueror what we had fought to avert. Victory assured for us the continuity of our democratic institutions, but continuity of rights and blessings seldom suggest the initial sacrifice. We made an investment in America. We do not regret it.

Yet, in a larger sense, we did fail. We preserved our way of life, but we are at war again. Our sons make their investment now. Out of our mistakes, out of their sacrifice, we must set up an international control which will make a third World War impossible.

We must accept our share of the responsibility for the tragic pay-off of these twenty years. Germany dominated Europe before 1914. It was winning in the spring of 1917. We entered the struggle, swung the balance of power the other way, and, after victory, withdrew, permitting Germany, with its seventy million people and its industrial and military genius, again to threaten the Old World and the New. How can we justify our record? Where is the common sense of it? We fight to save a civilization we love, and then fail to support an international mechanism devised to protect that civilization by barring power politics from the world. More than that, we withdraw within the barriers of an economic nationalism and restricted immigration, particularly at a time when war-weary and sickly nations need a common blood bank to survive. Whether we like it or not, America is a world power, the greatest on the earth, and we cannot escape, even if we would, our political and economic and social involvement in and responsibility to the world. The boys who have died in the Pacific will have died in vain, if, when this war is over, we assume another "splendid isolation."

"No man is an Island, intire of it selfe; every man is a peece of the Continent, a part of the maine; if a Clod bee washed away by the Sea, Europe is the lesse, as well as if a Promontorie were, as well as if a Mannor of thy friends or of thine owne were; any mans death diminishes me, because I am involved in Mankinde; And therefore never send to know for whom the bell tolls; It tolls for thee." Along the road of moral defeat of the past ten years — Manchukuo, Ethiopia, Austria, Munich, Prague — John Donne could have told us that each time the bell tolled, it tolled for you and for me.

Isolationism is the twin of pacificism. Too many thought until Pearl Harbor that we didn't have to fight. The Russians thought so, too, and the unwilling French. All accepted the dictum that a country worth dying for was worth living for. Too few accepted the reverse — a country worth living for is worth dying for. The flower of the youth of France — a million and a half of them — exist in Nazi prison camps. Would they embrace today — would Occupied France accept — a policy of appeasement, of peace at any price? The democracies have learned since Munich that peace cannot be bought at any price, even that of slavery or death, when ruthless force wills to rule the earth. Force must be met with force.

Now to our most tragic and stupid error. Too many years we failed to recognize that Communism, and Fascism, and National Socialism were the facets of a rapidly developing world revolution which recognized no boundaries in its lust for territorial and ideological conquest. This rise to power of the dictators cannot be attributed entirely to the treaty of Versailles; that is an escapist rationalization. Exhausted and disillusioned peoples sought new leadership and new concepts and yearned again for the sense of self-respecting power. The world they had known before 1914 was gone beyond recall. A new world was struggling to be born. The sterile leadership of a Baldwin or a Daladier offered not bread, but a stone. We played the stock market behind our own high tariff wall. "We are not," we said, "interested in Europe's petty squabbles." To the hungry and receptive peoples of Europe, Democracy sounded smug, pacifistic, uncomprehending, hopelessly capitalistic. They misunderstood our overwhelming desire for peace, as we did theirs for change. In despair they turned to the self-appointed creators of a new order, which, through military effort if need be, would rule the world.

Still we were blind. We might have met successfully their dynamic philosophy with one not implemented by a gestapo or a concentration camp. For it is not merely with military weapons that the menace of totalitarianism is met, but with ideas which can arouse the enthusiasm of all peoples, irrespective of race or creed, and give them strength in days which are dark, and hope for an uncertain future. When war came it was too late. Now we must wait upon the peace — "a people's peace." "The century which will come of this war . . . must be the century of the common man," says Vice-president Henry A. Wallace, for the man who has been deluded by Hitler as well as by the Frenchman who saw no reason to fight because, he thought, there was little difference between his way of life and what the conqueror professed to offer.

> Where the bricks are fallen
> We will build with new stone
> Where the beams are rotten
> We will build with new timbers
> Where the Word is unspoken
> We will build with new speech.

President Roosevelt's four freedoms are the stones of a foundation reconstructed in this spirit. Two come out of our political past — freedom of speech and of expression and freedom of every person to worship God in his own way; two, out of our new social sense — freedom from want and freedom from fear. As war aims these freedoms are far more revolutionary than the general principles of that Atlantic Charter upon which Mr. Roosevelt and Mr. Churchill base their "hopes for a better future for the world": no aggrandizement or territorial changes not in accordance with the freely expressed wishes of the peoples concerned; the right of all peoples to choose their form of government, with the restoration of those which have been torn down; equal access for all, victor and vanquished, to the trade and to the raw materials of the world; improved labor standards, economic adjustment, and social security; freedom of the seas; and disarmament. We must implement this peace with a world organization of which the United Nations are the nucleus.

Mr. Sumner Welles suggests, as a first step, a "long Armistice" during which we can disarm the aggressor, participate in an international police force to restore and maintain order until a permanent system can be set up, and work out a world organization which will determine the final terms of peace "after the period of social and economic chaos which will come inevitably upon the termination of the present war and after the completion of the gigantic task of relief, or reconstruction and rehabilitation which will confront the United Nations at the time of the Armistice." No attempt would be made to work out a permanent peace settlement for months or years — not until passions cooled and hatreds became tempered, immediate economic and social adjustments were made, and the peacemakers could take a clearer view "of the enormous problems in the fields of national ambitions and economic pressures and over-all security before they attempted to draft a blueprint for a new post-war world."

It is too early to draft that blueprint. Many questions are being settled for us as the struggle proceeds. With our accelerating effort, our purposes are taking a more definite shape, and we insist that those purposes be permanently secured. The settlement lasts longer than the war. We are now prepared for any sacrifice. Are we prepared for the sacrifice of peace? Certainly the costs of a continuing world federation are less than those of this second World War, or a third World War to come. Under the shadow of a great threat, we are unified and unselfish. We must discipline ourselves to a continued and unstinted effort, to a continued co-operation when the war is ended. It guarantees a better world of freedom and of peace at a far lesser price.

In *Pilgrim's Progress,* Christian says to one who falters: "If you will go with me, you must go against wind and tide." In a similar spirit the pioneers carried the flag we honor, as do the boys at Midway and Dutch Harbor today. The flag speaks to us of the courageous past, and of this present, and of the future we must build. Let us go along the road of the future together, though it be against wind and tide. Then do we pass on the heritage, pioneers of a new world beneath the flag of freedom.

LeRoy S. Buffington and the Minneapolis Boom of the 1880's

Muriel B. Christison

WHOEVER SPEAKS of the "gay nineties" is mistaken, according to Mr. Edward C. Gale, at least so far as Minneapolis is concerned. In Minneapolis it was the "gay eighties" instead; those were the city's boom years. Other Midwestern cities were booming in the 1880's too, but in Minneapolis the tempo of expansion was faster, almost reckless. Statistics and the amazing architectural output of LeRoy S. Buffington corroborate Mr. Gale's memory. The census figures are typically impressive. By 1880 the population of Minneapolis had reached 46,887, and by 1890 it had jumped to 164,738, an increase of over two hundred and fifty per cent. This growing citizenry with its demand for housing facilities had, in turn, a dynamic effect upon the real-estate trade. There were 54 real-estate brokers or agencies in Minneapolis in 1880; just three years later, the *Minneapolis City Directory* listed 213! The consideration on real-estate transfers rose from $4,500,000 in 1880 to the staggering amount of $27,500,000 in 1883.[1]

The decade from 1880 to 1890 was characterized by the "Minneapolis idea"; civic enterprise absorbed the boundless energies of the local businessman and served as an outlet for the rash optimism that attracted him to the West. The following excerpt from a report written in 1882 by the secretary of the Minneapolis Board of Trade expresses the wonderment and excitement felt by those who were taking part in this great development: "The extraordinary increase in its [*Minneapolis'*] population; the rapid advance in the value of its realty; the number and value of new buildings erected; the astonishing growth of both its retail and jobbing trade; the constant yet rapid extension of its manufacturing industries, and its marvelous progress in every department of business and social life, are facts

---

[1] *United States Census,* 1890, *Population,* part 1, p. 198; Minneapolis Chamber of Commerce, *First Annual Report,* 1883, p. 115.

which, unsupported by the solid array of absolutely reliable statistics
... might well challenge the credulity of those not personally familiar
with the phenomenal growth and progress of Minneapolis." [2]

In 1883 the man walking along one of the new stone sidewalks
on Hennepin Avenue might well look up at the Boston Block or the
rising West Hotel and reflect upon the grandeur of his city — and
the genius of Buffington, the architect who designed these structures.
It is doubtful if there could be more revealing testimony to the
phenomenal character of those years than the work of this one man.
Among his designs for Minneapolis buildings in the 1880's are competitive projects for the Exposition Building, the Hennepin County
Courthouse, the Minneapolis Public Library, the Northwestern
Storage Warehouse, a ten-story bank and office building, churches,
flour mills, university buildings, and mansions for some of the city's
first families.[3]

Such a list, partial though it may be, indicates that the citizens
of Minneapolis in the 1880's had confidence in their city's future and
surplus wealth which they were willing to invest in that future. In
the ten years beginning in 1880, Minneapolis enjoyed a period of
physical growth and civic improvement unparalleled in any other
decade of its history. The increasing concentration of capital, the rise
of the city to first rank as an industrial and commercial center, the
expanding retail trade, and the general accessibility of the region,
all combined to make Minneapolis capable of physical expansion to
an unlimited degree. It was an ideal place for an ambitious, progressive young architect to settle.

Buffington was born on September 22, 1848, in Cincinnati. That
city, known in the 1880's as the "Paris of America," was a propitious
spot for the future architect to form his early impressions and receive
his education. After being trained in engineering, he joined the
architectural firm of Anderson and Hannaford, first as a student,
then as a delineator. There Buffington acquired a sound knowledge

[2] Minneapolis Chamber of Commerce and Board of Trade, *Joint Annual Report*,
1882, p. 17.
[3] Original drawings for these projects are preserved in the Buffington collection of
the University of Minnesota Library.

of structural problems as well as of artistic styles. In 1869 he went to St. Anthony to marry Mary Eleanor Depew, the daughter of a former Cincinnatian. They returned to Cincinnati immediately after their marriage, but they did not remain there long, for Buffington removed to St. Paul in 1871 and his wife followed him later in the same year.[4] In St. Paul, he became associated with the architectural firm of A. M. Radcliffe, and attained prominence through his collaboration on the designs for the Kelly Block, the Plymouth Congregational Church, the First Methodist Episcopal Church, the residences of Maurice Auerbach, William R. Marshall, and Henry P. Upham, and other important structures.

In 1874 Buffington opened an office in Minneapolis. During the 1870's his reputation grew steadily, and by 1877 he was commonly referred to as the best architect in the state. Buffington's success, though professionally deserved, was partly the result of his remarkable personality. The following quotation reflects the general esteem in which he was held by his contemporaries: "Personally, Mr. Buffington possesses in eminent degree those social qualities which are a necessary attendant upon commercial or artistic success. He is a brilliant conversationalist, and of a ready tact. . . . Herculean in his resources and ability, his own staying powers, coupled with indomitable courage, have placed him in the front rank of the profession to which he belongs. In fact, Mr. Buffington is an excellent example of what energy, enterprise and brains will accomplish when properly utilized."[5]

Buffington's role in the booming eighties is revealed somewhat by the remarks of a *Chicago Times* correspondent who, writing in 1884 of the architectural development of Minneapolis, said that he was "the one architect who more than any other has stamped the impress of his artistic personality upon the finest and most costly structures" and that "his own abilities . . . have pushed him to the front in the wild race of competition which is characteristic of the

[4] *National Cyclopedia of American Biography*, 22:364 (New York, 1932); Isaac Atwater and John H. Stevens, *History of Minneapolis and Hennepin County*, 2:1022 (New York, 1895).
[5] Minneapolis Board of Trade, *Minneapolis Illustrated*, 63 (Chicago, 1889).

great Northwest, particularly so in Minneapolis, the city whose fortunes and those of a few of her enterprising, hard working citizens, of which number Mr. Buffington is one, are so inseparably connected." [6]

Buffington's office in the 1880's was one of the busiest spots in town. His firm occupied a suite of rooms and employed some thirty draftsmen. So unusual was the size of the firm, and so impressive the decoration and furnishings of its offices, that they were regarded as show places and were frequently mentioned with wonderment and amazement by the press. People from out of town or new clients who visited the establishment were baffled by the youthful appearance of the man who greeted them when they asked for Buffington, for at the peak of his career he was only in his thirties.

Buffington's luxurious offices were in the new Boston Block at Third and Hennepin. The building was under construction in 1880, when Hennepin Avenue was hardly more than a muddy lane. Buffington, who was already interested in the structural use of iron, incorporated cast-iron columns in the walls of the Boston Block. The story goes that, one weekend in the fall, when building operations were suspended, an iron column weighing three thousand pounds, which was lying on the ground, sank from its own weight into the mire until it was completely obscured. No one could explain the disappearance of an object so difficult to move and to conceal until the wheel of a wagon running down Hennepin Avenue struck against it some six months later, after the ground thawed.[7] Stylistically, the Boston Block belongs to the category of Victorian architecture with its typical liking for broken surfaces. The chastening influence of the Romanesque revival was beginning to appear, however, and it was evident in the moderately restrained design of the façade. Minneapolis was proud of the Boston Block; it was large, tall, stylish, and impressive. A few more such buildings would give the city a metropolitan air.

The cost of the Boston Block has been estimated at approximately five hundred thousand dollars. The Pillsbury A Mill cost over a

[6] Quoted in the *St. Paul Pioneer Press*, January 12, 1884.
[7] *Minneapolis Daily Star*, December 10, 1926.

million.[8] Plans for this new mill, also under construction in 1880, called for the largest and most complete flour mill in the world. But more than that, the Pillsbury firm wanted to erect a mill of the best architectural design. To insure the accomplishment of these intentions, Buffington was engaged as architect. Charles A. Pillsbury made a careful study of the most famous European mills, especially those in Budapest, so that no desirable mechanical or architectural feature might be omitted from the new Minneapolis mill. The external appearance of the building was a credit to Buffington, as well as to the taste of the firm for whom it was designed. In planning the mill, Buffington was thinking primarily in terms of function. By so doing, he showed that he certainly was not provincial in taste, but definitely progressive. At so early a date he was able to side-step Victorianism and proceed in the direction of utilitarianism, a herald of the modern theory that form follows function. The mill looks today essentially the same as it did when it was completed in 1883. The interior has been rebuilt to meet the demands of modern production, but the exterior has not been changed. The massiveness and simplicity of its appearance suggest somewhat that landmark in the development of American commercial architecture, the Marshall Field Wholesale Store, built in Chicago from 1885 to 1887 by Henry Hobson Richardson.

The building of the Pillsbury A Mill was of great local significance. In 1883 it was estimated that the new mill had stepped up the daily producing capacity of the Minneapolis mills from 15,200 barrels to 20,400 barrels. It was symbolic of the economic development of Minneapolis and the concentration of capital that went hand in hand with this development. And the mill was of immeasurable artistic significance because of its influence upon public taste. The very importance of the building and the convincing suitability of its design prepared the way for a large-scale acceptance of Richardson's version of the Romanesque style, which characterized Minneapolis architecture between 1885 and 1893.[9]

---

[8] *Minneapolis Illustrated*, 63; *Pioneer Press*, January 12, 1884.

[9] *Tribune Hand-book of Minneapolis*, 70 (Minneapolis, 1884). Among Minneapolis buildings constructed in the same style in this period were the Masonic Temple, the

Before the Pillsbury A Mill was completed, Buffington had begun work for a Cincinnati capitalist whose belief in the future of the growing city of Minneapolis ultimately led him and his associates to invest' over a million and a half dollars in the West Hotel. That building, which was hailed as the "Minneapolis Miracle," was a tangible acknowledgment of the city's greatness. Extravagant praises were written of the West. One commentator described it as: "The ne plus ultra of hotels . . . considered the finest hotel in the West." "The finest hotel building on the continent," wrote another.[10] Visitors from far and near agreed that claims made for it were just, and Minneapolitans who toured England were proud to find a picture of the West Hotel hanging in the London agency of Thomas Cook and Son, an example of the wonders awaiting the lucky traveler in America.

Buffington proved himself progressive both in his design for the Pillsbury A Mill and in the structural features of the West Hotel. It was estimated that he used some 2,300,000 pounds of iron in the West's construction, at a time when conservative architects were neglecting this promising material. Furthermore, his use of the then new clay tile in the fire-resisting construction of the interior was probably the first example west of Chicago of modern fireproofing, certainly the first on a large scale. The traditional fame of the West was eloquently verified by nostalgic remarks in the press when the old hotel was torn down in 1940.[11] It can be said that its own grandeur destroyed it. Had the hotel been smaller and less expensive to operate, it might still have been standing, like many less significant but equally aged landmarks.

By the time that the West Hotel was completed in 1884, Buffington was a nationally known architect. While he was still at work on

Lumber Exchange, the courthouse, and the Guaranty Loan, now the Metropolitan Life Building.

[10] *Tribune Hand-book of Minneapolis*, 126; *Minneapolis Illustrated*, 7; *Pioneer Press*, October 25, 1883; Chamber of Commerce, *First Annual Report*, 108. Buffington later said that the cost of the West Hotel, including the furnishings, was $900,000, and that the lot cost $45,000. See *Minneapolis Journal*, February 23, 1908.

[11] Robert C. McLean, "LeRoy S. Buffington, F.A.I.A., An Obituary," in *Western Architect*, 40:9 (March, 1931); A. J. Russell, "The Long Bow," in *Minneapolis Times-Tribune*, March 18, 1940.

this gigantic project, his office was flooded with other commissions. With the incorporation of the Minneapolis Chamber of Commerce and the assured rise of the city as an important grain market, much outside capital and many business firms were attracted to the city. Consequently, after 1881, commercial and residential building increased by leaps and bounds. In 1882 over nine million dollars were spent on building, and in 1883 some ten and a half million.[12]

Among the noteworthy commissions that Buffington handled in 1883 were the Sidle and the Eastman blocks. The Sidles were a banking family, having been connected with the oldest bank in Minneapolis, the First National, from its incorporation in 1857. W. W. Eastman, owner of the new Eastman Block, began his career in the 1850's in the flour milling business at St. Anthony. He had been one of the charter members of the Millers' National Association, and he was active in the lumber industry. Eastman also operated a woolen mill which later formed the nucleus of the North Star Woolen Mills. While his business block on Nicollet Avenue was in the process of erection, Eastman became one of the charter members of the first Minneapolis board of park commissioners. With the formation of the park board, a systematic plan for the beautification of Minneapolis was drawn up which included the laying out of public parks and parkways. The main areas and arteries to be developed in the 1880's, according to this plan, were Central Park, Lake Calhoun Boulevard, Minnehaha Falls, the East River Road, Lake Street, and Riverside Park.[18] The year 1883 also saw the incorporation of another notable organization whose chief purpose was to "foster and promote educational, artistic and scientific interests"—the Minneapolis Society of Fine Arts.[14] With William Watts Folwell as its first president, the society sponsored the exhibition of works of art and conducted lecture courses on art. Both endeavors aided in the

---

[12] McLean, in *Western Architect,* 40:9; Chamber of Commerce, *First Annual Report,* 108.

[13] Chamber of Commerce, *First Annual Report,* 84; Horace W. S. Cleveland, *The Aesthetic Development of the United Cities, Saint Paul and Minneapolis* (1888), and *Suggestions for a System of Parks and Parkways for the City of Minneapolis* (Minneapolis, 1888).

[14] See the "Articles of Incorporation," in a booklet on the *Minneapolis Society of Fine Arts* (Minneapolis, 1922).

maturing and improving of public taste, a development which was to find an expression in the handsome buildings erected in Minneapolis in the last half of the 1880's.

Buffington's new Tribune Building on Fourth Street and First Avenue South was completed in 1884. The occupation of the new structure was announced in the *Minneapolis Tribune* for July 19 of that year: "The new Tribune Building is one of the most handsome and substantial business structures in the northwest, besides being the most complete and best arranged building for newspaper purposes west of Philadelphia." In praise of the location and the architect, the article goes on to say: "The location is one of the very best in the heart of the city. It could not be more central, allowance being made for the rapid development and extension of the business quarter. . . . Whatever credit results from the elegance of the design and the thoroughness with which every detail of the immense structure has been carried out, belongs to Mr. L. S. Buffington of this city, one of the most experienced and competent architects in the country." The *Tribune's* admiration for the architect of its new building is understandable. Evidence that he was being recognized elsewhere appeared in a St. Louis paper for 1885, when Buffington attended the meeting of the Western Association of Architects in that city. The *St. Louis Daily Globe Democrat,* in its issue for November 21, remarked that he had "more buildings standing to his credit than any architect" in the Northwest.

When Buffington returned from St. Louis, talk of the Minneapolis Exposition was in the air. The idea, which had its birth in an editorial appearing in the *Tribune* in the fall of 1885, was fostered by W. M. Regan of a firm of bakers and restaurant proprietors. Regan Brothers was a phenomenal establishment, catering to hungry business and professional men. The restaurant, which started in 1882, was soon forced to expand until it could serve on an average of fifteen hundred people daily. It was said that the businessmen who assembled there consumed a hundred and thirty pounds of roast beef, sixty gallons of milk, and twelve bushels of cantaloupes at a single noonday meal. The restaurant was important as a gathering place where ideas were exchanged across the tables. Among those who met there each day were many who thought that Minneapolis had been cheated in losing the Midway district and the State Fair to St. Paul. They were particularly receptive to Regan's idea of a great exposition. Plans grew, money was raised, a site was chosen, and a competition for an architectural award was opened. Buffington, at this date filled with dreams of iron construction, designed a building modeled on the Exposition Building for the New York World's Fair of 1853, a metal frame with a screen of glass. He lost out in the competition.[15] Was his design too ornate, or was it too expensive? Probably both.

Another competitive design that Buffington prepared in 1886 was that for a public library building. Again he was a loser, though his design bears a strangely close resemblance to the building actually erected. The state legislature passed an act in 1885 authorizing an issue of a hundred thousand dollars in bonds for the building of a public library in Minneapolis, providing an additional fifty thousand dollars be raised by private subscription. By the fall of 1886 the necessary sum was available, and work on the foundation had begun. When Buffington's competitive sketch for the public library was drawn up, he was working in the Romanesque style, and he produced a number of Romanesque designs after 1885 which are masterpieces of architectural composition.[16]

In the 1880's a number of charitable and private hospitals were opened in Minneapolis. Buffington had his hand in planning a number of hospital buildings, just as he had it in the building of mills, office blocks, retail blocks, hotels, and other public buildings. In 1886 he supervised the rebuilding of a mansion for use by St. Mary's

[15] *Minneapolis Illustrated*, 28, 77. A preliminary sketch for the Exposition Building is in the Buffington collection of the University of Minnesota Library.

[16] *Minneapolis Illustrated*, 20. Buffington's design for the library is reproduced in the *Northwestern Architect*, 6:994 (November, 1888). Critics have tended to give credit for the excellence of Buffington's designs in the late 1880's to the influence of Harvey Ellis, an artist in his own right, who was working for Buffington at the time. The evolution of Buffington's work, however, seems to have been fairly consistent, and he adopted the Romanesque style before Ellis, who had known Richardson in Albany, joined the Minneapolis office as a draftsman. But it must be said that the sketches of Ellis showed an understanding of the Richardsonian Romanesque and possessed a distinction and beauty of design which surpassed the work of many of his contemporaries.

Hospital. Churches did not lag behind hospitals. So many new religious structures appeared in Minneapolis in the 1880's that it was called the "City of Churches." Through the interest of one of his most enthusiastic clients, Samuel C. Gale, Buffington designed and supervised the construction of the First Unitarian Church on Eighth Street and Mary Place. This, too, was completed in 1886.

By 1886 Samuel Gale was well aware of Buffington's versatility, knowledge of his profession, and foresight. As far back as 1876 Buffington had worked for Harlow Gale on the new City Market; he had built tenements for Samuel Gale, who furnished housing for some of the city's swelling population. It was not surprising, then, that Samuel Gale chose Buffington to build a house for him on Sixteenth Street and Harmon Place. The *St. Paul Pioneer Press* for September 16, 1888, published a description of the residence which assures one of its astounding richness and makes its estimated cost, a hundred thousand dollars, seem not unreasonable. Parts of the description are worth quoting, since they picture the type of house prominent Minneapolitans were building in the 1880's.

"The style of the architecture is the Romanesque. . . . The roof will be of red slate. . . . The stone in the building is almost entirely rock-faced. . . . The archway of the entrance is not a complete one, but dies away into the tower. . . . The barn is connected with the residence by an arch which forms a porte cochere. The barn is about as handsome as the residence itself. . . . To return to the residence. Passing under the heavy arch of the entrance the stone niche in the wall commands attention. Within the niche will be a life size bronze statue. . . . Off from the hall and partially separated by Moorish screen work is an alcove divan. On one side of the hall is an alabaster and mosaic mantel extending from the floor to the wooden-beamed ceiling. At the central point of the mantel is a beautiful silver plaque. The stair case will be . . . elaborate in construction. About two feet from the floor is a newell post terminating in a three-fourths life size statue. The entire hall will be wainscoted to the ceiling in oak, stained and finished to a pale amber green. . . . It will be the most imposing room in the house. . . . Opening from the hall is the drawing room, library, morning room and dining room. . . . The library and morning room are finished in mahogany with elaborate plaster ceilings. The dining room . . . is elaborately finished in antique oak, and has at one end a buffet and breakfast alcove and at the other end a mantel. . . . The conservatory opens from the dining room. . . . In the center . . . is to be a marble fountain. The drawing room is finished in white and gold, with a ceiling of pale yellow silk with a pattern in plush of a pale blue appliqued thereon, the pattern emphasized with silver-headed nails of a hemispherical shape. . . . The floors of all the above mentioned rooms will be of hard wood, except that of the conservatory, which will be of mosaic of a more or less emblematic nature. . . . The heating is to be by hot water and the apparatus will be located in the barn."

It is significant that Gale's residence, while it was admired, apparently was not considered extraordinary. Probably this was because a good number of imposing residences were arising at about the same time, many of them shaped by the careful genius of the same architect. There was the residence of Fred C. Pillsbury on the corner of Tenth Street and Third Avenue, just across the street from the George A. Pillsbury house. There was a new house for Francis B. Hart on Clifton Place, another for Frank E. Little on Harmon Place, and many more. The domestic architecture of L. S. Buffington has been overlooked in the past because of its private character and because of the great amount of publicity given to his commercial and public buildings. It would seem, however, that many of Buffington's best and most original designs were for dwellings. Even a cursory examination of these houses of the 1880's explains the frequent references to Buffington's "exquisite taste" by his contemporaries.

While Buffington had been engaged on these many commissions, a momentous project had been taking shape in his mind. In the middle eighties he began to work out the technicalities of the problem, and finally, in 1888, he patented a system of construction which earned for him the title of "Father of the Skyscraper." His patent provided for a braced skeleton of metal with masonry veneer supported on shelves fastened to the skeleton at each story. If Buffington had not been so occupied with other buildings in the eighties, he might have patented his invention at an earlier date and, in that case, his claim to the title of "inventor of the skyscraper" would have been more secure.[17] It is certain that he was thinking in terms of iron construction before 1888, and it is now generally acknowledged that he was the first to think out systematically the details and ultimate possibilities of this method of building.

Buffington's patent was regarded with anything but complacency in 1888. By some it was ridiculed; others were not so ready to deny its logic. One of the more favorable notices asserted that "Architect L. S. Buffington, of Minneapolis, has brought forward an invention which he thinks will revolutionize the world of building. . . . By it buildings can be constructed of any desired height. A 'syndicate of capitalists' is also backing his system, and will erect in Minneapolis a building . . . twenty-eight stories high. Architect Buffington says: 'The syndicate which is backing me includes some of the best men of the city, who control plenty of capital, and as soon as a few details are settled we shall publish our plans'. . . . The land at the corner of Wall and Broad Sts. is worth somewhat more than $30,000,000 per acre. . . . It will be seen that at these prices a landlord might welcome even twenty-eight stories to keep down his ground rent. . . . The highest buildings now in New York are about thirteen stories, which is about the limit of the rational use of brick and stone walls." Buffington later admitted that he never really intended to put up the twenty-eight story building, but was using it only as a publicity device. Minneapolis had to wait for its first skyscraper. A recent writer asserts that "it was the publicity given to his twenty-eight story building which was responsible in large part for the spread of the knowledge of this form of construction in the architectural world." [18]

[17] Buffington applied for his patent on November 14, 1887, and it was granted as patent number 383,170 on May 22, 1888. His work on the skyscraper is discussed in the *Minneapolis Journal* for December 30, 1928, and in the "Memories of LeRoy S. Buffington," a manuscript owned by his daughter, Miss Ella D. Buffington of Minneapolis. A copy, which has been edited and annotated by the present writer, is in the University of Minnesota Library.

[18] *Engineering News* (New York), March 31, 1888; *Chicago Tribune,* December 4, 1892; E. M. Upjohn, "Buffington and the Skyscraper," in *Art Bulletin,* 17:70 (March, 1935).

Another project that occupied much of Buffington's attention during the 1880's was the erection of buildings for the University of Minnesota. Several of his buildings still are standing on the campus. He designed the university Coliseum, which was used both for military drill and for concerts, and a farmhouse and barn for the agricultural school, all built in 1884; the Mechanic Arts Building, now Eddy Hall, erected in 1886; and the farm Home Building, completed in 1888.[19] His work for the university was closely associated with the regency of John S. Pillsbury, another pioneer business leader whose vision and indefatigable energy did so much to shape the course of the business, municipal, and educational development of Minneapolis. For many years Pillsbury was engaged in the local milling industry and the hardware trade, and he was also associated with two Western railroads, the First National Bank, and other business and financial organizations. He still found time to devote to public duty and was perhaps more closely connected with the growth of the University of Minnesota than any other one man. His most generous act in the closing years of the 1880's was the contribution of over $150,000 for the completion of a science building, now known as Pillsbury Hall.[20] This, too, was designed by Buffington, although his scheme for the building was drawn up by his assistant, Harvey Ellis. This may account for its marked similarity to Austin Hall on the campus of Harvard University, which was built after a design by Richardson between 1881 and 1883.

By 1890 the boom had spent its force. The financial surplus available for building in the 1880's was frozen or drained away. The ominous cloud of the oncoming panic of 1893 was already beginning to cast its shadow on the spreading city beside the Falls of St. Anthony. In the ten years that elapsed from 1880 to 1890, Minneapolis had changed from a sprawling frontier town to an integrated metropolitan center, ready to assume the burdens of civic maturity. The harvest festival of 1891 was just an echo of the earlier optimism, which disappeared in the quietude of gloom.

[19] For a discussion of the Coliseum, see William W. Folwell, *A History of Minnesota*, 4:103–108 (St. Paul, 1930).
[20] Isaac Atwater, *History of the City of Minneapolis*, 2:593 (New York, 1893).

Buffington lived until 1931. He continued his work for many years, following the changing currents of architectural taste. With a few exceptions, it seems fair to state that he never surpassed the excellence he had displayed in his work of the late 1880's. The spirit of that decade seemed to call forth the best from all who participated in its surging activity.[21]

[21] In 1889 it was estimated that Buffington had erected buildings valued at more than twenty million dollars in Minneapolis and its vicinity. See *Minneapolis Illustrated,* 20. Over half of Buffington's commissions were for buildings outside Minneapolis. The writer is compiling a catalogue of his work.

With Cass in the Northwest in 1820

Edited by Ralph H. Brown

[THE SECOND *installment of the journal of Charles C. Trowbridge, a member of the expedition under Governor Cass which explored the wilderness of frontier Minnesota in the summer of 1820, is presented herewith. The first section, with an introduction by Professor Brown, appears* ante, p. 126–148. *It covers the period from May 14 to June 18 and carries the party from Detroit to a point on the south shore of Lake Superior a little beyond the Sault de Ste. Marie. The present section continues the journey westward to the mouth of the St. Louis River, up that stream, and over the difficult portages that mark the divide between the rivers emptying into the Great Lakes and the southward flowing waters of the Mississippi system.* Ed.]

Monday June 19th. As we were about starting this morning our indians brought us intelligence that boats were in sight. This was very gratifying news, for we anticipated the arrival of Mr [William] Morrison, a clerk in the employment of the American Fur Comᵖʸ, and we were not disappointed. Mr M. had a brigade of five barges loaded with Furs, on his way to Mackinac. The interview was not only pleasing but very important to us, for on the information received from him depended in a great measure our route. We had determined, provided the season would permit, to visit the Lake of the Woods; but Mr Morrison informed us that more than a month additional time would be required for that purpose, and considering the lateness of the season, combined with other powerful causes, we have concluded to take another route vis, to ascend the Fon[d] du Lac [of Lake Superior] or Sᵗ Louis River, by which a communication is had with the Mississipi.[40] After our conference with

[40] The Lake of the Woods had earlier been assumed to be the source of the Mississippi. The import of this meeting between Schoolcraft and Morrison, two claimants to the discovery of the true source, has often escaped attention. If Morrison knew in 1820 that he had been to the headwaters of the Mississippi, surely this was the time for him to speak out. It cannot be supposed that he would withhold such information from an official exploratory party on its way to the headwaters. It was thirty-six years later, on January 16, 1856, that Morrison wrote to his brother, saying, "For the information of the H[istorical] Society, I will state to you all about what came to my knowledge, by which you will perceive that H. R. Schoolcraft is in error and that he was not the first

Mr Morrison was ended we embarked, but had not made more than 13 miles when a violent wind arose, and we were obliged to land.[41] Nothing could be more disagreeable to us than to be subject as we are to the winds on this Lake, for the waves roll so wonderfully, that it would evince in us little regard for personal safety, should we attempt to proceed. This stop however was productive of agreeable consequences, as an express with letters sent on by Mr [Ramsay] Crooks of the Am. fur C° overtook us at this place, and the satisfaction of hearing so directly from our friends was an ample compensation for the loss of time.[42]

We met this afternoon 14 canoes loaded with indians on their way to Mackinac. They appeared highly gratified to see their great father, and after we had given them what most could please them, some tobacco, we continued on, but only made to day 20 miles. To day we experienced one of these dreadful mists so common on this Lake: it is dangerous to travel in them, for the most prominent objects are scarcely distinguishable at a short distance, and unless the guides are competent we are every moment running the risk of lozing our canoes.

Tuesday June 20th. We made a very early start this morning and stopped not until we arrived at the Two hearted River, or La Riviere du deux coeurs, (a small stream 47 miles from Shell Drake River,) where we breakfasted. We thence continued our voyage as usual for 21 miles when we were gratified with a sight of Lagrand Sable or grand Sand Banks, a place much spoken of by Voyageurs. These Banks are from 100 to 250 feet in height, and present not a single indication of vegetation; one of our Indians whom curiosity induced to ascend them had much the appearance of a child when running on the summit of the hills, and when he returned to the canoe he was almost exhausted with fatigue.

person who made the discovery." Morrison states in this letter, which is one of three published versions, that in 1803–04 he went up La Biche or Elk River to "near Lac La Biche," and that "Lac La Biche is the source of the Great River Mississippi, which I visited in 1804, and if the late Gen. [Zebulon M.] Pike did not lay it down as such when he came to Leech lake it is because he did not happen to meet me." See J. V. Brower, *The Mississippi River and Its Source*, 122 n.–124 n. (*Minnesota Historical Collections*, vol. 7 — Minneapolis, 1893); Folwell, *Minnesota*, 1:116 n. Schoolcraft announced his discovery of the river's source following his second trip into the region in 1832. Lac la Biche of the early maps is the body of water he named Itasca. Folwell, in his *Minnesota*, 1:116, concludes that Morrison's "claim may well be just, but the failure to make any report or record, and a silence of forty years or more, debars Morrison from credit as an exploring discoverer."

[41] This encampment was probably at Whitefish Point, the western limit of the great bay of that name.

[42] For an article on "Ramsay Crooks and the Fur Trade of the Northwest," by J. Ward Ruckman, see *ante*, 7:18–31.

We passed the Grand Sable and encamped about 5 miles distant from them on a narrow sandy beach, unprotected from the winds and waves. (The G. Sable extend nine miles.)

Wednesday June 21st. We experienced last night the most violent Thunder Storm I ever knew; our tents were blown down, our canoes carried from their resting places by the wind, and every person was obliged to exert himself to save the baggage from the impending destruction. Fortunately however nothing was lost or injured, though we saved the articles at the expence of our rest; and the sea ran so high this morning that we considered it imprudent to set out. we therefore waited until 11 o'clk when the waves having in some measure subsided, we ventured to launch our little barks and brave the rolling waters.

It is only 12 miles from LaGrand Sable to the Pictured Rocks, one of natures works of grandeur and sublimity. These rocks extend 13 miles, are perpendicular, and generally about the height of 150 feet. They are of that kind of Rock called by Geological men "Gra[y]wacke", which resembles sand stone, and is of a dusky white colour, it is easily worn and the action of the waves has caused as far as their influence extend, a succession of caverns, in many of which a boat of considerable size might be safely moored.

They are called the pictured rocks from the circumstance of their being variegated with the veins of different kinds of ore running through, and colouring the surface, and among these the carbonate of copper is most pleasing. On the whole, the natural colour & height of the Rocks, the numerous caverns, arches and variegations and the beautiful cascades which here abound, render it one of the most romantic and picturesque views possibly imaginable. The traveller is lost in amasement, and the insignificance of man is pourtrayed in the most striking manner. Near the middle of these rocks, is an alluvial flat of some extent, on which in a central location is a singular arch, which from its appearance we named the Doric Arch.[43] The French boatmen call it "Portail" "Arch". This is

[43] The fame, now somewhat faded, of the Pictured Rocks was extended by an account in the *Detroit Gazette* for February 16, 1821, which says that they furnish "one of the most astonishing and magnificent natural curiosities that can be found in this country. An intelligent gentleman, who accompanied Governor Cass in his tour last summer, describes them as surpassing, in grandeur, the far-famed Cataract of Niagara." The item concludes with a poem "composed a short time since by a young lady after hearing a description of the Pictured Rocks." The frontispiece of the Trowbridge journal is a view of the "Dorick Arch, in the Pictured Rocks of Lake Superior," clipped from the elaborate title page of Schoolcraft's *Narrative Journal*.

an arched rock, supported by two pillars on each side, of the doric order, and bearing on its summit very large pine trees — it may be about 30 feet high, and resembles at a distance the arch of a fire place, by which name or "mantle piece" it is generally known.

What renders it more curious is, that no other rocks are nearer to it than ½ a mile, and it is plainly seen at the distance of one mile from the shore. It is said by those of our company who have seen the Niagara falls, that the scenery there will bear no comparison to the Pictured Rocks.

Near the Doric Arch, Miners River empties its waters into the Lake. By this river th[r]o' a long and difficult route, a communication is had with the Mississipi River — it is not often used and may be termed an injudicious course.[44]

It is six miles from the end of the Portaille to Grand Island. This island lays about 3 miles from the shore and is 9 miles in length — it contributes, with the shape of the opposite shore, to form one of the safest and most commodious harbors on the waters of the west.[45] Vessells of any sise may ride here without the least apprehension from wind or waves, and the beauty of the scenery renders it an enchanting place.

As it had grown late we landed on the foot of the island and encamped: we had not been ashore many minutes before we were visited by ten or a dozen indians who had come to pay their respects to the great Father, as the Gov. is universally called by them. They were dressed in their best apparel, and one who spoke the french language fluently, and appeared from his dress to be a young chief, brought us the pipe of peace, and desired us to smoke. This was soon accomplished, and they then assembled around our flag where they danced and related their achievements in war, until we were heartily tired of their company. Their object was to get Tobacco & Whiskey, but we could not make them satisfied with a reasonable quantity and were obliged to send them away. They parted with many expressions of gratitude and attachment to the Americans, and promised to call on us again, which promise the[y] punctually adhered to.

Their music consists of a drum constructed of a hollow log and covered with the skin of the deer, and a kind of rattle made with the Hoofs of the same animal.

[44] This route extended to Green Bay, and thence followed the Fox and Wisconsin rivers to the Mississippi at Prairie du Chien.
[45] The harbor of the present city of Munising.

Thursday 22nd June. At 6 o'clock we parted with our friends, for so they style themselves, and continued our journey — nine miles from Grand island, in the bottom of a deep bay [*Train Bay*] La Riviere aux Trene or Sleigh River empties its waters. The Shore of the Lake on either side of Grand island is rocky, principally sand stone; near Sleigh [Train] river is another called Laughing fish River, a very deep stream, but only 12 yds wide and rises in a march [*marsh*] a few miles back. From every appearance at the mouth, this river is well named, for there were many lodges left standing and the ground was covered with the bones of the fish caught. Here we stopped to eat, and proceeded 18 miles to Chocolate [*Chocolay*] River, from thence 6 miles to Dead River both of which empty into a deep bay near presque Isle which is 25 or 26 miles from Laughing fish River.[46] The Country near presque Isle is very mountainous and presents a handsome prospect. About 2 hours before dark we landed on Presque isle near a small River, which bears no name.

Friday 22nd June. This morning we passed a number of small Rivers, vis: Garlic River 15 miles from Dead River, River St Jean, 15 miles further, Salmon Trout River 12 miles from that, and Pine River distant from the last 6 miles. About 3 p. m. it commenced raining very hard and we were under the necessity of landing at Huron River, which is narrow at the mouth, but widens to about 70 yards, above the bar which obstructs the entrance, and is very deep. These rivers are all too small to be navigable for larger vessels than canoes, and even they cannot be made to ascend a great distance, as they generally rise in swamps a short distance from the lake.

Soon after our landing we discovered the grave of an indian very handsomely constructed, of cedar bark and enclosed with pickets of the same: at the head was placed a narrow board on which was carved the figure of a Beaver, which we were informed was the sign or mark of the person buried there; and also several curious marks denoting the number of persons he had slain in battle. A Bow, dish and other necessaries for his passage were deposited with the body of the deceased.

Saturday 24th June. We left Huron river early this morning after passing a sleepless night on account of the musquitoes and a small gnat. This little insect is venomous beyond description — it is not larger than the head of a pin, and consequently nothing can be constructed to prevent them from committing their depredations. They crawl into the hair

---

[46] The bay is the harbor of the present city of Marquette.

and under the clothes, and every place they touch is instantly inflamed.

From Huron river we crossed a deep bay to Point au beigne or Cake-point, succeeding which is the bay called Keewenahneh, which is 12 miles wide, and from Cakepoint 45 miles deep; [47] from which point also it is 45 miles to the extreme end of Point Keewenahneh, make [*making*] the whole length of that Point on this side 90 miles. From Point au beigne we crossed to Portage River, (directly opposite to P^t au bene); during our passage across this bay the wind blew so violently that three of our canoes were obliged to return to the shore from whence they set out and remain until the next morning. Our canoe (The Gov$^{r s}$ had crossed before the storm rose) was very large and strong, though heavily loaded, and we were obliged to use our utmost exertions to enliven the spirits of the Voyageurs, who tho't of nothing but crossing themselves and going to the bottom. We succeeded however after buffetting the waves for 5 hours, during a part of which time we gained hardly an inch, in make [*making*] the mouth of the River, where we arrived in safety to the surprise of the Govr and his party. During our passage we kept one man constantly at work to throw out the water.

The Portage river like most others emptying into this Lake is narrow at its mouth but soon widens and becomes very deep. Here we landed & encamped for the night, and

on Sunday 25th June about 9 a. m. our canoes having crossed we proceeded up Portage River 6 miles to a lake of the same name which is 12 miles in length and 3 in breadth.

From the extreme end of this Lake the communication with the portage is by a very small and almost wholly artificial stream, the outlet of a swamp, the channel of which is so narrow, so crooked and so much obstructed that we found much difficulty in getting our canoes through. Our men were obliged to get out and wade in the mud up to their breasts, and it was only by dint of the most obstinate perserverance that we at last succeeded with our largest canoe.[48] The portage which is 1½ miles long leads through a swamp about ¾ m, and then the land changes into a fine high country.

At 7, we arrived at the Lake, where we found about one half of our

---

[47] The reference is to Point aux Baie, now known as Point Abbaye, a peninsula that forms the eastern limit of Keweenaw Bay.

[48] The cities of Hancock and Houghton are situated in this vicinity. The western section of the portage route, which the journalist terms "almost wholly artificial," is now in fact an excavated channel.

lading. The usual load on the portages is 2 packs or 180 pounds, but our Yankees cannot bear burdens so great.

Here Mr Schoolcraft found many very interesting specimens, one of virgin copper ½ a lb in weight, and a number of pieces of agate and cornelian, quite as beautiful as those brought from India. He tells us we shall probably find them abundant on the head waters of the Mississipi.

Tuesday 27th June. The early part of yesterday was taken up in transporting our lading across the portage, after which a rain commenced accompanied by high winds and prevented us from Setting out; but this morning we rose at 4 and with a fair wind embarked and steered for the River Ontonagon, one of the moving springs of our expedition, for here is deposited the enormous mass of copper so much spoken of in the civilized world.

In our passage to day we saw as usual a number of Rivers — vis, The Salmon trout, Grave rods, and Fire Steel — all small — at 2 o'clock we arrived at the Ontonagon a distance of 51 miles from the portage.

At the mouth of this river are five permanent lodges of indians, who seldom leave this place, but subsist chiefly on sturgeon which they take in great quantities.

There number is 60, including men women & children. Immediately after our arrival we were visited by the men of the village who welcomed us to their country, made some long speeches and presented as is customary the pipe of peace. The men had no sooner gone than their wives came, and brought us sturgeon in such profuse quantities that we could not do ourselves the pleasure to accept of all.

We learned that the mass of copper so celebrated is about 30 miles up the River, and our party this afternoon left us in two canoes with some indian guides, Mr Forsyth Mr Chase & myself staying behind to regulate the camp. We were anxious to accompany the gentlemen, but as it was absolutely necessary to stay and regulate the camp in their absence, we could not but lose the anticipated & so much wished for pleasure of seeing that wonder of the North western world.[49]

---

[49] Schoolcraft, in his *Narrative Journal,* 171, points out that this deposit "has been known from the earliest times, and is noticed by all the travellers of the region. La Hontan, Charlevoix, Henry, Carver, and McKenzie, have successively published accounts of it, which have served at various periods, to arrest the public attention, and to confer a notoriety upon the country, which it had otherwise certainly lacked." Following his visit, Cass wrote to Calhoun that "Common report has greatly magnified the quantity, although enough remains, even after a rigid examination, to render it a mineralogical curiosity." Cass to Calhoun, October 21, 1820, in Schoolcraft, *Summary Narrative,* 281.

Thursday 29th June. This morning, our party returned, fatigued beyond description and disappointed in their expectations. They ascended the river about 30 miles, nearly all of which distance they were, on account of the rapids and rocks in the river, obliged to walk, and over mountains too of immense height. When they arrived at the spot sought after they found, instead of a mass of pure native copper weighing from five to ten tons, a rock of the kind called *serpentine,* through which copper of a pure and maleable nature ran in veins. The greatest length of which is 3 8/12 feet, the greatest breadth 3 4/12 feet, and the average thickness 1 foot, estimated by Captain Douglass to contain 12 cubic feet & to weigh one Ton.[50] Thus ended all the marvellous stories we have heard about the copper mines of Lake Superior, which some have gone so far as to represent inexhaustible. Some specimens of copper were procured, but they were very small. The Rock bears evident marks of having been frequently visited, and the ground is strewed with old chissels, &c.

On this return the Governer succeeded in procuring a piece of [copper] the indians found on the bank of the Lake near this which weighed 7 pounds, and was perfectly pure.

The River Ontonagon is computed to be 120 miles in length, and is supposed to be connected with the Menomini, by which a communication is had with Green Bay — it is about 160 yds. wide, at and near its mouth, is very deep, & its waters, like those of all rivers emptying into Lake Superior, are thick and muddy.

About 6 miles from the mouth of this river the Indians have constructed a weir, by means of which they take all their sturgeon — it extends entirely across the stream, and on the lower side seats are constructed on which they sit with perfect ease, holding in their hands a long pole to which is attached an iron hook, and with this when the fish are dropping down against the weir, the[y] make a dexterous and sudden pull which fastens it in the body of the finny prisoner. This manner of taking

[50] Apparently by the time Schoolcraft prepared his narrative for publication, some of the disappointment which attended the finding of this ore was forgotten. He says that the rock was possibly "much diminished since its first discovery," but "notwithstanding this reduction, it may still be considered one of the largest and most remarkable bodies of native copper upon the globe, and is, so far as my reading extends, only exceeded by a specimen found in a valley in Brazil, weighing 2666 Portuguese pounds." Furthermore, "it is, indeed, notwithstanding the exaggerated accounts, a wonderfull mass, and viewed in connexion with the mineral appearances of the surrounding country, leaves little doubt that extensive mines of this metal exist in the vicinity. But to explore it with any degree of satisfaction, a week or a fortnight affords a very inadequate period." *Narrative Journal,* 176, 181.

their food, is peculiarly adapted to the indolent habits of an indian, and here they sometimes sit from morning till night imagining themselves if we may judge from appearancés, the happiest mortals in existence.

After they have caught a considerable quantity of fish they return to the village, where [it] is immediately delivered to the women, whose office is to slice and dry it for preservation. Every article of food besides these fish is esteemed by these indians as a luxury, for they are too poor to supply themselves with ammunition at the extravagant price demanded by the Traders and the wooden traps in which they sometimes catch wild animals, is a very inefficient mode of supplying themselves with food. They informed us that they were obliged to pay a Beaver Skin for a gill of powder, the same for a shirt, 3 do for a Blanket, one for 30 Balls.

The Otter is seldom taken here. From the mouth of the Ontonagon the Porcupine Mountains are distinctly seen, which rising in the south west and running to the very banks of the Lake, present a pleasing contrast to the low sandy plains by which they are surrounded.

Friday June 30th Agreeably to their promise and our anticipation, the indians of the village came over to our encampment, and amused us for a long time with their different dances, of which they have as many kinds as a modern french dancing master could find names for in all his vocabulary. They have the War Dance, which is, as we would say, the most fashionable, the pipe dance which is used only in peace, the Bear Dance & the Buffalo Dance, descriptive of their respective achievements in the chase. In one of these dances our attention was attracted and our affections excited towards a young chief, whose conduct clearly demonstrated to us, that greatness of mind, suavity of manner and filial affection are not altogether confined to the civilised world.

He made a speech of some length to the Governor, in which after apologising for his ignorance, and awkwardness of manner, he said, that he was the son of [a] powerful chief of the north; that his father had died while we was very young, but that he could distinctly recollect his earnest endeavours to inculcate in him the strongest affection and respect for their fathers the americans, and his advice to him never to go to war with any nation if an honorable way could be found to avoid it. That, he had always sincerely followed the advice of his father, that he loved & respected the american people; that he had shown many marks of fidelity to their traders, but that he had never received a single proof of their confidence. He then presented the Gov. with an elegant belt of wampum, which he had received from his father while on his death bed, and which had hitherto served to remind him of the advice & instruction received with it, and he concluded by observing that in return he hoped to receive something which would still serve to remind him of his duty towards his fathers the Americans.

His modesty and sense of propriety induced the Gov. to give him a medal and a flag; the latter he immediately attached to a pole which he prepared in anticipation and so long as we saw him he carried it, promising to sit under and guard it for life. The other indians after receiving some presents of tobacco &c returned to the village.

Saturday 1st July. This morning we succeeded in getting under way at four, well pleased to leave a place where we had met with so much disappointment and fatigue. In a few hours we passed the mouth of Iron River, a small stream, 15 miles from which is Carp River, which rises in the Porcupine Mountains. From Carp River to Presqu' Isle River is 6 miles, thence to Black River 6 miles. There is so much sameness in the sise and appearance of these rivers that a minute description of each would be unnecessary.

At 7, in the afternoon we landed on a very rocky shore, about 8 miles beyond Black River much more fatigued than interested with the events of the day. The Shore from the Ontonagon to this river is generally low, sandy, & thickley wooded.

We made to day 50 miles without wind.

Sunday July 2nd 1820. At 5, we left our encampment, and at 9 had arrived at Montreal River, where we landed for breakfast. this is 30 miles from Black River. About 200 yds from its mouth this river has a bea[u]tiful fall of 70 feet, over rocks, and directly below in the eddy a weir similar to the one on the Ontonagon is erected, which serves not only to facilitate the convenience of taking fish, but adds much to the scenery around. By the Montreal river a communication is had with Green Bay, tho' the difficulties attending the route are so great as to deter most traders from the undertaking.

After breakfast we continued our voyage to Mauvais or Bad River, 12 miles, thence 6 miles to Point Cha-goni-ma-gon.[51] This is a long sandy point, from which a bay runs in about 15 miles to the south; it is laid

[51] Chequamegon Point and its insular extension, Long Island, partly enclose Chequamegon Bay, at whose head the city of Ashland is located. Across the bay is the Bayfield peninsula, which was frequently confused with Keweenaw Point by early cartographers.

down on no map but that of Charlevoix, a french Historian who many years since was a missionary in this country. Directly opposite Point Cha-goni-ma-gon, and distant 3 miles, is situated the trading establishment of Monsr Cadotte on Isle au[x] Chené or Oak Island. This island is one of that cluster called by Carver the twelve apostles, but their number is much greater than he represented them.[52]

We landed at Mon^r Cadottes trading house or fort, (all trading houses in the indian country are enclosed by pickets) but we had not the pleasure of seeing Monsieur, he having sailed for Mackinac. The indians however were very well pleased to see us, particularly our old pilot Monsieur Roi, whom they knew; they fell on his neck and wept for joy.[53]

These islands form an excellent harbor for shipping.

After distributing a little tobacco among our indian friends we proceeded on about 5 miles and landed, having made 39 miles.

Monday 3rd July Got under way at 6 o'clock, and 10 miles from our encampment passed the mouth of Raspberry River, from which it is only five miles to another called Sandy River. Here we landed for breakfast, but the wind rose and detained us until

Tuesday 5th July at 1 p.m. when we embarked, and determining to make up lost time, we continued on till we had made 33 miles, when the fatigue of the men obliged us to land and pitch our tents.

Here we were much troubled by our little enemies the gnats which assisted by their allies the musquitoes made terrible work with our already vexed dispositions. Indeed we often wished ourselves out of the power of these tormenting little insects.

Wednesday July 5th We rose this morning as much overcome with fatigue as if instead of fighting musquitoes, &c we had been celebrating the birthday of our national independence, in the usual dissipated man-

[52] There are nineteen charted islands in the Apostle group, the largest being Madeline, Stockton, Oak, and Outer. Cadotte was probably "Kind-hearted" Michael Cadotte, one of the sons of Jean Baptiste Cadotte. Trowbridge appears to have erred in stating that Cadotte's post was on Oak Island. Doty and Schoolcraft independently state that the post was on St. Michaels, now Madelaine, or Madeline. The authentic map drawn about 1840 by Dr. Douglas Houghton, and now preserved in the University of Michigan Library, shows a "factory" on Madeline Island. The subject is fully discussed by R. G. Thwaites in "The Story of Chequamegon Bay," in *Wisconsin Historical Collections*, 13:397–425.

[53] This was probably Jean Baptiste Roi, who was engaged as a boatman and interpreter by the American Fur Company at Mackinac on July 8, 1818, and employed in that company's Fond du Lac department. He joined the party during its Lake Superior passage. His name is included on a list of "American Fur Company Employees, 1818–19," in *Wisconsin Historical Collections*, 12:166.

ner of carousing over a wine table — but the cause of our feelings was
far from "the feast of reason & the flow of soul" — (or the other feast
either.) However we left our encampment at the early hour of 3 a m,
and soone came to La Riviere Broulé, or Burnt River, 48 miles from
Sandy River, and a short distance from the mouth of the Fon[d] du Lac
River, which is the principal, and the last one I have to name, as emptying into this Lake on this side.[54]

About 2 miles from the mouth of this river is an indian village containing 7 lodges, and here we landed for the purpose of engaging the
indians to assist us in transporting our goods &c over the portage which
we expect to make to morrow.

They engaged to assist us, and we continued to ascend the River with
a fine wind, for twenty four miles, when we arrived at the Establishment
of the Am. Fur Company, under the command or charge of Mr Coti a
very gentlemanly frenchman.[55]

M Coti received us with all that politeness and respect characteristic
of the french in general and proffered his services to us in any way that
we might feel disposed to command them. We landed.

This is the principal establishment of the Am. Fur-Company.[56] They
have some houses built, and a few acres of land cleared, on which they
raise potatoes. We saw a number of cows, Bulls, & horses, [which had
been brought from Mackinac in batteaux.] [57] Each of the canadians here
(we saw 5) has a squaw and family, & they enjoy themselves if we may

[54] The Fond du Lac is now known as the St. Louis River. There and elsewhere the
explorers depended largely upon hearsay information relative to the river routes connecting the upper Great Lakes with the Mississippi and Green Bay. Despite Calhoun's
injunction to inspect the river routes, the party ascended only the Ontonagon to a distance of thirty-five miles. Possibly realizing this deficiency, Cass later proposed a second
and more detailed exploration of the inland routes by several parties to be dispatched
from the frontier forts. Each party should comprise, in his view, an officer and eight or
ten men. Cass to Calhoun, September 27, 1820, Department of War, Letters Received,
National Archives.
[55] This was doubtless Pierre Cotté, who was employed in the Fond du Lac department. That his position was one of some responsibility is indicated by his annual salary
of $2,400. See *Wisconsin Historical Collections,* 12:158. The name is spelled "Cotes"
by Doty, in *Wisconsin Historical Collections,* 13:202, and "Cotte" by William W.
Warren, in his "History of the Ojibways," in *Minnesota Historical Collections,* 5:381,
383. The latter refers to Cotté as a trader, on salary, for the American Fur Company,
and notes that he was employed earlier by the old Northwest Company.
[56] This post, according to Folwell, *Minnesota,* 1:104 n., "was on the site of the
present village of Fond du Lac" near Duluth.
[57] In the original journal, the passage enclosed in brackets was crossed out by the
author.

judge from appearances, quite as well as those whom in contrast with them we would term civilised beings. In fact it is dangerous for a man to live here unless he takes a wife, for the natural jealousy of the indians induces them to go all lengths, if he thinks his bed dishonered, to gratify his passion for vengeance.

On the other hand an alliance of this kind if with a considerable family in the tribe, gives the trader perfect security in his property and much influence over the nation.

The Fond du Lac River, or the River at the Extremity of the Lake, is for some miles above its mouth about a mile in width; it then narrows considerably, and at the establishment is only about 80 rods; its general course is west, tho' it is very crooked.

The length of Lake Superior, from Point Iroqouis, at the head of the river S[t] Marys, to the mouth of the Fond du Lac, is agreeably to our computation, which is made from the Voyageurs accounts, *484* miles.

Thursday July 6th We found on enquiry from M[r] Coti, that our large Canoes would be no longer serviceable to us, on account of the difficulty in transporting them across the portages: we therefore concluded to leave them and take smaller ones in exchange on the opposite side of the first, which is called the Grand portage of Fond du Lac.[58]

The indians about 30 in number, including their squaws, came this morning according to agreement, and we loaded our canoes, and set out. We carried all our baggage in the canoes for two miles, where we unladed, and the canoes alone were pushed up 3 miles further, while at the first landing place, the men commenced their difficult and truly laborious task.

The whole of Thursday, Friday and Saturday were taken up in transporting our Goods, &c across the Grand portage, and the labor was rendered much more unpleasant than it would have been, by a violent storm which commenced with our setting out; and in consequence of which the men, who had never been in the habit of transporting their goods and furs in rainy weather, murmured at what they termed their hard lot, to remedy which we were obliged, after having carried our own baggage across, to return and assist them with their burdens.

[58] To avoid possible confusion with the more famous Grand Portage of the Pigeon River, it is desirable to use the early expression "Grand Portage of the Fond du Lac." See Grace Lee Nute, ed., "A Description of Northern Minnesota by a Fur-Trader in 1807," *ante*, 5:32 n.

This maneuvre, while it facilitated the accomplishment of our task, caused perfect satisfaction in the minds of the men.

The usual load of a French Voyageur is about 180 pounds, or two packs, which weight they carry without great fatigue, through the mud, sometimes (as on this portage) up to their knees. But we found an astonishing difference between these men and our soldiers and indians, who seriously felt the consequences of their exertion, altho' they carried only about half the weight of the others.

The method of transporting goods is rather singular. The portage is divided into "Pauses" or resting places, distant from each other in some places a quarter of a mile, in others half a mile, the same being regulated by the state of the road. From the commencement, the[y] carry *all* the goods to the first pause, thence to the second, and so on. We supposed this to be a waste of time, and the Governor made a different regulation, but was soon obliged to abandon it, for we found little improvement could be made in the "ancient usages" of these men of the forest. They asserted, and it was satisfactorily demonstrated to us, that in returning from their usual short pauses, they were a good deal relieved from the fatigue of carrying to them, but that to continue with their monstrous burdens for three or four pauses, was an excess of exertion, and rendered them incapable of performing the same journey immediately. So that we were well pleased to give that part of the management up to the Engagées.

The Grand Portage is 19 pauses in length, which agreeably to our computation make about 7½ miles, and the road for the whole distance is very narrow.

Sunday 9th July. While the men were employed last evening in repairing the canoes, (which is done by applying a composition extracted from the young pine and boiled down to the consistency of pitch, when it is called gum. This is heated and applied to all the seams or openings in the boat, and renders it altogether impervious to water.) we delivered the presents promised to the indians for their services, and left a medal and flag for their Chief who is absent, with Mr Coti the Agent &c

So that we were prepared this morning to bid adieu probably for ever to the Grand Portage of Fon Du Lac. This we very willingly did about 7 o'clock, and ascended the River 4½ miles to another portage called La Portage aux Couteaux, or Knife Portage, so called from the abundance of Slate, which lays in perpendicular strata, shooting above the ground, and greatly incommoding the traveller, particularly the Voyageur, who is obliged to travel so often over it. Altho' we used all imaginable caution, we unfortunately ran one of our canoes on a rock of this Slate, which lay hid, (some of them only 6 inches under the surface of the River) yet imperceptible from the Black and muddy nature of the water.[59] Fortunately for us however we have an excellent guide in the person of Mr Defour, an engageé of the Am Fur Co, sent on to us by Mr Crooks with his express on Lake Superior. This man is a native of this country, of french & indian extraction, and I am convinced that without him we would find it dangerous to proceed, for our guides are destitute of that correct knowledge of every part of this country, which from his long residence here and his pursuits he possesses in an eminent degree.

There are many rapids between these two portages, and we were much pleased to see the expertness of these men in managing the canoes; sometimes in the water up to their necks, lifting them over rocks, and the next moment in the Boat, setting with their poles, to save our whole cargo from apparent destruction.

Contrary to the information received we found this portage not only better than the first, but tolerably good; and by one o'clock everything was ready for another move up stream, but as our men were excessively fatigued, it was thought advisable to devote this afternoon to rest.

We learned of M Defour, that the river above this portage is very rapid and difficult of ascent; that our soldiers are too unskilful to manage a canoe with facility, and that if some of our party could walk to Sandy Lake, it would be a great relief to the balance: we therefore made enquiries of Mr Coti respecting the practicability of such a jaunt, and he informed us that in the winter one of his men had travelled through in one day, but that the Country was interspersed with small Lakes, which we would be obliged to travel around, in this season, whereby the distance would be made greater, by one day. He told us however that he would send us two young men who had hunted in that country, from whom we could get better information, and who could act as guides, if we chose to employ them.

[59] Schoolcraft refers to this rock as argillite. "Some idea may be formed," he says, "of the singular appearance of the rock, by comparing it to the leaves of a book standing edgewise. The effect of this arrangement of the strata, upon the mockasins and feet of the voyageurs . . . has led to its name." See his *Narrative Journal*, 208. A good description is contained in William Johnston's "Letters on the Fur Trade 1833," in *Michigan Pioneer and Historical Collections*, 37:170.

Accordingly the young indians came, and after representing the country as very open and dry, and the road direct, said that we might travel it in two days at most; upon which representation it was resolved that the soldiers at all events should go, and as many of the Govr suite as would consent.

Mr Schoolcraft, Mr Mackay, Mr Doty, Mr Chase, Ryley Interpreter, and myself volunteered with pleasure, to undertake such an agreeable walk — and prepared ourselves with Knapsacks, & provisions for five days.[60]

Monday 10th July. At 5 this morning we took leave of the Govr & our companions, and set out for Sandy Lake, 16 in all, including the guides. We had not proceeded more than 6 miles, when to our great surprise the path ended, and we found ourselves at the edge of a horrible swamp, covered with water or mud, in which we sunk to our knees at almost every step. The travelling was more difficult on account of the trees which had been blown down in great numbers by a violent wind. Over these we were obliged to climb, sometimes to a great height and not infrequently at the risk of our necks.

We succeeded after a painful struggle, in getting through this swamp about the middle of the afternoon, but it was succeeded by another much worse.

This was of a kind called Tamarack Swamp, from the timber that grows in it, tho' we found very few trees of this kind here. These swamps are covered with water as the others, on which lays a thick moss, so tender that it will not bear the weight of a man. Consequently at every step we took we were entangled in the moss, and often prostrated headlong in the water.

It is only necessary to say that these two kinds of swamps continued

[60] The immediate objective was the post on Sandy Lake, southwest of present-day Floodwood in St. Louis County. This post, according to Irving H. Hart, "was the first enduring establishment of its type west of Fond du Lac on Lake Superior, and, from the date of its erection in 1794 to the close of the period of British occupancy of the region after the War of 1812, it was one of the most important fur-trading stations in the Northwest." See "The Site of the Northwest Company Post on Sandy Lake," *ante,* 7:311. The post maintained its importance for many years after the time suggested. A fur trader wrote, on September 17, 1833, that "Sandy Lake is considered as the central trading post, of the Fond du Lac department, from which clerks separate for Upper and lower Mississippi; and occupied by the principle trader. It is only for the above cause that it is occupied, and the clerks having always to rendevous at this place before proceeding to the Lake." But by 1833 the Indian population had so dwindled that "in point of trade the proceeds of this post, are the least in the whole department." Johnston, in *Michigan Pioneer and Historical Collections,* 37:173, 174.

alternately for three days, when on the evening of the third day we found to our inexpressible joy, a hunting path which our guides told us led directly to Sandy Lake. We could hardly content ourselves to lay down, so great was our anxiety to see the end of this injudicious journey. However, the fatigues we had endured, having been heightened by a heavy rain which had continued for two days to fall in torrents, overcame every other feeling, and we placed ourselves before a large fire, with nothing but our cloaks for a Bed & covering, and under the influence of patient dispositions, (which were now much more so than a few days before,) we received the rain as it fell.

On Thursday the 13ᵗʰ at 2 p m we arrived at the Lake, but unfortunately on the side opposite to the Fort.[61] We commenced firing our guns, as signals of Distress, but the indians who were at the fort became alarmed at so much noise, and refused to come for us. About two hours after we commenced firing a canoe approached us containing two men, and as we soon found them to be, white men too: A joyful sight! These were two of the Clerks of the [American Fur] Company, Mr Ashman and Mʳ Fairbanks; by them we were taken to the fort where we found a number of indians assembled to witness our arrival, a circumstance altogether novel to them, and as we had reason to believe, not a little gratifying.[62]

The Distance from La Portage aux Coutou to this Lake is about 70 miles by land. The timber in the first mentioned swamps principally cedar. We saw no wild animals on our route, tho' the tracks of the Moose and Bear, were visible in many places, and in one particularly, where the track made by a Bear, would with great ease admit the foot of a man,

[61] Trowbridge and his companions had followed what was known as the long portage between the St. Louis River and Sandy Lake, where the American Fur Company was occupying a post in 1820. The precise site has been identified as Brown's Point on the northwestern shore. Mr. Hart's study, *ante,* 7:311–325, includes a detailed map and plan reconstructed from descriptions and a few vestiges.

[62] Samuel Ashmun, Jr., and John H. Fairbank, clerks, who had been stationed at Sandy Lake since 1818, tell of the arrival of the explorers in letters written to a correspondent in Champlain, New York, on July 24, 1820. The letters have been published in the *Moorsfield Antiquarian,* 2:19–22 (May, 1938); film copies are owned by the Minnesota Historical Society. "After having passed 2 Month in solitude," writes Ashmun, "you may judge My surprize at seeing such a Brigade arrive. The Govʳˢ Suit consists of 7 or 8 Proffesional Gent Mostly from New York. They appeared Much surprized after so long a voyage to find a fort and Conveniences in this wilderness but More particularly Chairs and Beds." Fairbank reported that "the Governor is trying to make a peace between the Chippewys and the Soux," and referred to the brigade, using the fur-traders' terminology, as consisting of forty-five men including "11 passengers, the interpreter and cook."

These animals are very strong in this Country, and we are told that they frequently kill the largest Buffalo.

We passed several small Lakes in our journey, In some of which the water was transparent as crystal.

Immediately after our arrival at the fort we were invited [to] take supper; welcome news to us, for our provisions were exhausted before our arrival at the Lake. We found on the table a plate for each person, containing each a Boiled Duck and a large slice of Buffalo meat, dried in the sun.

The quantity seemed repelling, but we had learned to eat, as well as the indians, and we were astonished at looking at our plates in a little time, to find them all empty. The principal food of these voyageurs, consists of the meat of the Buffalo, and wild Rice, which latter grows in great quantities in this Country; and for these they are dependant on the natives. Buffalo meat is easily cured, by being cut in thin slices as soon as killed, and dried on poles.

The taking and curing of the Rice is attended with more difficulty — it is gathered by the squaws, who go to the Lake in a canoe, and while one manages the boat, the other with a stick bends down the Rice and beats out the young grain.

After a canoe load is collected they return to their encampment, where it is cured. For this they have two different methods, one by parching it in a kettle, the other by drying it in the sun, or on platforms over a slow fire. The latter mode, tho' the most tedious is yet the best, as the grain is much more nutritious than when cured in the other way.

It is threshed in a singular manner: This is by digging a hole in the ground, which after being lined with a moose skin, is filled with Rice, and then a man treads on it until the hulls are entirely off — a very laborious manner of performing this process.

Friday 14th July. Viewed the situation. The fort is situated on a point of land extending some distance into the Lake, and is very handsomely enclosed with pickets 25 feet high, and flanked by Bastions of the same height. It was built by the old N[orth] West Company, (who employed experienced workmen) and at the time of its erection was absolutely necessary, on account of selling liqour to the indians. It is now useless, the indians being perfectly peac[e]able in their behaviour.[63]

Adjoining the fort is a large garden under cultivation, but they suc-

---

[63] For a reconstructive sketch of the fort, see *ante*, 7:322.

ceed in nothing but potatoes, on account of the curiosity or perhaps the unrestrained disposition of the indians, who leave nothing untouched.

In the winter season one of these young gentlemen is stationed at Leech Lake, by water 300 miles distant from Sandy Lake, in a N. W. direction — Tho' it is supposed to be only 100 miles by land.[64] They transport no goods, nor do they trade much in the Summer and in the winter all their goods are drawn by Dogs, even to the most remote parts of the Country.

These animals are of a mixed breed and remarkably strong. Attached to a sledge peculiarly constructed for the purpose, they are capable of drawing a small outfit for trade, the baggage, and even the person of the trader; and they generally travel 60 miles in a day; but this is always on a hard snow crust, or on the ice. Generally two dogs are attached to each sledge, but sometimes three and even four. When travelling they are fed raw fish, which they take in the streams on which they travel. Even on this simple and unwholesome food they subsist and are capable of enduring great fatigue.

Saturday 15th July. This afternoon Mr Schoolcraft and M[r] Mackay who had set out yesterday to meet the Gov[r], returned accompanied by His Excellency and party — very much fatigued but all in good health and Spirits.

The Governor ascended the Fon Duc Lac from La Portage aux Couteaux 58 miles, to a small branch called the Savanah; which they also ascended 7 miles to a portage of 13 pauses or about 6 miles, after crossing which they found themselves on another branch of the *Savan* (which empties into Sandy Lake,) and only about 24 miles distant from the Lake. "La Portage du Savann" is much worse than either of the others, owing to the swampy nature of the soil, from which circumstance it derives its name.[65]

[64] The canoe distance between the two lakes is only about a hundred miles; an overland journey in winter probably would measure seventy-five miles. Fairbank wintered at Leech Lake in 1818–19, according to Ashmun's letter of July 12, 1819. *Moorsfield Antiquarian*, 2:18.

[65] This portage path was carefully described and mapped by Irving H. Hart in 1926, and in the summer of 1940 the trail was located, cleared of underbrush, and marked by Eagle Boy Scouts from Minnesota, Montana, and North and South Dakota. See Hart, "The Old Savanna Portage," *ante*, 8:117–139. It may clarify the present narrative to state that the section of the party under Cass traveled up the East Savanna, a tributary of the St. Louis River, and portaged to the West Savanna, an affluent of the Sandy River. Both this route and that followed by Trowbridge, Schoolcraft, and their companions are indicated on the map, *ante*, p. 138.

In descending the Savann the party were obliged to make two or three dechargés, or half portages,[66] and its general character is represented to be much the same with the Fon du Lac, on which they experienced wonderful fatigue; and in fact were obliged to get into the water and assist the men in their labors.

[To be concluded]

[66] Mackenzie offers the following definition: "The place where the goods alone are carried is called a *Decharge*, and that where goods and canoes are both transported overland, is denominated a *Portage*." See *Voyages from Montreal*, 1: xxxi n.

Reviews of Books

A Short History of Canada for Americans. By ALFRED LeROY BURT.
(Minneapolis, The University of Minnesota Press, 1942. xvi, 279 p.
Illustrations, maps. $3.00.)

Professor Burt is one of those inconsiderate historians who, having
written a book, leave the reviewer between the horns of a dilemma. He
must either lean heavily upon the publisher's blurb or make what mountainous errors he may of the writer's molehills. And that is a hard choice.
Even the most hardened reviewer shrinks from the charge that he has
been too lazy to read the book and therefore is reduced to quoting the
blurb. And, in this case the other horn of the dilemma is equally uncomfortable, because Mr. Burt has left next to nothing to cavil at. What's the
use of reviewing a book if you cannot pick holes in it!

It would be difficult indeed to find a man better equipped to describe
the history of Canada to American readers. Born and largely educated in
Canada, with the scholarly background and the experience of one who has
filled the chair of history in both a Canadian and an American university,
with knowledge of what the average American needs particularly to be
told about the story of his northern neighbor, with the advantage of several books in the same field that had already been accepted as authoritative
on both sides of the international boundary, and with the far from negli-
gible gift of a clear and agreeable style — how could A. L. Burt fail in
interpreting Canada to the people of the United States?

It has been particularly interesting to compare this book with Mr.
Burt's *Romance of Canada,* prepared for use in Canadian schools, and to
see how the emphasis has been shifted from one thing to another. Certain
matters are taken for granted by Canadians because they have become part
of their lives; but even educated Americans are often confused by their
recollection of conditions in Canada that had disappeared many years
ago, or that in some cases had never existed. Other questions, such as the
extent to which Canada has become completely self-governing by reason
of the Statute of Westminster, are made more understandable to both
Canadians and Americans by Mr. Burt's admirably clear and concise
interpretation.

Not less important is the light thrown upon the little-understood character of the French-Canadian habitant, both in the days of New France and today. He was, in the Canada of the seventeenth century, a very different person from the peasant of France, a well-dressed fellow with good manners, instead of a coarse and boorish rustic, and very far from servile in his attitude toward the governor, the seignior, and the church. "He was a typical farmer of the North American frontier, where nature made men free and equal by enabling all to become economically independent. A man who thus stood erect on his own feet and could look the whole world in the face was not likely to be a hewer of wood and a drawer of water for his church, no matter how much he might be devoted to it, and there can be no question of his devotion. Every Sunday, unless he happened to be away off in the woods, he went to church with all his family; and throughout his life the best and wisest friend he ever had was the curé. Yet the habitant was no slave of the clergy, as a glance at the history of the tithe will show."

Other characteristics besides an independent spirit, among French Canadians, may be traced back to early colonial days. The great Intendant Talon "encouraged early marriages and large families by generous bounties," and he taught the people to be self-supporting. He was able to report to the home government, "I am now clothed from foot to head with home-made articles."

Particularly commendable is the way in which Mr. Burt has handled a story that happens to be rather disjointed both geographically and politically. Without straining the facts he keeps in true perspective the relationship between east and center and west, French and English and New Canadian; and he succeeds where other historians have failed in doing reasonable justice to the history of the Maritimes and of western Canada.

Still, one must make some effort to redeem one's reputation as a hard-boiled reviewer. There seems here to be an assumption, in dealing with conditions in Nova Scotia in the latter part of the eighteenth century, that the sentiment of the people was decidedly sympathetic to the revolution in the thirteen colonies and that the Nova Scotians were "unwilling prisoners of British power." Does this not take too little account of the loyal element? Is there sufficient evidence that no considerable proportion of the New Englanders in Nova Scotia were loyal?

Also one is inclined to cavil at the statement, in connection with the events that led to the War of 1812, that the "impressment of men sailing under the Stars and Stripes was the British counterpart of the unrestricted submarine campaign launched by the Germans a century later, in that it touched American lives." Surely it touched American lives in a very different way. Indeed one had the idea that, so far as Americans were concerned, the impressment of men — assumed to be British seamen — found on United States ships was rather a matter of American *amour-propre* than of American lives.

In telling the curiously involved story of the international boundary Mr. Burt obviously could not find room for some minor details; indeed it is amazing that he has managed to get so much real meat into such a small sausage. One of these minor details has to do with the fragment of Minnesota that was cut off when it was decided to drop the boundary due south from the Northwest Angle to the forty-ninth parallel; and another was the still smaller isolated fragment of Point Roberts that became United States territory when the boundary reached the Pacific.

In contrasting the rival fur-trading companies of Canada, Mr. Burt rather gives one the impression that the Northwest Company was an organization of French Canadians, while the Hudson's Bay Company was Scottish. The canoemen were of course French, and so were some of the clerks, but the bourgeois or partners bore such names as McGillivray, Mackenzie, Fraser, McTavish, McLeod, Shaw, Grant, McKay, McGill, Macdonell, Cameron, McDonald, Finlay, Leith, Ellice, and Forsyth, and one finds only two French names, Rocheblave and Chaboillez.

The opinion attributed to the Hudson's Bay Company that the establishment of the Selkirk colony "meant that in a few years food might be produced there more cheaply than it could be bought on the other side of the Atlantic" may be correct, but one recalls the famous Parliamentary inquiry in which Sir George Simpson found himself in an awkward predicament when asked to explain two conflicting statements. He had just testified, as governor of the company, that the land was useless for settlement, being permanently frozen a short distance below the surface. It was pointed out to him that in his *Narrative of a Journey Round the World* he had described the country along Rainy River as an earthly paradise, and had become lyrical in his enthusiasm over its colonization possibilities. Now Simpson's difficulty was that he was suspected of having engaged the services of a literary ghost in preparing his book for publication, and he must now either admit that someone else had written his book or that his opinions as an individual and as governor were hopelessly at variance. As I recall the incident he tried to play safe, and convinced no one; but there does not seem to be any doubt about the company's policy to discourage settlement.

Also some students of the history of the period will not altogether agree with Mr. Burt's picture of the conflict between the Northwest Company on one side and Selkirk and the Hudson's Bay Company on the other. The villainy was not all on the side of the Nor'Westers, as witness the account of the death of Benjamin Frobisher in Masson's *Bourgeois de la compagnie du nord-ouest*.

Among the book's many merits is the really admirable collection of illustrations that the author has managed to get together; and the book is in other respects very creditable to the University of Minnesota Press.

LAWRENCE J. BURPEE

The Republic of the United States: A History, vol. 1, 1493–1865. By JEANNETTE P. NICHOLS and ROY F. NICHOLS. (New York, D. Appleton-Century Company, 1942. xvii, 638 p. Illustrations, maps. $3.50.)

The teacher of history is sometimes almost bewildered by the numbers of new textbooks that come to his desk at the request of those personable young men, the publishers' college representatives. Some of the books, one is inclined to suppose, were written hurriedly with the thought of royalty checks uppermost in the mind of the author. Occasionally, however, a volume appears which is delightful in its treatment of a familiar theme and which gives a timely interpretation to a well-known story. In the latter class is the first volume of this two-volume history of the *Republic of the United States*.

The Nichols' account of the history of our country is not in the tradition of Von Ranke, but rather it follows the pattern of the "new" history, exemplified, for example, by the volumes in the *History of American Life* series. Political and diplomatic history are not neglected. In fact, much emphasis is placed on the way in which Americans have learned to govern themselves; but the political aspects of the story have been interwoven with the economic, social, and cultural developments. The West and Southwest have received adequate treatment, yet in their desire to do justice to those sections the authors have somewhat slighted the East. The style is clear and readable, although it lacks the literary quality of that possessed by a Samuel E. Morison or an Edward C. Kirkland.

Justification for the volume is found in the interpretation given to the history, an interpretation of particular significance today. The emphasis is on "the reasons for, and the course of, the growth of this spirit of common endeavor," of democracy, of each citizen's responsibility for effective government. The authors feel keenly the value of the American experiment in self-government, and believe that a knowledge of its growth and the dangers that threatened it in the past will help insure its continuance and expansion in the future. The last sentence in the book is typical of the constant attention given the theme of the republic: "His [*Lincoln's*] idealized figure was to become symbolic in the national ethics, a force for the preservation of the democratic experiment."

The book is divided into three main sections of roughly two hundred pages each. The first, entitled "Creating a Society," covers the years from 1493 to 1763; section two, "Establishing Independence," deals with the period from 1763 to 1819; and the final section, "Multiplying and Dividing," treats of the years 1819 to 1865. For the benefit of the student and general reader there are introductory paragraphs at the beginning of each chapter, cross references to subject matter dealt with in different parts of the book, forty-one illustrations, and twenty-one maps. Selected references for further reading are found at the end of each chapter, and a reading plan and bibliography are included in the back of the volume. The appendix contains the Declaration of Independence, the Constitution, and tables of presidential elections and cabinets.

If the second volume of *The Republic of the United States* maintains the high level achieved by the first, the work will take its place among the best surveys of American history.

MERRILL E. JARCHOW

The Continental Congress. By EDMUND CODY BURNETT. (New York, The Macmillan Company, 1941. xvii, 757 p. $6.00.)

The annals of our Revolutionary period are greatly enriched with the publication of this volume. The reasons are not far to seek. Dr. Burnett has given many years of scholarly activity to the study of the Continental Congress. Under the aegis of the Carnegie Institution of Washington, he assembled the known letters written by the members of Congress between 1774 and 1789 and culled from them the more significant passages. These he edited with excellent judgment and meticulous care. Issued between 1921 and 1936 in eight stout volumes and equipped with copious footnotes and cross references, *Letters of Members of the Continental Congress* immediately became a major source for this period. That monumental work supplemented the meager official journal of Congress, cast a penetrating light on obscure transactions, and uncovered many a spring of human action. Most editors of documents, their tasks completed, retire from the field. Not so Dr. Burnett. In the volume under review he has used his unsurpassed knowledge to impart to the general reader, as well as to the scholar, the distilled essence of his researches.

In *The Continental Congress* the author seeks to "present the more significant phases of the drama called the American Revolution as they were enacted on the central stage." In Congress "most of the great actors in the drama played their stellar parts," and "many of the lesser actors ofttimes strode or strutted." Having long communed with the actors, the author describes their activities with masterly skill. The method is chronological rather than topical. There are no footnotes, but the curious can turn with little trouble to the basic source described above. The literary style is clear and richly interpretative. It is adorned moreover with touches of humor — delightful to the reader and especially so to those who have known the warm glow of Dr. Burnett's personality. This book surpasses anything we have hitherto had on the subject. If it is not definitive, the reason is that the subject is too vast to be treated in one volume. Six concluding chapters deal with the period of neglect following the Revolutionary War when the states were "wrapped in the deceptive mantle of supposed self-sufficiency" or preparing to try their fortunes under the Constitution. Dr. Burnett is convinced that the old Congress made a greater positive contribution to our governmental structure than is usually conceded. That he has projected a further work on this aspect is welcome information.

Clarence W. Rife

The Man Who Sold Louisiana: The Career of Francois Barbe-Marbois. By E. Wilson Lyon. (Norman, University of Oklahoma Press, 1942. xix, 240 p. Illustrations. $2.75.)

In the author's words, this is the "first full-length study" of Barbé-Marbois. Of particular interest to students of American history are the chapters on Marbois' residence in the United States from 1779 to 1785, first as secretary to the French minister Luzerne and subsequently as French chargé d'affaires, and on his role in the sale of Louisiana. Separate chapters are also devoted to his tenure as intendant in St. Dominique (modern Haiti), to his experiences during the French Revolution, and to his long service in the French government under the Directory and under Napoleon and succeeding governments until near the end of his very long life.

Marbois' prime interest in government was in finance. And it was in his capacity as finance minister to Napoleon that he handled the details of the sale of Louisiana. An interesting side light in this connection is the account of the arrangement Marbois made with the English banking house of Baring to take the American bonds floated to raise the purchase price; England and France were at war at the time. A moderate in politics, he suffered but one period of exile. And it is a remarkable phenomenon that such a public figure should have escaped the guillotine during the excesses of the French Revolution. His well-known honesty and efficiency as a financial administrator and a fairly well-defined sycophancy are the probable explanations. He was a convenient, servile, and trustworthy tool for any party or faction in power at the moment.

The book, well written and based on a wide study of sources in France and in the United States, is a distinct contribution to knowledge. But the absurd practice of relegating footnotes to end pages cannot be condoned.

CLARENCE E. CARTER

The Old South: The Founding of American Civilization. By THOMAS JEFFERSON WERTENBAKER. (New York, Charles Scribner's Sons, 1942. xiv, 364 p. Illustrations. $3.50.)

The moonlight-and-roses-on-the-old-plantation school of historians, suh, is destined to receive a shock when its members read Professor Wertenbaker's book. Long years of careful study have made the author more familiar with colonial Virginia than any back countryman who followed Bacon as he bore the torch of the Revolution, or any councilman crony of Governor Berkeley, could ever have been. Professor Wertenbaker knows the Tidewater, the Piedmont, and the Valley of Virginia. He knows the people and understands their speech. He knows how they planted their corn and tobacco, how they got their crops to market, what they got for them, and how they spent the money. In the same intimate way, he knows and understands Maryland and the Carolinas. His book is a distillate of long study and careful scholarship.

This volume's thesis is that the roots of the present South run deep into the colonial period. Neither the New South nor the Old was a unit. "No part of the country was more complex," says Professor Wertenbaker, nor "had a larger number of conflicting groups and interests." It was homogeneous neither in nationality, nor religion, nor economics. Slavery and the soil gave a superficial unity, but in the various regions the patterns of culture were diverse.

Professor Wertenbaker wastes no effort in pedantic elaboration of this thesis. Instead, he illustrates it in independent essays on subjects ranging from the intellectual life of the tobacco aristocrats to the development of colonial architecture, the western migration, the arts and handicrafts of the colonial artisan, and the ownership, use, and abuse of the good earth. These essays show no solid South, no cavalier migration, but a land of middle-class and poorer folk. Here is a penetrating examination of the extent of commercial and industrial activities of the Southern colonials. Here, too, is an excellent summary of the way the colonial land system worked to create a landed aristocracy and an unsound economy. And here, above all, is the best available survey of Southern architecture. In fact, Professor Wertenbaker believes that Southern architecture was the only contribution which the American colonies made to the fine arts.

The book should be required reading for all those who have been bemused by the folklore of the Old South. They will, however, probably ignore it. But those who would understand the complex forces lying at the foundations of American civilization will give the volume a hearty acclaim.

W. B. Hesseltine

The Coming of the Civil War. By Avery Craven. (New York, Charles Scribner's Sons, 1942. ix, 491 p. $3.75.)

Professor Craven has written an argumentative book, which invites an argumentative review. The author's preface is much more modest than the blurb on the jacket. Mr. Craven disclaims any desire to be included among "revisionist" historians of the Civil War and affirms that he has not been interested in defending or attacking any section. In his zeal to set forth "new findings" that upset "orthodox" or Northern interpretations, however, he becomes militant and lays himself open to the same sort of criticism that has been leveled against the "old school." He has been remarkably successful in capturing the spirit of the times by piling up a wealth of detail in "quotes" gathered from widely scattered sources. It all adds up to the "irrepressible" conflict, which revisionists, including Mr. Craven, have tried to prove was "repressible." Two chapters alone — "The Northern Attack on Slavery" and "The Southern Defense of Slavery" — furnish convincing testimony that the conflict was "irrepressible," humanly speaking, and historians have to do with human conduct.

In his quest for the explanation "why Americans only two generations away from the formation of their Union should have held positions so uncompromisable that only a war could alter them," Mr. Craven presents the familiar story of growing sectional antagonism in which slavery occupies the center of the stage. The familiar landmarks and personalities are there. No historian can escape them. Laws, compromises, resolutions, abolitionists, politicians, clergymen, journalists, teachers, and jurists are given a hearing. There are excellent accounts of political maneuvering and sparring, sectional crosscurrents, eddies of public sentiment, and sectional and political bullying. The author's treatment of the defenders of the institution of slavery, while critical, is more lenient than in the case of the abolitionists. There is a tendency to exaggerate the less intelligent antislavery propaganda and to find flaws in the personal lives of the propagandists and to slight levelheaded men like William Ellery Channing.

Why did the Wilmot Proviso, in which an insignificant member of Congress formulated the substance of the final form of the slavery controversy, stir the public and give sleepless nights to politicians? Mr. Craven guesses at Wilmot's motives, but that is beside the point. The important thing is that the member of Congress touched a vital nerve; and twelve years later the greatest American of all, who as an insignificant member of Congress voted for the proviso at every opportunity, gave it the sanction of his maturing mind in his prophetic "House Divided Speech."

In his discussion of the momentous Kansas-Nebraska Bill, Mr. Craven quotes with approval Douglas' vigorous and clever defense. The author thinks the "Little Giant" made a telling argument when he pointed out that Northern men had voted more than four to one against the Missouri Compromise and thereby accused Chase, Sumner, and Seward of playing politics in 1854, when they called it a sacred compact. The argument recoils on Douglas and proves, if it proves anything, that at the time Northern men were opposed to the extension of slavery. Where, then, was the inconsistency of Northern men in 1854 opposing a bill that opened more territory to slavery? The realistic old Texan, Sam Houston, as Mr. Craven quotes him, perceived that the enactment of the Kansas-Nebraska Bill would convulse the country from Maine to the Rio Grande.

Viewing the Dred Scott decision from the vantage ground of the present, Mr. Craven finds little in it to excite public passions. At its worst the decision was nothing more than "a fatal error of judgment." A fatal error committed at a fateful moment by the Supreme Court is serious business. Lincoln thought so at the time and continued to think so when he wrote his cautious inaugural address. Douglas thought so, too, when he tried to reconcile it with his doctrine of popular sovereignty. It is true, as Mr. Craven points out, that Justice Taney had freed his own slaves; but he went a mile out of his way to complicate the efforts of moderates in both sections to find a way to a better understanding.

These items have been selected from among several to illustrate Mr. Craven's interpretation of major issues in the slavery controversy. It is a bit unfair to make such a selection, however, because a book should be judged in its entirety. Let us therefore give attention to the reactions after the reader has laid down the book.

It is obvious that there were moderates and extremists on both sides; that the abolitionists were never more than a small minority; that secession was engineered and put through by a minority; but beneath the vituperation that gushed forth, and the conflicting economic and social differences, was the moral iniquity of human bondage, which the abolitionists never lost sight of. As compared with contemporary systems of labor — and the men of the South were fond of making this comparison — slavery does not come off so badly; but the South cannot escape the reproach of attempting to silence the prophets of a better day for men and women who toiled and who were given a hearing in the North.

Which section completely fastened slavery to the sectional controversy? Which section was blinder to the natural frontiers of slavery? Who paved the way for the sectional Republican party and its successful candidate for the presidency in 1860? What historian can justify the rashness of the secessionists in 1860-61, who maneuvered a minority president — a wise, calm, just, and charitable man — into a position where he had no course other than to defend the integrity of the Union and the authority of the government? The fact remains that the South seceded after the election of a conservative president, who had been cautious and moderate in statement to the point of exasperation from the radicals, and who continued to be tender of the feelings of sections and individuals throughout four bloody years.

Pearl Harbor should teach a lesson to historians of the Civil War: An act of violence can arouse and unite a people who had previously been divided by propaganda infinitely more subtle than that which was broadcast in the twenty years before the Civil War. "The old North Carolina soldier at Appomatox was right," says Mr. Craven. "It is a serious thing to love a country."

No truer words were ever written by a historian than were those spoken by Abraham Lincoln on March 4, 1865: "The slaves constituted a peculiar and powerful interest. All knew that this interest was, somehow, the cause of the war. To strengthen, perpetuate and extend this interest was the object for which the insurgents would rend the Union, even by war; while the government claimed no right to do more than to restrict the territorial enlargement of it."

GEORGE M. STEPHENSON

Papers of Edward P. Costigan relating to the Progressive Movement in Colorado, 1902–1917 (University of Colorado, *Historical Collections,* vol. 4, *Political Series,* vol. 1). Edited by COLIN B. GOODYKOONTZ. (Boulder, University of Colorado, 1941. xiv, 379 p. Portrait. $2.50.)

"When bad men combine, good men should associate; otherwise they will fall, one by one, useless sacrifices in a contemptible struggle." In writing these words, Edward P. Costigan was warning Americans that their cherished democracy was first endangered by assault from within. Between 1900 and America's entrance into the first World War in 1917 Costigan and his colleagues of the Progressive movement were conducting a vigorous crusade against what they felt to be a betrayal of the principles of democratic government. The scope, purposes, and spirit of this crusade are faithfully revealed in this collection of letters, speeches, legal briefs, and political manifestoes, culled from the Costigan Papers in the possession of the University of Colorado. In selecting the documents, Professor Goodykoontz of the university's department of history has aimed "to set forth Costigan's social and political principles, and incidentally to describe and illustrate the progressive movement in Colorado." This goal he has admirably achieved, and surpassed, for there are numerous letters with interesting information on Roosevelt, La Follette, and other

Progressive leaders. In editorial capacity, Professor Goodykoontz has supplemented the material with brief but adequate historical and explanatory notes.

Costigan's contribution to the movement during the period covered by these papers was largely educational. Defeated in 1912 and again in 1914 as the Progressive candidate for governor, he held no political office until his appointment to the federal tariff commission in 1917. As a speaker, organizer, and people's attorney, his influence was, however, considerable. Like Roosevelt, he was a college graduate, a man of broad culture, who spoke and wrote with charm and knowledge, and who felt keenly his responsibilities as a citizen. He was no excessively optimistic or shallow reformer. He agreed that there was little hope for "absolute relief" until human nature was "considerably altered, or very differently controlled in its expression," but he would not stand pat while democracy staggered painfully among its foes.

In his adopted state he found representative government "a jest and a contemptuous by-word among the officers, agents, and attorneys of certain large aggregations of capital." He believed that the "claim of necessary self-defense" by which special interests justified the corruption of politics was "rather a cloak to cover unjust aggrandizement." To meet the situation, to make civilization more humane, and to distribute wealth and opportunity more equally, Costigan devoted his energies to numerous issues. There are documents relating to civil service reform, the State Voter's League, the direct primary, the direct election of senators, feminine suffrage, limitation of judicial powers, and many lesser aspects of the machinery of democracy.

He was also interested in economic issues, believing that "economic justice, logically as well as strategically, precedes much moral betterment through government." In quest of social and economic justice he fought to protect the public interest in Denver utility franchises, to conserve natural resources, to secure fair railroad rates, and particularly to win more rights for labor. Colorado was racked with labor strife during much of this period, and many of the later documents of this collection are concerned with this problem. Costigan's position was clear: "Labor represents manhood, womanhood, and childhood. Capital represents machinery and earnings. Labor is therefore more important." The labor problems of Colorado were the result of years of denial of social, industrial, and political justice, which Costigan believed should be corrected through recognition of the unions, and just governmental policing of industrial relations.

Costigan's career did not, of course, end in 1917, but his later years have been covered in another volume of papers, issued in 1940 under the title *Public Ownership of Government*. Progressivism as a party program of national importance failed to survive the first World War and public preoccupation with international issues, yet a nation now engaged in a second World War to protect democracy may profitably remember the purpose and spirit of men like Edward Costigan, to whom citizenship in peacetime was a high responsibility.

WILFRED O. STOUT, JR.

The Minnesota Commission of Administration and Finance, 1925–1939: An Administrative History (Public Administration Training Center, University of Minnesota, *Studies in Administration*, no. 1). By LLOYD M. SHORT, PH.D., and CARL W. TILLER, A.M. (Minneapolis, The University of Minnesota Press, 1942. xiii, 160 p. $2.00.)

Fresh evidence of the strong movement to make government service a profession is offered in this interesting booklet prepared by the director of the public administration training center of the University of Minnesota and his associate.

In 1925 Minnesota viewed with pride the establishment of a three-man administrative commission designed to modernize the business of the state, to secure efficiency and economy, and to prevent corruption. Not all these results were achieved, primarily because the legislature was never very co-operative and consequently appropriations were usually inadequate; difficulties arose between the members of the commission and the auditor and, in the later period, between the members of the commission; the personnel division became a "central employment and patronage office"; and the organization was inherently weak in several respects, particularly in the lack of a complete budgetary accounting system. Nevertheless it accustomed legislators and departments to centralized budgeting and thus paved the way for further improvements incorporated in the establishment of a centralized business office under the commissioner of administration in 1939.

The authors show in some detail the long pull to secure efficient government and cite the effective help of such citizen organizations as the

League of Women Voters, the Minnesota League of Municipalities, and the Minnesota Taxpayers Association. Analysis of the work of the commission covers organization, budget procedure, personnel problems, and the administrative practices.

This publication is of more than historical importance; it points the way to better government in the future. Throughout the chronicle, but particularly in the concluding chapter, emphasis is laid on the necessity for efficient personnel, for selection of administrators who work together harmoniously, for adequate appropriations, and for a merit system to keep selection of employees out of party politics. The book will be valuable to students of state government and will evoke keen interest among citizens of the state.

GLADYS C. BLAKEY

Minnesota Historical Society Notes

IN PLANNING its twentieth summer tour and convention, which was scheduled for 1942, the society gave due consideration to the wartime situation, involving curtailment of travel and the saving of tires. Consequently the meeting was held near the Twin Cities, at Fort Snelling, and was confined to a single session on Sunday, June 14, Flag Day. The program, which was arranged jointly by the society and the commissioned and enlisted personnel of the fort, was appropriately built about military and patriotic themes. Attendance figures left little doubt of the appeal of these themes, for no less than twenty-five thousand people witnessed the ceremonies that preceded the program in the Field House, where a capacity audience of five thousand assembled.

The Flag Day celebration opened at 2:00 P.M. on the polo field before the marquee, which was occupied by officers and their wives, members of the society's executive council, and a few invited guests. Passing in review before the marquee and the vast audience that lined the field were companies of the Third United States Infantry, a regiment that has been closely identified with Fort Snelling for more than half a century, and the 701st and 710th Military Police battalions. In an impressive ceremony, the recently established 710th Battalion received a regimental color from Colonel Sidney Erickson, assistant chief of staff of the Seventh Corps Area with headquarters at Omaha. He represented the commanding general of the area, Major General F. E. Uhl, who was unable to be present.

The program that followed in the Fort Snelling Field House opened at 3:00 P.M. with a brief address of welcome by Colonel Harry J. Keeley, commandant of the fort. He called attention to the ties that bind the military post and its neighbor cities of St. Paul and Minneapolis, noting that the settlement of what is now a great metropolitan area began with the establishment of the fort in 1819. He mentioned also the pleasant relationship between the Fort Snelling authorities and the Minnesota Historical Society, as exemplified in their joint sponsorship of the Round Tower Museum. Colonel Keeley then turned the meeting over to Dr. Lester B. Shippee, president of the society, who presided. After noting the appropriateness of the fort as a meeting place for the society and expressing his appreciation for the co-operation of the men stationed there, Dr. Shippee introduced Colonel Erickson. He extended to the audience the greetings of General Uhl and announced that, as a native son of Minnesota, he specially appreciated the privilege of representing his commanding officer on this occasion. The importance of Flag Day in this year of crisis, in the midst of a war whose history "is being written in sacrifice," was emphasized by Colonel Erickson. He pointed out, however, that tribute is due to the Minnesota State Guard as well as to forces from the state in service overseas, to industrial workers and farmers as well as to soldiers and sailors.

After the playing of the *Stars and Stripes Forever* by the Fort Snelling Reception Center Band, Dr. Shippee called upon Brigadier General Harold E. Wood of the Minnesota State Guard for the principal address of the afternoon. Taking as his subject "The Shape of Things to Come," the speaker showed how the history of Minnesota and, particularly, of Fort Snelling is related to the war in which we are now engaged. His address appears in full elsewhere in this issue. The singing of the national anthem by the audience brought the meeting to a close.

Hundreds of the visitors remained at the fort, however, to visit the Round Tower Museum, where a special exhibit relating to the Third Infantry had been arranged by members of the society's staff. This regiment, which traces its history back to 1784, has been stationed with headquarters at Fort Snelling almost continuously since 1888. Among the interesting items on display were regimental colors, including a battle flag with the names of the battles in which the regiment has participated; battle streamers, also bearing the names of such encounters; rifles and other firearms typical of various periods in the regiment's history; a souvenir of its participation in the Mexican War of 1846 in the form of a wooden baton mounted with silver, acquired in Mexico City; a series of photographs illustrating the trek of the Third from Fort Sheridan, Illinois, to Fort Snelling in the fall of 1921; and four cases of manuscript records relating to the movements of the regiment. Copies of a folder describing the murals in the Round Tower were distributed to visitors. The pictures, representing episodes in the history of the fort, are the work of Richard Haines; the text of the folder was prepared by Dr. Grace Lee Nute, the society's curator of manuscripts.   B. L. H.

The society's secretary and superintendent, Dr. Arthur J. Larsen, has been granted a leave of absence to accept a commission as first lieutenant in the Army Air Force. He will leave St. Paul on September 16 and report for duty at Miami Beach, Florida, where he will enter the Army Air Force Officers' Training School.

Dr. Nute has signed a contract with Bobbs-Merrill and Company for the writing of a volume on Lake Superior to be included in that company's projected series on the Great Lakes.

Two life members, Louise T. Dosdall of St. Paul and William G. Purcell of Pasadena, California, and one sustaining member, Walter C. Coffey of Minneapolis, joined the society during the quarter ending on June 30. Annual members enrolled during the same period are Edward A. Boyden of St. Paul, Everett F. Collins of Coldwater, Michigan, Abbott J. Gould of Minneapolis, Frederick W. Lasby of Minneapolis, Ensign William N. Rom of the U.S.S. "Maryland," Nellie Sloan of Chisago City, and B. A. Webster of Mason City, Iowa.

In the first six months of 1942 the society lost three active members by death: Gertrude Ann Jacobsen of Minneapolis on March 3, Dr. Hallward M. Blegen of Warren on April 1, and Dr. Victor Nilsson of Minneapolis on April 7.

Members of the society's staff presented fifteen talks and addresses before audiences in various parts of Minnesota and the Northwest in the quarter ending on June 30. Mr. Larsen spoke on "Minnesota in the Defense of America" before the Lion's Club of Stillwater on April 7, on "The Historical Society in Wartime" before a meeting of the McLeod County Historical Society at Silver Lake on April 20, on "The Historical Society and the Community" before the Lake Pepin Valley Historical Society at Lake City on April 27, and on "The Records of the People at War" before the Fourth District Federation of Women's Clubs meeting in St. Paul on April 28. "The History and Natural History of Northeastern Minnesota" was the subject of a talk presented by Miss Nute before the Minnesota Bird Club at the University of Minnesota on April 8. She spoke also before the Minneapolis Audubon Club on "Birds in England" on May 1, before the Radcliffe Club of the Twin Cities meeting in South St. Paul on "Voyageur Land" on May 27, before the Zonta Club of St. Paul on "Bird Life of Minnesota" on June 9, before the Thunder Bay Historical Society at Fort William, Ontario, on "Radisson and Des Groseilliers" on June 29, and before the Fort William Rotary Club on the Webster-Ashburton treaty on June 30. At Bayport on April 29 Mr. Babcock spoke on "The St. Croix Valley in Days of Yore" before a meeting of the Washington County Historical Society; he gave talks entitled "Introducing Minnesota" before the Adrian Club of St. Paul on May 12 and before a Methodist ladies aid society at Crookston on May 27; and he spoke again at the latter place on the same day before the Polk County Historical Society on "Community Memory." Miss Jerabek attended the Silver Lake meeting of the McLeod County Historical Society on April 20, speaking on the early history and Czech backgrounds of the village.

CONTRIBUTORS

Widely known for his writings in the field of Canadian exploration, as well as for his services as Canadian secretary of the International Joint Commission, is Mr. Lawrence J. Burpee of Ottawa. His paper on "A Hundred Years of North America" was presented at Fort William, Ontario, on a program designed to mark the centennial of the Webster-Ashburton treaty of 1842. As a result of that treaty, Minnesota's northern boundary from the mouth of the Pigeon River to the Northwest Angle of the Lake of the Woods was defined, and the Arrowhead country, with its vast iron deposits, became part of the United States. Since the commission of which Mr. Burpee has long been a member deals with boundary disputes, it was peculiarly appropriate that he should represent his government on the Fort William program. Mr. Burpee has published numerous books and articles and he has edited the journals of several explorers and traders, including La Vérendrye. He has contributed to this magazine an article on "Grand Portage" (*ante,* 12:359–377), and several book reviews. In the present issue he is represented, in addition to his article, by a review of Professor Burt's newly published history of Canada.

Brigadier General Harold E. Wood, whose Flag Day address, "The Shape of Things to Come," is presented herewith, is an officer in the Minnesota State Guard. In the first World War he served with the United States Marines, and he had attained the rank of captain before his discharge in 1919. In St. Paul, where he resides, General Wood is known as a leader in business and civic affairs. Among the offices he has held is that of president of the St. Paul branch of the Foreign Policy Association.

The structures designed by a progressive Minneapolis architect of the last century drew the attention of Mrs. Muriel B. Christison while she was working as a graduate student in the department of fine arts of the University of Minnesota. Her paper on "LeRoy S. Buffington and the Minneapolis Boom of the 1880's" reflects her interest both in architecture and in the economic history of her home city. She received her master's degree from the University of Minnesota in 1941, and she is now a lecturer on the staff of the Minneapolis Institute of Arts. The second installment of Charles C. Trowbridge's journal of the Cass expedition of 1820, which has been edited by Professor Ralph H. Brown of the department of geography in the University of Minnesota, appears in this issue (see *ante,* p. 169). During the past summer, Dr. Brown has been engaged in field work in the vicinity of Park Rapids.

Eight writers, including Mr. Burpee, have contributed book reviews to the present issue of *Minnesota History.* Dr. Merrill E. Jarchow of the history faculty of the South Dakota State College of Agriculture at Brookings is the author of an article on "Early Minnesota Agricultural Societies and Fairs" in the issue of this magazine for September, 1941. Professor Clarence W. Rife teaches history in Hamline University at St. Paul. Since 1931 Dr. Clarence E. Carter has been engaged in editing the gigantic series of *Territorial Papers of the United States* now in the process of publication under the supervision of the department of state. Dr. William B. Hesseltine is professor of history in the University of Wisconsin and the author of a *History of the South* and other works in the field of Southern history. Professor George M. Stephenson of the history department in the University of Minnesota is a frequent contributor to this magazine and the author of several books in the fields of general American history and of Scandinavian-American history. Mr. Wilfred O. Stout, Jr., is a member of the history faculty in the University of Chattanooga. Mrs. Gladys C. Blakey of Minneapolis has collaborated with her husband, Professor Roy Blakey of the University of Minnesota, in the preparation of several books on taxation.

ACCESSIONS

A wealth of material about the history of the Third United States Infantry, which has been stationed at Fort Snelling almost continuously since 1888, is included in its archives, recently placed with the society for safekeeping. The regiment is known as the oldest infantry unit in the United States Army, since it can trace its origins back to 1784 and it was organized as the Third in 1815. Its records, covering more than a century of military activity, consist of twelve boxes of letter books, descriptive lists, pay rolls, muster rolls, printed army regulations, and other items. Included in the collection also are insignia, trophies, and flags. Records of service in many parts of the United States and in Cuba, Mexico, and the Philippines are to be found in these archives.

Photostatic copies of approximately a hundred and twenty-five documents of Minnesota and Northwest interest have been received from the Public Archives of Canada. They relate mainly to the period between the American Revolution and the close of the War of 1812 and afford information on the fur trade, exploration, boundary claims and disputes, the War of 1812, the Red River settlements and Lord Selkirk, Prairie du Chien, Robert Dickson, and such traders as Charles Chaboillez, Joseph Renville, John Macdonell, and William McGillivray. Included are a metereological record kept by a "Mr. McCrae" at "Lac la Mecam" in the winter of 1806–07, and a journal kept by William McGillivray in the Canadian Northwest about 1793. Fort William was named in McGillivray's honor.

Twenty-eight volumes of fur-trade records kept by Alexis Bailly at St. Peter's and Wabasha have been added to the collection of his papers already in the possession of the society by Mr. William H. Amerland of Wabasha (see *ante,* 5:61, 7:180). Daybooks, ledgers, accounts, inventories of goods used in the fur trade, and a few letters are included in this valuable collection, which covers the period from 1826 to 1851. Mr. Amerland also has presented a package of autographs.

A substantial addition to the papers of the Riggs family (see *ante,* 18:210, 444), pioneer missionaries in Minnesota and the Dakotas, is the gift of a grandson of the Reverend Stephen R. Riggs, Mr. H. S. Morris of Sisseton, South Dakota. It consists of 117 letters written from 1854 to 1883 chiefly to and by Mrs. Martha Riggs Morris, the donor's mother. She received many of the letters from her father, Stephen R. Riggs. In them the Minnesota missionary discusses such matters as his work on behalf of the Sioux, books prepared and published both in English and in Dakota, his translation of the Bible into Dakota, his experiences as chaplain with the Sibley expedition of 1862, and life at Beloit, Wisconsin, where he lived from 1865 until his death in 1883. Mrs. Morris' letters were written between 1854 and 1860 from Lac qui Parle, Hazelwood, and Oxford, Ohio, where she attended the Western Female Seminary. In a letter of June 9, 1857, she describes the ransoming of Mrs. Margaret Ann Marble, who was captured by Indians in the Spirit Lake uprising of that year.

Information on land speculation in St. Paul from 1857 to 1880 is to be found in four account books and a few business papers of Charles A. and Caleb Morgan, recently received from Mr. Charles Everitt of New York.

Manuscripts of speeches and addresses, account and memorandum books, diaries, and other items filling four filing boxes have been added to the papers of Senator Knute Nelson through the estate of his daughter, the late Mrs. Ida G. Nelson of Alexandria (see *ante,* 14:437, 22:319). Included are the manuscript of a valedictory address presented at Albion Academy on June 28, 1865, notes for an autobiography, and a diary kept on a trip to Alaska in 1903. The account and memorandum books cover the period from 1872 to 1920. With the gift are two albums of views of Alexandria and about ninety portraits and other photographs illustrative of Senator Nelson's career. Many costumes, medals, pieces of silverware, and other personal items also were received from the Nelson estate.

The reminiscences of John DeLaittre, banker, miller, and mayor of Minneapolis from 1877 to 1878, have been presented by his son, Mr. John DeLaittre of Minneapolis. They cover the years from 1832 to 1910 and include information on DeLaittre's lumber milling activities at St. Anthony; the state prison at Stillwater, of which he was an inspector for six years; his activities as a member of the state board of capitol commissioners; and on gold mining in California.

The activities of the Architects Small House Service Bureau, Incorporated, from 1920 to the present are recorded in thirty-nine boxes of correspondence and other papers presented by its officers. The organization, which began in Minneapolis and became national in scope under the control of the American Institute of Architects, provides standard plans and expert advice at low costs to the builders of small houses.

A note for one dollar issued by the treasurer of West St. Paul on March 4, 1859, has been presented by Mrs. Imogene B. Ossmann of St. Paul. She is a granddaughter of G. W. H. Bell, the first mayor of West St. Paul.

Objects illustrative of pioneer life recently received include a nose pincer used on cattle and a sausage gun, from Mr. A. R. Johnson of St.

Paul. Mr. Warren Pladsen of St. Paul has presented a machine used by his great-grandfather for cutting clock gears.

A carved mixing bowl of basswood, three feet in diameter, is the gift of Mrs. C. C. Bovey of Minneapolis. She has also presented an old-fashioned rocking chair, a number of bedspreads, and some pieces of early china and glassware. From Miss Georjeannie Hamilton of Minneapolis the society has received a number of handsome shawls, a hand-woven blanket, several bedspreads, some pieces of Chelsea china, and a number of other items.

A guest ticket for the Democratic national convention held at Denver in 1908, issued by Fred Lynch at the request of Governor John A. Johnson, is the gift of Mr. Charles H. Evenson of Minneapolis.

Epaulets worn by Colonel Josiah Snelling when he was a captain in the United States Army have been added to the military collection by Miss Marion Snelling Hall of Cincinnati.

An oil-burning stereopticon lantern with slides has been presented by Mrs. Edith M. Whitman of St. Paul, through the courtesy of Mr. Ira C. Oehler.

A white lace and georgette parasol that belonged to Mrs. James J. Hill has been presented by Mrs. C. E. Lindley of New York. A child's dress of wool worn about 1850 has been received from Mr. Frank L. Braden of Minneapolis.

Oil portraits of Dr. and Mrs. William W. Folwell and of Russell H. Heywood of Buffalo, New York, are the gifts of Miss Mary H. Folwell of Minneapolis.

Genealogies received during the second quarter of 1942 include: John A. Barksdale, *Barksdale Family History and Genealogy* (Richmond, Virginia, 1940. 634 p.); Glenn C. Barnhart, *Genealogical History of the Families of Orrin Henry Barnhart and Carra Cobb Barnhart* (Oakland, California, 1931. 44 p.); Jacob W. Bittner, *History of the Bittner-Werley Families* (Kutztown, Pennsylvania, 1930. 239 p.); Mrs. Elma Butler Gordon, *Incomplete Roster of Nine Generations of the Butler Family* (Albany, Missouri, 1941. 23 p.); Maurice L. Carr, *The Story of John Karr* (Avon, Illinois, 1938. 32 p.); G. R. Carter, *Joseph Oliver Carter, The Founder of the Carter Family in Hawaii* (Hawaiian Historical Society, *Genealogical Series,* no. 1 — Honolulu, 1915. 16 p.); Paul L. Clugston, *Clugston Genealogy* (New York, 1932. 25 p.); Michael F. Costello, *The Cook Family of Rhode Island* (Pawtucket, Rhode Island, 1942. 8 p.); volume 1 of Elizur Yale Smith, *The Descendants of William Edwards* (New York, 1942. 50 p.); Eva Turner Clark, *Francis Epes* (New York, 1942. 309 p.); Myrtle M. Morris, *Joseph and Philena (Elton) Fellows* (Washington, 1941. 404 p.); Alfred L. Becker, *The Ancestors of Nicholas van Vranken Franchot (Except Those of the Franchot Name)* (New York, 1941. 47 p.); Byron K. Hunsberger, *A Portion of the Genealogical History of a Few Swiss Hunspergers* (Norristown, Pennsylvania, 1941. 828 p.); V. Gilmore Iden, *Sons and Daughters of Randall Iden* (Mount Vernon, Ohio, 1941. 99 p.); Pauline K. Skinner, *The Lt. Moses and Jemima Clement Kimball Family* (Wilmington, Delaware, 1941. 152 p.); Roscoe L. Whitman, *Kline and Young Families of the Mohawk Valley* (Westfield, New Jersey, 1941. 68 p.); Irma L. Moorman, *History of the Lathrop Family* (Swanton, Ohio, 1940. 32 p.); Emily L. Noyes, *Leavitt, Descendants of John, the Immigrant, through his Son, Moses* (Tilton, New Hampshire, 1941. 354 p.); Walter J. Coates, *The Lee Family of Hounsfield, New York* (North Montpelier, Vermont, 1941. 102 p.); Grace M. Marshall, *The Marshall Family Tree* (Rutherford, New Jersey, 1940. 18 p.); Baldwin Springer Maull, *John Maull (1714–1753) of Lewes, Delaware* (New York, 1941. 241 p.); Spencer Miller, *Joseph Miller of Newton, Massachusetts* (New York, 1942. 62 p.); Robert D. Mowry, *The Descendants of Augustus Mowry, 1784–1941* (Chicago, 1942. 94 p.); William B. Mowry, *A History of the Mowry Family of Pittsburgh* (Pittsburgh, 1941. 61 p.); George M. Pearson, *Benjamin and Esther (Furnas) Pearson* (Los Angeles, 1941. 538 p.); James Oscar Prude, *An Historical and Genealogical Record of the Prude and McAdory Families* (Tuscaloosa, Alabama, 1937. 328 p.); *Famille Alexis Reau* (Three Rivers, Quebec, 1923. 69 p.); Alfred Andrews Starbird, *Ancestors and Descendants of Winfield Scott Starbird and Emeline Hardy (Roberts) Starbird* (Burlington, Vermont, 1941. 61 p.); and *A Genealogy of the Wilder Family of Hawaii* (Hawaiian Historical Society, *Genealogical Series,* no. 2 — Honolulu, 1916. 7 p.).

Three recently received genealogies that include material on Minnesota residents are Evangeline L. Halleck, *Descendants of George Linn* (Ann Arbor, Michigan, 1941. 220 p.); Edmund J. Longyear, *The Descendants of Jacob Longyear of Ulster County, New York* (New

Haven, Connecticut, 1942. 622 p.); and Bonnelle William Rhamy, *The Remy Family in America, 1650–1942* (Fort Wayne, Indiana, 1942. 492 p.).

Volume 2 of the *American Genealogical Index* (Middletown, Connecticut, 1942) is now available in the society's library. In it surnames from Anthony to Barows are indexed. Other useful compilations acquired recently are *Montgomery County Soldier Dead* (Crawfordsville, Indiana, 1941. 23 p.), with a revision corrected to May, 1942; volume 26 of the *Lineage Book* of the Daughters of Founders and Patriots of America (West Somerville, Massachusetts, 1940. 429 p.); *A First Supplement to the 1922 Index of Ancestors and Roll of Members of the General Society of Colonial Wars* (Hartford, 1941. 2 vols.); and volume 2 of the *National Register* of the Sons of the American Revolution (New York, 1902. 428 p.). Genealogists also will be interested in an *Index to the Vermonter, 1914 through 1939* (Montpelier, Vermont, 1941. 108 p.).

Those working in the field of Canadian genealogy will find useful a recent compilation by Pierre-Georges Roy, *Inventaire des testaments, donations et inventaires du regime francais conservés aux archives judiciaires de Quebec* (Quebec, 1941. 3 vols.), and Antoine Roy's extensive "Bibliographie de généalogies et histoires de familles," which appears in the *Rapport* for 1940–41 of the archivist of the province of Quebec (p. 95–332). Other bibliographies received include *Genealogical Material and Local Histories in the St. Louis Public Library* (St. Louis, 1941. 219 p.) by Georgia Gambrill, and *An Index of the Source Records of Maryland* (Baltimore, 1940. 478 p.) by Eleanor P. Passano.

Ten states are represented in the local histories and source materials of value to genealogists added to the library during the second quarter. Publications about the New England states include four pamphlets by Grace M. Limeburner issued under the title *Vital Statistics of Surry, Bluehill, Brooksville, Sedgwick, Maine* (North Brooksville, 1942); Henrietta D. Wood, *Early Days of Norridgewock* (Skowhegan, Maine, 1941. 124 p.); *Vital Records of Ashfield, Massachusetts to the Year 1850* (Boston, 1942. 273 p.); Massachusetts Historical Records Survey, *History of the Town of Ashland* (Framingham, Massachusetts, 1942. 141 p.); Danvers Historical Society, *Collections*, vol. 30 (Danvers, Massachusetts, 1942. 96 p.); *The History of South Congregational Church, Springfield, Massachusetts, 1842–1942* (Springfield, 1942. 134 p.); Edward T. Fairbanks, *The Town of St. Johnsbury, Vermont* (St. Johnsbury, 1914. 592 p.); C. E. Harris,

A Vermont Village (Yarmouthport, Massachusetts, 1941. 105 p.); and Carrie K. Harvey, *History of Bristol, Vermont, 1762–1940* (115 p.). Other eastern states are represented by Annie Walker Burns, *Maryland Genealogies and Historical Recorder,* vols. 5–6 (Washington, 1942); Maryland Historical Society, *Archives of Maryland,* vol. 58 (Baltimore, 1941. 614 p.); Annie Walker Burns, *Kentucky Genealogies and Historical Recorder,* vol. 2 (Washington, 1942); James D. Magee, *Bordentown, 1682–1932* (Bordentown, New Jersey, 1932. 145 p.); William C. Mulford, *Historical Tales of Cumberland County, New Jersey* (Bridgton, New Jersey, 1941. 197 p.); Cornelia F. Bedell, *Now and Then and Long Ago in Rockland County, New York* (Suffern, New York, 1941. 368 p.); Raymond T. Sant, *Fair Haven Folks and Folklore* (Red Creek, New York, 1941. 145 p.); Ethelyn Weller, *North Collins Remembers* (Gowanda, New York, 1941. 42 p.); Harold D. Eberlein, *Historic Houses of the Hudson Valley* (New York, 1942. 208 p.); *The Biographical Encyclopaedia of Pennsylvania* (Philadelphia, 1874. 672 p.); Harold D. Eberlein, *Philadelphia, 1670–1838* (Philadelphia, 1939. 580 p.); George MacReynolds, *Place Names in Bucks County, Pennsylvania* (Doylestown, 1942. 474 p.); *The Huguenot,* no. 10, 1939–41, issued by a Huguenot society of Virginia (171 p.); and Millard K. Bushong, *History of Jefferson County, West Virginia* (Charlestown, West Virginia, 1941. 438 p.).   E. J.

News and Comment

IF "AMERICAN INSTITUTIONS are worth fighting for abroad, they are certainly worth working for at home," writes Richard L. Beyer in an article on "The Historical Society in War Time" in the *Journal* of the Illinois State Historical Society for June. He believes that "the home front would be guilty of gross neglect if it refused to preserve in America those very institutions and ways that our boys have gone all the way to Australia, Burma, Iceland, the British Isles and other distant places to defend." Dr. Beyer reminds his readers that if we are fighting to defend our way of life and preserve our culture, it is important to maintain and strengthen our historical societies, for they not only take "high rank among the cultural institutions that have helped to make America what it is," but their activities "are concerned with . . . the past, the knowledge of which fosters national pride and contributes to better citizenship." The writer suggests that "instead of retreating in the present crisis, the historical society "might well multiply its activities" by sponsoring "exhibits, patriotic lectures, and radio broadcasts," publishing "literature that will influence all elements in this nation," collecting and preserving records of the present conflict, and sponsoring "programs devised to assist newcomers," especially enlisted men and workers in defense industries, "in adjusting themselves to their unfamiliar environment."

A similar theme was stressed by L. Hubbard Shattuck, director of the Chicago Historical Society, in a stimulating address on "Wartime Duties of Historical Museums" presented before a meeting of the American Association of Museums at Williamsburg, Virginia, on May 18. "To bring before our people in a vital and convincing manner the virtues as well as the failures of the past is the important task which confronts our historical museums today," said the speaker. That "it is our responsibility to educate donors as well as visitors" was only one of the concrete and useful suggestions made by Mr. Shattuck. Most museum visitors today, he said, "are not easily impressed by some objects just because they have been associated with pleasing but unimportant persons or events." He asserted that we must accept the changes wrought by the world crisis "in the spirit of true pioneers," and must "interpret our museums in the light of this changing world."

Since "libraries, archival institutions, and museums have important functions to fulfill in connection with a nation's war effort, both from an immediately practical standpoint and from the long-range point of view as aids in the maintenance of national morale," it is of utmost importance that "every effort should be made to keep holdings available," according to a booklet recently issued by the National Resources Planning Board. It bears the title *The Protection of Cultural Resources against the Hazards of War: A Preliminary Handbook,* and it was prepared by the Committee on Conservation of Cultural Resources (Washington, 1942. 46 p.). "The Role of Libraries, Museums, and Archival Agencies in Wartime" is the theme of the opening chapter. Others deal with the hazards to which cultural resources are exposed in wartime, the classification of materials and the selection of those calling for special protection, methods of protecting buildings in which cultural resources are housed, the protection of collections in such buildings, and the removal of collections when necessary, with suggestions as to the selection of depositories and methods of packing, transportation, and storage. In his introduction, Dr. Waldo G. Leland, chairman of the committee, announces that it "has initiated a survey of space suitable for the temporary deposit of cultural material removed from areas of danger," and that it "will be glad to give any assistance it can by way of information or advice toward the protection of cultural materials in the possession of any person or institution." The booklet, which contains many useful suggestions for both state and local historical leaders, may be purchased from the superintendent of documents at Washington for ten cents.

In an address on "History for the People" presented before the Pennsylvania Federation of Historical Societies at Harrisburg on April 10, 1941, and recently published as a pamphlet, C. C. Crittenden contends that "In planning a broad program of history for the people, we must realize that our greatest opportunity lies in the field of local history." He believes that "Nowhere is the current popular interest in history more real than in the local field," and that "for arousing and maintaining the interest of the masses of the people there is nothing like the history of one's immediate locality." He discusses some of the many things we can do in developing a program of history for the people, such as preserving physical remains, marking historic sites, conducting programs of archaeological work, establishing and maintaining museums, collecting and preserving written and printed sources, writing and publishing community histories, and holding meetings and conferences. "Just as local self-government must be the foundation of the democratic state," Dr. Crittenden concludes, "so local historical interest and activity must be the chief means of support of a general, popular historical program."

"Archaeology enables us to visualize the Greeks and the Romans of classical times — to see them and their lives reflected in other than literary creations, in their pictorial and plastic art, their temples and houses, their furniture and jewels." Thus writes Professor M. Rostovtzeff in an article explaining "How Archaeology Aids History," which appears in the *Yale Review* for June. The writer draws his examples from the field of ancient history and the classical world with which he is familiar, but many of his remarks may well be applied to Midwest America, and more specifically to Minnesota, where such sites as Grand Portage and Fort Ridgely have been excavated by archaeologists in recent years. "Every turn of the spade on well-chosen sites will bring new facts to light that will open new vistas and pose new problems to the historian," suggests Professor Rostovtzeff. In the study of Minnesota as well as of Hellas, it is the historian's "duty to register these facts, to co-ordinate them, to grasp their meaning, and out of them to build the lofty and well-balanced edifice which we call history."

A brief article on "Jacques de Noyon: nouveaux détails sur sa carrière" by E.-Z. Massicotte, appearing in the *Bulletin des recherches historiques* for April, is of interest to students of Minnesota exploration, for it tells the facts — many of them newly discovered — of the career of the earliest known explorer in the Minnesota country. He made his first voyage into the interior in 1688, and a document written thirty years later shows that he got at least to the Lake of the Woods and probably to Lake Winnipeg. In 1690 De Noyon was engaged for a fur trading expedition, and three years later he was one of twelve voyageurs leaving for "the Ottawa" under the direction of Pierre le Sueur. Since the latter was in the Minnesota country shortly afterward, it is fairly certain that De Noyon was there also. The author has found references to De Noyon in court records, he notes the record of his marriage, and in at least one instance he finds evidence of the explorer's whereabouts in the record of the birth of one of his children. De Noyon left for Detroit in 1704, and for many years thereafter he probably was in the interior on trading and military expeditions.

G. L. N.

"Did Daniel Defoe base his immortal story 'Robinson Crusoe' on the true adventures of one of Canada's most famed explorers — Pierre Radisson?" This question is raised and discussed by R. T. Byers in the *Montreal Standard* for July 4, which presents an article entitled "Was Radisson Robinson Crusoe?" The writer points out a number of similarities between Radisson's narrative and Defoe's tale.

In an interesting article on "Voyageur Songs," which appears in the June number of the *Beaver*, Marius Barbeau points out the fact that "these vocal compositions were first of all working songs. Their function consisted in marking the motion of the many paddles in the water and sustaining the energy of the canoemen throughout their tiring journeys in the wilderness." The author quotes the remarks penned by some of the early chroniclers after hearing these songs, and he notes that they were impressed not only by the "length and usefulness of the songs," but by "their genuine musical quality." He groups the voyageur songs under several classifications and quotes both the music and the words of a few typical examples. In the same issue of the *Beaver* the process of making the "Birch Bark Canoe" is described by Lynus R. Pattee, who illustrates his text with a series of fourteen photographs.

A charming narrative of "Audubon's 'Journey up the Mississippi' " to the frontier river settlements of Missouri in 1810 has been provided with an introduction and annotations by John Francis McDermott and published in the *Journal* of the Illinois State Historical Society for June. Professor McDermott, who frequently contributes articles and reviews to *Minnesota History*, found this account of Audubon's first visit to the Mississippi in a rare annual for 1829 known as *The Winter's Wreath*. A description of a hunting trip with the Indians east of the river in Illinois and Tennessee is included in the narrative. Among other interesting contributions to this issue of the *Journal* are a discussion by Jay Monaghan of the question, "Did Abraham Lincoln Receive the Illinois German Vote?", a history of the Northwestern Female College at Evanston by Dwight F. Clark, and a review of the "Unique Career of an Illinois Musician," Albert M. Bagby, by Lorene Martin.

The contributions of scientists, including physicians, to the exploration and opening of the frontier Northwest were discussed by Dean Theodore C. Blegen of the graduate school in the University of Minnesota before a meeting of Sigma Xi at the Mayo Clinic, Rochester, on April 9. Dr. Blegen, who was formerly superintendent of the Minnesota Historical Society, reviewed the exploits of such exploring scientists as David Thompson, Dr. John McLoughlin, and Joseph N. Nicollet.

The influence of N. P. Langford of St. Paul upon the "Governmental Exploration of the Upper Yellowstone, 1871," is brought out by W. Turrentine Jackson in the *Pacific Historical Review* for June. Langford is described as an "outstanding member and diarist" of the Washburn-Doane expedition of 1870. His lecture tour in the East in the early months of 1871 was, according to Mr. Jackson, part of a "vigorous promotional scheme" planned by members of the 1870 expedition, who "desired an official governmental exploration in 1871 to confirm their discoveries." The resulting expedition under Professor F. V. Hayden, a trained geologist, is the subject of the present article.

"The First Winter Trip through Yellowstone National Park" is described in the *Annals of Wyoming* for April by Jack Ellis Haynes, whose father, F. Jay Haynes of St. Paul, was the official photographer for the party that made the hazardous journey in January, 1887. Five of the thirty-five photographs made at that time are reproduced with Mr. Haynes's article.

"Captain Fisk's Expedition from Minnesota to Fort Benton and Bannack City in 1863" is the subject of an extended article in the *Rocky Mountain Husbandman* of Great Falls, Montana, for May 14. A detailed account of the journey from St. Cloud westward is presented, and meetings with Red River hunters, Indians, and gold hunters are noted. When the party reached Bannack City, it was greeted by two former Minnesotans, N. P. Langford and James Fergus.

A collection of *Legends of the Mighty Sioux* has been compiled by workers engaged in the South Dakota Writers' Project of the WPA and published in a volume intended for youthful readers (1941.   158 p.). The opening sections deal with the "Land of the Sioux" and with their social life and customs. The legends are grouped under several headings — "Traditional Lore," "Campfire Tales," "Legends of Places," and "Hunting and Battle Stories." Many of the stories here recorded were recited in the original Dakota tongue by reservation Indians.

Under the title "The Frontier and American Institutions," George Wilson Pierson presents "A Criticism of the Turner Theory" in the *New England Quarterly* for June. He poses the question, "How much of Frederick Jackson Turner's frontier hypothesis is reliable and useful today?", asserting that "this problem has begun to trouble economists, sociologists, geographers," and historians. Mr. Pierson believes that "frontier legends of one kind or another have now so permeated American thought as to threaten drastic consequences," and he contends that "in what it proposes, the frontier hypothesis needs painstaking revision."

A booklet entitled *Some Landmarks in the History of the Department of Agriculture,* by T. Swann Harding, has been issued by the United States department of agriculture as number 2 of its *Agricultural History Series* (1942. 94 p.). Several pages are devoted to the services as commissioner of agriculture from 1877 to 1880 of William G. Le Duc of St. Paul. The establishment in 1879 of a veterinary division "to carry out fully the work on animal diseases" is noted, and credit is given to Le Duc for emphasizing the importance of food and drug regulation by his department.

A biography of *John S. Wright, Prophet of the Prairies,* by Lloyd Lewis, has been published by the Prairie Farmer Publishing Company of Chicago to mark the centennial of the founding of the *Prairie Farmer* by Wright (1941. 215 p.). The files of this pioneer agricultural periodical reflect the history of western agriculture. Reproduced in the volume are many interesting illustrations that appeared originally in the periodical.

"Conflicting Trends in the Populist Movement" are analyzed and discussed by Harlan R. Crippen in the spring issue of *Science & Society.* The writer contends that "The populist movement has been interpreted and 'defined' in almost as many differing fashions as there have been historians," and that the "significance of the agrarian unrest of the last decades of the nineteenth century is still a matter of controversy." He divides Populism into "three categories, namely wheat-belt Populism, southern Populism and western Populism," giving his attention chiefly to the first of these categories, since he believes that "Populism developed most clearly, and advanced farthest, in the wheat-belt states of Kansas, Nebraska, North and South Dakota." Agrarian unrest died down in these areas after 1900, according to Mr. Crippen, who notes that "It rose again with the

organization in the Dakotas and Minnesota of the Non-Partisan League."
In the latter state, he points out, the league "made little headway until it
entered into an open political alliance with labor, forming the Farmer-
Labor party."

"Food habits certainly should be as worthy of record as many other
social, economic, or political aspects of our history," writes Richard Osborn
Cummings in the preface to his recent book on *The American and His
Food: A History of Food Habits in the United States* (Chicago, 1941).
The author's discovery that a "systematic account of food habits during
the past century was lacking" led him to prepare this volume, which could
well serve as a guide for interesting and valuable local studies. The influence upon the food habits and physical welfare of Americans of the introduction of the middlings purifier in the Minneapolis mills of the early
1870's is discussed in a chapter entitled "An Indefinable Loss." "As white
flour and white sugar rolled like a flood over the land, the nutritive value
of the diet of millions changed," writes Mr. Cummings, for the "refining
of sugar and flour . . . meant the subtraction of qualities which had
formerly been present in customary food."

In the introduction to a recent volume entitled *The Story of Everyday
Things* (New York, 1942.   428 p.), Arthur Train, Jr., defines his subject
as "really the story of houses, furniture, food, clothes, transportation and
communication," adding that "it is also, to a certain extent, the story of
agriculture, handicraft, and industry, community life and the life of the
intellect, and amusements." The arrangement of the volume is chronological, with a prologue dealing with Indian life, and sections on the seventeenth, eighteenth, and nineteenth centuries. Much of the narrative deals
with the eastern seaboard, and there are only occasional references to the
Middle West. In discussing libraries in community life, for example, Mr.
Train notes that "Children were served along with adult readers until
1889 when the Minneapolis Public Library set aside a shelf with books
for minors and three years later gave them a room of their own."

A new arrival among state historical magazines is the *Arkansas Historical Quarterly,* the first number of which was published in March. It
opens with a review of historical work of the past in Arkansas and an
appeal for the preservation of material relating to the history of the state —
archives, personal papers, newspapers, and museum items. "Such material

should be preserved and made available to people engaged in research work," writes the editor. He suggests that "county historical societies could render invaluable service in locating such material," and that "items of more than local interest should be made available to a larger public by being deposited with the History Commission or some college or University library." Unfortunately, the Arkansas Historical Association, which publishes the *Quarterly,* does not have fireproof quarters in which to house such collections.

In an article on "Emerson in Michigan and the Northwest," which appears in the spring number of the *Michigan History Magazine,* Russel B. Nye gives some attention to Emerson's lecture tour in Minnesota in the winter of 1867. On this trip, which was "one of the longest tours of his career," Emerson "visited every one of what are now the middle western states," writes Mr. Nye. The Minnesota visit was discussed by Hubert H. Hoeltje in the issue of this magazine for June, 1930 (see *ante,* 11:145–159).

Articles on the development in Iowa of two modern methods of communication appear in the April number of the *Annals of Iowa.* In the first, Charles C. Deering surveys the history of "The Telephone in Iowa" from 1879, when an exchange was opened at Dubuque. Included are sections on early toll lines, early equipment used in the state, companies operating telephone lines, and rural service. A. G. Woolfries, the author of the second article, reviews the story of "A Radio Pioneer: WOI-Ames, 1923–1940." The leading article in this issue of the *Annals* is Ora Williams' history of the Iowa Department of History and Archives, which is marking its fiftieth anniversary this year.

A contribution to Middle Western political history is Allen Fraser Lovejoy's study of *La Follette and the Establishment of the Direct Primary in Wisconsin, 1890–1904,* which has been published by Yale University as volume 1 of the *Patterson Prize Essays* (New Haven, 1941). For this study, Mr. Lovejoy received a prize in American politics established at the university by the bequest of Frank Miner Patterson.

Nearly half of the Reverend Peter Leo Johnson's recent volume entitled *Stuffed Saddlebags: The Life of Martin Kundig, Priest, 1805–1879* (Milwaukee, 1942) has its setting in Wisconsin, where the missionary priest served after 1842. Early Jesuit and other Catholic missionary activity in Wisconsin and the upper Mississippi Valley is the subject of one chapter, which includes a brief account of Bishop Loras' trips to the frontier settlements of Wisconsin and Minnesota.

"St. Nazianz, a German Settlement" in Manitowoc County, Wisconsin, is the subject of an article by John Eiselmeier in the *American-German Review* for June. The settlement, which "was developed on a communal basis," was established in 1854 by Father Ambrosius Oschwald and more than a hundred German Catholic colonists. They made all implements "necessary for their existence," and some of these with quaint "furniture which appears to be indestructible" are now preserved in a local museum. In the same issue of the *Review* is an account of the "German Drama in the Middle West" by Horst Frenz, who gives special attention to theatrical performances in German playhouses at Cincinnati, Milwaukee, Chicago, St. Louis, and Davenport.

Students of Czech settlement in the Northwest will be interested in a booklet, compiled by the Reverend Paul J. Monarski, presenting the *Golden Jubilee History of St. John Nepomucene's Parish, Prairie du Chien, Wisconsin, 1891–1941* (54 p.). This Catholic parish was established in 1891 to serve former parishioners of St. Gabriel's Church who "could speak and understand only Bohemian."

The story of the construction of "The Prairie du Chien Pontoon Bridge," which connected the western terminal of a Wisconsin railroad line with North McGregor, Iowa, and gave access to the Minnesota settlements farther north, is reviewed by Alden E. Miller in number 58 of the *Bulletins* of the Railway and Locomotive Historical Society, issued in May. The writer gives credit for designing the bridge and supervising its construction to Michel Spettel, a German shipbuilder who had settled in Prairie du Chien. Patents on the design, however, were held by John Lawler, who financed the building of the bridge. The structure, which is described as the "largest and only one of its kind on the main channel" of the Mississippi, was completed in the spring of 1874 and is still in use. Some interesting pictures of the bridge accompany the article.

Antoine d'Eschambault is the author of two sketches of the voyageur appearing in the January and February issues of *Le Canada français*. In them Mr. d'Eschambault describes, as does Dr. Grace Lee Nute in her volume on the same subject, the life and customs of the voyageur, including his role in the wars, exploration, and settlement of the Northwest. Some descendants of François Rolet, who is identified as the first Rolet in Canada, are traced by E.-F. Surveyer in an article on "La Famille Rolette," appearing in the June number of the *Bulletin des recherches historiques*. Among Rolet's grandsons the author lists Jean-Joseph Rolette, the well-known fur trader of the Northwest.　　　S. A. D.

Sister Ursula Dunlevy's monograph on the "Canadian Halfbreed Rebellions of 1870 and 1885" is concluded in the April number of the *North Dakota Historical Quarterly* (see *ante*, p. 186). Many Minnesota connections are brought out, and the St. Paul newspapers are used as an important source of information. A memorial addressed to Governor Ramsey in 1849 by Father Belcourt and a group of half-breeds from the Red River colony is reprinted as an appendix. Other articles in this issue of the *Quarterly* are a description of a "Dakota Indian Victory-dance" observed in 1918 near Fort Yates, North Dakota, by Aaron McGaffey Beede, and a "Study of Population Trends in North Dakota" by J. M. Gillette.

GENERAL MINNESOTA ITEMS

The faculty of the University of Minnesota is well represented among the authors contributing to volumes 21 and 22 of *Minnesota History,* and their contributions are in turn listed in a bibliography of *Publications of the Faculties* for 1940–41 issued as volume 45, number 10, of the university's *Bulletins* (1942. 209 p.). It therefore seems appropriate to quote herein some passages from the foreword to the latter publication. It was written by President Coffey, who gained the impression from his examination of this bibliography that we are now at war and "are fighting in order that a way of life may survive that will permit the continued free and untrammeled study of just the kind of problems that these books and articles represent. No one has told a single author represented here what he must write or think," he continues; "no one has told a single author included between these covers that his ideas are politically unacceptable." Thus, for the president of our state university, the publications in this list "symbolize the freedom of thought that characterizes the democratic way of life." He expresses the belief that "This volume should engender in all of us a better understanding of what we are struggling for, and a deeper appreciation of the fact that the struggle is worth all the sacrifices it may impose."

A valuable compilation recently published by the Minnesota Historical Records Survey is a *Directory of Churches and Religious Organizations in Minnesota* (1942. 583 p.). The arrangement is by denominations, and under each heading the communities in which churches are maintained are listed alphabetically. Names of congregations and clergymen, information about the incorporation of the church, items on parochial schools and other church institutions, and many other useful bits of information are included. Indexes of names of persons and of names of organizations add to the value of the volume. Another notable publication prepared and issued under the auspices of the survey is a *Guide to Church Vital Statistics Records in Minnesota: Baptisms, Marriages, Funerals* (1942. 253 p.). The arrangement in this volume is by counties and communities. A volume listing the archives of Aitkin County that are preserved in the courthouse at Aitkin has been issued in the survey's *Inventory of the County Archives of Minnesota* (no. 1 — 172 p.). A historical sketch of the county, twenty-two pages in length, precedes the inventory.

The April issue of the *Minnesota Archaeologist* is devoted to a series of illustrated articles by Burton W. Thayer on Indian beadwork and design. Among the subjects considered are " 'Black' as a Preferred Color in Ojibway Art," "Some Examples of Red River Half-breed Art," and "The Algonquian Trait of Asymmetry in Ojibway Art." The assertion is made that "Minnesota is an interesting crossroad of Indian beaded art," since several groups lived and worked in the area. The state is therefore described as a "particularly fertile field for research in beadwork ornamentation."

A letter written from Fort Snelling on November 30, 1835, by S. C. Stambaugh after a hazardous journey on foot from Prairie du Chien is published in the *Chatfield News* for June 4. The writer, who notes that he has made arrangements with the "sutler to take possession the first of January," describes in detail the difficulties encountered during a trip of sixteen days northward to the Minnesota post. Stambaugh's letter has been preserved in the form of a copy made by his wife, to whom it was addressed. She sent it to her sister, in order to give the latter "some idea of going to St. Peter's (or Iceland I think would be more appropriate) in November." Accompanying the letter is a note from Mrs. Stambaugh, who remained in Prairie du Chien. "I stay with Mr. Rolette and daughter, a rich old French trader," she relates. "They are very kind and attentive to me, and I spend my time pleasantly." Mrs. Stambaugh notes that a "splendid horse and sleigh" with a driver had been placed at her disposal.

A brilliant characterization of George Edgar Vincent, who served as president of the University of Minnesota from 1913 to 1917, is contributed by Professor L. L. Bernard of the University of Washington to the April number of *Social Science*. The author did graduate work in sociology at Chicago under Dr. Vincent's direction, and he joined the Minnesota faculty just after Vincent left to take up new duties as president of the Rockefeller Foundation. At the time the "memory of a great presidency still persisted at Minnesota among the more enlightened members of the faculty," writes Dr. Bernard. He explains the reasons why Dr. Vincent failed in his attempt to carry out some of his educational ideas at Minnesota, but notes that the "regents liked Vincent's plans to expand the services of the University in the direction of extension activities." As a result, under Dr. Vincent's administration, Minnesota became "one of the leading extension states, perhaps the leading one."

A record of the commemorative exercises conducted to mark the *Twenty-fifth Anniversary of the Mayo Foundation for Medical Education and Research* in the Mayo Civic Auditorium at Rochester on October 23, 1940, has been issued in the form of a booklet (1941. 34 p.). Among the addresses and other documents here brought together and preserved in published form are a review of the accomplishments of the foundation from 1915 to 1940 by its director, Dr. Donald C. Balfour; an account of its growth by Dr. Lester D. Powell, president of the Alumni Association of the Mayo Foundation; a discussion of "The Pioneer Tradition" as it is exemplified in the work of the Mayos at Rochester by Dean Theodore C. Blegen of the University of Minnesota graduate school; a tribute to four leaders in the establishment of the foundation by Dr. Guy Stanton Ford, president of the university; and a letter from Dr. George E. Vincent, who was president of the university in 1915 when the foundation was established.

Dr. Arthur S. Hamilton continues, in the issues of *Minnesota Medicine* for April, May, and June, his "History of the Minnesota State Medical Society," which forms part of a "History of Medicine in Minnesota" (see *ante,* p. 190). These installments consist merely of brief reports of meetings, semiannual and annual, held by the medical organization from 1871 to 1890.

Historical accounts of many Norwegian settlements in Minnesota and sketches of scores of Minnesota residents who emigrated from the Nordfjord district of Norway are included in a volume entitled *Nordfjordingernes historie i Amerika,* by the Reverend L. M. Gimmestad and others (Minneapolis, 1940.   508 p.).   Included are chapters on the Faribault County settlements of Bricelyn, Frost, and Kiester Township; on Belview, Clarkfield, Stony Run, and Granite Falls, in Redwood and Yellow Medicine counties; on Swift Falls and Benson in Swift County; on the Big Stone County settlements; and on some widely distributed groups, including those in St. Paul and Minneapolis.

Three useful *Bulletins* recently issued by the Minneapolis board of education in its series of *Social Studies* deal with *Bridges of Minneapolis and the State of Minnesota* (no. 56 — 30 p.), *Notable Buildings of Minneapolis* (no. 57 — 74 p.), and the *Story of the Minnesota State Fair* (no. 58 — 40 p.). All were prepared with WPA assistance, and all have been issued in multigraphed pamphlet form. They aim to place at the disposal of teachers and pupils in the high schools and teachers in the grades material not readily available elsewhere. In addition to brief accounts of individual bridges in Minneapolis, St. Paul, and Duluth, the first of these pamphlets presents notes on bridges at Zumbrota, Hudson, Hastings, Winona, Henderson, Stillwater, Wabasha, La Crosse, and Osceola. Among the *Notable Buildings* described in the second booklet are such early structures on the site of Minneapolis as the government mill at the Falls of St. Anthony, the Pond cabin on Lake Calhoun, the Godfrey and Stevens houses, and the Round Tower at Fort Snelling outside the city limits. There are brief historical sketches also of some of the city's "famous houses," churches, hotels, schools, university buildings, libraries, art galleries, public buildings, business and industrial structures, theaters, auditoriums, and clubs.

A bicycle with wooden wheels, "flat steel tires," and pedals that resembled "large wooden spools," which was used in Madelia about 1885 by a local blacksmith, is the earliest machine described by George Wilson in a series of articles on bicycling appearing in the *Mankato Free Press* from April 22 to 29. By the end of the century, Mr. Wilson recalls, bicycles with rubber tires were in use in Madelia. In succeeding installments he tells of improvements in the machine, of bicycle races, of trips from town to town, and of the relation of the bicycle to the good roads movement in Minnesota. Material on the area about the Twin Cities is included with many interesting items relating to Madelia and Mankato.

In the second of a series of articles in the *Conservation Volunteer* dealing with Minnesota's "Memorial Parks and Waysides," Harold W. Lathrop describes some that "commemorate the 1862 Indian uprising" (see *ante*, p. 192). Included in the May issue are brief explanations of the significance of Traverse des Sioux and Camp Release state memorial waysides, of Monson Lake State Memorial Park, and of the Wood Lake and Sam Brown state monuments. Monuments erected to commemorate the battle of Birch Cooley and the Old Crossing treaty with the Chippewa and the Joseph R. Brown State Memorial Wayside are described by Mr. Lathrop in the June number of the *Volunteer*.

WAR HISTORY ACTIVITIES

The Minnesota War History Committee, established by Governor Stassen on May 18 as one of the agencies of the Minnesota Office of Civilian Defense (see *ante*, p. 148–153), held its first meeting on May 25, when a comprehensive general plan for its work was presented and approved. The plan calls for the collection of all types of war records having research value for Minnesota, including photographs, motion pictures, radio transcriptions, microfilms, processed material, and the like, as well as printed and written documents. The records of the war activities of individual Minnesotans and of all organizations having local units, an appreciable number of members, or a following in Minnesota are to be collected.

The War History Committee is not attempting to collect immediately certain classes of war records. One of the fundamental records of the war, a roster of Minnesota men in the armed services, it believes, can best be compiled through collaboration with the Minnesota adjutant general and the war and navy departments in Washington. The correspondence and other office records of public and private agencies are not available for collection until their usefulness to such agencies is past. The committee, however, is stimulating the preservation by agencies of all materials resulting from their war activities, whether they are office records or items issued to the public, such as speeches, news releases, manuals, certificates, badges, posters, or the like. If public war agencies preserve all their records in their own files, the committee's objective with respect to their records will have been achieved. The office files of some private organizations may never become available for collection by the committee; consequently, it is asking such organizations to send in currently all possible material. Thus the War History Committee is attempting to assure the preservation of office records, to collect from private organizations all kinds of ephemeral material, and to collect the records of individuals. The committee will avoid as far as possible the duplication of material collected by other depositories in the Twin Cities. It will not collect, for example, Minnesota newspapers and periodicals and federal publications received by the Minnesota Historical Society, or books, pamphlets, and other printed materials to be found in public, college, and university libraries of Minneapolis and St. Paul.

The appointment of local war history chairmen in forty-six of the hundred and six Minnesota counties and communities that have local defense councils has been announced by the chairmen of the latter organizations. Contact between the state War History Committee and the local chairmen is being maintained through instructions and suggestions published in the *Minnesota Defense Council Bulletin.* Through the co-operation of the local chairmen and their committees, the state committee expects to build up collections of local war records in communities throughout the state and to obtain for itself a mass of valuable war records of local Minnesota origin.

Lists of organizations and individuals from whom material is desired have been compiled in the office of the War History Committee. Gifts from 107 donors, nearly all of whom will continue to send the committee material, were received before August 1. Among the donors are the American Jewish Committee, the American Legion, the American Legion Auxiliary, the Council for Democracy, the Friends of Democracy, the Minnesota Federation of Womens Clubs, the Minnesota Anti-defamation Council, the Minnesota Mutual Life Insurance Company, the League of Women Voters, the Russian War Relief, the *St. Paul Pioneer Press,* the *St. Paul Dispatch,* the Union for Democratic Action, the United American Slavs of Minnesota, and the Veterans of Foreign Wars.

Through the co-operation of the Labor Volunteers for Victory, thirteen international unions with locals in Minnesota are sending the War History Committee their publications. Nine newspapers published by the army at places where Minnesota men are stationed are coming to the committee. Minnesotans in Alaska are sending the *Kodiak Bear* and other material. The Military Railway Service, commanded by Brigadier General Carl R. Gray, Jr., with headquarters in St. Paul, is contributing various items. Numerous letters from Minnesota soldiers have been received. A representative collection of antiwar and defeatist literature is being accumulated.

LOCAL HISTORICAL SOCIETIES

During the past two years the Carver County Historical Society has built up the impressive collection of pioneer objects now on display in its museum at Mayer. In two large rooms on the second floor of the Mayer school, the museum was formally opened to the public on April 12, 1940. Mr. O. D. Sell, the president of the society, whose energy and enthusiasm has resulted in the building up of the society's collection, is on hand every Wednesday and Friday afternoon to receive visitors and explain the exhibits.

Mr. Sell's success in assembling specific types of materials and his ability to organize these materials for purposes of display are exemplified in some extensive special collections on view in the Carver County museum. Outstanding among these is a collection of firearms, consisting of no less than 225 guns. Among them are many handmade pieces, chiefly of European origin. Exquisite wood carvings and finely wrought metal work decorate many of these items, making them worthy of careful and detailed examination. Included are numerous guns of primitive types, and the collection as a whole illustrates the development of small firearms over a period of more than a century. The guns are arranged on specially constructed racks, and each is carefully numbered and labelled. Supplementing the exhibit, and adjacent to it, are displays of hunting and military accessories — powder bags, powder horns, holsters, saddle bags, and many similar items.

A number of other special collections might be mentioned. There is, for example, an archaeological exhibit, consisting chiefly of Indian implements of stone, arrowheads, and other objects of Indian origin found in the county. An exhibit of smokers' equipment consists not only of pipes, many of which are of unusual design, but of tobacco pouches, flints used for lighting tobacco, and the like. There is a special display of razors and shaving equipment. An exhibit of frontier lighting devices includes candle molds, candle snuffers, whale oil lamps, lanterns of various types, and the like. As is to be expected in an agricultural community, a large proportion of the objects displayed are of an agricultural nature. Scores of agricultural implements, many of them handmade, are included. The equipment used in making maple sugar and a straw beehive dating from the 1850's are reminders of some activities of frontier farmers. Among the larger pieces on display are a fire engine used at Norwood in 1879, the switchboard used in 1903 to inagurate telephone service in Carver County, and a sewing machine dating from 1868.

Painted chests of Scandinavian origin, wooden shoes and pewter mugs used at Cologne by Dutch settlers, and clocks and musical instruments from the homes of German pioneers suggest the racial composition of the county's population. The museum collection as a whole provides convincing evidence that the Germans are the dominant European group of the vicinity, for a large proportion of the items of foreign origin were brought in by German immigrants. Evidences of their cultural interests and activities are particularly numerous. Most of the musical instruments in the Carver County society's large and varied collection, for example, once belonged to German settlers. Of outstanding interest and value in this connection is the collection of the Carver County German Reading Society or *Leseverein*. A scarlet and gold banner that hung in the association's headquarters at Carver reveals that it was organized in 1858 and incorporated in 1865. It continued to function as a local library association until 1941, when its library and records were turned over to the county historical society. The library consists of more than a thousand volumes, many of them in German, though a large number of recent acquisitions are in English. A study of the titles would reveal much about the reading tastes and literary interests of residents in a typical German community of the Middle West. With the books were received the reading society's manuscript records, including lists of members, minutes of meetings, records of the payment of dues and of books withdrawn and returned, and financial accounts. Here is the raw material on which can be based a cultural study of unusual interest and value.

More than three thousand objects have been acquired by the Carver County society since it opened its museum in the spring of 1940. They are listed in accessions books and are well identified by typewritten labels. Each label gives information about the nature of the object, the date of its origin, the time that it was brought into the county, its former owner, and the donor. Several hundred pictures are filed alphabetically in a special case. Pictures on display are changed from time to time.

In the brief period of its existence the museum at Mayer has received nearly thirty-five hundred visitors. Groups of school children accompanied by teachers frequently view the exhibits; thus the museum has become an important educational factor in the county. Co-operation has been given to an unusual degree by newspapers at Chaska, Norwood, Waconia, Watertown, and Young America, which frequently publish articles about the museum and the activities of the historical society.   B. L. H.

Plans for the erection of markers and the expansion of its museum after the war were discussed at a meeting of the Thunder Bay Historical Society at Port Arthur on April 8. Mr. Carson F. Piper, who has charge of the society's museum, announced that since its opening in January it has received more than a thousand visitors. A bequest left by the society's first president, the late Peter McKellar, made possible the successful establishment of the museum, Mr. Piper revealed. He urged that collecting activities should continue during the war in order that at its close the museum might be ready for expansion. The society's president, Mr. J. P. Bertrand, listed and described the historical significance of four sites that should be marked when normal conditions prevail once more.

More than two hundred people attended the annual dinner meeting of the Brown County Historical Society, which was held at New Ulm on May 7. The program, which consisted of papers on various aspects of the Sioux Outbreak of 1862, commemorated the eightieth anniversary of that tragic event in the history of the Minnesota Valley. Five papers and addresses presented on this occasion later were published in the *New Ulm Daily Journal*. They are an account of the murder of the Humphrey family and of the escape of the twelve-year-old boy, John A. Humphrey, by Judge Russell L. Johnson, appearing in the issue for May 8; a review of the "Outbreak at the Lower Agency," by Victor P. Reim, May 9; a description of the battles of New Ulm, by Dr. Carl Fritsche, May 11; accounts of Indian raids in sections near New Ulm in the month following the outbreak, by George Hage, president of the Watonwan County Historical Society, May 12; and a summary of a report prepared for the government after the outbreak by Major Thomas Galbraith, in which he discussed its causes, by Fred W. Johnson, president of the Brown County society, May

13. At the business session of the meeting, Mr. Johnson was again named president. Other officers include A. G. Loomis, vice-president, Louis G. Vogel, secretary, and William Brust, treasurer.

Motion pictures of the Lac qui Parle area and of some of Minnesota's state parks were presented by Mr. Harold Lathrop of the Minnesota division of state parks to illustrate a talk before the Chippewa County Historical Society at Watson on June 12. The speaker gave special attention to the state park at Lac qui Parle and to the reconstruction of the chapel used in connection with the mission there. The work on the chapel has now been completed and plans for its dedication on July 12 were announced.

The historical societies of Douglas and Todd counties held a joint meeting and picnic at Osakis on June 14. A feature of the program was a pageant reviewing the history of the counties, written especially for the occasion by O. B. DeLaurier.

An entire page of the Red Wing *Daily Republican Eagle* for April 2 is devoted to pictures, with explanatory notes, of the museum of the Goodhue County Historical Society in the courthouse at Red Wing. They record the visit to the museum of members of the teacher-training class in the Red Wing public schools. Both general views and specific exhibits are depicted in the photographs.

The bequest by the late Dr. F. W. Powers of Barrett of his collection of firearms and military equipment to the Grant County Historical Society is announced by the society's secretary, Mr. W. H. Goetzinger, in the *Grant County Herald* of Elbow Lake for April 30. A cabinet in which the collection can be displayed and kept intact has been presented by Dr. Powers' widow. With other exhibits arranged by the Grant County society, the Powers collection is now on display in the rotunda of the courthouse at Elbow Lake.

Professor A. L. Burt of the department of history in the University of Minnesota was the speaker at the annual meeting of the Hennepin County Historical Society, which was held at the Coffman Memorial Union on the university campus on April 14. He took as his subject "The Center of Patriotism Today." On May 17 the society dedicated a monument at Layman's Cemetery in Minneapolis commemorating the services of Charles W. Christmas, pioneer Hennepin County surveyor. Brooklyn Center was the scene of the society's annual outing on June 6. About a hundred people made the trip, which included stops at the Minneapolis water-softening plant at Fridley and the Half-way House near Robbinsdale. Mrs. Herbert Ward received the visitors, telling them that the house was built by Jesse Ward in the 1850's and that it was well-known to travelers on the stage line between St. Anthony and Monticello, for there stagecoach drivers stopped to change horses. At Brooklyn Center the tourists visited the farm of Mr. Earle Brown, where they were given an opportunity to view his extensive collection of horse-drawn vehicles and a reconstructed logging camp. The tour ended at the Brooklyn Center Methodist Church, where dinner was served and a program of papers and talks centering about the history of the community was presented.

The annual meeting of the Kandiyohi County Historical Society was held at Willmar on June 16. Among the speakers was Mr. Victor E. Lawson, who explained the work of the organization, and Mr. Roy Hendrickson, who made an appeal for the preservation of the county's war records.

The Kittson County Historical Society held its annual meeting at Hallock on June 19. An illustrated talk on Minnesota history was presented by Mr. Paul O. Hanson, president of the society.

"The Historical Society and the Community" was the subject of an address presented by Dr. Arthur J. Larsen, superintendent of the Minnesota Historical Society, before a meeting of the Lake Pepin Valley Historical Society at Lake City on April 27. Following the meeting, the society's museum in the public library building was opened for inspection. The museum is open to the public regularly on Tuesday and Friday evenings.

The Czech backgrounds of the village of Silver Lake were featured in a program presented before a meeting of the McLeod County Historical Society at that place on April 20. Descendants of a number of Czech pioneers recalled the experiences of members of their families who helped to found the community. Among them was Miss Esther Jerabek of the library staff of the Minnesota Historical Society, who reviewed the early history of the village. The role of the local historical society in time of war was discussed by Dr. Arthur J. Larsen, superintendent of the state society. A local chapter of the McLeod County society was organized;

Mrs. Henry Hawlish was named president, and Mr. James Zavoral, secretary-treasurer. More than eighty people attended the meeting. Brownton was the scene of another well-attended meeting of the McLeod County society on June 23. Reminiscent talks and papers were presented by Mrs. Sophia Pollard of Morgan, Mrs. Nora Dwinnell of Brownton, and others.

The secretary of the McLeod County society, Mrs. Sophie P. White, who presents a column under the heading "Pioneer Pictures" in the *Hutchinson Leader,* quotes from an interesting letter of Abby Hutchinson in the issue for May 8. It was written on July 14, 1867, shortly after this youthful member of the musical Hutchinson family arrived in the Minnesota community that her relatives founded. She comments upon family possessions that had been shipped from the East, including an organ purchased in Boston, and notes that "Our old carriage we expect soon, coming by the lakes." She made haste to enter into the social life of the frontier village. "Tomorrow afternoon we have a croquet party in honor of a Mr. Durand and a Mr. Bonniwell from Milwaukee who are rusticating here," she writes. "Expect to have some horseback rides before they leave."

A picture of Fort Ripley in 1878 and a review of its history by Val E. Kasparek of the Morrison County Historical Society appear in the *Little Falls Herald* for April 24. The local historical society is given credit also for an article, appearing in the *Little Falls Daily Transcript* for May 16, about Lieutenant Zebulon M. Pike's trip up the Mississippi in 1805 to a winter post near Little Falls.

The summer meeting and picnic of the Otter Tail County Historical Society, which was held at Prairie Lake, near Pelican Rapids, on June 28, "drew one of the largest crowds in the history of the society," according to the *Fergus Falls Daily Journal* for June 29. Among the papers presented were a review of the early history of Pelican Rapids and Scrambler by John R. Quamme, and a series of reminiscences by a pioneer Otter Tail County teacher, Mrs. R. R. Bogstad. These papers are published in full in the *Journal.* Another item of more than usual interest on the program was the reading by Mr. Hilding Larson of Pelican Rapids of several brief township histories written by students in the seventh and eighth grades of rural schools in Otter Tail County. Reports of the meeting and other items about the society and its activities that appeared in the *Journal* for

June 29 and 30 have been reprinted in a four-page news sheet for members of the society.

About two hundred people attended the annual meeting of the Pipestone County Old Settlers Historical Society at Pipestone on June 13. The principal speaker, Senator J. V. Weber of Slayton, discussed the place of the society in the life of the county. All officers of the organization, including H. A. Petschow, president, were re-elected.

The curator of the state historical society's museum, Mr. Willoughby M. Babcock, was the speaker at a meeting of the Polk County Historical Society at Crookston on May 27. He took as his subject "Community Memory," emphasizing the role of the local historical society in preserving the records of the past.

A program planned to commemorate the seventy-fifth anniversary of the founding of Carleton College was presented before a meeting of the Rice County Historical Society at Northfield on May 12. Among the speakers were Mr. Carl L. Weicht, president of the society, Dr. Donald J. Cowling, president of Carleton, and Miss Isabella Watson. The latter drew upon her experiences as a student at Carleton in the 1880's and as a member of its faculty for thirty-nine years for her interesting reminiscent talk. About sixty people attended the meeting.

The log cabin museum of the Waseca County Historical Society was open to the public on Saturday afternoons during the summer months. Members of the society volunteered to be in attendance at times when the museum was open.

Papers on "The St. Croix Valley in Days of Yore" by Willoughby M. Babcock, curator of the museum of the Minnesota Historical Society, and on the early history and settlement of Bayport by Mrs. Grace McAlpine, superintendent of schools in Washington County, were read before a joint meeting of the Washington County Historical Society and the Bayport Improvement Club at Bayport on April 29. Mrs. McAlpine's paper, which drew attention to the centennial of the beginning of settlement on the site of Bayport, appears in full in the *Bayport Herald* for May 7. Miss Helen Clapesattle of the University of Minnesota Press was the speaker at a meeting of the Washington County society held on the grounds of its museum in Stillwater on June 18. About a hundred and fifty people heard her address on the "Horse-and-Buggy Doctor" and inspected the museum, which was reopened for the summer season. An informal tea followed the meeting.

LOCAL HISTORY ITEMS

The finding at Graceville of the register for 1881 and 1882 of an early Browns Valley hotel, the Traverse House, is the occasion for an article about the volume in the *Graceville Enterprise* for May 26. The names of many western Minnesota pioneers as well as of numerous visitors to the region appear in the manuscript volume.

The history of the Brown County Farm Bureau, which was organized in 1918, is outlined in the *New Ulm Daily Journal* for May 5. Its organization is described, and a chronologically arranged list of its activities during twenty-four years is presented.

Under the auspices of the Carlton County Old Settlers Association, an interesting mill, built in Thomson Township in 1878, has been removed piece by piece and reassembled in Jay Cooke State Park, according to an article in the *Carlton County Vidette* of Carlton for April 23. The story of the mill, which was built by a group of Finnish pioneers for the grinding of rye meal, is reviewed in this issue by J. A. Mattinen. He obtained information about it some years ago by interviewing Isaac Raattaamaa, one of the original builders. Included in the account is a list of the nineteen Finnish pioneers who built the mill in order that their families might enjoy the rye bread and rye porridge to which they had been accustomed in their native land. A series of pictures of the razing of the mill accompanies the article. Another account of the mill and its removal appears in the *Barnum Herald* for April 9.

The "Story of Albert Lea's First Newspaper, Published 85 Years Ago" is reviewed in some detail by Lester W. Spicer in the *Evening Tribune* of Albert Lea for May 23. The author describes the founding of the *Southern Minnesota Star,* gives some biographical information about Alfred P. Swineford, the frontier journalist who established it, and analyzes the contents of the first issue, dated July 9, 1857. He notes that a copy is preserved by the Minnesota Historical Society. Thirty-eight numbers of the *Star* were issued before it ceased publication in May, 1858. In the following September Swineford launched a second paper, the *Freeborn County*

Eagle, which continued to appear until February, 1859. How these frontier news sheets reflect the early history of Albert Lea and Freeborn County is demonstrated in Mr. Spicer's narrative. A "Chapter of the Early History of the Albert Lea Co-operative Creamery" is the subject of a reminiscent article by H. E. Schuknecht, who was connected with the plant in the 1890's, in the *Evening Tribune* for June 4.

The constitution, by-laws, and minutes of the Cannon Falls Lyceum, which was active in the Goodhue County community from 1857 to 1860, are contained in a manuscript volume recently discovered by Mr. Richard Nelson in a shed, according to an announcement in the *Cannon Falls Beacon* for May 22. Lists of members, programs of meetings, and subjects of debate before the lyceum's sessions are to be found in this interesting record of frontier cultural activity.

The issue of the *Little Falls Daily Transcript* for April 4 is a fiftieth anniversary edition, two sections of which are devoted to articles about local history. Included are accounts of schools and churches in the community; of such institutions as the local library, which, like the newspaper, was founded in 1892; and of banks and business concerns. One article reviews in some detail the story of the Pine Tree Lumber Company, which was organized by a group of prominent lumbermen in the early 1890's. The story of Lindbergh State Park is outlined in another article.

With a three-day program of commencement exercises from June 5 to 7, Gustavus Adolphus College at St. Peter marked its eightieth anniversary. Features of the celebration were a historical pageant, a baccalaureate service conducted by Dr. O. J. Johnson, retiring president of the college, and a commencement address by President Walter C. Coffey of the University of Minnesota. A number of articles about the history of the college appear in the *St. Peter Herald* for June 5, and a volume by Professor Conrad Peterson of the school's department of history, in which he reviews *A History of Eighty Years,* was published in commemoration of the anniversary. This permanent record of one of Minnesota's pioneer institutions of higher learning will be reviewed in a future issue of this magazine.

Episodes in the history of Rochester, stories of pioneer life in its vicinity, sketches of its distinguished citizens, accounts of its business firms and institutions, and the like have been selected from various sources and assembled by Flora McGhee in a little book entitled *Know Rochester Better*

(St. Paul, 1940.   112 p.). Some of the sections have been reprinted from local newspapers, some are drawn from reminiscent narratives, and others are based upon interviews with pioneers recorded by students in the Rochester Junior College, where Miss McGhee is a member of the faculty. Among the more interesting chapters are those dealing with music in Rochester, entertainment and social life, and horse racing. A number of excellent illustrations are included.

A "History of Methodism at Little Prairie" in Rice County, prepared by Mrs. H. A. Illsley in connection with a home-coming celebration held on April 12, is published in the *Northfield Independent* for May 7. Credit is given to Jacob Emery, a pioneer settler of 1855, for promoting the establishment of the Methodist community at Little Prairie. When the Reverend William McKinley began to conduct regular services in Northfield in 1856, writes Mrs. Illsley, "Emery hauled all the folks from Little Prairie and Dundas that his ox team could handle" to hear McKinley preach.

Pioneer reunions and celebrations held in St. Louis County rural communities in 1940 and 1941 resulted in the publication of some significant multigraphed booklets containing sketches of local historical interest. They make available information about communities which were settled chiefly in the present century. Historical sketches of Brookston, Culver, Brevator, Grand Lake, and Stoney Brook appear in a booklet entitled *Brookston Region Pioneers* (August, 1940.   27 p.).   In the same month were issued pamphlets on the *Elmer Pioneer Reunion* (9 p.), containing an account of the settlement of Elmer Township, and of the *Shaw Pioneer Reunion* (9 p.), with brief reviews of the history of that community and of its school. Historical sketches of Alborn and New Independence townships, which were settled in the later decades of the nineteenth century, and some notes on Industrial Township appear in a pamphlet entitled *Alborn Region Pioneers* (15 p.). Brief accounts of pioneer experiences at Linden Grove and of "pioneer school days" in the same township are presented in a booklet issued for that community in August, 1941 (20 p.).

To commemorate the eighty-fifth anniversary of the organization of Waseca County, the *Waseca Journal* of June 24 devotes three sections to articles about the history of the county. Most of these are part of a chronological series, each of which deals with one year in the county's history, from its establishment in 1857 to 1942. Articles on the years previous to

1905 are based on James E. Child's history of the county; material for the accounts of more recent years has been gleaned from newspaper files. The series begins with a review of settlement in the Waseca County area from 1854 to 1856. Following the chronological series are articles dealing with such subjects as schools, fire departments, industries, churches, lodges and other organizations, and mail service.

MINNESOTA HISTORY

VOLUME 23 · PUBLISHED IN DEC. 1942 · NUMBER 4

Theatrical Personalities of Old St. Paul

Frank M. Whiting

ACCORDING TO veteran troupers of the modern theater, there are three bad weeks in the show business — Christmas week, Holy week, and St. Paul. Whether Minnesota's capital city deserves such a reputation is largely a matter of opinion, for there is evidence that poor and mediocre companies have often played to empty theaters in St. Paul, while productions of outstanding merit draw packed houses. Whatever St. Paul's present reputation may be, this much is certain — skepticism regarding the city's ability to support the theater did not arise until after the 1850's, for during that feverish decade St. Paul was one of the best towns for summer theatricals in the entire nation. The financial boom, the flood of summer immigrants, the territory's reputation as an ideal vacation spot, and the Mississippi, which provided steamboat transportation for theatrical troupes from St. Louis, New Orleans, and Cincinnati, seem to have been primarily responsible for the theatrical prosperity of the period. At the same time the contributions of a few outstanding personalities should not be overlooked, for without them the first chapter in St. Paul's theatrical history would lose much of its color and fascination.

Perhaps the first to deserve mention is none other than the frontier Jack-of-all-trades, Joseph R. Brown. His achievements as a fur trader, lumberman, land speculator, legislator, politician, newspaper editor, inventor, and founder of cities are well known, but his unique place as an actor has been overlooked. Brown seems to hold the dubious distinction of having been Minnesota's first "leading lady," according to his own account of the performance in a news-paper of 1856.[1] In a review of a production of "Pizarro," which he had recently seen at Market Hall in St. Paul, Brown recalled his own part in a performance some thirty-five years earlier at old Fort Snelling. "The representation of this tragedy," he mused, "caused our mind to wander back to the winters of 1821 and 1822, when a thespian corps used to murder *Rolla* in the barracks at the mouth of the St. Peters. We were one of the performers, and in the play of *Pizarro* we done Elvira," the tragic heroine. "From what we can recollect of our manner of representing the character, however," Brown continues, "we are inclined to believe there was some little difference between our performance, and that of Miss Deering," who played the role in St. Paul.

The date given by Brown in this bit of personal reminiscence stands as a landmark in the westward expansion of the American theater. Pittsburgh, New Orleans, Cincinnati, Detroit, and St. Louis appear to have been the only other localities west of the Allegheny Mountains where theatrical performances were staged at so early a date.[2] It is unfortunate that Brown did not reveal more about early dramatic productions at Fort Snelling. Perhaps he was restrained by the unsuppressed glee with which some of his contemporaries seized upon his account.[3] One St. Paul journalist remarked that Brown "must permit us to indulge in a 'larf'. . . . He measures nearly six feet in height, and about as much in circumference. . . . We don't think even thirty-five years ago, he was very delicately formed or strikingly handsome. The idea of his representing tragedy, at any time of his life, or in any character, strikes us as being sublimely ridiculous. But to attempt the personation of a female character; to bind himself up in stays and boddices, and shroud himself in petticoats, and other unnameable female gear . . . to try to pass himself off as a woman . . . why, Brown, it was the most gracelessly impu-

---

[1] *Henderson Democrat,* June 12, 1856. See also Theodore C. Blegen, *Building Minnesota,* 115 (Boston, 1938).

[2] William G. B. Carson, *The Theatre on the Frontier: The Early Years of the St. Louis Stage,* 2–5 (Chicago, 1932).

[3] *Weekly Pioneer and Democrat* (St. Paul), June 26, 1856.

dent imposture ever perpetrated by you in any character you ever assumed."

In passing it might be added that the performance recalled by Brown was only one example of early dramatic activity at old Fort Snelling. The record is very incomplete, but enough evidence has been gathered to indicate that amateur dramatics constituted a major form of recreation at the post. At least one actor of some importance, Harry Watkins, began his career by playing leading ladies in post theatricals while serving as a "fifer boy" with the Fifth United States Infantry in the late 1830's.[4]

Professional drama made its bow in St. Paul with the arrival in the summer of 1851 of George Holland and his troupe from Placide's Varieties of New Orleans. Local historians seem to agree that Holland gave the first professional production of legitimate drama in Minnesota. Even T. M. Newson, an ardent crusader against the evils of the stage, devotes space to the subject. Although Holland was typical of the theatrical tradition that was to develop in St. Paul, he was not an average frontier trouper. As one of the foremost comedians of his day, his regular engagements were confined to New York, Philadelphia, and New Orleans.[5]

The effect of Holland's opening performance at Mazourka Hall on August 12, 1851, can be better appreciated if one imagines the

---

[4] Some interesting references to experiences at old Fort Snelling are included in a recent book based upon Watkins' diary — Maud and Otis Skinner's *One Man in His Time: The Adventures of H. Watkins, Strolling Player*, 1, 52, 206, 250 (Philadelphia, 1938). Other sources of information about Fort Snelling theatricals include the entries for October 1 and 6, 1836, in Major Lawrence Taliaferro's journal, in the possession of the Minnesota Historical Society; Bertha L. Heilbron, "The Drama at Old Fort Snelling," *ante,* 7:274; Marcus L. Hansen, *Old Fort Snelling,* 100 (Iowa City, 1918); John H. Bliss, "Reminiscences of Fort Snelling," in *Minnesota Historical Collections,* 6: 335, 342; and Charlotte Ouisconsin Van Cleve, *Three Score Years and Ten,* 10 (Minneapolis, 1888).

[5] Newson, who was editor of the *St. Paul Daily Times,* engaged in at least two newspaper wars on the drama. See the issues of his paper for July 18, 20, and 21, 1855, and the *Daily Minnesotian* (St. Paul), July 25 and September 15, 1857. Holland's engagement is mentioned in Newson's *Pen Pictures of St. Paul,* 260 (St. Paul, 1886). For information about Holland, see T. Allston Brown, *History of the American Stage,* 181 (New York, 1870), and Joseph Jefferson, *Autobiography,* 336–340 (New York, 1897). Jefferson was a close friend and an admirer of Holland. Among other things, he relates how the death of the comedian resulted in the naming of the Little Church around the Corner in New York.

sensation that would be created if Eddie Cantor, for example, were to drop in for a personal appearance at some remote town today. On the opening night, when he played in "A Day After the Fair," Holland maintained his reputation for robust comedy and broad versatility by portraying six different characters ranging from a grouchy old man to a French maid! James M. Goodhue, the editor of the *Minnesota Pioneer,* who attended the performance, described Holland as "a wonderful Protean actor, whose versatility is such that he alone amounts to a dramatic company." Although St. Paul numbered but slightly over a thousand inhabitants, houses were crowded for this and the eleven performances that followed.[6]

Brown and Holland were the pioneers who introduced drama, amateur and professional, into the territory, but it was a woman, Sallie St. Clair, who brought the art to its first climax of popularity. Sallie was the glamour girl of the 1850's. She was born in England in 1831, went to America as a child, and shortly thereafter made her first stage appearance at the Park Theater in New York as a child dancer.[7] During her St. Paul engagements, in 1855 and 1857, she was at the height of her popularity. Young men fell in love with her, critics lauded her, and the public flocked to see her. The extravagance of the praise heaped upon her is well illustrated by a long article in the *Daily Minnesotian* for June 22, 1857. "This accomplished lady," reads the account, "proudly stands upon the very summit of that gorgeous temple of renown, the priestess of its glories, and guardian of its fame. . . . The highborn genius of Miss St. Clair flings a glory upon the drama. . . . To all these she adds a perfect *physique* and charming grace — a fine musical voice, and clear enunciation — which make her the embodiment of that ideal, which only one in a thousand of candidates for histrionic honors can ever attain."

It should be made clear, however, that not everyone in St. Paul held such high opinions of the lady. Another St. Paul editor, Joseph

---

[6] For an advertisement of Holland's first performance, see the *Minnesota Democrat* (St. Paul), August 12, 1851. His play is reviewed in the *Minnesota Pioneer* (St. Paul), August 14, 1851.
[7] Brown, *History of the American Stage,* 323.

Wheelock, challenged the writer for the *Minnesotian* in his paper: "If she has enthusiastic admirers in more appreciative circles, it is not the first time that an enchanting figure and a ravishing ankle have created a sensation among very young men," remarked Wheelock. "She simply capers gracefully. She holds her head well, with a superb arching of the neck, and prances with a splendid curvette through the routine of the Thespian menage. . . . Yet it must be confessed that Sally has some talent. If her powers had been concentrated in a particular line of characters, instead of being squandered in ambitious but shallow displays of versatility it is not impossible that she might have become an artiste." [8]

The truth about Miss St. Clair's talent undoubtedly lies somewhere between the two extremes expressed above. There is ample evidence that she loved to indulge in what Wheelock termed "shallow displays of versatility." In one of her favorite farces, "Actress of All Work," she portrayed six different characters. When she grew tired of such light fare and the usual leading ladies, it was not uncommon for her to don male attire for the portrayal of such dashing heroes as Claude Melnotte, Jack Sheppard, and Pizarro.

Though Sallie St. Clair may not have been an actress of the first rank, she still was a glamorous stage personality. Her companies prospered. At the close of her first season, in 1855, the prominent citizens of St. Paul, headed by Governor Willis A. Gorman, gave her a great farewell benefit. At Muscatine in 1856 a gentleman offered to fight a duel on her behalf. In 1857 her power over young men became a choice topic of local gossip. A youthful St. Paul belle remarked, in a letter to her sister, that Joe Rolette was suffering from "Sonny Dayton's disease," a malady the nature of which may be surmised when one learns that "Sonny" followed Sallie St. Clair as far as Galena before being persuaded to turn back. Clara Morris spoke of her as "the lovely blond star," saying, "I adored Miss St. Clair, as everyone else did." [9] Many people believed that her husband's

---

[8] *St. Paul Financial, Real Estate and Railroad Advertiser,* June 27, 1857.
[9] For advertisements of some of Sallie St. Clair's St. Paul performances, see the *Minnesotian,* July 6, 16, 1856, May 20, July 23, 1857. See also *Pioneer,* July 14, 1855; *Pioneer and Democrat,* September 15, 1856; George C. D. Odell, *Annals of the New York Stage,* 7: 41 (New York, 1931); Clara Morris, *Life on the Stage,* 140–154 (New

death, which followed closely upon her own, was not an accident but the deliberate suicide of a grief-stricken man.

In 1857 the attractions of the St. Louis Varieties, the company with which Miss St. Clair appeared, were enhanced by adding to the programs music by the Old Gent's Band. This was a local organization consisting of W. H. Munger, violinist, R. C. Munger, cornettist, R. S. Munger, cellist, and D. W. Ainsworth, flutist. If a second violin was needed, Dan Emmett or George Siebert was called in. For years the Munger brothers ran a music store in St. Paul, where they were highly respected for their musical talent. Emmett became famous as the composer of "Dixie" and he had long been known as a performer in minstrel shows. Siebert organized one of the earliest orchestras in the Northwest.[10]

There were several good actors in the troupe. Outstanding was C. W. Couldock, who was a guest star for part of the 1857 season.[11] He is best remembered for his brilliant performance as Dunstan in "Hazel Kirke," Steele Mackaye's record-breaking success of the 1880's. But even a quarter of a century earlier, when he first went to St. Paul, he enjoyed a national reputation as a tragedian and the city had reason to be proud of his visit. According to Clara Morris: "The strong point of his acting was in the expression of intense emotion — particularly grief or frenzied rage. He was utterly lacking in dignity, courtliness, or subtlety. He was best as a rustic and he was the only creature I ever saw who could snuffle without being absurd or offensive."[12] His one weakness was an ungovernable temper, but this trait probably gave fire and conviction to such roles as Dunstan Kirke, Macbeth, Petruchio, and Lear. Manton H. Luther, dramatic critic of the Pioneer Press in the late 1880's, relates the following incident: "One night while the company was giving a heavy Shakespearean play the stage manager took occasion to cut out a small

York, 1901); Lizzie Fuller to Abby Fuller, September 4, 1857, Fuller Papers, in the possession of the Minnesota Historical Society.

[10] Manton H. Luther, "Theatres of Old St. Paul," in Daily Pioneer Press (St. Paul and Minneapolis), April 8, 1888; "The Old and the New," in Pioneer Press, January 22, 1889; Minnesotian, July 1, 30, 1857.

[11] This was not Couldock's first visit to St. Paul, for he played a season with the Hough and Meyer Company at Market Hall in 1856. Minnesotian, July 10, 1856.

[12] Morris, Life on the Stage, 130.

scene from the last act without consulting him. This completely broke the actor up. In a broad-sword scene, closing the play, he went for his innocent stage antagonist so savagely and viciously that the audience feared there would be blood spilled, and the innocent actor had to actually defend himself with his best skill to avoid being run through. When the curtain went down Couldock, still frantic, tore off the elegant costume he was wearing and rent it into shreds, apparently oblivious of all around him. A member of the orchestra was looking on, with eyes starting from their sockets in holy horror. Couldock suddenly looked up, and, seeing the young man's affrighted look, became instantly calm. 'My young friend,' he said to the musician, 'you have done your part very well; good evening.' Then he gravely rolled up his tattered costume and walked off with it." [13]

Couldock's visit not only meant good acting but also good plays. Previous companies had dabbled in an occasional scene or two from Shakespeare, but it was not until the arrival of Couldock that St. Paul had an opportunity to see such plays as *Othello, Macbeth, Hamlet,* and the *Merchant of Venice* reasonably well performed.[14]

One factor that undoubtedly retarded St. Paul's dramatic development during the early 1850's was the lack of an adequate playhouse. Prior to 1857 the only available theaters were crude frontier amusement halls. Some of the difficulties encountered when such halls were used for theatrical purposes may be surmised from a letter of Sara Fuller, a member of a pioneer St. Paul family, in which she tells of attending a performance in the Empire Block. "There were no windows," she writes, "excepting in front, and the stageing took those off, and all the air there was for the audience were the skylights overhead. We had been there about ten minutes when it commenced raining and they closed the skylights, and it was an oppressive warm night and they had been closed about five minutes when I began to grow faint and Sam [Abbe] went out with me to the door, and went for a tumbler of water for me and when he came

[13] Luther, in *Pioneer Press*, April 8, 1888.
[14] For reviews of earlier Shakespearean productions, see the *Minnesota Pioneer*, July 24, 27, 1854. Couldock gave such productions on July 12, 14, 17, and 18, 1856.

back I had fainted and fell upon the doorstep. . . . My bonnet was completely covered with mud, lamed one side of my face and had to wear a patch for more than a week. I did not attend any more theatre parties." [15]

The first man actually to do something toward improving theatrical conditions in St. Paul was Henry Van Liew. Unlike most of the theatrical managers who preceded him, Van Liew went to St. Paul for the purpose of making the city his home and providing it with a permanent theatrical company. When he arrived, in the spring of 1857, the city was nearing the climax of an extravagant financial boom. Van Liew immediately set to work on the construction of a temporary playhouse, which was intended to serve only until arrangements could be completed for a really first-class theater, but financial panic, fire, and civil war combined to defeat his plans. His temporary structure, the People's Theater, consequently holds the distinction of being the only building in St. Paul constructed primarily for theatrical purposes before the completion of the Opera House in 1867.[16]

According to one description, Van Liew's theater "cost the modest sum of $750. The sides were of rough boards, the roof of canvas. . . . The interior of the theater was as primitive as the days. There were no galleries. The floor raised gradually toward the rear, was seated with benches. The stage was cramped and small, and there was little attempt at decoration." A photograph of the exterior, in the possession of the Minnesota Historical Society, seems to bear out this description. The statement that it had no galleries, however, appears to be an error, since daily advertisments listed admission to the "colored gallery" at twenty-five cents. Nothing is known of the lighting except that there were footlights, a fact deduced from an ac-

---

[15] Sara Fuller's letter, which is undated, is near the end of a group for 1852 in the typewritten copies of letters among the Fuller Papers. For an account of early amusement halls, see Frank Moore, *Reminiscences of Pioneer Days in St. Paul*, 68–83 (St. Paul, 1908).

[16] *Pioneer and Democrat*, August 6, 1857, February 24, 1867; Luther, in *Pioneer Press*, April 8, 1888. The manager of the St. Louis Varieties, Lionel Bernard, made plans in 1857 to stay in St. Paul, but changed his mind before the season was over. See the *Minnesotian*, May 18, 1857. For an account of the dedication of the Opera House, see the *Pioneer*, February 24, 1867.

count of how a Chippewa Indian walked to the footlights and presented the star, Miss Henrietta Irving, with a diamond ring valued at seventy-five dollars. Van Liew brought an extensive wardrobe, good properties, and stage settings from Dubuque, Iowa, where he had been associated earlier with the Julien Theater.[17]

The People's Theater was completed and ready to open on June 27, 1857. Van Liew had assembled a capable company, which included William S. Forrest, brother of the great Edwin Forrest, as stage manager, and R. E. J. Miles, later a producer of national importance, as prompter. For the first six weeks Van Liew encountered keen competition. Sallie St. Clair and her Varieties were at the height of their popularity, a third theater was opened by D. L. Scott, and variety entertainment was abundant.[18] Then early in August the financial panic struck the town. All other forms of entertainment quickly melted away, but Van Liew continued, keeping his doors open in spite of hard times and empty seats. Finally, on October 19, 1857, even Van Liew had to give up, but not permanently. With the return of warm weather he was ready for the opening of a new season. Most of his original players returned, and to these Van Liew added the Old Gent's Band. Dion Boucicault's new drama, "The Poor of New York," which had the timely subtitle "or, the Panic of 1857," was one of the important productions of the season. Another highlight was "Mazeppa," which reached a sensational climax when a trained horse with Miles strapped to its back dashed wildly across the stage. The feat won the plaudits of both audiences and critics and it was soon to make the name of Bob Miles famous throughout the nation.[19]

On September 27, 1858, the season came to a close, but on April

[17] *Minnesotian*, September 17, 1857; *Pioneer and Democrat*, June 19, 1858; *Pioneer Press*, April 8, 1888, January 22, 1889.
[18] Brown, *History of the American Stage*, 236, 248; *Pioneer and Democrat*, July 29, 1857. Luther, in the *Pioneer Press*, April 8, 1888, quotes an "old-timer" as saying: "I remember going the rounds of the amusements on the Fourth of July in 1857 . . . and I can tell you I had to be mighty spry so as not to miss any of the shows. There were three theaters, a negro minstrel show, a big circus and an acrobatic tent show — all running full blast on that national anniversary."
[19] *Pioneer and Democrat*, May 26, August 20, 1858; Brown, *History of the American Stage*, 248.

23 of the following year the People's Theater was reopened for its third season. Apparently Van Liew planned to make this a banner year. From May 9 to June 2 he featured Mr. and Mrs. James W. Wallack in the best season of drama and tragedy the city had yet seen. But as soon as the Wallacks left, attendance dropped off. General business conditions seem to have entered that darkest phase just before the dawn. Newspapers often printed extra pages to take care of foreclosures. Toward the end of July the company ceased to give regular performances, although special benefits continued into August.[20]

The final blow came on September 8, 1859. A Republican political rally was in progress, with Schuyler Colfax and Galusha A. Grow as the speakers, when flames were discovered under the stage. The cause of the blaze was never determined. Some believed that sparks from a lamp or a lighted cigar had fallen through the rickety stage floor onto the combustible material beneath; others openly accused the Democrats of having fired the building in order to break up the rally. In any event a heavy wind soon swept the flames through the building and, although the audience escaped, nothing else could be saved. Van Liew lost everything — properties, costumes, scenery, and effects.[21]

During the following winter he and his foster daughter, the beautiful Azlene Allen, danced, sang, and entertained whenever and wherever possible in an effort to make a living. At last Van Liew gathered up his few remaining belongings and started down the river on a barge loaded with Minnesota sand. Somewhere along the way the barge sank, leaving Van Liew penniless, but in spite of everything he went to Memphis and started over again. It is little wonder that, upon learning that he had become a proprietor of the Memphis Burlesque Opera House, a writer for a St. Paul paper lauded Van Liew as a man of irrepressible "courage and enterprise." Many years later "a St. Paul gentleman ran across him at Deadwood,

---

[20] *Minnesotian,* May 11, June 2, 14, 30, 1859; *Pioneer and Democrat,* June 30, 1859. The last performance of the season seems to have been a benefit for the Radcliffe sisters. *Pioneer and Democrat,* August 7, 1859.

[21] *Pioneer and Democrat,* September 10, 1859; *Minnesotian,* September 9, 1859.

gray and grizzled but almost as cheery as in the days when he ca-
tered to the elite of St. Paul in the amusement line." [22]

With the passing of Van Liew, the first period in the history of
the St. Paul theater came to a close. Civil war soon intervened and
cut short all thoughts of stage entertainment. It was not until 1864
that a regular theatrical company was again seen in St. Paul, and
by that time the old plays, the old players, and the old playhouses that
had stirred audiences with excitement, laughter, and tears during the
1850's had disappeared.

[22] *Pioneer and Democrat,* September 23, October 7, 29, December 31, 1859, September 13, 1860; *Pioneer Press,* January 22, 1889.

Farm Machinery in Frontier Minnesota

Merrill E. Jarchow

ONE OF AMERICA's main contributions in agriculture has been the invention and development of laborsaving devices which have enabled farmers of the United States to cultivate more land per man than has been possible in any other country. The story of this development is a fascinating one. The easing of the toil of the farmer, better farming, the displacement of horses and mules, the freeing of acres formerly devoted to forage crops, the relation of farmer and machine agent, improved machines — these are only a few of the topics related to the history of farm machinery. It has been marked by almost constant improvement and development, and one of its most amazing features has been the fact that most of the action has taken place during a little over a hundred years. It was only in July of 1831 that Cyrus McCormick tested his reaper before a little group of interested, if skeptical, spectators on a Virginia farm. Before that date agricultural mechanization had made little advance, but it has since proceeded to such an extent that practically every farm job can be done by a machine. Playing a role by no means passive in this drama were many pioneer Minnesotans of the 1840's and 1850's.

Little is known about the agricultural implements used by Minnesota pioneers of the 1840's, but one student of local agricultural history believes that "most of their implements were made of wood." It is quite possible, however, that metal tips and other small pieces of metal were used to reinforce the wooden parts. William R. Brown, who farmed near Red Rock on the Mississippi River in the 1840's, recorded in his diary on May 20, 1846: "Davis plowing. Struck a Bolder & broke 2 inches off the point of the Boston plow - ground it & went to work." Again, on May 30, Brown wrote: "yesterday Harrison commenced plowing for potatoes & Rutabagas   plows 10 to 12 inches deep. . . . We hoed the Beets parsnips & Carrots." And on June 1 he recorded: "Sold my Large Prairie Plow to B. L. Rockwood he agrees to Break next year between the 20 of May & 20 June 8 acres for me for the Plow." [1] Thus it is evident that some crude machines were used in Minnesota in the 1840's, notably a breaking plow, perhaps a smaller plow, and a hoe. In addition to these implements, Brown and the other farmers of his day probably had sickles or cradles, spades, wagons, flails, and a few other primitive agricultural devices to aid them in their efforts to wring returns from the land. On the other hand, a lack of adequate tools was undoubtedly a real handicap.

Few of the earliest settlers in any part of the state had many farm implements when they arrived. Lurett Whiting, who left Fremont County, Iowa, early in the summer of 1865 and reached Clitherall, Minnesota, on July 31, gives an interesting account of farm machinery in the middle sixties, but the essentials of his story will fit the case of many Minnesota farmers of earlier decades. Whiting and his party took with them only a few plowshares, one breaking plowshare, a small set of blacksmith's tools, and some carpenter's tools. For plow beams and handles they were dependent upon their own skill, fashioning them out of wood cut in the forest. Their breaking plow "had a large beam about six feet long made of wood, with a piece framed into the back end of the beam to fasten the plow-share to. There were four-and-a-half-inch rods bolted above the share to take the place of a moldboard, and a wooden axletree about four feet long. To this was fastened the plow with two wagon-wheels attached to the axletree and a gauge made out of wood, so arranged that one could set it at any depth desired. Two yoke of oxen were hitched to this plow. It would run without being held up by hand and worked fine, all our land being broken in this way." [2]

The drags used by Whiting's group were made of wood, teeth and all, as iron teeth were not available. One was called the A drag, and it was hinged in the middle so that it could be cleaned by raising only half of it at a time. One member of the group fashioned a drag

[1] Rodney C. Loehr, ed., *Minnesota Farmers' Diaries,* 15, 78, 80, 81 (Minnesota Historical Society, *Narratives and Documents,* vol. 3 — St. Paul, 1939).

[2] Hallie M. Gould, *Old Clitherall's Story Book: A History of the First Settlement in Otter Tail County,* 18 (Battle Lake, 1919).

from a forked tree and drove teeth about twenty inches long into holes which he bored through the two prongs of the fork. "This was surely a comical looking affair," Whiting recalled, "and on account of its being so narrow and high it would often upset on the side-hills. This drag was drawn by oxen, and they had to work very steadily all day to smooth up an acre." Sometimes, when Whiting used it, he "let it run lying on its back . . . for it did just about as good work that way." Another invention used at Clitherall was a corn cultivator, which "never gave satisfaction. It went twice in a row and was never known to scour. After using it a while" the colonists "decided to call it a 'corn aggravator' for it lived up to that name to perfection." For cutting their grain, the Clitherall settlers used cradles with which "a man who was good at it" might cut five or six acres a day. After the grain was cut it was raked with a hand rake and bound by hand into bundles with straw. One other device mentioned by Whiting was a pair of wool cards, used in the process of getting wool ready to be spun into yarn.[3]

Such inventions as Whiting used and difficulties as he encountered probably were typical of the experiences of thousands of other early farmers. He mentions threshing with a horsepower machine, but even earlier, in the 1840's and 1850's, horses or oxen were commonly used to tramp out the grain.[4] Edward B. Drew, who farmed near Winona in the early 1850's, tells of the latter method in his reminiscences: "We stacked our wheat of course," he writes. "We wanted our winter wheat threshed for seed. We knew the primitive way was to tread it out with oxen. We had never seen anything of the sort done, except shelling out corn in Indiana by horses treading it out on the barn floor. . . . We fixed a place by the side of the stack, smoothing off a circular piece about twenty feet in diameter, and making the ground as smooth and hard as we could by using a maul made for that purpose. We made a temporary fence around it to keep the cattle off from it. . . . We were not long in threshing out the stack and it was very satisfactory too. But when it came to

---

[3] Gould, *Old Clitherall's Story Book*, 18, 19.
[4] Loehr, ed., *Minnesota Farmers' Diaries*, 17. J. S. Minor used cattle to thresh his oats, according to the *Minnesota Pioneer* (St. Paul), October 16, 1851.

cleaning the grain without a mill it was very poor business. . . . We watched for a windy day. We heard of a fanning mill in Winona. A man had sold his farm . . . and brought his mill to Minnesota. I found the man and borrowed or hired the mill. It was a streak of good luck." [5]

Another common method of threshing was to beat out the grain with a flail. This instrument was composed of two rods of hardwood of varying lengths, one about four and the other about two and a half feet long, fastened together at one end with a cord or a piece of rawhide. The operator held the loose end of the longer piece in his hand, whirled the shorter piece over his head, and brought the flail down upon the grain. In order to perform this task a person needed a certain amount of skill to avoid hitting himself over the head. A Mower County pioneer recalled that as a boy in 1858 he did not know how to use a flail, so he and his brothers and sisters "took the grain by the handful and whipped it out on the sides of a wagon box, letting the grain fall in the box." [6]

But hand labor on the part of the frontier agriculturist was not confined to threshing time. Most of his work had to be performed by hand. He often cut his hay and grain with a scythe, sickle, or cradle; he raked his hay and grain by hand; he bound his bundles in the same way, and shocked them without benefit of machine; his corn was planted, picked, husked, and often shelled by hand; and his fences, home, and barn were the products of his ingenuity and skill. Such tasks could and did become deadening, but they might also provide occasions for co-operative effort and social get-togethers. Cabin raisings and husking bees were common. In speaking of the latter, a Minnesota newspaper of 1858 remarked that they "have been in vogue, of late, and were the means of enlivening the spirits of old and young. On several occasions within a fortnight, and especially at the mansion of our neighbor Clayborne Chandler, one evening last week, the men had no occasion to sigh and wish they were

[5] Edward B. Drew, "Pioneer Days in Minnesota," 102. This is an unpublished reminiscent narrative; the Minnesota Historical Society owns a typewritten copy.

[6] Leo Rogin, *The Introduction of Farm Machinery,* 178 (University of California, *Publications in Economics,* vol. 9 — Berkeley, 1931); *History of Mower County,* 213 (Mankato, 1884).

boys again, for they were apparently young, in feeling at least . . .
the ladies, too, were all young equally with those of 'sweet sixteen.'
Better corn; ladies with healthier bloom upon their cheeks; gentlemen more worthy to be — ahem! — sweeter kisses; better people —
cannot be found elsewhere." [7]

The village blacksmith was a mighty figure. He was very necessary to the farmer, not only as a maker of implements, but as a re-
pairman as well. As late as 1925 one Minnesota pioneer liked his old
shovel plow, made in 1856 by David Smith, a Belle Plaine blacksmith. This plow was similar in shape to a cultivator shovel, but was
much larger and more convex. A strip of iron sharpened on one side
was attached to the beam perpendicularly ahead of the plow to cut
the sod. It was recalled that in his shop Smith turned out hundreds
of farming implements for the early settlers of the Big Woods area.[8]

Neither the inventiveness and ingenuity of the farmer himself nor
the hammer and anvil of the blacksmith, however, were sufficient to
meet the needs of Minnesota's growing rural population in the late
1840's. The earliest territorial newspapers frequently mention the
importation into the region of agricultural implements. One rather
typical item notes the fact that a certain Irishman who traveled up
the Mississippi by boat had on board three plows brought from Ireland. With them he expected to break the prairie, and they were
made of iron — beam, handles, and all. "Such plows will be of no
manner of service breaking prairies," was the newspaper comment.
And some early settlers recall in their reminiscences that the river
boats transported many implements to Minnesota, Iowa, and Wisconsin in the early 1850's. One pioneer recalled "seeing grain cradles
carried off the boat" in 1852.[9]

An essential implement was the breaking plow with which the
tough prairie sod was made ready for agriculture. Sometimes, also,
city lots were broken. Drew recalls that he "started the breaking-
plow" at Minnesota City early in May, 1852. "We made it quite a

[7] *Glencoe Register,* November 6, 1858.
[8] *Minneapolis Tribune,* May 17, 1925.
[9] *Pioneer,* November 15, 1850; Drew, "Pioneer Days in Minnesota," 30.

business breaking city lots for members [of the Western Farm and Village Association], or half a lot for some," he writes. "We got $3 per acre for breaking, and called a lot two acres." It was no easy job to cut the prairie sod, and sometimes as many as ten yoke of oxen were used to pull one giant breaking plow. Another difficulty was the failure of many of the plows to scour in the rich prairie soil. Joseph Haskell and James Norris, probably the first farmers in Washington County, used wooden and cast-iron plows which would not scour; so the plowmen had to carry paddles with which to clean the plowshares frequently.[10]

Another implement prized by the farmer fortunate enough to possess one was a reaper. There seems to be some doubt as to the exact date on which the first reaper made its appearance in Minnesota, but it probably was not later than 1854. In February of that year George W. Farrington of St. Paul wrote to Cyrus H. McCormick of Chicago, stating that the prospects were favorable in the vicinity of St. Paul for an increased demand for the latter's reaper. By talking to farmers during the winter of 1853–54, Farrington was led to believe that several of them planned to order reapers in the spring. Later in the spring J. C. Burbank and Company of St. Paul wrote to Norton and Hempsted of Chicago about obtaining reapers. The Minnesota concern had orders for two reapers manufactured in 1853 without mowers attached and for two complete machines. And in August, 1854, Farrington complained to McCormick that he had received a bill of lading for a McCormick machine which had been shipped from St. Louis but had arrived too late to be sold that year. This was regrettable, as Farrington had had many earlier opportunities for disposing of it. "Shall I pay charges on it and hold it until next season?" he asked. The freight charge incidentally was $55.95. The first reapers were crude machines designed for cutting both grain and hay, the hay mower being optional on a reaper. The reaper proper in 1854 was still rather crude, though it was equipped with

[10] Drew, "Pioneer Days in Minnesota," 41; Loehr, ed., *Minnesota Farmers' Diaries,* 11, 15; William A. Benitt, "Introduction to the History of Agriculture in Southern Washington County," 9. The latter is a manuscript narrative in the possession of the Washington County Historical Society, Stillwater.

seats for both the driver and the man who raked the cut grain from
a platform to the ground. The grain was bound by hand.[11]

It is thus apparent that McCormick early invaded the Minnesota
market. Farrington acted as his agent at St. Paul as early as 1854,
and other agents were appointed at various places in the 1850's and
later. These agents wrote numerous letters in longhand to the Mc
Cormick Harvesting Company of Chicago, giving not only details
of sales, but also information on market conditions, rival machines,
weather, and a host of other matters. In return came replies from
McCormick urging the agents to expand their business, telling how
to keep books, directing the disposition of machines neglected by incapable agents, and giving other information and advice.[12]

But McCormick did not have the Minnesota reaper business all
to himself in the 1850's. James J. Hill later recalled that a Manny
reaper was used in the territory at an early date. Mention is made of
this reaper in Illinois in 1851, but no record has been found to tell
when the first Manny machine appeared in Minnesota. The Manny
reaper seems to have been crude, however, until 1854, when a greatly
improved machine was placed on the market. Another reaper and
mower that competed with McCormick's machine was the Esterley.
George Esterley originally patented a header in 1844, but in the early
1850's he abandoned that device and began to manufacture a combined reaper and mower. A good deal of rivalry existed among the
agents representing the various implement manufacturers. In 1858,
one of McCormick's agents complained that other agents had the
advantage over him. It was claimed that the McCormick machines
were older and that they ran harder than the Manny and Esterley

[11] Rogin, *Farm Machinery*, 89–91; G. W. Farrington to C. H. McCormick, February
22, August 22, 1854; J. C. Burbank and Company to Norton and Hempsted, April 15,
1854. The letters are in the papers of the McCormick Harvesting Company, in the
possession of the McCormick Historical Association of Chicago. Filmslide copies of all
letters from this collection used in the preparation of this article are owned by the
Minnesota Historical Society.
[12] On May 31, 1856, for example, McCormick wrote to G. W. Farrington: "As we
have now little time to look please advise us whether you will be able to sell machines
this season. Will it be safe for me to ship you any and if so how many?" And on
December 15, 1856, he wrote to William Constance: "I . . . trust you can make large
sales. Can't you make arrangements and canvass Minnesota or part of it thoroughly?"
See also McCormick's letters to Timothy Chapman, March 21, 1857, and W. H. Harrington, April 17, 1858, McCormick Harvesting Company Papers.

reapers, and the writer noted that the latter especially had taken well during the season just past.[13]

In addition to the reaper, other implements found their way to Minnesota in the 1850's. A Fillmore County pioneer enumerates the various farm machines owned by the farmers of his neighborhood in that decade. He lists "lumber wagons, bob sleighs of home manufacture, sleds with long runners of home manufacture, 'A'-shaped harrows, wood beam crossing and breaking plows, cradles to cut the grain, scythes to cut the grass, hand rakes to rake the hay and the grain from the swath, single and double shovel corn plows, spades, shovels, axes, hoes, iron wedges, bettles or mauls used to split rails for fencing, frows to rive out the shakes or clapboards to cover the log cabin, and a limited number of carpenter tools." Often "five or more settlers would own a fanning mill to clean their grain, and in the first few years of settlement an eight-horse sweep power separator threshed all the grain grown in two or more townships." Corn was dropped by hand, covered with a hoe, and plowed with a one-horse shovel plow; the weeds in the cornfield were kept down with a hand hoe; and when the corn was picked the stalks were cut by hand and then shocked.[14]

Although many of the plows were homemade or were fashioned by the local blacksmith, some were factory made. By 1860 cast-iron plows were being made in numerous foundries and factories in the Middle West; and steel plows, which would scour, though they were often brittle and inclined to warp, were being manufactured in various places, notably by John Deere at Moline, Illinois. Breaking plows manufactured in Galena, Illinois, were extensively used in Minnesota in the early 1850's. Gradually, plow factories began to

[13] James J. Hill, "History of Agriculture in Minnesota," in *Minnesota Historical Collections,* 8: 278; Rogin, *Farm Machinery,* 77, 103; W. H. Harrington to McCormick, August 26, 1858, McCormick Harvesting Company Papers. Two machines manufactured by John H. Manny were purchased in St. Paul and taken to McLeod County in 1859, according to Franklyn Curtiss-Wedge, ed., *History of McLeod County,* 272 (Chicago, 1917).

[14] See William Willford's narrative, in Franklyn Curtiss-Wedge, comp., *History of Fillmore County,* 1: 117, 118 (Chicago, 1912). The *St. Croix Union* of Stillwater for January 16, 1855, offered for sale "Salmon's Improved Patent Grain and Grass Seed Separator," which won the first premium at the New York World's Fair and the New York State Fair of 1852. In Minnesota it was sold by McCloud and Brothers of St. Paul.

appear in Minnesota itself. The date of the first one is unknown, but in 1856 a St. Paul newspaper mentioned the fact that a plow factory was in operation at Cannon City in Rice County. This plant was owned by Honeyman and Andyke, and its breaking plows were said to be better than those made in Galena. The factory, however, unfortunately could not supply half the demand for plows in its vicinity. New developments in plows were being made constantly, some practical and some not, and many people had visions of great and rapid future progress. Governor Henry H. Sibley, in an address before the Dakota County Agricultural Association at Nininger, on October 8, 1858, predicted that the steam plow would soon supersede all others. Though his prediction was incorrect, there was an element of truth in it. On farms today steam is not the motivating power for plows, but another force, gasoline, furnishes fuel for the tractors that pull many Minnesota plows.[15]

Another machine that reached Minnesota in the 1850's was the mechanical thresher. Although the West lagged behind the East in the use of the threshing machine, the Case thresher was manufactured at Racine, Wisconsin, as early as 1844, and the better-known Pitts machine, at Alton, Illinois, in 1847. In 1852, the Pitts Company produced machines at its new plant in Chicago. Thus, the thresher became easily available in the West at about the same time that Minnesota was beginning to fill in with settlers.[16]

According to James J. Hill, the first threshing machine in Minnesota was operated by John Cormack, a river raft pilot, at Eden Prairie, back of Fort Snelling. Another pioneer, however, recalled that the first threshing machine brought to the territory arrived between 1853 and 1855, and belonged to Leonard Aldrich. Whether either is correct is uncertain, but it is probably true that the thresher made its advent about the same time as the reaper, in 1853 or 1854. The Pitts Company was early in the Minnesota field, and Hill's company made a contract with it "to try to sell three threshing machines."

[15] Rogin, *Farm Machinery,* 30, 33; Benitt, "Agriculture in Southern Washington County," 9; *Weekly Pioneer and Democrat* (St. Paul), May 29, 1856, November 4, 1858.
[16] Rogin, *Farm Machinery,* 165.

Hill was asked if he thought he could set up a thresher, and after going to Eden Prairie to watch Cormack's machine run, he was convinced that he could. Soon he had a customer near Shakopee.[17]

Most of these early threshers were little horsepower treadmill machines, which separated the grain and the straw, but threw them out together. Then all the straw had to be pitched on to a stack by hand, and the grain had to be cleaned with a fanning mill. Still this was better than using a flail. The Pitts thresher, however, from the first combined the three operations of threshing the grain, separating the grain and the straw, and winnowing the grain. Gradually other machines added shakers, which separated the wheat from the straw, to the cylinders; and then fanning mills, which cleaned the grain of chaff, became integral parts of the threshers. Nearly all machines seem to have had winnowers attached by the early 1860's.[18]

Many a farmer, however, did not have access to an improved thresher. Small machines provided with separators were much more common than the larger type. Before grain was fed into the cylinder, the bands on the bundles were cut by hand. Then the bundles were thrown into the machine by a feeder, who wore goggles to protect his eyes from stray kernels of grain flying from the cylinder. The feeder's task was considered the most laborious of all the operations connected with threshing. To operate the early threshing machines, from one to eight or ten horses were used. In the late 1860's, threshers "with from one to four-horse powers" were generally used in the East, but at the same time and even earlier, in Minnesota, eight and ten horsepower machines were frequently employed.[19]

Operating a horsepower machine was not always easy, as Lurett Whiting later recalled. "I well remember that the first threshing done in Otter Tail County was with a second-hand horsepower ma-

[17] Hill, in *Minnesota Historical Collections*, 8: 278; Franklyn Curtiss-Wedge, *History of Dakota and Goodhue Counties*, 1: 649 (Chicago, 1910).

[18] Curtiss-Wedge, *Fillmore County*, 1: 118; Rogin, *Farm Machinery*, 168–171; *Caledonia Journal*, October 2, 1929; *United States Census*, 1860, *Agriculture*, 23. John R. Cummins, a pioneer farmer living near Eden Prairie, made the following entry in his diary on August 20, 1858: "Threshing machine came today and threshed out 102 bus of winter wheat. This machine threshes and cleans at the same time, using 8 horses at a time." The Cummins Diary is owned by the Minnesota Historical Society.

[19] Loehr, ed., *Minnesota Farmers' Diaries*, 18; Rogin, *Farm Machinery*, 171, 174, 175.

chine which Uncle Lewis Whiting bought near Sauk Center," he writes. "As we had only a few horses we hitched in two yokes of oxen and started up, but the merry-go-round, so to speak, was too much for the oxen and they would get dizzy after two or three rounds and lie down, so we took them off and managed to thresh out what little we had with the horses by feeding the machine light. After a year or two farmers began to settle all around us, and we were then able to get all the horses we needed." [20]

The introduction of a thresher into a pioneer community was heralded with delight. Typical was the notice of the purchase of a machine at Glencoe: "This is an institution that was required, it being the second one introduced into the county. The proprietors will find plenty of work for their machine. We hope to hear it 'rattle' before another month rolls around. There will be some fun in threshing grain this year. It will not be all chaff." [21]

Another device much needed by farmers who did not live near an adequate water supply was a well-drilling machine. In Fillmore County in the 1850's, for example, some farmers hauled water five miles or more before well drillers became available. Finally, in 1858 and 1859, a drilling machine was put in operation on a local farm. "It consisted of a kind of spring pole arrangement and was operated by the foot. The hole drilled was about four inches in diameter, and about twelve inches a day constituted a day's work drilling." When water was reached, only about four pails a day could be drawn.[22]

As the decade of the 1850's came to a close, the United States government, for the third time through its census bureau, inquired into the status and progress of agriculture in each of the states. By studying the census findings it is possible to gain at least a rough picture of the place occupied by farm machinery in Minnesota's agricultural pattern in the decade. The total population, according to the census of 1860, was 172,023, as against 6,077 in 1850, a gain of 2,730.7 per cent. In the same decade, the rural population increased 3,119.4 per cent; the number of farms, 11,364.4 per cent; the value of

[20] Gould, *Old Clitherall's Story Book*, 20.
[21] *Glencoe Register*, July 23, 1859.
[22] Curtiss-Wedge, *Fillmore County*, 1: 116, 117.

farms, land, and buildings, 16,884.4 per cent; and the production of field crops, 12,248.4 per cent. Thus the number of farms, the value of farm property, and the total volume of field crops each increased four or five times faster than the total population. Although the average value of agricultural implements per farm decreased from $102.00 in 1849 to $56.00 in 1859, farm machine values for the state as a whole increased by 6,271.2 per cent in the same decade. Nearly all the farm machinery used in the state was imported at heavy expense from the East, for only such simple utensils as plows and fanning mills were manufactured in Minnesota in 1860. All grain cradles, horse rakes, forks, spades, shovels, straw cutters, and hoes were imported, and only about thirty of the thousand reapers sold in Minnesota in 1861 were manufactured there. This represented expenditures amounting to about $150,000, a "pretty large sum to go out of our State in one year for a single implement used by the farmer," according to the state's leading farm journal, which asked, "When will these machines be made at home?" [23]

Fifteen years later the state had many farm implement plants, and manufacturers from other localities had developed elaborate distribution agencies in Minnesota. Then loud complaints from Granger orators, debt-ridden farmers, and crusading editors were voiced against the machine manufacturers and agents. Some urged that the farmers scrap their machinery and return to the cradle and the hoe. But whatever the evils associated with the production, sale, and distribution of farm machinery, one thing is certain — man's, and later woman's, lot was eased and the constant fear of famine was removed by the invention, production, and use of mechanical devices on the farm. Even today we may be only on the threshold of agricultural mechanization, and a century hence observers probably will consider our farming methods just as primitive as we do those of 1850.

[23] Edward V. Robinson, *Early Economic Conditions and the Development of Agriculture in Minnesota,* 45, 55, 56 (University of Minnesota, *Studies in the Social Sciences,* no. 3 — Minneapolis, 1915); R. W. Murchie and M. E. Jarchow, *Population Trends in Minnesota,* 7 (University of Minnesota, Agricultural Experiment Station, *Bulletins,* no. 327 — 1936); *Minnesota Farmer and Gardener* (St. Paul), 1: 120, 267 (February, September, 1861). The latter publication notes that a plant in Winona manufactured threshing machines.

With Cass in the Northwest in 1820

Edited by Ralph H. Brown

[HEREWITH *is presented the third and final installment of the journal kept by Charles C. Trowbridge while traveling as a member of the Cass expedition in the summer of 1820. Earlier sections of the journal, recording the writer's adventures and impressions of the country between Detroit and Sandy Lake in what is now northern Minnesota, appear in the issues of this magazine for June and September, ante, p. 126–148, 233–252. In the concluding section, Trowbridge describes the voyage down the Mississippi to the newly established post at the mouth of the Minnesota, thence to Fort Crawford at Prairie du Chien, by way of the Wisconsin and Fox rivers to Green Bay, and back to Detroit.* Ed.]

Sunday 16th July. To day the Governor held a council with the Indians residing at this Lake, and after giving them the usual advice respecting their conduct generally, and receiving in return, reiterated promises of friendship and affection to the American gover[n]ment, we proceeded to distribute a number of presents, among the most acceptable of which was ammunition, they having fired the last round of powder in saluting the Governor on his arrival. After the pipe of peace was presented, (which ceremony always attends a council) the Governor proposed to the Chiefs, that some of them should accompany him to St Peters, with a view to conclude a peace with the Sioux with whom they have been at war from time immemorial.[67] They consented to have a meeting for the purpose of determining by the arrival of the Govr from the head of the Mississipi for which they understand he is to set out to morrow.

Monday July 17th Every thing was prepared for an early start to see the head waters of one of the longest Rivers in the world, and the great Northern Boundary of our expedition. The Governor set out in three canoes, accompanied by all the party except Mr Doty, Mr Chase and

[67] For a comprehensive view of the advance of the Chippewa into what had been Sioux territory and the resulting long-continued conflict, see Folwell, *Minnesota,* 1: 80–88.

myself, who are left to superintend the remaining part of our brigade consisting of 12 white men & 8 indians, it being contemplated to return in a barge and two canoes from this place.

They took nothing but their blankets & provisions; being determined that weight of lading should not retard their progress.

Tuesday July 18th. On walking through the indian encampment this morning I observed a large number of old people assembled, and on enquiry found that it was a council convened to deliberate on the proposition made to them by the Gov'. Tho' such a question might be settled without any difficulty, it is characteristic of the indians, that they duly weigh the most trivial matters before a decision is made.

Thursday 20th July, Being a day devoted to the collection of information: [68]

On enquiry of M' Ashman, I learn that there are 3 principal places of residence of the Indians of this country: these are, Fon du Lac, Sandy Lake, and Leech Lake.

The Fon du Lac Indians are in consequence of the paucity of game and fish, obliged to wander about in bands, on the small Lakes and Rivers with which this Country abounds; for they have neither Buffalo, Deer, Wolf, Fox or Racoon.

Their tribe consists of 45 men, 60 women & 240 children, besides 30 Half breeds. They do not partake of the genius and spirit of the Northern Indians; and although they consider the Sioux as their common enemy, yet their natural indolence prevents them from freely engaging in the scenes of war and bloodshed common to the other parts of their tribe.

The Sandy Lake Indians are more numerous than those of Fon du Lac: There are 85 men, 243 women & children and 35 Half breeds. They

[68] The material recorded by Trowbridge under this date closely parallels the account of Doty in *Wisconsin Historical Collections*, 7:195–206. Doty says that he occupied himself "in surveying the lake and acquiring information relative to the country" during the absence of Cass. He also implies, p. 195, that Cass specifically requested him to secure the information. The similarity of this portion of the accounts of Doty and Trowbridge, extending to the misspelling of words then in common usage, suggests that one was copied from the other, or that both were copied from the same source. The data, according to Doty, were "obtained from persons who have traveled over and resided in the country, almost from their infancy," a designation that excludes Ashmun, whose arrival was of comparatively recent date. The source of the map of river routes in Doty's report, p. 204, is not given, thus detracting from its authenticity. In estimating the Indian population, the informants may have known of similar tables included by Zebulon M. Pike in his *Account of Expeditions to the Sources of the Mississippi*, Appendix, part 1, p. 66 (Philadelphia, 1810). These data are summarized by Warren, in *Minnesota Historical Collections*, 5:459.

are divided into 3 parties, one of which resides at Sandy Lake, one at Rice Lake, and the third between Sandy and Leech Lakes.

These Indians hunt as far north as the Vermilion Lake, the head waters of the Fon du Lac River, on which the Am. Co. have an establishment. They take Bear, Otter, Muskrats, Beaver, Raccoon, Fishers, Martin, and sometimes Red & Gray foxes and Deer. The only Buffalo they kill are taken on the borders of the Sioux Country, which is the great bone of contention between the two nations.

The Lakes Winnipec [*Winnebagoshish*], Cross [*Bemidji*], Red Cedar [*Cass*], Leech, and Sandy, abound in white fish, but none are so rich as those of Leech Lake. They are never known to ascend the Rivers.

Some other kinds of fish are caught, among which are Pike, Carp, Blk Bass, Catfish, and a kind resembling the white fish in colour and shape, but smaller, called the Telibee.[69] Without these very necessary animals, together with the wild rice, the trade could not be conducted in this country, for it would be utterly impossible to transport provisions from the South.

The white fish are taken in autumn, & the Telibees in the spring of the year, in nets of 60 to 100 fathoms in length. Among the Water fowls, we saw the Bustard, Wild Goose, (both of which are similar) several kinds of Ducks, the Swan, Pelican, Loon, Gully & co[r]morant. The pheasant, pa[r]tridge & pigeon are found here, the latter numerous.

The Rein & Common Deer and the Moose are killed in the vicinity of this Lake, but it is a saying among these wise people, that he who kills a moose is perfect master of his trade.[70]

This animal does not depend on its eyes, but their sense of hearing is very acute; and if once fairly raised from its bed will run sometimes 100 miles before it rests.

When an indian finds a fresh track of this animal, he follows it until

[69] In an interview in November, 1941, Dr. Samuel Eddy of the department of zoology in the University of Minnesota identified the pike as the northern pike, not the walleyed pike; the carp as the quillback or carp sucker, not the fish commonly called the carp today; the black bass as the largemouth bass; and the catfish as one of several species of bullhead. The tullibee is a type of whitefish familiar to present-day fishermen. Doty, in *Wisconsin Historical Collections,* 7:196, records that it was "called by the savages the too-nee-bee, and by the French, 'telibees.' "

[70] In the expert opinion of Dr. Thomas S. Roberts of the Museum of Natural History, University of Minnesota, Trowbridge's bustard was the Canada goose; his pheasant, the ruffed grouse; his partridge, the Canada or spruce grouse; and his pigeon, the passenger pigeon. Dr. Roberts also suggests that the "rein and common deer" would now be known as the caribou, and the white-tail or Virginia deer, respectively.

he comes near the spot where he expects to find him, from which he proceeds with all imaginable caution until he gets sight of his object, when he drops on his knees, and removing every obstruction .however trifling, advance[s], until he can fire with certainty, when by breaking a twig not larger than a pipe stem he starts the moose from his bed, which is the proper time for him to secure his remuneration for the toils of the chase. It is remarkable that if the wind blows never so hard it is necessary to use the same precaution as if no air was stirring. No Snakes are found here except the small striped snake.

The Leech Lake Indians are more numerous and more warlike than either of the other bands, and are divided, each division having its own chief.

There are 200 men, who have 350 wives, & about 1100 children.

The Brachu, who resides at Sandy Lake is acknowledged to be the general leader of this part of the tribe as well as the others, but maintains little influence over those who are distant from him.[71] The Chieftanship descends from father to son, and the women are always excluded, so that the line becomes extinct on the death of the last male of the old line. When this happens to be the case, (but I believe it seldom happens,) the vacancy is filled by election of the man most valiant, brave and powerful, or the most celebrated for wisdom and eloquence; and he inherits the title of chief together with all the honors of the last in power. This practice is never deviated from except by some daring fellow, who usurping the authority, holds the tribe in awe by his ferocity or the influence of numerous relatives devoted to his interest.

Such an one however is soon disposed of by his enemies.

The Brachu or present acknowledged Chief of all these tribes, raised himself to his present advanced station by his superior eloquence alone, and is said to be the first general ruler they ever have had.

The Game and fish are *generally* much the same at Leech Lake as at Sandy and the other lakes, but the white fish are thought far superior to those caught at the Saut de St Marie.

As the indians are extremely improvident, they are sometimes obliged

[71] Other Cass journalists spell this name differently. The name presumably derives from "De Breche," identified by Pike, in his *Expeditions,* 45, and later by other visitors, as "Broken Tooth," reigning chief at an earlier time. The context and usage suggests that "the Brachu" had become the title, not the specific name, of the Sandy Lake chieftain.

to subsist on the Wau-be-se-pin. It is a root resembling the potatoe, is mealy when boiled, and grows in clay soil.

They have also the Sitch-auc-wau-besepin, which resembles the other, but is inferior in quality, and grows in every part of the Country. When these cannot be found, the Watapine is eaten by them: this is a small root, frequently pulled 3 feet in length and for preservation dried in the sun: it is most abundant on Lake Superior.[72] The only way of cooking these is by boiling. In cases of extreme necessity they use a wood which resembles Bitter Sweet, growing to the tops of the highest trees; which when boiled is very palatable.

They eat every animal, *and every part* of it, and it is not unusual for them to season their rice with the intestines of Rabbits and other small game; a practice almost incredible were it not familiar to us.

Winter in this country commences about the first of December and closes about the first of April. The climate at Sandy Lake is similar to that of Montreal, but it is much colder at Fond du Lac, where the season is 15 days later. The snow on Lake Superior is often 3 feet in depth, but decreases to the west, so that they frequently have 3 feet snow at Fond du Lac when it is only two or three inches deep at Sandy Lake — and while a South wind may prevail 3 days at Fond du Lac without decreasing the snow, 12 hours of the same wind invariably produces a thaw at Sandy Lake.

The summer season is generally very warm and pleasant and so soon as winter disappears vegetation progresses very rapidly.

The traders here suffer nearly as much in the summer season from

---

[72] Consultation of many Chippewa and Sioux vocabularies has not been rewarded by positive identification of the plants whose phonetic spellings are given in this passage. It may be said, at least, that *waub* is white and *sepin* root in the Chippewa tongue. In the informed opinion of Dr. C. O. Rosendahl of the department of botany in the University of Minnesota, expressed in a letter of April 14, 1941, it is "fairly certain" that "Wau-be-se-pin is the common Arrowhead — *Sagittaria latifolia*. Sitch-auc-wau-be-se-pin seems likely to be another species of Arrowhead, but this surmise may be wrong. Watapine might be the Ground nut — *Apios tuberosa*," but Dr. Rosendahl is "rather doubtful of this species being common along the south shore of Lake Superior, hence it is more likely to be some other plant." Henry H. Sibley, in the "Life and Adventures of Joseph Jack Frazer," in the *St. Paul Pioneer* for January 20, 1867, tells of a Sioux camp that "subsisted on the dried meat *cached* during the winter, and the *wap-si-pin,* or small bulbous root of the nature of a potatoe, found in the shallow ponds. These roots are a favorite food of the larger wild fowl, such as geese and mallard ducks. They have a slightly saccharine flavor, and are by no means in-nutritious, or unpleasant to the taste." This doubtless was the arrowhead. Doty, in *Wisconsin Historical Collections,* 7:198, says that the bittersweet is also named "bois retors," and that "sitch-auc-wau-be-sepin" is the "crane potato."

the Musquitoes as from the want of provisions. Tho' they have none of the gnats mentioned on Lake Superior, yet the difference in the sise, numbers, and venomous sting of the former insect are a sufficient counterbalance to any deficiency on that score.

Indeed we are obliged not only to use our nets, but to keep a smoke in our room during the night, or we should be serenaded by millions of these unwelcome visitors: and in the day time if we walk towards the woods it is necessary to use veils.

Goods are sold here at enormous prices, but owing to the indolence or dishonesty of the indians, very little is eventually realized.

All the goods are sold and reckoned by skins — a [*beaver?*] skin is estimated at $2. a Blanket is sold for 4 to 6 skins. ½ p^t powder 1 skin, 30 balls the same, a knife 1 skin, 1 fathom of twist Tobacco 2 skins, 3 plugs do 1 skin, a hatchet 1 skin, and in proportion for other articles.

If an indian obtains credit for these articles, he expects to be furnished gratis, with a flint, needle, awl, gun worm, rings, tobacco, and a little vermilion; and in a credit of 600 skins, the trader considers himself recompensed (because he is obliged to do so) if he receives 300 in return.

The indians pay for their goods in Rice, Sugar or furs. A Mocock of Sugar of 40 lbs is equivalent to 4 skins, a Sack of Rice (1 Bus) 2 skins, a large Beaver 2, a large Otter 2, 2 prime Buck skins 1, 3 Racoons, 1, 2 Lynx, 1, 2 fisher, 1.

One very necessary article to the indian hunter he never fails to pay for: this is his axe. When he returns from his hunting ground to the trading post, his best skins are selected and given to the trader for this instrument which he is sensible he cannot do without.

The Am Fur Compy have almost all the trade in this Section of the Country, tho' they are not unfrequently harrassed by petty traders.

Monday 24. July. About noon we had the pleasure of witnessing the return of our party.

They ascended the Mississipi to Upper Red Cedar Lake, distant from Sandy Lake about 350 miles.[73]

They were prevented from ascending any farther on account of the difficulty of the navigation. The Country above is represented as very uninteresting: Mr Schoolcraft collected nothing in the mineralogical way

[73] The narrative shows clearly that the party laid no claim to having reached the final source of the river. The explorers reached Cass Lake, which Schoolcraft named Cassina, on July 21, and concluded that the Mississippi entered that lake from the south. The mileage given here is, of course, far in excess of the actual distance.

and Capt Douglass was equally unsuccessful in Botany. Red Cedar Lake
is about 9 miles in circumference and situated in Lat ——. The River
from Sandy to Cedar Lake is about 60 yds wide.

Mr Chase who has been out to survey & delineate Sandy Lake has also
returned, and has probably the most correct chart that was ever made of
it.[74] The shape is very singular: its width is in no one place more than
4 or 5 miles, but there are many deep indentations, and its circumference
cannot be less than 30 miles. The shores are not generally sandy as has
been supposed, but gravelly, abounding in the most beautiful Cornelians
and agates, of which we have collected specimens in abundance. The
point on which the Fort stands is one exception — and it was this point
in all probability that gave the Lake its name.

Tuesday July 25. When our party returned from above we had everything in readiness for a start. The Barge which we repaired or rather
finished, was one which the engagées had made during the summer season, when they could find no other manner of passing their time; and
we collected a parcel of old fish nets and gum (which served as substi-
tutes for oakum and pitch) with which we made it tolerably tight & fit
for use.

Accordingly we left Sandy Lake at 3 p m, in the Barge & 3 canoes,
leaving 2 behind as useless; and we were soon on the Missisipi, pulling
away with light hearts and anxious hopes. I do not know when I have
felt more happy than this afternoon, in the prospect of seeing again my
much loved friends: and although we are still 1700 miles distant from
them, yet we feel comparatively near to them.

The communication between the Lake and the Missisipi is two miles
in length and about 30 yds in width.

We made to day 28 miles and encamped on a small Bottom, in the
midst of swarms of musquitoes which promise to give us little rest.

We are accompanied by the Chief of the Sandy Lake tribe and 15 of
his principal men, who are going to treat of a peace with the Sioux. On
our passage this afternoon we observed another singular custom of the
indians, which had not before presented itself to us.

The wife of the old chief had attached to a board (such an one as they
bind their children to for the purpose of making them strait) a roll of
cloth in the shape of an infant, which she had decorated with beads and

[74] No map that could be attributed to Chase was found among the documents consulted by the editor.

other ornaments, among which was the medal presented by the Governor; and this on landing was the first object of their care.

On enquiry we learned by our interpreter that it was intended to represent a young child of the chief's lately deceased, and that it was customary to carry this with them for two years from the period of its death, unless before that time he should be blessed with another, to which the image would give place — a singular superstition!

Wednesday July 26th. Last night to have the benefit of room & air we pitched our nets outside of the tent, and about one o'clock the rain suddenly commenced falling in torrents, and before we could collect our bedding &c, the tents were blown down; so that we were obliged to retreat for a time to the lodge of our indian friend the chief, where I remained until morning sleeping soundly in a puddle of water at least four inches deep in some places; yet I experienced no ill from it, perhaps because we are more enured to hardships than some time since.

At sun rise we started in the canoes, but the barge (and its party were left behind,) she having sprung a leak. During the day we shot at a Deer, some Ducks & a Heron, but only succeeded in getting two Ducks.

Passed during our course 3 small rapids, which tho' not dangerous would retard the progress of ascending boats very considerably. We find the Current very strong & rapid, the banks generally low and spreading into extensive bottoms, but sometimes very high & barren. We have seen today, Elm, Birch, Black walnut, a little Butternut & Pine.

At 7 in the evening we landed, and about 10 had the pleasure of seeing our barge come on pretty well repaired.

About 2 miles above our encampmt, Pine River has its confluence with the Mississipi, and tho' a small stream considerably augments the latter, so that it is now nearly of an average width of 120 yds. We made to day as nearly as we are able to judge 100 miles, which with the distance yesterday makes us 128 from the Lake.

Thursday 27th July. At 5 we embarked, and about noon we passed La Riviere au Corbeau or Crow River, a considerable stream flowing through a low open Country.[75]

We find the scenery dull and uninteresting, well calculated to remind the traveller that he is far from the haunts of civilised beings.

At 5 we arrived at the encampment of those indians who left Sandy

[75] This is the Crow Wing River of today, not to be confused with the Crow River, a tributary of the Mississippi entering at Dayton.

Lake to hunt, immediately after receiving ammunition from the Govr.
They have killed only 5 or 6 Buffalo, not daring to go far south, on account of their differences with the sioux. We proceeded on two miles
from their encampment and landed. Here they came with their squaws
and presented us with fresh and dried Buffalo and venison in abundance.

In our descent to day we passed many rapids, some of which are rather
dangerous.

Mr Forsyth while walking out this evening saw a herd of Buffalo,
and to his great satisfaction killed one of them.

The E. side of the River from the River de Corbeau to our encampment is one immense prairie with very high banks, while the W. is
generally Low and well timbered. On the shores we find occasionally
some of our favorites, agates and cornelians.

We made to day about 90 miles.

Friday July 28th We got under way at an early hour this morning and
soon fell in with our indian friends, without whose assistance we should
find the navigation of the River very dangerous.

Having now got into the Buffalo Country, we landed about noon to
enjoy the pleasures of a hunt.[76]

Immediately on ascending the bank we saw three or four droves of
these animals, containing from 20 to 30 in each, which is considered as
a number unusually small. We divided our party and took guides or instructors, intending to do the business systematically, and went in pursuit.

Doct Woolcott, Mr Mackay and myself approached within 30 yards
of a drove by crawling through the grass on our hands & knees, and
after having taken deliberate aim, fired; but to our astonishment *every
one* scampered *off apparently unhurt.*

The other droves were fired at with almost as little success, and we
began to despair, until one of the indians brought a Bull down with a
single ball; and afterwards two more were killed, together with an Elk
and a Deer. The difficulty of killing a Buffalo is very great: I saw one

[76] In a letter written to Calhoun from Detroit, February 2, 1821, Cass states that
"In this debatable land the game is very abundant. Buffaloes, Elk, & deer range un-
harmed and unconscious of harm. The mutual hostilities of the Chippeways & Sioux
render it dangerous for either, unless in strong parties, to visit this portion of the
Country. The consequence has been a great increase of all the animals, whose flesh
is used for food or whose fur is valuable for market. We found herds of Buffalo
quietly feeding on the plains. There is little difficulty in approaching sufficiently near
to kill them." Department of War, Letters Received, National Archives.

shot seven or eight times without bringing him down, until an indian ran up to him and shot him through the head. The Elk is very large and strong, resembling a Deer only in shape and colour. The meat is much finer than that of the Buffalo which we yesterday tho't delicious. We landed at sun down very much fatigued, on a large prarie, where herds of Buffalo were seen feeding, but the temptation was not so great as it would have been in the morning, and we did not attempt to disturb them. These Prairies as well as we can judge are about 15 miles wide and extend from the River de Corbeau to the falls of St Anthony, with little interruption. They show few indications of vegetation, and are generally destitute of trees.

Saturday 29th July. This morning two of the Sandy Lake indians set out before us on foot, as they told us to hunt, but as we afterwards learned, to act as spies, for this is an invariable practice with either nation when approaching the Territory of another.

About 12, they returned to the Bank of the River, bringing with them a large piece of Bark, containing a communication in hieroglyphics from the Sioux Indians. Here a consultation was held and the contents of the letter explained to us. First, the Mississipi & St Peters [*Minnesota*] rivers were delineated, then the fort at the mouth of the latter, the sentinels at their posts, The principal chief, with a sword in one hand and a pipe in the other. On the river M, at different points the remains of 19 lodges were drawn, the number of warriors that had lately been at those encampments, with the Am. flag, and their object.[77]

From all this we were made to know that the Sioux desired a peace, that the Am. officer wished it, that they had been hunting in this country, and had made 19 encampments, consequently had spent much time; and that their object in leaving this piece of Bark was to inform the Chippeways that no evil was intended them should they be on their journey to St Peters for the purpose of holding a Treaty.[78]

Our indians were much pleased at the receipt of this intelligence and we saw nothing but manifestations of joy during the day; particularly when we passed the remains of the Sioux encampments, of which we saw 8 or 10 to day.

[77] The exchange of peace notes between the Chippewa and the Sioux is also treated by Doty, in *Wisconsin Historical Collections*, 13:215, with the additional comment that the birchbark letter was preserved by the governor.
[78] The names St. Peter's, Mendota, and New Hope were often used interchangeably. The entire region about the mouth of the Minnesota was known as St. Peter's.

We stopped frequently to find Buffalo and cornelians, but both are growing scarce as we approach the falls.

Encamped at 6 p.m.

Sunday 30th July. At 9 this morning we arrived at the Falls of S[t] Anthony, (in Sioux Minee Hah Hah.) [79] These afford a most romantic prospect, which is not a little heightened by the green foliage of a small island laying nearly in the centre of the perpendicular fall. The descent in the distance of ½ a mile is 58 feet, but the perpendicular fall is only about 20 feet.

The rocks over which this body of water is precipitated are very beautiful white Sand stone. We made a portage of ¾ of a mile around the falls and about noon were ready to reembark for S[t] Peters. Immediately after passing the falls a visible change takes place in the appearance of the country. The shores become Rocky, the Cliffs in many places perpendicular & very high.

In about two hours we arrived at the Fort. We found the troops stationed about one mile above the mouth of the S[t] Peters, on a commanding eminence, chosen as a summer situation in consequence of the salubrity of the air.

The Officers are living in log huts, covered with bark, and rendered tolerably comfortable. The Soldiers are in tents. The troops erected a cantonement on their arrival here, near the mouth of the S[t] Peters, but it was found to be an injudicious selection, on acc[t] of a swamp in the neighborhood.

The permanent work is to be built on a very high & commanding point of land formed by the junction of the two Rivers.[80]

Much of the land is said to be highly susceptible of cultivation, and

---

[79] The names of the Falls of St. Anthony and of Minnehaha Falls were sometimes confused, as here, by early writers.

[80] The Cass party arrived at a transitional stage in the development of this post, which was soon thereafter to bear the name Fort St. Anthony and finally Fort Snelling. The Fifth United States Infantry left Detroit in the spring of 1819 and proceeded by way of Green Bay and Prairie du Chien to the mouth of the Minnesota River, which was reached in the latter part of August. The first encampment was on the east bank of the Minnesota, near the present site of Mendota. In May, 1820, the troops were removed to a new location on the west bank of the Mississippi, north of the Minnesota River, forming a cantonment named Camp Coldwater, and there the explorers found them. No permanent buildings were erected at the Camp Coldwater site. As the journalist states, preparations were being made to build the fort on the high bluff at the junction of the two rivers. "It is in fact," says Schoolcraft in his *Narrative Journal*, 292, "the same point of land which first suggested to Lieutenant Pike the idea of its being an eligible situation for a fort." For a map of these sites, see Folwell, *Minnesota*, 1:424.

there can be no doubt of this fact if it resembles that adjacent to the present cantonement, where every garden vegetable grows luxuriantly. Peas were eaten in june and Corn on the 20th July, which is earlier than many of the States can boast of.

The Country back of the Fort is a handsome rolling prairie, abounding in small Lakes, where fish are caught in abundance.

Here we found Lieu^t [Andrew] Talcott & Capt [Matthew J.] Magee of the Missouri Expedition, who had travelled from the Council Bluffs by land, across the country, and owing to the ignorance of their guide were on the route 21 days. Tho' Mr Talcott estimates the distance to be no more than 300 miles. Their provisions & baggage, and that of their Soldiers, of whom they had 12, were caried on Pack horses. Their object is, to mark out a road for expresses, but they expect to find it a very difficult task, as most of the Country is a low prairie.[81]

Monday 31. July. This day the indians of the Sioux and Chippeway nations met each other at the council House of L^t [Lawrence] Taliafer[r]o the indian Agent at this place, and after a council of some length, a peace was concluded, which they protested should be lasting as the Sun.[82] This however may *not* be a lasting peace, for as it appears, it was only made between 3 of the Sioux Bands and one of the Chippeways, and of course, agreeably to their customs does not affect the distant bands of either nation.

Besides the Sioux tho' a cowardly race, are very tenacious of their right to the hunting grounds on the Mississipi, and easily take umbrage.

The Sioux Indians hunt the Buffalo with the horse and bow; a plan more efficient than the other, as their horses are well trained, and their arrows, which shoot with great force are barbed with steel.

It is said that they drive these arrows entirely thro' the fleshy parts of the Buffalo. They also have guns, which they use for common hunting purposes; if they can procure ammunition.

---

[81] The officers mentioned by Trowbridge and Captain Stephen W. Kearny, with a command of a dozen soldiers, had been at the cantonment for five days. The "Journal of Stephen Watts Kearny," kept on this trip, has been edited by Valentine M. Porter and published in the *Missouri Historical Collections,* 3: 8–29, 99–131. "Low prairie," in the specific meaning of the time, was descriptive of a wet or marshy terrain.

[82] Lawrence Taliaferro resigned his military commission in 1819 to become Indian agent at the Minnesota fort, a position which he occupied until 1840. Schoolcraft notes, in his *Narrative Journal,* 304, that on August 1 "A treaty of peace was this day concluded between the Sioux and Chippeways in the presence of Governor Cass, Colonel [Henry] Leavenworth, Mr. Tallifierro, the Indian agent at St. Peter's, and a number of the officers of the garrison." Leavenworth was the commandant at the fort.

They are a very ill looking race of beings and almost as indolent as the northern Chippeways.

Monday July 31st From the observations taken this morning by Cap[t] Douglass and Lieut. Talcott the latitude of this place (S[t] Peters) has been ascertained to be 44° 45′ north.

S[t] Peters may boast of many curiosities. M[r] Schoolcraft has procured some handsome specimens of native copper from the cliffs on the east side of the river; and we have seen curiosities in natural history. The Gofer [Gopher] [83] is one of them. This animal is nearly of the sise of a black squirrel, but much in appearance like a rat, and is very destructive to the gardens. It lives and moves altogether under ground and works it[s] way with great ease and swiftness. Its teeth and claws are very long, and, they are provided with a bag on each side of the head, capable of holding a gill each, in which as they progress they draw the earth; when these are full they return to the mouth of the hole and discharge their burden; and from repeated observations it has been ascertained that only three seconds of time are necessary for collecting and discharging each load, feeding themselves at the same time on the roots of such vegetables as come in their way.

A singular bird has also been found here, of which no account has been seen in history. It is much of the size of a robin and has a long bill and webbed feet, and is of a beautiful white colour.[84]

Wednesday August 2nd. About 9 we left S[t] Peters and descended the river 7 miles, where we stopped to view a cave, of which [Jonathan] Carver spoke as of a great curiosity. About 80 yards from the bank of the river we found its mouth, and having lighted a number of torches we proceeded to explore. A broad entrance of the height of eight feet, led us to a large chamber, through which ran a little brook, whose water was clear as crystal and very cold: from this we passed through a low, narrow passage into another chamber less than the first. These are the only rooms which we discovered, and after penetrating a distance of 400 yd′rs from the last, in all which distance we were obliged to crawl on our hands and knees, we turned about, well satisfied that no other opening could be found, and that the water which had ran through and

---

[83] The word enclosed in brackets was written by the author above the line, and was doubtless intended as a correction. The reference is to the pocket gopher.

[84] Dr. Thomas S. Roberts, in a letter to the writer dated November 19, 1941, suggests that this bird was probably "a young black tern which is so largely white that it would appear white on the wing."

caused the excavation through which we had made our way with so much difficulty, proceeded from a spring perhaps not far distant from the place at which we turned about. The name of Carver had been cut on the soft sand stone of which this cave is formed, but tho' we searched, we could not find it, and after leaving our names marked on the rocks at its mouth we reembarked and continued our course, not a little elated with the idea of soon seeing our home & friends. About noon we arrived at a Sioux village, containing 8 large houses or wigwams, and a number of small ones.[85] On landing we were saluted by the Chiefs and ushered into a large wigwam, where Buffalo robes were spread for us to sit on, and after some time, an old warrior commenced a speech which he continued nearly half an hour, and the purport of which was, to inform us that they were pleased with our attention in calling at their village, &c, that they entertained a strong attachment for the Americans, and to conclude, in the ordinary way, said that they were poor, and hoped their father the Gov. would give them some of his Tobacco and milk, (whiskey); which request was granted, and we received in return a large quantity of green corn, which is in the summer Season almost their only food, for they are too indolent to hunt when they can possibly subsist without, and their squaws do all the labor of the field.

This was a feast day, and we were admitted (which is an unusual condescension,) in the hut where the Indians were collected. Here were four or five fires, over each of which hung a large brass kettle filled with corn: around these fires they danced and sang until the corn was sufficiently boiled, when having made an offering of a small part of it to the Great spirit, each one filled his wooden bowl, holding probably two gallons, and commenced eating. Here the scene ceased to be interesting and we improved the opportunity to depart, lest we might be importuned to grant more favors.

The current being rapid and our men considerably refreshed, we made a distance of 49 miles although we had stopped frequently, and landed about 5 miles above the river St Croix.

Thursday 3 Augt 1820. About sun rise we were at the mouth of the

[85] The village, which was known as Kaposia, was that of Chief Little Crow, near the present site of South St. Paul. Schoolcraft, in his *Narrative Journal*, 315, notes that the party "stopped to examine a remarkable cavern on the east banks of the Mississippi called *Wakon-teebe* by the Narcotah or Sioux Indians, but which, in compliment to the memory of its first European visitor, should be denominated Carver's Cave." The cave, which was explored in 1766 by Jonathan Carver and is commonly known by his name, is located below Dayton's Bluff in St. Paul. Folwell, *Minnesota*, 1:57.

St Croix, which empties into the M. on the east side, and is a very handsome stream, at its mouth nearly 200 yards wide. In the afternoon we arrived at another Sioux village, beautifully situated on the west side of the river.[86] Here we landed and after a short discourse with the Chief of the village continued our journey. From this village it is nine miles to lake Pepin, which, tho' called a lake is nothing more than the expansion of the waters of the M. to the width, (generally) of four miles.

The water of this lake is extremely pure and the Cliffs by which it is bordered, approaching nearer to the river than above, where the bottoms are from one to three miles wide, present a succession of the most delightful scenery imaginable.

Here dwells a remarkable fish, vulgarly called the shovel mouthed sturgeon, but Doct[r] Mitchill I presume would feel somewhat vexed at such a pervertion of scientific terms.[87] The projection from the head resembles in shape the bill of a Duck and is from 8 to 12 inches in length; we saw many, but having no good spears, were unable to take one.

Cornelians are found in greater abundance on the shores of this Lake than above, and are of a better quality than any we have before seen.

We made to day 65 miles.

Friday 4 Aug. At the remains of an indian encampment we found the bones of one of the sturgeon, and intend to transmit it to the learned Doctor; it will at least serve to excite his curiosity.

Nothing remarkable occurred to day & we landed at sunset, having made 60 miles.[88]

Saturday Aug. 5, 1820. Being very anxious to see Prairie Du Chien to day we set out before day break, and at 5 in the afternoon we arrived at the village, having travelled in that time 111 miles.

Between the falls of S[t] Anthony and the Prairie, we found instead of the numerous rapids which so often threatened destruction to our Canoes, sandbars without number, which extending in every direction from the shores very much impeded our progress; and indeed we were fortunate if we did not strike 15 or 20 of them in a day: so that difficulties present

[86] The village of Chief Red Wing, on the site of the city that bears his name.

[87] Samuel L. Mitchill, distinguished scientist, prolific author, and editor from 1802 to 1808 of the *Medical Repository,* was an influential outlet for papers in many scientific fields.

[88] Curiously, no mention is made of a stop at the large Sioux village of Wabasha, about fifty miles south of Lake Pepin on the present site of Winona. Schoolcraft notes that a "short halt" was made there on the afternoon of August 4. See his *Narrative Journal,* 334.

themselves as well below as above the falls, tho' they can be more easily surmounted.

From the foot of Lake Pepin (which is computed to be 30 miles in length,) to Prairie du Chien, the bluffs are about four miles distant from each other, and the intervening land is a rich bottom, timbered principally with Cotton wood.

The principal rivers between St Peters & the Prairie, are, the St Croix, Cannon, Chippeway, Buffalo, Drift wood, Wing Prairie, Black, Root, Racoon, Bad Axe, Tower, & Garlick Rivers: none of these however are very considerable except the St Croix.[89]

Village of P. du Chien Aug 6. This village is situated three miles above the mouth of the Ouisconsin river, on a Prairie about 2 miles in width, and contains (including the adjacent settlement,) about ninety houses, and as many families. (492 inhab. including 131 troops.)

The native inhabitants are all french, whose ancestors migrated to this Country in the Early settlement of Louisania by that nation, A.D. 1719. Most of them support themselves in a very miserable manner, subsisting in part, during the summer, on corn &c procured from the indians. Some however have seen more of the world and live comfortably.

Fort Crawford, so called, is handsomely built and is the only ornament to the place.[90]

There are at present only 2 companies of the 5th Regt infy, stationed here; and the post is under the command of Major [Peter] Muhlenberg a very gentlemanly officer.

The U. S. have a "Factory" here for the purpose of supplying the indians with goods; the object was in its origin to prevent imposition by the traders, but it is tho't to be an unprofitable establishment.[91]

[89] The journalist probably did not intend this to be an exhaustive or discriminating list. The Buffalo River is the Beef River of today, which was known earlier as the River des Boeufs and also as the Bonsecours; it enters on the Wisconsin side. See Winchell's map, in *The Geology of Minnesota*, 1:2. Not mentioned among the major tributaries are the Trempealeau, the Zumbro, which was named the River des Embarras by the French explorers, and the Upper Iowa rivers.

[90] Fort Crawford was one of a series of frontier forts erected in 1816. "The site chosen for the structure was the spot occupied by Fort Shelby or Fort McKay, which had burned down after the departure of the British," according to Bruce E. Mahan, *Old Fort Crawford and the Frontier*, 71 (Iowa City, 1926). Fort Crawford was rebuilt on a new site, on elevated ground, between 1829 and 1834.

[91] Located at Prairie du Chien was one of the more important units in the chain of stores owned and operated by the government in the Indian factory system. Twenty-eight factories were established at frontier forts between 1795 and 1822, but not more than seven or eight were active at any given time. Their purposes were many: to protect the Indians against exploitation, to strengthen the military front, to promote

The state of society here is a very unhappy one — no schools — no church — & no ministers.

Monday Aug. 7. Having learned that an indian of the Win[n]ebago nation had some years since discovered a remarkable cave about twenty miles from this place, he was accordingly sent for, and the Gov, dispatched me with an interpreter to ascertain the truth of his story. We started on horseback (for in this country there is no difficulty in travelling through the woods in that manner,) and travelled 18 miles, to Kickapoo river, a small stream emptying into the Ouisconsin. Here we stayed at night and on the morning of the 8th travelled five miles further by a circuitous route to the Cave, which is of Limestone, about 40 feet square and 20 ft high. As is usual with savages they had, with a view to get some presents, told us a false tale, and instead of silver ore, which we were told we should find in abundance, we saw nothing but the petrifactions usually found in Limestone Caves, called Stalactites.

The result was, that I returned, much dissapointed, and the guide lost his conditionally promised compensation.

Wednesday 9th Aug. Mr Schoolcraft, who had been down the river about 70 miles to visit a lead mine, returned this morning, with a good collection of specimens, mineralogical and geological.[92]

He represents the Country below as highly interesting. The lead ore in the mines on the Mississipi lays on and near the surface of the earth, a singular fact, known in no other part of the world.

At the mine which he, [( ]Mr Schoolcraft) visited it is dug by the squaws, of the Fox nation, who inhabit that part of the Country, and

peace, and to offset the influence of other countries. The Prairie du Chien post was typical in its ill success, which was caused by the high cost of freight, limitations placed upon the superintendents, and the frequent necessity of selling to the Indians on credit. The government stores were abolished in 1822. Edgar B. Wesley, in *Dictionary of American History*, 2:238.

[92] Schoolcraft's three-day tour, a kind of sequel to his earlier exploration of the Missouri lead mines, took him to the vicinity of present-day Dubuque, Iowa, and Galena, Illinois. An area of some sixty square miles on the Iowa side was then known as Dubuque's lead mines. Julien Dubuque, to whom the Fox Indians had granted the privilege of working the mines, died in 1810, and after that the Indians showed increasing jealousy of the whites. Within the area, the most active mining had long been concentrated in a small district, known as the Indian diggings, near the mouth of the River Tete de Mort. By the 1820's, many of the mines had been abandoned and the Indians were forced to the necessity of searching for lead metal in the ash heaps of earlier, perhaps even ancient, smelting sites. Schoolcraft found that the Indians delivered the ore in baskets to traders, who paid two dollars for 120 pounds, payable in goods. Schoolcraft, *Narrative Journal*, 343–346; Thwaites, in *Wisconsin Historical Collections*, 13:279–289.

they also trade with the merchants. Few persons are so industrious as to dig deep into the earth, rather choosing to abandon the digging when it becomes laborious, thereby losing perhaps the richest fruits of their perseverance.

The french people here, use sleigh bells on their harness at all seasons, and think it quite a mark of distinction.

Wednesday Aug 9th We left Prairie du Chien and proceeded to ascend the Ouisconsin, which we found very difficult, on account of the sand bars, which are more numerous, and render the ascent more tedious than the descent of the Mississipi. The water being very low makes our travelling more irksome, for we are frequently obliged to wade.[93] The width of the river varies, according to the abundance or fewness of the bars, but is generally 100 yds wide. There are many handsome bluffs, on this as well as on the Mississipi, but generally much sameness in the appearance of the country.

There are in this river some of the "planters" of the Missouri.[94]

On Monday the 14th Aug we arrived at the portage between the Ouisconsin & fox rivers, having made in 4½ days, against a rapid current and other difficulties, 165 miles.

We had no sooner arrived at the portage, than we discovered twenty or thirty indians coming towards us on horseback at full speed, (They had no lances, but bows, in modern fashion,). They were Winebagoes, of whom there are a large number residing near this portage.

We landed our goods & employed a frenchman, (who is the only white person residing here,) to assist us in transporting them across — which was expeditiously done with oxen, & for which we paid $2 per load. The portage is made through a low prairie, much infested by Rattle Snakes. It is little more than 1½ miles in length, and as the Ouisconsin has been ascertained by an accurate calculation of Cap[t] Douglass, to be 2⁸⁄₁₂ feet higher than the Fox, no one can dou[b]t of the practicability of constructing a Canal, which would save much time and expense.[95]

[93] The party was now following the much traveled Fox-Wisconsin route, connecting the Mississippi and Great Lakes systems. "By all odds the most important topographic feature of Wisconsin in relation to its history is the diagonal valley which extends from Lake Michigan to the Mississippi," writes Lawrence Martin in the *Physical Geography of Wisconsin,* 21 (Madison, 1932).

[94] A "planter" or "sawyer" was, to the riverman, a log or tree that had become lodged in the river's bottom or bank, creating a hazard to navigation.

[95] This is a surprisingly precise measurement. The Cass party was not the first to recognize the possibilities of a canal at this place. A small connecting ditch was dug perhaps as early as 1766; the government canal, passing through the city of Portage,

At the opposite side of the portage we were visited by all the indians of the Village, about 100 in number, whose object was to procure whiskey, which we gave, and they departed.

Tuesday Aug 15th 1820 We bid adieu to the waters of the Ouisconsin & the great tributary of the Gulph of Mexico, with sincere pleasure. The Fox at the portage is not more than 10 yards wide, but is different in its nature from the Ouisconsin — its waters are very deep, and flow through immense fields of Wild rice, which are from one to four miles wide, and greatly obstruct the navigation in some places, for the country is so level that near its head the river has no channel. On the 16th we passed through Lac Le Beuf 53 miles from the portage, & Lake puckaway, 9 miles farther, both small, and only 2 miles wide, so that they may be called more properly expansions of the river to the solid banks.

On Friday the 18th Aug we passed through Lac Des Puants* or Winebago Lake, 161 miles from the portage. This lake is 18 miles long and from 4 to 8 broad, with high, mountainous shores: its waters are very shallow & rocky.

At the east end of the Lake are two Winebago villages, (one on each side of the river,) where we stopped a short time, and procured some assistance in the persons of two indians, to guide us down a rapid, which commences at the end of the Lake. From this place to Green Bay the river is very rocky, and at present in consequence of the lowness of the water, very dangerous. We were obliged to make a constant succession of *decharges* to the Bay, and in addition to our other ill fortune, we broke our barge on the rocks, so that we were under the necessity of employing indians to carry its lading, in their Canoes; to which act of industry nothing would tempt them but the promise of a barrel of whiskey.

On Sunday the 20th of Aug we arrived at the Fort, distant from Lac Des Puants about 33 miles.[96]

Fort Howard is situated about three miles above the mouth of the Fox River, and for the distance of three miles above it, the shores are

was commenced in 1849; and the first recorded steamboat passage was in 1846. Martin, *Physical Geography of Wisconsin*, 355.

* The Winnebagoes are called Puants or "Stinkers" [*author's note*].

[96] This fort, named in honor of General Benjamin Howard, was built in 1816 on the left bank of the Fox River, about a mile above the junction with the Duck River. Its site, now within the city of Green Bay, was occupied earlier by a French fort, known as La Baye. "Fort Howard (1824-1832)," in *Green Bay Historical Bulletin*, vol. 4, no. 5, p. 3 (September–October, 1928); Louise P. Kellogg, "Old Fort Howard," in *Wisconsin Magazine of History*, 18:125-127 (December, 1934).

thickly settled. There are 54 houses, containing in all about 60 families.

Most of the inhabitants are either of french alone, or of french & indian extraction, and appear very poor.

There are some *americans* however, but this is not their permanent place of residence, their only object being to trade with the indians.

There are now upwards of 600 men at this post, under the command of Cap[t] Whistler, by whom we were treated with much kindness during our stay.[97]

The present fort is built on a low sandy plain, which is a very unhealthy as well as inconvenient situation, and most of the troops are now employed in erecting another fort, about 3 miles above this, on a very beautiful & commanding eminence.[98]

Tuesday 22nd Aug 1820. At the mouth of the Fox, a division took place in our brigade; the Governor, Cap[t] Douglass, Mr Schoolcraft, Lieut Mackay, R. A. Forsyth, with the frenchmen, steered for Chicago, while Mess[rs] Doty, Chase & myself took the north shore of the Lake for Mackinac.

Soon after we parted, the wind rose, and we were compelled to labor excessively hard, as the indians of whom our crew was composed, were determined to work very little, having now no *Great father* to control them.

We continued to buffet the waves to our great vexation & fatigue, until Tuesday the 29th Aug, when we were so fortunate as to arrive in safety at Mackinac, where we were very hospitably received by our friends Col Boyd,[99] Mess[rs] Crooks, [Robert] Stuart and Capt Pierce.

The Country on the north shore of Lake Michigan is very barren, & little susceptible of cultivation. Nothing important occurred to us in the voyage.[100]

[97] Identified as Captain William Whistler by M. M. Quaife, in *Checagou, From Indian Wigwam to Modern City, 1673–1835*, 83 (Chicago, 1933). Whistler was temporarily in command of Fort Howard during the absence of Colonel Joseph L. Smith, the commandant. Schoolcraft, *Narrative Journal*, 370.

[98] Colonel Smith wished to remove the post to a spot known as Camp Smith, and much of the garrison was there when the Cass expedition arrived. Smith "kept the garrison there for over a year. He was, however, superseded in 1821 by Colonel Ninian Pinckney of the Third United States Infantry, who immediately revoked Smith's orders and concentrated all the troops once more at Fort Howard." Kellogg, in *Wisconsin Magazine of History*, 18:130.

[99] Perhaps reference is to George Boyd, Indian agent at Mackinac.

[100] The journey of Trowbridge, Doty, and Chase from Green Bay to Mackinac was more leisurely than the quickened tempo of the narrative suggests. They had sufficient opportunity to collect geological specimens of use to Schoolcraft in the preparation of

At Mackinac we remained until the 9ᵗʰ September, when we were once more gratified with the sight of our friends Capt D. and Mr Schoolcraft, from whom we learned that the Gov and the other gentlemen had proceeded by land from Chicago to Detroit.

Note: The distance from Green Bay to Mackinac is 230 miles. From Chicago to M. 300 miles.

The Country from Chicago to M. on the east side of Lake Michigan is represented as extremely uninteresting.[101]

On Wednesday 13 Sepᵗ we left Mackinac for Detroit where we arrived in ten days overjoyed to meet once more our friends.

And thus ends my dull, uninteresting, ungrammatical &c. &c. &c. &c — of a four months voyage, in which time we travelled in Bark Canoes 4388 miles! [102]

his report. The routes of the parties that went from Green Bay to Detroit may be followed by reference to Schoolcraft's *Narrative Journal* and Cass's manuscript report to Calhoun. The division led by Cass coasted the western shore of Lake Michigan to Chicago, a settlement described by Schoolcraft in his *Narrative Journal,* 383, as consisting of the garrison and "ten or twelve dwelling houses, with an aggregate population, of probably, sixty souls." There the group again divided, and one of its members, Wolcott, remained to continue his duties as Indian agent. Cass, with Mackay and Forsyth, accompanied by John Kinzie, who had substituted for Wolcott during the summer, set out on horseback for Detroit, following the beach road to the Chemin River, near the present site of Michigan City, Indiana. This route led the travelers to the Sauk Trail, later known as the Chicago Road, which ran from the vicinity of Rock Island, Illinois, to Detroit. Early routes to and from Chicago have been carefully considered by M. M. Quaife, in *Chicago's Highways, Old and New* (Chicago, 1923). Cass's arrival in Detroit was announced in the *Gazette* for September 15, 1820. Douglass and Schoolcraft journeyed by canoe along the eastern coast of Lake Michigan to Mackinac, where they joined Doty and Trowbridge.

[101] Dull and unsatisfying, certainly, is Schoolcraft's narrative of this portion of the exploration, which was apparently done in haste.

[102] This mileage suggests a precision of measurement that could not possibly be attained. Cass, in his letter of September 14, 1820, reported to Calhoun that he returned on September 10 "after a very fortunate journey of four thousand miles, and an accomplishment, without any adverse accident, of every object entrusted to me." The two divisions which returned via Mackinac and St. Ignace necessarily traveled a greater distance.

Notes and Documents

A MISSISSIPPI PANORAMA

READERS of a little book on Henry Lewis and his moving panorama of the Mississippi Valley, published by the Minnesota Historical Society in 1936,[1] will be interested to learn that one of the huge rolls of painted canvas which unfolded the mysteries of Mid-America for delighted audiences of the 1850's has come to light recently. It is preserved in the anthropological museum of the University of Pennsylvania at Philadelphia, which received it in 1899 with the collection of Dr. Montroville Wilson Dickeson, a local physician and scientist. The enormous picture, which was painted by I. J. Egan "from drawings made on the spot" by Dr. Dickeson, depicts chiefly the mounds and other archaeological remains of the lower river.

Dickeson's panorama, which probably was painted about 1850, was only one of perhaps a dozen "travel movies" of the Mississippi offered as entertainment in the East and in Europe in the middle decades of the last century. Until November, 1941, however, when the University Museum at Philadelphia displayed the Dickeson panorama, the Minnesota Historical Society had been unable to learn of the survival of a single Mississippi panorama. At that time the Eastern States Archaeological Federation met in Philadelphia, and the panorama was placed on view for the visitors. Because it "covered the walls and some of the cases in several halls" of the museum, "it was shown for only three days," according to Dr. J. Alden Mason, curator of the American section of the institution. He expresses the hope that the Dickeson panorama "may later be placed on permanent exhibition, if a suitable place can be found for it." The November display, he reveals, "was probably the first . . . in ninety years."

Like other panoramas of the period, Dickeson's evidently was unrolled to the accompaniment of a lecture explaining the significance of

[1] Bertha L. Heilbron, ed., *Making a Motion Picture in 1848:Henry Lewis' Journal of a Canoe Voyage from the Falls of St. Anthony to St. Louis* (St. Paul, 1936).

MONUMENTAL GRANDEUR

OF THE

MISSISSIPPI

VALLEY!

NOW EXHIBITING FOR A SHORT TIME ONLY,

WITH SCIENTIFIC LECTURES ON

American Ærchiology.

Dr. Dickeson, late Professor in Philadelphia College of Medicine ; Member of the Academy of Natural Sciences, and Fellow of the Royal Society of Copenhagen, &c., &c., will Lecture THIS EVENING on the

ANTIQUITIES & CUSTOMS OF THE UNHISTORIED INDIAN TRIBES,

who dwelt on this Continent 3,500 years ago, and also on the leading peculiarities in the construction of those *Mounds, Tumulii, Fossas,* &c., with the Geology, Mineralogy and Botany of this beautiful country.

Dr. D. has devoted twelve years of his life in these investigations, having in that time explored the whole Valley of the Mississippi, and opened over 1,000 Indian Monuments or Mounds, and has now a collection of 40,000 *relics* of those interesting but unhistoried Native Americans.

During the entertainment, the Doctor will unroll a most magnificent *Scenic Mirror*, covering 15,000 feet of canvass, illustrating the Monumental Grandeur of the Valley, with the splendid scenes that occur upon the *Father of Rivers*

His Lecture, which accompanies each moving of the Tableaux, abounds in invaluable information, and is worth alone, double the price of admission.

BROADSIDE ISSUED TO ADVERTISE DICKESON'S PANORAMA

[On this and the following page is reproduced in two sections a descriptive advertisement preserved with the panorama in the University Museum, Philadelphia. A copy of the broadside was presented to the Minnesota Historical Society by Dr. J. Alden Mason, curator of the museum's American section.]

THIS GORGEOUS PANORAMA,

WITH ALL THE

ABORIGINAL MONUMENTS

Of a large extent of Country, once roamed by the RED MAN, was painted by the

Eminent Artist I. J. EGAN, Esq.,

AND COVERS OVER 15,000 FEET OF CANVASS!

It has been pronounced by our Celebrated Artists to be the most

FINISHED AND MAGNIFICENT PICTURE

Ever presented to

THE AMERICAN PUBLIC.

Each View and Scene is taken from DRAWINGS MADE ON THE SPOT, by

Prof. M. W. DICKESON, M. D.,

Who spent TWELVE YEARS of his Life in opening

Indian Mounds.

SECTION I.

Marietta Ancient Fortification—A grand view of their Walls, Bastions, Ramparts, Fossa and Walls, with the relics therein found—Circleville Aboriginal Tumuli—Cado Chiefs in full costume—Youths at their War Practice—Hanging or Hieroglyphical Rock—Colossal Bust at low water mark, used as a metre by the Aborigines—Portsmouth Aboriginal Group in a Storm—Cave in the Rock, Stalagmitic Chamber and Crystal Fountan, Desecated and Mummied Bodies in their burial places—Magnificent effect of Crystalization—Terraced Mound in a snow storm, at sunset—Twelve gated Labyrinth, Missouri—Indians at their piscatory exploits.

SECTION II.

Bon Hom Island Group—Distant view of the Rocky Mountains—Encamping Grounds of Lewis and Clark—Louisiana Swale Group, with extensive Wall—Lakes and Sacrificial Monuments—Natchez Hill by Moonlight—Indian Encampment—Distant view of Louisiana—Indians preparing supper—The Tornado of 1844—Destruction of Indian Settlements—Horrid loss of Life—Louisiana Squatter pursued by Wolves—Humorous Scene—Prairie with Buffalo, Elk, and Gigantic Bust on the ledge of a Limestone Rock—Spring Creek, Texas—Fort Rosalie—Extermination of the French in 1729—Grand Battle Scene—Mode of Scalping.

SECTION III.

Chamberlain's Gigantic Mounds and Walls—Natchez above the Hill—Indians at their Games—Baluxie Shell, Mounds—Ferguson Group—The Landing of Gen. Jackson—Lake Concordia and Aboriginal Tumuli—Huge Mound and the manner of opening them—Cado Parish Monument—De Soto's Burial at White Cliffs—Mammoth Ravine —Exhuming of Fossil Bones—Temple of the Sun by sunset.

Exhibition to commence at 8 every evening, and at 3 o'clock every Wednesday and Saturday afternoon.

Admission - - - - - - - - 25 cents.
Children under 12 - - - - - 12½ "

During the week a FREE ENTERTAINMENT will be given in the Afternoon, for the examination of the *Indian Museum.*

PRINTED AT THE MERCURY OFFICE—NEWARK, N. J.

the successive scenes. The texts of such lectures frequently were available in printed booklets, which were sold in connection with the exhibition. So far as is known, no booklet of this type was published for the Dickeson panorama.[2] It is, however, known that when Dickeson showed his panorama he also displayed his collection of "relics of those interesting, but unhistoried Native Americans" who built the mounds of the lower Mississippi Valley. Admission to his panorama doubtless included permission to examine his archaeological collection.[3]

Although the University Museum does not have the text of Dickeson's lecture, it does own several hundred copies of a descriptive broadside evidently issued to advertise the panorama. One of these broadsides was presented to the Minnesota Historical Society by Dr. Mason and is reproduced herewith. It was through his courtesy and interest that the survival of the Dickeson panorama was called to the attention of the Minnesota organization. He also made available a short account of Dickeson and his panorama which he prepared for publication in the *Pennsylvania Archaeologist*. With the permission of the editor of that periodical and of Dr. Mason, extracts from the latter's article are reprinted herewith.   B.L.H.

[From the *Pennsylvania Archaeologist: Bulletin of the Society for Pennsylvania Archaeology*, 12:14–16 (January, 1942).]

THE [DICKESON] panorama was one of the first acquisitions of the [University of Pennsylvania] Museum, but was forgotten until several years ago, when it was discovered in the Museum storage. It came as a part of the archaeological collection of Dr. Montroville Wilson Dickeson, who

[2] Only two Dickeson publications are listed in Joseph Sabin's *Dictionary of Books relating to America*. He is the author of an *American Numismatic Manual* (Philadelphia, 1859) and, in collaboration with Andrew Brown, of a *Report on the Cypress Timber of Mississippi and Louisiana* (Philadelphia, 1848). A copy of the third edition of the former work (1865) is owned by the Minnesota Historical Society.

[3] A detailed account of the "Dickeson Collection of American Antiquities" by Stewart Culin appears in the Free Museum of Science and Art of the University of Pennsylvania, *Bulletin*, 2:113–168 (January, 1900). Included is a list of items in the archaeological collection. The author reveals that the collection was displayed in 1842 at agricultural fairs at Washington and Natchez, Mississippi. He notes also that Dickeson's reports on excavations of mound groups in Mississippi were published in *The Lotus*, a periodical issued at Philadelphia for a few months in 1848. References to these publications, which are not available in Minnesota libraries, were furnished by Dr. Mason.

was born in Philadelphia in 1810 and died in 1882. Dr. Dickeson was greatly interested in natural science and was one of the first to travel through the Mississippi Valley for scientific observations. He was especially interested in archaeology, and made some of the earliest excavations in the mounds of the southern Mississippi Valley. . . . From 1837 until 1844 he spent most of his time traveling and excavating in the mound region. He took notes and made many sketches which were used in the painting of the panorama; these are the more valuable because a number of these mounds and other archaeological features have long since disappeared.

Dr. Dickeson apparently traveled through the country exhibiting the panorama and his archaeological collection. A clipping from a Philadelphia newspaper of 1851 shows the following advertisement: "A Grand Moving Diorama of the Mississippi Valley and its Indian Antiquities is now open at Fotteral Hall, corner Fifth and Chestnut Streets. The diorama will be explained by Professor M. W. Dickeson, who will also exhibit his cabinet of Indian Curiosities. The Diorama was painted by I. J. Egan, Esq., one of our best artists, from drawings taken on the spot by Professor Dickeson. To commence at a quarter before 8 o'clock. Admittance 25 cts."

After 1851 I have been unable to find any certain reference to the exhibition of the panorama, but the archaeological collection — and possibly the panorama — were shown at several later periods. Scharf and Westcott, in their *History of Philadelphia* (1884), speak of the collection as shown in the City Museum, on the north side of Callowhill Street between Fourth and Fifth Streets, in 1854, and note that "the Professor of Natural Sciences having charge of the museum was Dr. Montroville W. Dickeson." Apparently the venture was not profitable and the museum did not long exist. In 1867–68 the objects were shown in the Swaim Building, Seventh Street below Chestnut, and again in the Main Building at the Centennial Exposition in 1876. After this Exposition the objects remained in Memorial Hall until 1885, and soon thereafter they were acquired by the Department of Archaeology and Palaeontology of the University of Pennsylvania, which later became the University Museum.

A century ago, when photography was in its swaddling clothes, lantern slides very rare, and the movies and the radio undreamt of, visual education was limited to a few media, and prominent among these was the painted panorama. Also the West was just being opened up, the Forty-niners were crossing the Great Plains with their immense herds of buffalo and their savage Indians, and interest in the strange and unknown West was very great. Panoramas of the Mississippi Valley were apparently very popular, and some of them were advertised as being several miles in length. This statement must be discounted with many grains of salt, however, as advertising "blurbs"; for instance the Dickeson-Egan panorama is advertised as covering "more than 15,000 feet of Canvass," whereas it is actually about 2,500 square feet. . . .

Preserved with the panorama in the Museum are many of the handbills advertising it, banners, posters, notices of admission price, ordinary tickets, and tickets to a "Complimentary Benefit to the Reading Rifles." All are in the archaic printing or painting of the pre-Civil-War period. The handbills are superb examples of the advertising of a century ago. . . . Fortunately the handbill describes each scene, so that they may be identified on the panorama, which contains no lettering. The scenes, archaeological, ethnological, historic, and scenic, blend one into another. . . . In keeping with Dr. Dickeson's interest, however, a large part of the panorama is devoted to scenes of Indian mounds and of excavations in them. . . .

The panorama is in two sections, each about eight feet in height; one is about 190 feet in length, and the other about 130 feet. The colors are as bright as the day they were painted, evidently a sort of tempera on thin muslin so that the whole can be wound on a roller and weighs only a hundred pounds or so.

To date I have been able to obtain little information on the "eminent artist" I. J. (elsewhere given as John J.) Egan, but hope to secure more. He was apparently an Irish artist, born about 1810, who was in this country for only a short time around 1850. In that year he exhibited two paintings at the Academy of Fine Arts in Philadelphia. Though of course the immense scene was painted too rapidly for him to show his best work, he was evidently a painter of great ability.

Reviews of Books

The Long Ships Passing: The Story of the Great Lakes. By WALTER
HAVIGHURST. (New York, The Macmillan Company, 1942. viii,
291 p. Illustrations. $3.00.)

The subtitle of Mr. Havighurst's book, *The Story of the Great Lakes,*
is somewhat equivocal, since Lake Ontario is almost ignored and the
history of Lake Superior is only partly told. The volume focuses on
Lakes Michigan and Huron and on the famous locks at the Sault.
Through the last the long ships pass, one every twenty minutes throughout the eight-months ice-free season, bearing grain and iron ore down
the lakes, coal and manufactured articles on their return. For well over
a century vessels have carried the commerce of the lakes, vessels ranging
from bateaux and sloops and schooners to the steel-hulled passenger boats
and freighters of today. This long period of inland trade has seen many a
tragic foundering, many a battle against fires, explosions, ice, and November gales. The men who built the boats, the captains and the crews
who navigated them, have a sympathetic chronicler in Mr. Havighurst.

But the story of the Great Lakes is a big story, and the present volume is too short and too impressionistic to tell all of it. The author
begins with Jean Nicolet and the French Jesuits, but omits Lahontan,
Major Rogers, Jonathan Carver; the story of Perry's victory at Put in Bay
is recounted, but there is no mention of Pontiac's savage attack on Detroit; Douglas Houghton's discovery of copper on the Keweenaw Peninsula is given due credit, but the Merritt brothers are overlooked; and
there is only one cursory allusion to Grand Portage. The immensely important fur trade on Lake Superior is only hinted at; the North Shore is
neglected in order to emphasize the littoral of Lakes Erie and Huron.
Thus the major weakness of the book is its lack of adequate historical
background.

When it comes to the narratives of the long ships themselves, the
author is on surer ground. He has a seaman's knowledge of and interest
in the channels, the reefs, the lighthouses, the docks, and ports. With
vividness and economy he tells of the building of the Sault canal and the
locks. He describes the type and career of a multitude of boats (the index

contains references to 155 different vessels) varying from La Salle's ill-fated "Griffin" to the huge freighters of today, measuring over six hundred feet in length and carrying a cargo in excess of fourteen thousand tons. Individual ships stand out in this saga of the greatest inland waterway in the world. There is the disaster of the "Mataafa," wrecked in Duluth Harbor in 1905 by a violent northeast storm which piled the ship up against the piers of the entrance and froze to death nine crew members in the very sight of the city's helpless populace. There is the "Independence," first steamer on Lake Superior, which was portaged past the rapids of the St. Mary's River and survived seven seasons on the biggest of the lakes; in 1853 the "Independence" left the Sault for Ontonagon, but its boilers exploded and put a swift end to the vessel. There is the exciting race of the belated grain fleet which left Fort William late in November, 1927, and scurried across to the Sault in sub-zero weather only to find the channel frozen solid. Twenty-two steamers, carrying six million bushels of grain, wintered at the Sault that year.

Mr. Havighurst writes with facility and color. Despite needless repetitions (Henry Clay's absurd taunt about the Sault appears three times in the text) and his fondness for certain trite superlatives ("most historic," "finest," "biggest"), he presents the reader with many a freshly-hued scene and terse incident. His depiction of Saginaw, Bay City, Alpena, the lumber towns of Michigan's east shore, is excellent, and no reader will be likely to forget his account of the Menominee fire of 1871. Equally compelling is the tale of the Mormon colony on Beaver Island at the head of Lake Michigan, a colony which once claimed America's only crowned king, James Jesse Strang, but which was obliterated by the exasperated sailors and fishermen of the vicinity. The book gains a rich personal flavor from the introduction of various celebrities of the Northwest: Douglas Houghton, Michigan state geologist and enthusiastic explorer of the shore lines; John Muir, the Scotch naturalist and conservationist who spent his boyhood in Wisconsin; Henry Rowe Schoolcraft, Indian agent and ethnologist; and many an intrepid lake skipper, marine architect, logger, and sailor, and voyager.

The illustrations by John O'Hara Cosgrave II provide a distinctive addition to this vivid and readable volume. The artist's sketches of sidewheelers, schooners, tugs, and ore carriers have unusual deftness and charm.

JOHN T. FLANAGAN

Western Ontario and the American Frontier. By FRED LANDON. (Toronto, The Ryerson Press, 1941. xvi, 305 p. Maps. $3.50.)

By virtue of its geographic position, the peninsula of western Ontario is very properly a focal point for the study of the interactions of Canadian and American peoples. The story of these contacts, as told by Professor Landon, offers fresh documentation for the view that historically the international boundary has been no barrier to the movement of settlers westward, nor to the spread of cultural influences and institutional patterns.

The author explores this thesis in a series of chapters devoted to American immigration, churches and schools, social and humanitarian influences, political reform, the antislavery movement, farms and farmers, and the labor movement. He points out the contribution of American mechanics and agriculturists to the economic development of the region, describes the activities of American evangelists and educators, and notes the impact of American democracy upon Canadian politics. Through population movements, organizations, and ideas, the pervasive force of things American was felt almost universally.

On the other hand, Mr. Landon makes it plain that the boundary was by no means a purely imaginary line. From his account, it is evident that governing officials in Ontario as well as in England conceived their plans of statecraft in terms of British policies and institutions, and labored to counteract the American penetration. Conservatives used the taint of Americanism to discredit their opponents. Canadian nationalism gained impetus from the Civil War and the threat of American annexation. The author's conclusion is that Ontario history has been marked as much by reaction against American influence as by a positive response to it.

In the opinion of the reviewer the book does not measure up to companion volumes in the series on the *Relations of Canada and the United States,* perhaps because of the limitations of the local approach, and because too many trails have been blazed before. It is, however, well worth reading.

CHARLES M. GATES

Iowa Public Land Disposal. By ROSCOE L. LOKKEN. (Iowa City, The State Historical Society of Iowa, 1942. 318 p. $3.00.)

Mr. Lokken's volume on federal land operations in the *Iowa Centennial History* series is a valuable addition to the historical literature of a great Midwestern state. Published under the excellent auspices of the State Historical Society of Iowa, it presents a form and style that will appeal to the general reader. Its deeper significance, however, especially for the student of history, is to be found in the outstanding quality of the author's research and the clarity with which he sets forth the many complicated problems of the public domain. Even a perfunctory examination of the text, maps, and notes will make evident the fact that Mr. Lokken, in his painstaking study of the large mass of private papers, archival documents, and frontier news sheets relating to his subject, has not only unearthed much fresh material, but also has written a work that will serve as a model for investigators in other public land states, in which, generally speaking, similar efforts still are needed.

The author appropriately begins his story with the first land surveys in 1836, and for this purpose he assembles an abundance of information about the activities of individual surveyors. He uses a similar method to follow the steps in the process by which the early land offices were created, as well as to describe the origin and development of the pre-emption policy under which most of the public lands in Iowa passed from federal to local jurisdiction and thereby into the hands of settlers. Adequate attention is given to questions of squatter rights, private and public land sales, land warrants or scrip, various kinds of federal grants to aid education and internal improvements, and the organization and operation of so-called settler or claim associations, the extralegal nature and processes of which cannot be clearly understood without a careful examination of local source materials like those used by the present author. The evidence points unmistakably to the fact that, regardless of Congressional acts and administrative decrees, the men of the soil, informally but effectively organized in claim associations, could and usually did succeed in circumventing national policy, thwarting the best efforts of federal land officials, and securing results more often than not favorable to their interests. The claim association was the most powerful frontier defense against the natural tendency toward a federal dictatorship of public land policy, especially in the period before homestead legislation was passed.

It is worth noting that of the approximately thirty-six million acres of Iowa lands in the hands of the federal government in 1836, only a little over nine hundred thousand acres were disposed of under the terms of the homestead acts. Before 1870, however, all but a million acres had been distributed, mainly by processes of pre-emption and federal grants to the state and the railroads, and in 1890 a mere five thousand acres remained.

VERNE E. CHATELAIN

A Reference Guide to Iowa History (State Historical Society of Iowa, *Bulletin of Information Series,* no. 17). Compiled by WILLIAM J. PETERSEN. (Iowa City, 1942.   151 p.)

Few organizations devote as much time and energy to making history available to the public as does the State Historical Society of Iowa. The extent of this service over a long period of years may be seen in Dr. Petersen's handy, accurate, and informative reference guide. The *Guide* lists not only the publications of the society, such as the *Iowa Journal of History and Politics,* the popular *Palimpsest,* and the volumes in the several series it sponsors, but also includes references to other publications, such as the *Annals of Iowa,* reports of the federal government, and even significant fiction pertaining to the Hawkeye State. The result is an indispensable handbook for almost anyone who wishes to work in the field of Iowa history or in the broader area of the upper Mississippi Valley.

The compiler arranged the main divisions of the *Guide* in "logical sequence beginning with the natural setting of Iowa history and proceeding through the periods of exploration and settlement to the principal fields of activity and to the people who have made history in this Commonwealth." In addition to the topics dealing with politics, government, land, Indians, travel, and the administration of justice, there are also sections dealing with the colorful life of the people — sections that tell the story of education in early Iowa, that lead the student to the pageant of religious activities, that cite chapter and verse to folklore and odd tales, and that refer to amusements, health, publishing, business, and agriculture. Two sections deal with collections of biographical sketches and with references to prominent Iowans.

The present *Guide* is the result of many years of planning by the Iowa society, which in 1904 conceived the idea when it published a list of twenty-five topics in Iowa history. Three years later the original list was revised. Other enlarged guides were published in 1914 and 1915. In 1932, Dr. Petersen prepared his *Two Hundred Topics in Iowa History.* One has only to compare the 1932 list with the bulletin under review to gain an idea of the immense amount of creditable research in Iowa history accomplished within a decade. If other state historical societies would prepare similar reference guides, it would be a great boon to research throughout the United States.

PHILIP D. JORDAN

Teaching the Social Studies. By EDGAR BRUCE WESLEY. (Boston, D. C. Heath and Company, second edition, 1942. xviii, 652 p. $3.00.)

This is a revision of the most extensively used book in print on the teaching of the social studies. No one doubts that in the five years that have passed since the first edition of Dr. Wesley's book appeared the current of world events as well as trends in education have caused a shift of emphasis in the social studies field. The new edition reflects this tendency through the addition of a chapter on "Democratic Teaching and Learning," in which is stressed the teacher's need for understanding democracy in order to teach it. The chapter presents numerous suggestions for "materials, processes, and activities" in the curriculum and in the school organization and administration to further democratic learning. These suggestions are especially stimulating for teachers who would seek to foster one of the main functions of social studies in this period of strain. The chapter is so valuable that it alone is worth the price of the new edition.

The materials in the book have been rearranged, thereby strengthening the text for use in methods courses, and presenting materials in logical sequence for teachers who must adjust to curricular changes and trends. The placing of the historical summary of the social studies in the appendix has made possible a more practical arrangement of material.

The chapter in the new edition on "Teaching Reading and Study Skills" is a splendid aid to the teacher of the social studies who is troubled by the inability of pupils to understand what they read. What Dr. Wesley provides will serve both as a guide to improved work with pupils and as a valuable aid to teachers who may have suffered from lack of specific purposes and techniques in reading and study.

The new edition presents nearly two hundred new references that are of special value to the teacher of social studies techniques. The reviewer can speak with authority of the usefulness of the book even beyond the borders of the United States. It was continuously in demand by teachers of the social studies enrolled in a course that she gave recently in Canada, and it served those who teach in elementary and secondary schools alike.

ELLA A. HAWKINSON

Iron Pioneer: Henry W. Oliver, 1840–1904. By HENRY OLIVER EVANS.
   (New York, E. P. Dutton & Co., Inc., 1942. xiii, 370 p. Illustrations. $3.50.)

Several books have been written about the iron mining resources and
industry of northeastern Minnesota. The present volume deals with the
life of a man whose name is among the most famous in the history of
Minnesota iron ore. Despite his leadership and the fact that the great
mining subsidiary of the United States Steel Corporation still bears his
name, little is generally known about Henry W. Oliver. The book under
review gives some very interesting and important information about this
great industrial leader.

Oliver was an Irishman, born in County Tyrone in 1840. His parents
went to Pittsburgh two years later. Oliver attended school until he was
thirteen, and then worked for the Western Union and for various transportation companies. He was a successful iron and steel manufacturer at
twenty-three, became prominent in Pittsburgh civic and political affairs,
was a leading advocate of the Republican doctrine of high tariff, and an
associate of men of business and political power.

Of special Minnesota interest are sections of Oliver's biography on the
Vermilion and Mesabi ranges, including references to the Merritts and
many others who left their marks on the mining communities and operations of the state. Oliver's first Mesabi Range lease was on the Mountain
Iron mine, the most important discovery of the Merritts. This was located on school property and the fee belonged to the state. The lease
expired in 1942, after a half century during which the operations on the
mining property paid royalties of approximately a hundred thousand dollars per acre.

There was early skepticism by the iron and steel industry of the value
of the Mesabi ores. John D. Rockefeller, who at one time threatened to
be as great in iron and steel as he was in oil and who acquired the Merritt interests, was pessimistic. Oliver had a hard time interesting Andrew
Carnegie and his associates. Said Carnegie in 1892: "Oliver's ore bargain
is just like him — nothing in it. If there is any department of business
which offers no inducement, it is ore. It never has been profitable, and
the Messaba is not the last great deposit that Lake Superior is to reveal."
The old iron master was made to swallow those words within a few
years. Although Oliver kept his Mesabi operations going through the

great depression of 1893, he needed money. He gave a half interest in his company to Carnegie in 1894 as a bonus for a loan of five hundred thousand dollars. In 1897 the Carnegie Steel Company bought more of the holdings of the Oliver Mining Company, leaving to Oliver a sixth interest.

With the growth of the iron and steel industries, came a greatly increased demand for iron ore. Oliver's judgment of the value of the Mesabi ores proved to be correct. Ownership of the Minnesota iron ores helped to make the Carnegie Steel Company the leader in the steel industry and the most important factor in the creation of the United States Steel Corporation at the beginning of the century.

Oliver died in 1904. The book portrays him, as he doubtless was, an attractive, interesting, and aggressive personality, a leader in an age of aggressive personalities. Although the volume is well worth reading and owning, it fails to present adequately one of the greatest and most romantic stories of American industry.

L. A. ROSSMAN

This Circle of Earth: The Story of John H. Dietrich. By CARLETON WIN-STON. (New York, G. P. Putnam's Sons, 1942. ix, 271 p. $3.00.)

This is an unconventional and rather unusual biography of a man who is well remembered by Minnesotans, although his voice is no longer heard over the radio and he has discarded overcoat and earmuffs in favor of California, a state from which no Minnesotan is supposed to return. The author, who is Mrs. Dietrich, writes sympathetically and understandingly of her husband; but at several points she is "at wide variance" with his philosophy of life.

Dr. Dietrich's religious pilgrimage began in the orthodox Reformed church and ended in religious humanism. He was a very young man when he "broke through the shell of orthodoxy into the more spacious air of liberal religion." As in the case of many young men of inquiring minds, his experiences with certain misguided exponents of orthodoxy were disillusioning; and he began early to solve his problems as an intellectualist. He led his class in Mercersburg Academy in Pennsylvania and graduated as valedictorian. His predilection for the "social gospel" gave him employment with the *New York Tribune* Fresh Air Fund, a position which made it financially possible to enter Franklin and Marshall

College in 1896. On the campus he measured up to the definition of an "activity boy," even to playing football, but he was no mere seeker after popularity.

After graduation, he tasted the cup of poverty while job hunting and tramping the streets as a book agent, until he found employment as a teacher and later as a private secretary. Before enrolling in the theological seminary of the Reformed church, he had imbibed the freedom of thought of Unitarianism; and a flagrant example of "straddling" by a member of the faculty who lacked the courage of his convictions was disconcerting; but he was ordained and accepted the call to a church in the fashionable east end of Pittsburgh. His defiance of ritual and tradition aroused the indignation of a wealthy "patron" of the church and jeopardized a donation to his Alma Mater. His heresy trial was cut short by a confession of "guilt."

Dietrich's next pastorate was with the First Unitarian Society in Spokane, where his transition from mild theism to rationalism was so rapid that it brought disfavor with clergymen in the city. He devoured the writings of Darwin, Spencer, Huxley, Harnack, and others; and the word "humanism" took on a different connotation. His reputation, however, qualified him for the leadership of the First Unitarian Church of Minneapolis; and he was persuaded to accept the call largely through the efforts of the veteran professor of education in the University of Minnesota, Albert W. Rankin.

Dietrich assumed his duties in Minneapolis in 1916, when the politics of the state was seething with revolt in the form of the Nonpartisan League and the nation stood on the brink of the first World War. He plunged into controversy and threw the weight of his influence against the mounting war sentiment. After the die had been cast, there were whispers and shouts about his alleged pro-Germanism; but he weathered the storm and favored the entrance of the United States into the League of Nations, until at last he became convinced that no good could come of it. His attitude toward disarmament represented perhaps the group of liberals to which he belonged. He was ever the champion of free speech and of the oppressed and the downtrodden; and his sympathy for conscientious objectors during and after the war made him the target of Red baiters. He also entered the lists against the Fundamentalists, who favored a bill in the legislature which would prevent the teaching of the theory of evolution in tax-supported schools.

The concluding chapters of the book set forth the educational activity of the Unitarian Society, which sponsored distinguished lecture courses; Dr. Dietrich's radio broadcasts; the development of his humanist philosophy, and the publication of books and articles; the entrance of death into the family circle; the second marriage; and the close of his preaching career.

If not completely objective, the biography is pleasantly subjective. On the whole, the author writes understandingly, and sometimes even sympathetically, of her husband's adversaries and traducers. Readers who heard Dr. Dietrich's funeral "sermons" will understand the reference to the death of his first wife: "Many months he had lived with the knowledge that his wife must die; and no faith in God sustained him. There was no other world that would know her. . . . His stoicism was magnificent. Yet he knew that his interest in life was gone." These sentences read in connection with Dr. Dietrich's own statement in the years when the shadows were lengthening are significant: "I would still place all emphasis on reason and facts, but the older I grow the more I realize that by this method we lose much of life's radiance. . . . I sometimes wonder if we have not overdone making life reasonable, and serviceable, and seriously effective."

After reading this interesting biography, one cannot seriously question Dr. Dietrich's courage, integrity, and intellectual ability. One may reject humanism and differ with some of his objectives; but the sum total of his usefulness to the community is impressive.

GEORGE M. STEPHENSON

The Mayos: Pioneers in Medicine. By ADOLPH REGLI. (New York, Julian Messner, Inc., 1942. 248 p. Illustrations. $2.50.)

To those who would learn the main outlines of the lives of the Mayos in a pleasant evening or two, Adolph Regli's biography may be well recommended. The author sticks to the subjects of his biography closely, and includes the barest minimum of medical discussion and terminology, a feature to its advantage for young readers. The book, under two hundred and fifty pages of medium print, is obviously of vastly different character from the eight hundred pages of finer print which compose Miss Clapesattle's *The Doctors Mayo* (see *ante*, 22:404–408). Mr. Regli does succeed in telling a dramatic story with clearness and brevity, and for the most part in a style both colorful and accurate.

Many of the incidents are related in dramatic conversations. The story of the agents and traders' conference with the Sioux in 1862 reads like a novel. Mr. Regli writes that the angry trader snarled, "Let them eat grass," in answer to the agent's plea for credit. Yet this represents a fair picture of the stirring events. The author supplies conversation for all the characters in his book. Those for Dr. W. W. Mayo vary in quality in different situations. Those in his conflict with Cut Nose and in the defense of New Ulm seem plausible and fairly effective, those at the birth of his son overly prophetic, and those in chatting with a neighbor while summarizing his activities for several preceding years too obviously designed for the needs of the narrator. Mrs. Mayo's purporting to say in 1871, "I've been wondering why I never suggested this post-graduate work to you," sounds like a modern writer, not a pioneer housewife. The dramatic picture of Dr. Mayo's search for and recovery of the corpse of Cut Nose after the execution in 1862 is not quite in accordance with other accounts. The general sweep of facts is accurate, however, and the novel-like style is not as pronounced in the story of the sons as in that of the father.

There are no actual photographs, but the interesting drawings used as frontispiece, chapter headings, and end plates add much to the appearance of the book. It might well be added to biographical reading lists for high school students of Minnesota history, and it certainly can be enjoyed as a popular biographical study of Minnesota's famous doctors.

EVADENE BURRIS SWANSON

Minnesota Historical Society Notes

Dr. Lewis Beeson has been named acting superintendent of the society to serve while Dr. Arthur J. Larsen is on leave of absence from his duties as secretary and superintendent. Dr. Larsen left on September 16 to enter the Army Air Force Officers' Training School at Miami, Florida, with the rank of first lieutenant. For more than two years Dr. Beeson has been the society's curator of newspapers, and during the past spring and summer he organized and directed the work of the Minnesota War History Committee (see *ante,* 149–153). Mr. Jacob Hodnefield of St. Paul has been named acting curator of newspapers and supervisor of war history activities.

For the Clarence Walworth Alvord Memorial Commission of the Mississippi Valley Historical Association, the society has published a volume of *Documents Relating to Northwest Missions, 1815–1827* (xix, 469 p.). They have been selected, translated, and provided with an introduction and notes by Dr. Grace Lee Nute, the society's curator of manuscripts. Numerous reports and letters written in French are presented both in the original and in translation. Most of the documents relate to the activities of Catholic missionaries to the Indians of the Red River Valley and the Rainy Lake and Lake Superior districts. The preface was written by Dr. Solon J. Buck, archivist of the United States, who was superintendent of the society from 1914 to 1931; the work of preparing the manuscript for publication, seeing it through the press, and designing the volume was done by Mrs. Mary W. Berthel of the society's editorial staff. In return for its part in issuing the volume, the society is privileged to offer the book to its members at $2.50, which is half the regular price of $5.00. The book will be reviewed in the March issue of this magazine. With the publication of this volume, the Mississippi Valley Historical Association inaugurates a series of publications that will serve as a memorial to Professor Alvord, who was one of its founders. This distinguished American historian, who died in 1928, resided in Minnesota for several years while teaching in the University of Minnesota.

The society's reference librarian, Miss Lois Fawcett, was on leave of absence from July 15 to October 15. During that period Mrs. Irene B.

Warming had charge of the activities of the reference department in the library. A leave of absence for the month of September was granted to Mrs. Leone Brower of the catalogue department. Mrs. Florence Trelogan, chief clerk, was given a leave of absence for six months, beginning on September 16. Her work has been taken over by the office stenographer, Mrs. Phyllis Sandstrom. Miss Mary E. Palmes, former chief clerk who resigned on January 1, is temporarily serving as an assistant in the general office.

Wartime conditions have resulted in several permanent resignations and changes in the personnel of the society's staff. Miss June Day, a library assistant, resigned on August 15 to accept a position in a film record library at Wright Field in Dayton, Ohio. Her position was filled by the appointment of Miss Muriel Hoppe. An assistant in the manuscript division, Miss Phyllis Sweeley, resigned in August to accept a position at Hamline University, and Miss Ida Kramer was named to replace her. Another resignation in the manuscript division, effective late in October, was that of Miss Catherine Bauman, the curator's assistant. The museum assistant, Mrs. Henrietta B. Erickson, also has resigned.

To the series of articles on pioneer Minnesota leaders in various fields of activity, which has been appearing in the *Minnesota Journal of Education* since 1936, Mr. Babcock has contributed an account of "Some Minnesota Military Leaders." This appears, with a number of appropriate illustrations from the society's picture collection, in the September issue of the *Journal*.

Under the title "Highway of the Voyageurs," Miss Nute describes a canoe trip in northern Minnesota in the July number of the *Conservation Volunteer*.

Wartime activities have resulted in a greatly increased use of some of the society's collections and facilities. In the manuscript division, for example, more than six thousand readers were served during the first nine months of 1942, more than double the number recorded for the entire year of 1941. A decade earlier, in the early 1930's, from three to five hundred readers used the society's manuscript facilities annually. A large proportion of the recent readers of manuscripts are searching for records of birth or residence in the original schedules of the federal and state census in the society's custody. For similar purposes, large numbers of people each month are consulting the society's collections of city directories and Minnesota newspapers.

Newspaper readers who wish to use the *Minnesota Pioneer* for the years from 1849 to 1854 are now being referred to the manuscript division, where a microfilm copy of the file for those years is available. By using the copy, the society hopes to save wear and tear on the original file, much of which is unique. Among other newspapers for which the society owns microfilm copies are the *Boston Pilot* for the years from 1854 to 1875, and a number of Winnipeg papers for the period from 1859 to 1875.

Much attention has been given recently to the care and arrangement of archival material in the custody of the society. The records of the surveyor general of logs and lumber, which have been stored in the Historical Building for more than twenty years, were examined by Mr. Eugene Barnes and many of the earlier records, which date back to the 1850's, were arranged. Mr. Barnes also drew up a report on the use of microfilms as an archival aid in other states. The possibility in Minnesota of destroying huge accretions of archival material after they have been copied by the microfilm process is under consideration.

Four annual members joined the society during the quarter ending on September 30: Herbert C. Anderson of Hector, Ralph H. Brown of Minneapolis, Mrs. George G. Cowrie of Minneapolis, and Lieutenant Robert H. Fraser of Las Vegas, New Mexico.

During the third quarter of 1942 the society lost the following active members by death: Mary T. Hale of Minneapolis on July 28, John H. Darling of Duluth on September 12, Judge Royal A. Stone of St. Paul on September 13, George Bell of St. Paul on September 16, and Ross A. Gortner of St. Paul on September 30.

During the summer and early fall, members of the staff continued their speaking activities, though on a somewhat reduced scale. Dr. Larsen spoke on "The Missionary in the Development of Minnesota" at Lac qui Parle State Park on July 12, when the restored mission chapel was dedicated. At the first annual meeting of the Chisago County Historical Society, which was held at Center City on September 22, Dr. Beeson discussed the work of local historical societies. Dr. Nute gave talks and addresses on "The Voyageur" at Isle Royale on July 9, on "The Webster-Ashburton Treaty and the Voyageur" before the North Shore Historical Assembly meeting at Fort William on August 1, and on "The Farmer and History" before the short course for farm bureau women at the University Farm in St. Paul on September 24.

CONTRIBUTORS

While serving as technical director of the University Theatre and instructor in speech in the University of Minnesota, Dr. Frank M. Whiting became interested in the early history of the drama in Minnesota. His interest led to the preparation of a long and detailed study of the "History of the Theatre in St. Paul, Minnesota, from Its Beginning to 1890," which was submitted in the University of Minnesota as a doctoral dissertation in 1941. His present description of some "Theatrical Personalities of Old St. Paul" in the 1850's is based upon the early chapters of the longer study, which is unpublished.

Dr. Merrill E. Jarchow, the author of the article on "Farm Machinery in Frontier Minnesota" in the present issue, is an instructor in history in the South Dakota State College of Agriculture and Mechanic Arts at Brookings. His article on "Early Minnesota Agricultural Societies and Fairs" appeared in the issue of *Minnesota History* for September, 1941, and he occasionally contributes book reviews to the society's quarterly.

The third and final installment of the journal of Charles C. Trowbridge, who was "With Cass in the Northwest in 1820," appears in the present issue with annotations by Professor Ralph H. Brown of the department of geography in the University of Minnesota. His concern for the historical geography of Minnesota and the Northwest became evident some years ago, when he contributed to this magazine an article entitled "Fact and Fancy in Early Accounts of Minnesota's Climate" (see *ante,* 17:243–261).

The brief article on "A Mississippi Panorama" in the "Notes and Documents" section was prepared for a Pennsylvania periodical by Dr. J. Alden Mason, curator of the American section of the University Museum of the University of Pennsylvania. The fact that this "is purely an anthropological museum, and our possession of the panorama is merely due to the fact that it was part of the archaeological collection of Dr. Dickeson" was explained by Dr. Mason in a letter. The circumstances under which he wrote the account herewith reprinted are explained by the assistant editor of this magazine in a brief introductory note.

The name of Professor John T. Flanagan of the department of English in the University of Minnesota, which heads the list of reviewers, is familiar to readers of this magazine. His recent article on "The Middle Western Farm Novel" (*ante,* p. 113–125) attracted a wide audience. Dr. Charles M. Gates is a member of the history faculty in the University of Washington at Seattle. Mr. Verne E. Chatelain of Washington, D. C., is a former Minnesotan who made a special study of federal land policies and their operation in Minnesota. He has discussed several phases of the subject in earlier issues of this magazine. Professor Philip D. Jordan is associate professor of history in Miami University at Oxford, Ohio, and the compiler, with Lillian Kessler, of a recent anthology of *Songs of Yesterday* (see *ante,* p. 159). Dr. Ella A. Hawkinson is principal of the College High School and supervisor of history and the social studies in the Moorhead State Teachers College. Mr. L. A. Rossman, publisher of the *Grand Rapids Herald-Review,* is a member of the executive council of the Minnesota Historical Society. Professor George M. Stephenson of the department of history in the University of Minnesota has demonstrated his interest in the religious aspects of Scandinavian-American history by publishing a book and several articles on the subject. Dr. Evadene Burris Swanson of Minneapolis has contributed a number of articles and book reviews to this magazine.

ACCESSIONS

Forty-seven items from the papers of Robert Kennicott, a Chicago naturalist and ornithologist of the last century, have been copied for the society through the courtesy of Mr. Hiram L. Kennicott of Highland Park, Illinois. The papers copied, which relate to the years from 1855 to 1862, include information about visits to Minnesota in 1857 and 1859, with letters from St. Cloud, Pembina, and the Red River settlements. Kennicott, who was associated with the Chicago Academy of Sciences and organized the museum of natural history at Northwestern University, was a son of Dr. John Kennicott, editor of the *Prairie Farmer.*

The certificate of citizenship issued to Knute Nelson in 1866 is included in a mass of papers of the Minnesota Senator, consisting of five boxes and an account book and covering the years from 1861 to 1934, received from the estate of his daughter, the late Mrs. Ida G. Nelson of Alexandria. Among other personal items in this valuable collection, which adds considerably to the bulk as well as the interest of the Nelson Papers already in the possession of the society (see *ante,* 22:319), is a record of Nelson's service in the Civil War with the Fourth Wisconsin Volunteer Infantry. Throughout his life, Nelson corresponded with members of his regiment, and a large number of the resulting letters are among the papers recently presented. Other correspondents represented include President Theodore Roosevelt, William B. Dean of St. Paul, and Charles Whitney, a Minnesota journalist. There are a number of letters from H. E. Paine relating to the constitutional basis for state-owned elevators. Newspaper clippings reporting events in Nelson's career from 1886 to 1920 are included. The Senator's activities as a railroad lawyer, an estate administrator, and a land speculator are reflected in the records of twelve legal cases dating from 1868 to 1915. Of special interest are the records of a suit arising out of an attempt to remove the county seat of Grant County from Elbow Lake to Herman in the early 1880's.

The original minutes of the Furness colony, which was organized in the Furness district of northern England in 1872, and sent its members to settle on Northern Pacific Railroad lands near Wadena in 1873 and 1874, have been presented by Mr. George Masters of Brookings, South Dakota. The records were kept by the colony's secretary, Richard Bailey, whose son, Mr. T. J. Bailey of Sacriston, Durham, England, recently sent them to Mr. Masters. Seventeen pages of minutes open with a record of the organization meeting of the Furness colony on October 22, 1872. This is followed by the rules of the emigration group, notices of meetings and addresses, accounts of visits of inspection to Minnesota lands by representatives of the colony, and reports of negotiations with the railroad company.

The Trinity Lutheran Church of St. Paul has added to its records already in the possession of the society (see *ante,* 20:193) three volumes containing baptismal, marriage, and death records for the years from 1870 to 1923.

Clippings about the activities of Frank B. Kellogg, jurist, statesman, and diplomat, in 1907 and from 1924 to 1929, are contained in twenty scrapbooks presented by Mr. George Morgan of St. Paul. The earlier books relate to Kellogg's services as a United States attorney in the Interstate Commerce Commission's investigation of the Union Pacific trusts. The period when Kellogg was ambassador to England and secretary of state is covered in the later volumes, which contain material on the Kellogg-Briand treaty, the World Court, the League of Nations, and relations with Mexico and Nicaragua.

A mass of political information assembled by Lynn Haines and filling eight filing boxes has been added to his papers by his widow, Mrs. Dora B. Haines of Washington (see *ante,* 22:423). The newly acquired material includes the voting records of many Congressmen and relates to such subjects as the presidential campaign of 1928.

A German edition of Father Hennepin's *New Discovery of a Vast Country in America,* published at Bremen in 1698, has been added to the society's substantial collection of Hennepin items. This was Hennepin's second book about the journey to the upper Mississippi that resulted in the discovery of the Falls of St. Anthony. The society has several other editions of this work published in 1698, 1699, and 1704. The German version is entitled *Neue Reise-Beschreibung durch viele Länder weit grösser als ganz Europa.*

Two issues of a hitherto unknown St. Paul newspaper are included in a gift of Minnesota and Eastern newspapers recently received from Mrs. Levi M. Hall of Minneapolis. The paper, which is entitled the *North Star,* was a daily published in St. Paul to give support to John C. Breckinridge of Kentucky in the presidential campaign of 1860. The issues received by the society are numbers 45 and 47 of volume 1, and they are dated September 18 and 20, 1860. The editor was Harry H. Young, a journalist who came to Minnesota in 1859 and settled first at Henderson. After the Civil War he was employed on papers at Red Wing and Rochester, and he later served as secretary of the state board of immigration. Among other Minnesota newspapers in Mrs. Hall's gift that were not to be found earlier in the society's collection are the *Anoka Union* for November 16, 1865, the *La Crescent Plaindealer* for November 26, 1860, the *Minnesota Union* of St. Cloud for April 11 and November 28, 1862, and thirty-four issues of the *Minnesota Statesman* of St. Peter for 1860 and 1861. Represented also by issues for the 1850's and 1860's are three St. Paul papers, the *Pioneer,* the *Pioneer and Democrat,* and the *Press,* and newspapers published in Washington, Baltimore, Boston, and several places in Vermont.

Mr. Albert Steinhauser of New Ulm has presented substantial files of two German-language newspapers published in South Dakota from 1883 to 1915. A file of the *Dakota freie Presse* of Yankton covers the period from 1883 to 1900. The *Sud Dakota Nachrichten,* which was published at Mitchell until 1896 and later appeared at Sioux Falls under four different titles, is represented by a file for the years from 1891 to 1915. A single issue of the *Dakota Post,* published at Mitchell on May 14, 1896, is included in the gift. So far as has been determined, no other depository owns files of these newspapers.

Recent additions to the military collection include a Remington rifle that was used in the Revolutionary War, from Mr. W. E. Hickel of Birmingham, Alabama; a revolver patented by Otis E. Smith in 1873, from Mrs. G. P. Tuthill of St. Paul; and an American army bayonet of the 1880's, from the Goodwill Industries of St. Paul. The latter organization also has presented a number of tools, including an iron hames and a brace.

Miss Pauline Wold of Santa Barbara, California, has presented a beautiful lace handkerchief that was made by a Chippewa girl on the Leech Lake reservation in 1898. The handkerchief was a gift to Miss Wold from Miss Pauline Colby, who taught lacemaking on the reservation from 1892 to 1922. Among numerous items presented by Miss Edith Brill of St. Paul are two beaded bags made by Indians on the same reservation, a toy bank made in the form of a miniature iron safe, and an electric toaster of an early type.

A portable writing desk of mahogany with brass trimmings and a secret drawer, which is said to date from the period of the American Revolution, is the gift of Mrs. Annie Giblette of Mora. Miss Mary H. Folwell of Minneapolis has presented a pair of silver candlesticks, some rugs, and several pieces of furniture. Other items of household equipment recently received include a blue and white cotton quilt made in 1842, from Mrs. Raymond A. Jackson of Minneapolis; a number of iron trivets, wooden salad serving sets, a copper strainer, and a copper mug, from Mrs. C. C. Bovey of Minneapolis; a chopping knife with double blades, from Dr. J. C. Ferguson of St. Paul; and a coffee grinder, from Mrs. A. E. Ingberg of Sunrise.

A doll's rocking chair upholstered in horsehair, dating from about 1860, is one of the many interesting additions to the museum collection recently presented by Miss Georjeannie Hamilton of Minneapolis. Her gift includes samples of ribbons, trimmings, and materials used by her mother while conducting a millinery shop in Minneapolis in the 1870's and 1880's. Miss Hamilton also has presented numerous items of men's and women's clothing, accessories, jewelry, and lace; several patchwork quilts; and china, glassware, and other table appointments.

A bugle used in the Civil War by Albert Trost is the gift of his daughter and son-in-law, Mr. and Mrs. William A. McCreight of St. Paul. A guitar made in Germany in 1834 has been presented by Mrs. Charlotte Merrill of St. Paul.

Ninety tools used by John S. Ekman, a St. Paul cabinet maker, have been presented by his son, Mr. Lawrence E. Ekman of Rochester. Mrs. M. T. McEllistrem of St. Paul has presented some pieces of blacksmith's equipment used by her father, Dunoid Simard.

An interesting addition to the toy collection is a miniature model of a locomotive made in 1888 by Mr. H. T. Johnson of South St. Paul, who presented it. Originally, it was operated by steam, and later compressed air was used. A small doll with china head, hands, and feet, dating from about 1860, is the gift of Mrs. Julia Hintz of St. Paul.

An elaborately embroidered Swedish peasant costume consisting of a blouse, skirt, apron, jerkin, hood, and stockings has been presented by Mrs. Maria I. Wineberg of Akron, Ohio.

A brass medal issued for French orphans of the first World War has been added to the numismatic collection by Miss Marjorie Knowles of St. Paul.

Among the genealogies received in the third quarter of 1942 are several that contain up-to-date information about Minnesotans and their families. In one, *The Wells Family* by D. W. Norris and H. A. Feldmann (Milwaukee, 1942. 437 p.), there is an account of Captain Franklin Van Valkenburgh, a native of Minneapolis who met his death at Pearl Harbor on December 7, 1941. In another, volume 2 of *Our Pioneers Ancestors* by Henry E. Riggs (Ann Arbor, Michigan, 1942. 230 p.), a chart showing the descendants, as of January 1, 1942, of the Reverend Stephen R. Riggs, a prominent Minnesota missionary, is presented, and his work and that of his sons among the Sioux of Minnesota, South Dakota, and Nebraska is briefly sketched.

Information about the families of Harrison B. and Chauncey N. Waterman, based upon the Winona County federal census schedules for 1860 and 1870, appears in volume 2 of *The Waterman Family,* compiled by Donald L. Jacobus (New Haven, 1942. 784 p.). Another member of the same family who went to Minnesota, the Reverend Thomas T. Waterman, served as pastor of a Congregational church at Winona in 1856 and 1857 and helped to erect there a church building with a steeple and a bell, which is said to have been the first of its kind on the west bank of the Mississippi north of Dubuque.

Other genealogies received recently include: U. S. G. Bowersox, *Bauersachs Family History* (Longmont, Colorado, 1941. 168 p.); Winfield S. H. Engle, *The Melchor Engle Family* (Lima, Ohio, 1940. 243 p.); Harry F. Roush, *Family History of the Fenders and the Lances* (Lima, Ohio, 1942. 34 p.); David Graessle, *History of the Graessle-Gracely Family* (Lima, Ohio, 1941. 42 p.); Hugh C. Haynsworth, *Haynsworth-Furman and Allied Families* (Sumter, South Carolina, 1942. 333 p.); William O. Francis, *A History of the Holmes Family* (Chillicothe, Ohio, 1942. 11 p.); Loea P. Howard, *Ancestors of Joel and Maria Parker Howard of Reading, Massachusetts* (Boston, 1942. 62 p.); Alexander E. Hoyle, *The Story of William Hoyle and His Family, Told in Their Own Diaries and Letters* (Boston, 1942. 565 p.); George F. Ivey, *The Ivey Family in the United States* (Hickory, North Carolina, 1941. 113 p.); Edward S. Knapp, *We Knapps Thought It Was Nice* (New York, 1940. 211 p.); William J. Lodge, *A Record of the Descendants of Robert and Elizabeth Lodge* (Geneva, 1942. 150 p.); Ellsworth D. McEathron, *McEathron (McEachron, McEachran, Mc Eachern) Family* (San Pedro, California, 1941. 8 p.); Harrison M. Sayre, *Descendants of Deacon Ephraim Sayre* (Columbus, Ohio, 1942. 75 p.); Edith A. Rudder, *My Mother's Family, Shannon-Sill, Pennsylvania and Ohio, Hamilton-Robinson, Virginia and Indiana* (Salem, Indiana, 1942. 38 p.); Mary L. Graff, *Early History of Truby-Graff and Affiliated Families* (Kittanning, Pennsylvania, 1941. 367 p.); and Lewis C. Weldin, *History and Genealogy of the Weldin Family* (Pittsburgh, 1939. 163 p.). L.M.F.

News and Comment

THAT "the publication of a series of bulletins, covering different phases of local historical work," is one of the most significant phases of the work of the American Association for State and Local History is the belief expressed by C. C. Crittenden in a general introduction to its *Bulletins*. Since three numbers have now been issued by the association, it is possible to gain some idea of the value of these publications to local historians. In the first, published in October, 1941, Edward P. Alexander of the State Historical Society of Wisconsin deals with the question "What Should Our Historical Society Do?" His discussion "is intended to give a general résumé of possible activities for a local historical group." He divides his subject under four conventional headings — meeting, publication, library, and museum activities. Some of the activities included under these headings, however, are far from conventional. Under publications, for example, he discusses speeches, radio talks, and markers. Dr. Alexander's most useful suggestions probably are those relating to museums. Included is a definition of "principles of relevancy of material and changing display" that many a museum, large and small, might apply with profit. The Minnesota Historical Society should be flattered by the fact that several of Dr. Alexander's examples are drawn from its activities. For instance, after enumerating various types of meetings that historical societies might arrange, he suggests that the reader "examine the back numbers of *Minnesota History* or *New York History* . . . to see how these various suggestions are carried out." The local historical worker will do well to have a copy of this booklet at hand. Specific phases of the local history program are discussed in two *Bulletins* issued in 1942. In number 2 of the series, Sylvester K. Stevens deals with a timely subject, "Local History and Winning the War," giving emphasis to the "theory of local history as a morale resource." The experience of one local leader, Loring McMillen of the Staten Island Historical Society, in "Using Volunteers in the Local Historical Society's Program" is described in number 3 of the *Bulletins*. Other booklets planned for this series will deal with such topics as "the conduct of historical tours, planning and producing historical radio broadcasts, publicity programs for the historical society, the conduct of local historical forums, the writing of local history, the preservation and care of manuscripts by small libraries and historical societies, the restoration and care of historic buildings and sites, the marking of historic spots, the production of local historical plays and pageants, and the planning of suitable publication programs."

"No nation can be patriotic in the best sense, so people can feel a proud comradeship, without a knowledge of the past," writes Allan Nevins in the *New York Times Magazine* for May 3. He notes that "The Army camps are hastily organizing classes in historical instruction," and that "Our press is full of references to the devotion and heroism shown in former crises." This causes Professor Nevins to raise the question, "Have we done enough to teach American history in the lower schools, the high schools and the colleges, and has it been taught aright?"

A statistical study, by Professors William B. Hesseltine and Louis Kaplan of the University of Wisconsin, of "Doctors of Philosophy in History" who received degrees from forty-six American universities from 1873 to 1935 appears in the July number of the *American Historical Review*. Tables are presented to show the number of doctoral degrees in history granted by each university, the occupations of those holding such degrees, their distribution, and the number of books and articles they have published.

Four papers presented in a symposium on the question "Have the Americas a Common History?" at the annual meeting of the American Historical Association in Chicago on December 29, 1941, have been published in the June number of the *Canadian Historical Review*. Contributing to the discussion of this interesting question are William C. Binkley for the United States, George W. Brown for Canada, Edmundo O'Gorman for Mexico, and German Arciniegas for South America.

In an essay on "Frederick Jackson Turner, Historian," published in the *Wisconsin Magazine of History* for June, Avery Craven writes: "To reduce this first frontier essay to a hidebound thesis separate from the rest of Turner's work; to denounce it for its lack of exactness and its tendency to generalize; to criticize it because it does not contain everything which might conceivably be included in a complete formula for the writing of American history is to miss its whole purpose and value." Professor Craven defends Turner's theory by saying that it "was but a starting point, an approach. The end sought was research, not dictation."

"Those who have worked on the more comprehensive phases of agricultural history have long since realized that good agricultural history is unobtainable without good local history," writes Everett E. Edwards in an article on "Agricultural History and the Department of Agriculture," appearing in *Agricultural History* for July. Mr. Edwards contends that "it is a valuable and useful experience to write individually or collectively the history of one's own community. Good local histories can be prepared by school children," he continues, "and the Department may well assist in a 'write your own history' movement." The fact that the department has an opportunity to co-operate with 4–H Clubs and extension workers is stressed.

Viking tales containing references to America have been charmingly translated by Einar Haugen and published in a handsome volume that bears the title, *Voyages to Vinland: The First American Saga* (Chicago, 1941. 127 p.). Mr. Haugen is responsible not only for this new translation, "made directly from the original manuscripts of the thirteenth and fourteeenth centuries," but for the annotations, comments on historical evidence, notes, and interpretations that accompany the narrative proper. In one section he presents the evidence discovered by archaeologists and others "In Search of Relics," and there he comments on what he describes as the "most ambitious runic stone in all America" — the Kensington rune stone. "Whether one regards it as spurious or genuine," writes Mr. Haugen of the Minnesota stone, "its undeniable presence in Alexandria, Minnesota, is very hard to explain. If it is a hoax, it has not yet been unmasked," he continues; "if it is a voice from the past, its title to speak is still in doubt."

The literature that has arisen out of the Paul Bunyan tales is the subject of a revealing analysis by Gladys J. Haney appearing under the title "Paul Bunyan Twenty-five Years After" in the *Journal of American Folklore* for July–September. The author finds it "odd that such a short time as a quarter of a century ago, Paul was known almost entirely through oral tales, and to a comparatively small number of people." In the intervening years, Miss Haney discloses, "there have been at least 17 full-length books, five of them in poetry, published about Paul," and plays, "music, ballets, murals, wood-cuts, paintings, and statues have portrayed him." How recently the lumberjack hero has become generally known is illustrated by Miss Haney's list of "firsts," which includes "first written record, in 1914, by W. B. Laughead; first research recorded, in 1916, by Stewart and Watt; first continuous narrative, in 1919, by Ida Virginia Turney; and first book written especially for children, in 1927, by James Cloyd Bowman." And readers are informed that the "first encyclopedia to include Paul Bunyan was Brittanica, in 1929." Minnesotans will recall that Mr. Laughead recorded his tales in an advertising booklet issued by the Red River Lumber Company (see *ante,* 21: 177). Miss Haney's brief sketch is followed by a bibliography of eleven pages, which includes sections on music and art.

A contribution to the folklore of Lake Superior, in this case originating with the voyageurs rather than with the Indians, appears in the *Beaver* for September under the title "A Merman in Lake Superior." The narrative, which is reprinted from the *Canadian Magazine and Literary Repository* for May, 1824, describes a curious creature that a voyageur named Venant St. Germain is said to have seen "rising from the waters of Lake Superior." His account of the apparition is in the "form of a deposition before two of the judges of the Court of King's Bench." The experience that St. Germain reports occurred in 1782 while he was on a trip from Grand Portage to Mackinac.

The origin and significance of about three hundred *American Mottoes and Slogans* and their historical associations are explained by George E. Shankle in a recently published volume (New York, 1941. 183 p.). Included are "political campaign slogans, governmental slogans, colonial and revolutionary patriotic slogans, war slogans, personal slogans, religious slogans, the mottoes and slogans of patriotic organizations, and the state mottoes." The arrangement is alphabetical, with a profuse use of cross referencing.

The announcement that the State Historical Society of Missouri has acquired the library of "almost 3000 select items in the history and literature of the 'Middle Border,'" assembled over a period of more than forty years by J. Christian Bay of Chicago, accompanies Mr. Bay's address on "Western Life and Western Books" in the July issue of the *Missouri Historical Review.* Mr. Bay defines some of the principles that guided his collecting activities, relating that his library "was formed around the idea that our pioneer spirit, our western life, is worth preserving in record and by way of emulation." The pioneer spirit he asserts, "still unites us," and it still is true that "the Middle Border is our country's heart, and that heart remains sound, whatever comes, whatever passes." Incidentally, Mr. Bay pays a tribute to the American historical societies, which, he says, "prove that our best traditions are studied, made known, perpetuated. If history means anything to us," he continues, "we shall observe and obey the lessons of the past. I think we do this."

A "Conference on the Northern Plains" was held at Lincoln, Nebraska, on June 25, 26, and 27, with a number of historians and others from the Northwest participating. Minnesota was represented by Dean Theodore C. Blegen of the University of Minnesota; among those from neighboring states and provinces were Professor John D. Hicks of the University of Wisconsin, Professor Louis Pelzer of the University of Iowa, Mr. Richard C. Overton of Chicago, and Mr. George Ferguson of the *Winnipeg Free Press*. Dean Blegen contributed to the discussion many remarks based upon his long experience as superintendent of the Minnesota Historical Society and editor of its publications. At the final session he outlined a program consisting of ten points for the study of the Plains area, particularly its northern section.

In the *Bulletin* of the American Institute of Swedish Arts, Literature, and Science for September, Albin Widen makes the suggestion that a conference for the discussion of "Swedish immigration, local history, and history of denominations and organizations, personal and family history" should be held in the near future at the institute, which is located in Minneapolis. Mr. Widen stresses the importance of collecting and preserving material relating to the history of the Swedes in America, and he contends that "for that purpose, historical societies should be founded in all Swedish localities." One project suggested for workers in the field of Swedish-American history is the making of a "systematic inventory of Swedish settlements in Minnesota." The need for special Swedish-American archives also is noted. Mr. Widen fails to mention the vast collection of materials relating to the Swedes in America preserved by the Minnesota Historical Society, though a note elsewhere in the *Bulletin* calls attention to the society's resources in that field.

One of O. E. Rølvaag's boyhood friends in Norway, Mr. John Heitmann of Duluth, is the author of a charming sketch of the eminent Minnesota author appearing in volume 12 of the *Norwegian-American Studies and Records* (Northfield, 1941). Much of the article deals with Rølvaag's Norwegian background and his family, though a few Minnesota incidents are included. Among other interesting and informing articles in the same volume are Kenneth Bjørk's account of "Ole Evinrude and the Outboard Motor," Birger Osland's recollections of early "Norwegian Clubs in Chicago," and Marjorie M. Kimmerle's study of "Norwegian-American Surnames."

One chapter of the Reverend Vaclav Vojta's volume on *Czechoslovak Baptists* and their churches is devoted to religious organizations in Minnesota and Wisconsin (Minneapolis, 1941. 276 p.). Minnesota churches and church leaders in New Prague, Minneapolis, and St. Paul are considered. New Prague is described as a "typical Czechoslovak colony," where the "people speak the Czech language on the streets, in stores, in civic offices, and elsewhere."

The First Fifty Years of a midwestern institution of higher learning, the University of Chicago, are outlined in streamlined fashion in a pamphlet issued to commemorate its fiftieth anniversary (1941. 48 p.). In word and picture a record is presented of the founding, as the result of the gift of John D. Rockefeller, of an institution that was planned for concentration upon investigation and inquiry.

Some reverberations of the Northfield bank robbery of 1876 are to be found in an article on "The James Boys and Missouri Politics" by William A. Settle, Jr., appearing in the *Missouri Historical Review* for July. In 1880, four years after Frank and Jesse James escaped from Minnesota, the Missouri "Republican State platform contained two statements which were intended as reflections upon the Democratic administration for failure to capture the James band," writes Mr. Settle. One statement accused the Democrats of failure to "prosecute notorious criminals," and of "permitting a Republican state [*Minnesota*] to perform that duty." As late as 1885, "at the time of the dismissal of the last Missouri charge against Frank James . . . it was rumored that requisition for him would soon be made by Minnesota authorities"; and Republican papers printed "attacks upon the element of the Democratic party which wanted to prevent Frank James' trial in Minnesota and charged that political influence had been used to keep him from being punished." In the same issue of the *Review,* under the title "Lost Channels," Sue Hetherington writes of the old Mississippi River songs, most of which are now "forgotten because nobody thought to write them down." Among the types of songs mentioned are those to which "Norse lumberjacks set their dialect" while they "made large rafts of the logs up at Stillwater, Minnesota, then guided them down the river to St. Louis." The author notes that a song popular with raft pilots was " 'The *Fred Weyerhaeuser* and the *Frontenac,*' a ballad made entirely of the names of towboats." Miss Hetherington adds to her article an "index of first lines of such scraps of songs as were available to the compiler."

"David Dale Owen and the First Geological Survey," which began in Iowa in 1839, are discussed by Walter B. Hendrickson in the *Annals of Iowa* for July. It will be recalled that nearly a decade after he began work in Iowa, Owen extended his survey into the Minnesota country. His work there doubtless will be described in Professor Hendrickson's biography of Owen, which, according to an announcement that accompanies the present article, is soon to be published by the Indiana Historical Commission.

Conrad W. Leifur is the author of a newly published textbook on *Our State North Dakota* (New York, 1942.   621 p.), about half of which is devoted to geography and history. The volume meets the requirements and follows an outline provided by the state department of public instruction. Connections between the history of Minnesota and that of its neighbor to the west are brought out in many sections of the book, notably those dealing with the Indians, exploration, the fur trade, Indian wars, and transportation.

Nearly three hundred pages of volume 20 of the *South Dakota Historical Collections* are devoted to a detailed study by Charles Lowell Green of "The Administration of the Public Domain in South Dakota." The author, who is a member of the history faculty in the Moorhead State Teachers College, prepared this study as his doctoral dissertation in the University of Iowa. There are chapters dealing with Indian land cessions, surveys, and pre-emption, as well as with settlement, colonization, speculation, and railroad lands. Minnesota places and Minnesota residents frequently are mentioned in this narrative. Of Minnesota interest also is a sketch in the same volume of "Bishop Marty and His Sioux Missions," by Sister Mary Clement Fitzgerald. A brief statement about Father Martin Marty's service as bishop of St. Cloud in the 1890's is included.

Minnesota is well represented in a historical edition of a South Dakota newspaper, the *Sisseton Courier,* issued on July 2 to commemorate the fiftieth anniversary of three local events — the opening to settlement of the Sisseton and Wahpeton Indian Reservation, the founding of the city of Sisseton, and the establishment of its first newspaper. Browns Valley, across the border in Minnesota, was the gateway to the reservation, and it was there in April, 1892, that "hordes of eager home seekers, some on foot, some [on] horseback and others with every form of conveyance were packed . . . awaiting the discharge of guns of the soldiers, which were to signal the zero hour for the rush" for claims on the reservation. A sketch of the founding and early history of Browns Valley is included in the issue. There also are to be found accounts of Presbyterian and Catholic missions established by men who had been active earlier in the Minnesota mission field, and a biographical sketch of Hazen Mooers, a fur trader who was prominent both east and west of Lake Traverse.

The role played by N. P. Langford, who was known both in Minnesota and Montana, in bringing about "The Creation of Yellowstone National Park," is described by N. Turrentine Jackson in the *Mississippi Valley Historical Review* for September. That the first suggestion for the preservation of the wonders of the Yellowstone basin in a national park came from Cornelius Hedges, a member of the exploring expedition of 1870, is recorded in Langford's writings. Langford's own lectures on behalf of the park project and his untiring efforts to push a bill through Congress to provide for the park are described by the author in some detail.

One the most useful volumes issued by the Wisconsin Historical Records Survey deals with the *Origin and Legislative History of County Boundaries in Wisconsin* (Madison, 1942. 229 p.). Changes in boundaries are not only described in detail for each county in the state, with references to legislative enactments, but they are graphically illustrated on maps. Of special Minnesota interest are the sections relating to the border counties of Crawford, Pierce, Polk, and St. Croix. The volume is a reminder of the need for a similar study of county boundaries in Minnesota.

To "meet the needs of teachers, students, and study clubs interested in the history of La Crosse," Miss H. Margaret Josten, chairman of the department of social studies in a local high school, has prepared a useful study guide entitled *La Crosse: A Century of Growth 1842–1942* (1942. 53 p.). After disposing of the founding of the city and the establishment of its lumbering interests, Miss Josten outlines the growth of the city, dividing her subject into fourteen sections. Among the topics suggested for investigation are racial groups, local government, education, churches, cultural activities, recreation, social activities, and many phases of business and professional history. For each topic the author provides an outline, a list of references, and a number of suggested activities for students. When studying racial groups, for example, the author suggests that one student should "make a survey to learn what students had ancestors who were early settlers in La Crosse," and that another might "make a collection of songs, of recipes, of sayings, of holiday or other customs which one family or one racial group brought with it." Of timely significance is a section on "War and Defense," with divisions on La Crosse in wars of the past, on patriotic societies, and on "defense preparation 1941–1942," including local industries in the defense program and civilian activities.

An appeal to "Salvage Canada's Past," along with rubber, scrap iron, and paper, is made by Elsie McLeod Murray in the *Ontario Library Review* for August. "In the attics and cellars of our homes, in church vestries, in warehouses and stores, in municipal offices, and often even in our libraries," she writes, "lies unrecognized and completely abandoned the very stuff and substance of the past — original documentary accounts of the social life, business activities, cultural pursuits and political thought of earlier generations." The author is concerned chiefly with what she describes as the "new and sometimes baffling problems" that arise in making available to historians, genealogists, novelists, lawyers, and others who use libraries the manuscript materials relating to Canada's past.

Readers of Mr. Lawrence J. Burpee's article on "A Hundred Years of North America" in the September issue of this magazine will be interested in the same author's concise account of the founding, history, and accomplishments of the International Joint Commission, published by the Ryerson Press of Toronto under the title *Good Neighbours* (1940. 30 p.). He traces from sea to sea the international boundary over which the commission exercises jurisdiction, giving a detailed description of Minnesota's northern boundary.

The Canadian international boundary area that adjoins Minnesota to the north is given some consideration in an article on "The History and Status of Forestry in Ontario" by N. O. Hipel, appearing in the *Canadian Geographical Journal* for September. The forests of the Quetico region and the Rainy River country receive frequent mention. The many excellent pictures of lumber camps and logging activities that illustrate the article are as typical of northern Minnesota as of Ontario.

In an attractive volume entitled *Tadoussac Then and Now: A History and Narrative of the Kingdom of Saguenay* (1942. 23 p.), William Hugh Coverdale outlines the history of the ancient French settlement at the junction of the Saguenay and St. Lawrence rivers. He pictures Tadoussac as the center of a fabulous land where the French dreamed of finding unmeasured riches in the sixteenth century; as a "much-used base, where the fur-trade developed from being a side-line to the fisheries"; as a mission station; and, finally, as a summer resort. Among the many interesting illustrations is a picture of the chapel, still standing, which was erected in 1747.

A documentary film depicting the making of the birchbark canoe, produced under the direction of Mr. and Mrs. F. Radford Crawley, was given its first showing at the annual meeting of the Canadian Historical Society at Ottawa on February 25, 1942. The film inaugurates a series designed by the Canadian Historical Society to tell the story of transportation in Canada. Others dealing with various types of transportation, from the dogsled to the airplane, are planned for future production.

Dr. Grace Lee Nute, curator of manuscripts for the Minnesota Historical Society, was the speaker at a meeting of the Thunder Bay Historical Society at Fort William on June 29. She took as her subject the adventures of Radisson and Groseilliers in the Northwest, describing also some of the obscure sources of information on their careers that she had discovered in France and in Canada.

General Minnesota Items

The fiftieth anniversary of the Minnesota Library Association is fittingly commemorated in the September issue of *Minnesota Libraries,* which presents two articles on the history of the organization. The first, by Gratia A. Countryman, one of its charter members and founders, reviews the "Early History of the Minnesota Library Association, 1891–1900." She brings out the fact that the first suggestion for a state organization of librarians came from Dr. William W. Folwell in a letter of December 23, 1891, to J. Fletcher Williams, secretary and librarian of the Minnesota Historical Society. The role of these men in making the association a reality is described. It may be noted in passing that the "organization meeting was held in the directors' room of the Minnesota Historical Society on December 29, 1891." Miss Countryman describes the association's annual meetings in its first decade of existence, and she tells of some important cultural developments for which it was responsible. At its fourth annual meeting Dr. Folwell recommended that the university open a department of library science, at a time when there were only four library schools in the country. In 1899, as the result of constant agitation by the association in favor of traveling libraries, the legislature passed an act establishing a state library commission. Miss Clara Baldwin, who was named librarian of the commission, is the author of the second article about the history of the Minnesota Library Association, outlining the story of its accomplishments from 1900 to 1942.

The "Preservation of Local History" was the topic of a panel discussion held in connection with a short course for farm bureau women at the University Farm in St. Paul on September 24. The discussion followed an address on "The Farmer and History," presented by Dr. Grace Lee Nute, curator of manuscripts on the staff of the Minnesota Historical Society. Participating in the panel, which was led by Mr. Paul Johnson of the University Farm, were Dr. Nute, Dr. Ray Le May of the Winona County Historical Society, Mrs. Bunn T. Willson of the Olmsted County society, Mrs. O. M. Bollum of Goodhue County, and Dr. Lewis Beeson, acting superintendent of the state historical society.

Racial groups in Minnesota and the activities of certain industrial groups in the state are providing the subject matter for a series of articles by George L. Peterson on "Life in Minnesota," appearing from time to time in the *Minneapolis Morning Tribune.* The opening article, published on September 18, deals with "Askov's Danish Farmers" and their contribution to the war effort. The author gives an engaging picture of the orderly and comfortable community that developed after "the Danish People's Society took over the pioneer settlement of Partridge and all the country round in 1906, renaming the place for the town in Denmark where the first folk high school was established." The iron range country, with its Finns, Serbs, Slovenes, Croats, Lithuanians, Italians, and other "national groups that hurried from Europe a generation and more ago" is described in the article published on September 22; and life in the lumber camps of northern Minnesota, where an acute labor shortage exists, is the subject of the article for September 29.

Under the title "Range Court History Outlined," Judge Edward Freeman of Virginia reviews the story of the local judiciary in the *Hibbing Daily Tribune* for September 26. The account deals largely with the history of the Eleventh Judicial District, which has embraced St. Louis County since 1874, and which has held regular terms at Duluth, Virginia, Hibbing, and Ely since 1911.

"A Psychiatric Bulletin in Minnesota of Half a Century Ago" is the subject of a recent chapter, by Dr. M. K. Amdur of Cincinnati, in the "History of Medicine in Minnesota" that has been appearing for some years in *Minnesota Medicine.* Dr. Amdur, whose article appears in the September issue, calls attention to the fiftieth anniversary of a quarterly *Hospital Bulletin,* published from 1891 to 1893 by the medical staff of the Rochester State Hospital. Some interesting information about the early history of the hospital is included in this article. In the July and August issues of *Minnesota Medicine,* Dr. Arthur S. Hamilton completes his "History of the Minnesota State Medical Society." The final installment carries the story of the society's annual meetings to the turn of the century.

The Minnesota conference of the Evangelical church has set aside the year 1942–43 as a seventy-fifth anniversary year, since the conference was organized in April, 1868. To mark the occasion an illustrated pamphlet reflecting the history of the conference has been issued. In it are presented a brief account of the first conference, sketches of "pioneer personalities," a chronology giving the "high-lights" in the history of the conference, a list of "anniversary observances," and a sketch of the Lake Koronis Assembly Grounds, established by the church in 1922.

Students of history, sociology, and economics who attempt to interpret the 1930's will find much of interest and value in a booklet recently issued by the University of Minnesota Press under the title, *Economic Effects of Steady Employment and Earnings: A Case Study of the Annual Wage System of George A. Hormel & Co.* (Minneapolis, 1942. 75 p.). The author, Jack Chernick, reaches the "tentative conclusion that the annual wage plan" inaugurated in 1929 by Austin's leading industry, a meat packing house, "is at least in part responsible for the creation of new jobs" in the community, thus giving the city greater economic stability than its neighbors.

The fiftieth anniversary of the International Milling Company and Robin Hood Flour Mills Limited, as recorded in the April issue of the company's trade journal, *The Grist,* commemorates the opening of a Minnesota mill at New Prague in 1892. Some "Interesting Events in the Early Days of the Company" at New Prague are recorded by F. A. Bean, a son of the founder of the concern, and other incidents relating to the mill at that place are recalled by J. J. Kovarik. A record of the company's mills in Minnesota, Iowa, New York, Texas, and Canada indicates that in the past it operated plants at Blue Earth and Wells, as well as at New Prague.

In a bulky volume on *The History of the Oil Business of George F. and J. Paul Getty from 1903 to 1939,* J. Paul Getty includes a brief account of his father's career as a lawyer in Minneapolis for nearly two decades before he became interested in Oklahoma oil. When the elder Getty organized the Minnehoma Oil Company in 1903, he coined its name by combining the first two syllables of Minnesota with the last two of Oklahoma.

WAR HISTORY ACTIVITIES

Evidence that the federal government recognizes the need for "more adequate records of administrative activities . . . not only for historical purposes but to provide a clearer insight into problems of public management and to contribute to the more effective utilization of present experience in post-war administration" is to be found in the appointment by the director of the Bureau of the Budget, at the suggestion of President Roosevelt, of an advisory Committee of Records of War Administration. Included in its membership are Professor Arthur Schlesinger of Harvard University, president of the American Historical Association, Professor William Anderson of the University of Minnesota, president of the American Political Science Association, and Dr. Solon J. Buck, archivist of the United States. The functions and activities of the committee are explained by Harry Venneman in an article on "Records of War Administration" appearing in the fall number of *Military Affairs*. The writer reports that "several of the largest and most important departments and emergency war agencies have undertaken extensive programs for the development of current records of their war activities, in line with the objectives and in some instances at the direct instigation of the Committee."

Those who are working to assemble and preserve the records of the present war should profit by studying the work of *Historical Units of Agencies of the First World War,* as set forth by Elizabeth B. Drewry in number 4 of the *Bulletins* of the National Archives (1942. 31 p.). The writer confines herself to the federal departments and "agencies in which some germ of the idea of the development of a unit for historical work appears to have existed." Thus she gives consideration to historical units of the war and navy departments, the Marine Corps, the state department, the shipping and war industries boards, the fuel, food, and relief administrations, and the Council of National Defense. Miss Drewry notes that in the records of the war of 1917–18 there are "large gaps in important files that should explain policies and describe procedures," and that it often is necessary to "go through much worthless material for some small item of significance." The importance of keeping adequate records is well brought out by Miss Drewry when she notes that "we may well wish today that more attention had been paid to" the preservation of records "during and after the first war in order, if not to prevent this one, at least to prepare us better for it." A more optimistic viewpoint is taken by Professor John W. Oliver in an article on "The Role of a Local Historical Society in Times of War," which appears in the *Western Pennsylvania Historical Magazine* for March–June. Professor Oliver gives those organizations credit for taking the "lead in collecting, compiling, and preserving all papers, documents, leaflets, and other data of historical value that any historian would need when he set to work to compile the history" of the war. The writer praises the work accomplished in Minnesota "in collecting, compiling, and publishing the war history records" of the state, and he asserts that Franklin F. Holbrook and Livia Appel's "two volumes on Minnesota in the World War rank among the best of the state war histories."

On October 1, less than five months after Governor Stassen established the Minnesota War History Committee (see *ante,* p. 149) local committees were organized and actively functioning in twelve cities and forty-two counties of the state. A list of these committees and their chairmen appears herewith. As additional committees are organized, they will be listed in the section of *Minnesota History* devoted to war history work.

Albert Lea War History Committee, L. W. Spicer, chairman.

Austin War History Committee, Harry A. Anderson, chairman.

Beltrami County War History Committee, Harold T. Hagg, Bemidji, chairman.

Benton County War History Committee, Mrs. Felix Latterell, Foley, chairman.

Big Stone County War History Committee, E. N. Schoen, Ortonville, chairman.

Brainerd War History Committee, Grace E. Polk, chairman.

Brown County War History Committee, Fred W. Johnson, New Ulm, chairman.

Carver County War History Committee, O. D. Sell, Mayer, chairman.

Chippewa County War History Committee, Dr. Anna Amrud, Montevideo, chairman.

Cottonwood County War History Committee, O. J. Nelson, Windom, chairman.

Crookston War History Committee, L. L. Landberg, chairman.

Crow Wing County War History Committee, Mrs. R. J. Libby, Crosby, chairman.

Dakota County War History Committee, Mrs. William F. Feely, Farmington, chairman.

Douglas County War History Committee, Mrs. Wallace Dougherty, Alexandria, chairman.

Duluth War History Committee, Rev. Frank A. Court, 215 North Third Avenue, chairman.

Faribault County War History Committee, Mrs. Carrie A. Bachtle, Blue Earth, chairman.

Fillmore County War History Committee, George A. Haven, Chatfield, chairman.

Goodhue County War History Committee, C. A. Rasmussen, Red Wing, chairman.

Hennepin County War History Committee, Robert E. Scott, St. Louis Park, chairman.

Hibbing War History Committee, George Fisher, chairman.

Isanti County War History Committee, Mrs. Blaine B. Barker, Cambridge, chairman.

Itasca County War History Committee, O. E. Saxhaug, Grand Rapids, chairman.

Kandiyohi County War History Committee, Henry Southworth, Willmar, chairman.

Kittson County War History Committee, C. J. Hemmingson, Hallock, chairman.

Koochiching County War History Committee, Harriet Lloyd, International Falls, chairman.

Lac qui Parle County War History Committee, Lillian Fjelde, Madison, chairman.

Lake County War History Committee, Judge W. E. Scott, Two Harbors, chairman.

McLeod County War History Committee, S. S. Beach, Hutchinson, chairman.

Mahnomen County War History Committee, Harry C. Goodrich, Mahnomen, chairman.

Mankato War History Committee, Dr. M. R. Coulter, chairman.

Martin County War History Committee, E. L. Flygare, Fairmont, chairman.

Mille Lacs County War History Committee, Rev. John H. Hinck, Milaca, chairman.

Minneapolis War History Committee, Joseph Zalusky, 341 City Hall, chairman.

Morrison County War History Committee, Mrs. Bernard N. Peterson, Little Falls, chairman.

Mower County War History Committee, Mrs. N. V. Torgerson, Adams, chairman.

Nobles County War History Committee, Mrs. Inez Madsen, Worthington, chairman.

Olmsted County War History Committee, S. L. Lyksett, Rochester, chairman.

Pipestone County War History Committee, Fred A. Busse, Pipestone, chairman.

Pope County War History Committee, Charles Glantz, Glenwood, chairman.

Red Wing War History Committee, C. A. Rasmussen, chairman.

Rice County War History Committee, Frank Kaisersatt, Faribault, chairman.

Rock County War History Committee, A. G. Suurmeyer, Luverne, chairman.

St. Cloud War History Committee, Mrs. George W. Friedrichs, chairman.

St. Paul War History Committee, Judge Gustavus Loevinger, 1551 Courthouse, chairman.

Steele County War History Committee, B. P. Leary, Owatonna, chairman.

Swift County War History Committee, Nina Brown, Benson, chairman.

Virginia War History Committee, A. M. DeYoannes, chairman.

Wabasha County War History Committee, E. L. Hibbard, Lake City, chairman.

Washington County War History Committee, E. L. Roney, Stillwater, chairman.

Watonwan County War History Committee, George S. Hage, Madelia, chairman.

Wilkin County War History Committee, Clarence Gordhammern, Breckenridge, chairman.

Winona County War History Committee, Homer Goss, Lewiston, chairman.

Wright County War History Committee, Ray Yantes, Buffalo, chairman.

Yellow Medicine County War History Committee, Edwy O. Dibble, Granite Falls, chairman.

The executive secretary of the Wisconsin War Records Commission, Mr. Elmer Plischke, visited St. Paul on September 6 and 7 for the purpose of conferring with Dr. Lewis Beeson, director of the Minnesota War History Committee. A carefully prepared report of the conference was issued by Mr. Plischke on September 21. In it he points out differences in organization in the war history work that is being conducted in Minnesota and Wisconsin, and makes definite recommendations for the Wisconsin commission. A copy of Mr. Plischke's report has been received by the Minnesota War History Committee.

Most of the 107 donors reported *ante,* p. 292, have continued to send material to the Minnesota War History Committee. In addition, during August and September, it received gifts from 139 other sources, most of which are located outside Minnesota. The committee's policy of not duplicating material that is being received by the Minnesota Historical Society and other depositories in the state accounts for the preponderance of non-Minnesota items. Among the organizations from which periodicals, pamphlets, leaflets, and other printed and processed materials have been received recently are the American Legion National Headquarters of Indianapolis, the American Slav Congress of Pittsburgh, the American Youth Commission of Washington, the Association of American Railroads of Washington, the Belgian Information Center of New York, the Commission to Study the Organization of Peace of New York, the Jewish Welfare Board of New York, the National Education Association of Washington, the National League of Women Voters of Washington, the National Planning Association of Washington, and the Post War Council of New York.

Two of the twelve army camp newspapers received by the War History Committee have been issued under the editorship of Minnesotans. *The Bat,* published at Camp Croft, South Carolina, is edited by Private Rodney Loehr, formerly an instructor in history in the University of Minnesota and the author of several articles and reviews that have appeared in *Minnesota History.* In a letter to the acting superintendent of the Minnesota Historical Society, Private Loehr describes in detail the procedure followed in issuing a camp newspaper. Until recently Corporal Gene Newhall, who was formerly with radio station WTCN and the *Minneapolis Times,* served as editor of the *Kodiak Bear* of Fort Greely, Alaska, a paper that the War History Committee has received from its inception. Corporal Newhall has now been transferred to an officers' training school. The fact that the "activities of a good number of Minnesota men" are covered in the *Kodiak Bear* is indicated in a letter from Lieutenant Theodore B. Tufte, a public relations officer stationed at Fort Greely. He expresses the belief that camp newspapers "are bound to contain references of more than momentary interest" and are therefore worthy of permanent preservation.

Among the most interesting publications received by the War History Committee is *Hi Soldier,* a mimeographed monthly issued by the Minnesota Mutual Life Insurance Company for former employees who are now in the armed forces. It is made up largely of letters to those who remain in the home office at St. Paul from former employees now serving in widely separated localities. Through the medium of *Hi Soldier,* the men and women who once worked together in the company's office are enabled to keep in touch with one another. Included also are lists of men who are in the service, with their former and present addresses.

LOCAL HISTORICAL SOCIETIES

In a setting rich in historical associations, the Washington County Historical Society has established its museum. It occupies a large house in Stillwater that was erected in the 1850's for use as a residence by the warden of what was then the territorial prison. Since it is built against a steep bluff and faces the beautiful St. Croix River, the museum's surroundings add much to its interest and attractiveness. Furthermore, it is within sight of a ravine that was the scene of a fierce battle between the Sioux and the Chippewa in 1839. Thus the visitor becomes conscious of the past of the St. Croix Valley before entering the Washington County museum.

The ownership of the old warden's residence, which was used until the new state prison was completed in 1912, was transferred to the Washington County society by legislative action in the spring of 1941. It was dedicated as a museum with appropriate ceremonies on June 20 of the latter year, when the property was officially presented to the society. In a little more than a year the local organization has furnished many of the rooms in appropriate Victorian style, and it has installed many interesting and valuable exhibits.

Upon entering the house, the visitor finds himself in a narrow hall with a central staircase. The parlor to the left is typically Victorian, with lace curtains and elaborately figured carpet. An upholstered settee and two matching chairs have intricately carved frames of black walnut. There are a number of small side tables with decorative oil lamps, and several portraits in massive frames hang on the walls. An old-fashioned piano and a spinet add to the mid-century atmosphere of this room. Back of the parlor and opening into it is a library in which the society's books and manuscripts are arranged.

To the right of the entrance hall is the dining room, which is furnished with a table, chairs, and several side pieces. The table is set with china and silver, and interesting pieces of china and glassware are displayed on other tables and on the wide window sills. Back of the dining room is a small room, probably once used as an office or study. A large secretary is the chief item of furniture displayed there. Exhibits of silver, bags, and small accessories have been arranged in two display cases in this room. Hanging on the wall is an interesting button collection mounted on boards.

Five rooms on the second floor have been furnished or are used for exhibit purposes. Two of the rooms have been furnished in the style of the 1880's, with heavy wooden bedsteads, dressers, and chests. Other appropriate items in these rooms include a washstand, a cradle, a sewing machine, a spinning wheel, and a case filled with old-fashioned costumes. Perhaps the most attractive room in the house is the nursery, where a cradle, a child's bed, low and high chairs for infants, a baby buggy dating from 1873, and interesting collections of old-fashioned toys and children's clothing are on exhibit. A fourth room on this floor has been lined with shelves for the display of cooking and other domestic utensils, such as kettles, irons, butter molds, coffee grinders, and the like. Among the larger items in this room are an iron stove manufactured in Stillwater in the 1890's, a tin bath tub, and a sailor's chest. The fifth room is devoted to the society's picture collection, which is particularly rich in lumbering scenes. It includes also many interesting portraits and early views of Stillwater.

Some of the manuscripts assembled by the Washington County society deserve special attention. In this collection the lumber industry is well represented. It includes, for example, a little book kept in 1881 by Edward Rutherford, foreman of the St. Croix Boom Company, in which he recorded for his own convenience the stamphammer marks used by the lumber firms then operating on the St. Croix. Some account books for the 1860's of the lumber firm of Walker, Judd and Veazie also are preserved in the Washington County museum. Most of the manuscripts in this collection are in some way related to the region's chief industry. Thus the names of many pioneer lumbermen are listed in a manuscript copy of the Washington County census of 1850. Probably this was the original enumeration made by the census taker. The largest single collection in the society's possession consists of accounts, time books, and other items from the papers of William Willim, a pioneer contractor at Stillwater. Students interested in frontier economic conditions and in labor will find this collection of special value. The time books, covering the years from 1856 to 1880, give detailed figures on wages and hours of each employee; and other volumes record plans for buildings, costs, and prices charged, and list materials used.

The founding of the Washington County museum was in large measure a result of the effective leadership of its president, Mr. E. L. Roney. The exhibits were assembled and arranged by a group of special committees. One committee has collected furniture, another, pictures, another, books and manuscripts, still another, old glass, and the like. Miss Annie Connor acts as chairman of the museum committee, with general supervision over the special committees. During the summer the museum is open to the public three afternoons a week, when an admission charge of twenty-five cents is made. The funds thus raised help to maintain the property. In addition to exhibit rooms, the museum building contains an assembly room on the first floor, where meetings can be held and refreshments are served. When the weather is favorable, the society holds its meetings on the beautiful lawn that stretches out toward the river in front of the museum.   B. L. H.

A centennial of international significance was celebrated at Fort William on August 1 in connection with the fourteenth annual meeting of the North Shore Historical Assembly. It was appropriate that this organization, which is composed of the historical societies of St. Louis, Cook, and Lake counties in Minnesota and the Thunder Bay Historical Society of Ontario, Canada, should mark the one-hundredth anniversary of the Webster-Ashburton treaty, for by its terms the boundary between Minnesota and Canada was fixed. Boundaries as far south as the St. Louis River had been considered previously; thus the negotiations of 1842 gave to Minnesota the vast iron wealth of the Arrowhead country. At the dinner meeting that marked the centennial, Minnesota was officially represented by its state treasurer, the Honorable Julius E. Schmahl; and the Minnesota Historical Society was represented by its curator of manuscripts, Dr. Grace Lee Nute, who spoke on the treaty and the voyageur. Representing the Canadian government were Mr. W. J. Bennett, executive secretary of the department of munitions and supply, and Mr. Lawrence J. Burpee, secretary of the International Joint Commission. An address on "One Hundred Years of North America," presented by Mr. Burpee, is published in the September issue of this magazine. It was particularly fitting that Mr. Burpee should speak on this occasion, since the commission of which he is Canadian secretary deals with boundary disputes.

The dinner meeting was preceded by an afternoon session in the Thunder Bay society's museum in the Fort William library building. In response to the welcome extended by Mayor C. M. Ross of Fort William, Judge Julius E. Haycraft, a vice-president of the Minnesota Historical Society, spoke briefly. The four societies that comprise the North Shore assembly were represented by speakers on the program that followed. Papers were read by the Reverend Oswald Johannes of the Cook County society on "Catholic Missionary Work in Cook County"; by Bruce Elliott of the Lake County society on the "History of the Iron Ore Industry, Lake Superior Basin"; by Otto E. Wieland of the St. Louis County society on "Ontario and Minnesota"; and by Keith Denis of the Thunder Bay society on "The Silver King of the Eighties," Oliver Daunais, who discovered a profitable silver mine in the vicinity of Fort William.

Minnesota visitors, many of whom went to Fort William from Duluth by boat, also attended sessions arranged by the North Shore assembly on August 2 and 3. The program on Sunday, August 2, included a special religious service on Mount McKay and an evening session at Chippewa Park. Papers on the "Geological History of the Lake Superior Basin" by Jules Cross and on "Ojibway Legends" by Dr. Herman Bryan were presented. Following the latter paper a ceremony was staged by the local Chippewa, who conferred titles of chief and princess upon several of the visitors. A trip to Kakabeka Falls, visits to historic sites and trails in its vicinity, and a luncheon brought the meeting to a close on August 3.

A room in the new courthouse at Detroit Lakes has been reserved for use as a museum by the Becker County Historical Society. A membership drive arranged by the society early in September raised the membership roll to two hundred before the end of the month.

The acquisition by the Carver County Historical Society of the library and records of the Carver County Deutscher Leseverein was announced in a number of Carver County newspapers in July (see *ante*, p. 294).

Accounts of this important collection and descriptions of the activities of the reading society appear in the *Waconia Patriot* for July 9, the *Weekly Valley Herald* of Chaska for July 16, and the *Carver County News* of Watertown for July 30.

The dedication on July 12 of the restored chapel of the Lac qui Parle mission was the occasion for an elaborate program of religious services, talks, and addresses, arranged under the auspices of the Chippewa County Historical Society. Among the speakers were the Reverend Albert Henimger of Peever, South Dakota, who preached the dedication sermon; Mr. Harold W. Lathrop, director of the division of state parks; and Dr. Arthur J. Larsen, superintendent of the state historical society, who presented the principal address. He took as his subject "The Missionary in the Development of Minnesota." A historical sketch of the mission is contributed to the *Montevideo American* of July 10 by Dr. Anna Amrud, chairman of the committee which arranged the dedication program. In the printed program issued for the occasion are notes on the American Board of Commissioners for Foreign Missions, which established the Lac qui Parle mission in 1835, and brief sketches of the missionaries who served there.

The summer months brought an addition to the list of Minnesota's local historical societies with the organization, as the result of a series of meetings, of the Chisago County Historical Society. Preliminary meetings were held at Lindstrom on June 27 and July 14. At North Branch on August 18 a committee was named to draw up a constitution, which was adopted at Center City on September 22. At the latter place Dr. Lewis Beeson, acting superintendent of the Minnesota Historical Society, spoke on "The Local Historical Society and Its Work." The officers of the new society are Bert Merling, president, Theodore Norelius, vice-president, Mrs. Stanley Folsom, secretary, and Hjalmar Anderson, treasurer.

An exhibit arranged by the Fillmore County Historical Society at the county fair at Preston from August 29 to 31 attracted hundreds of interested visitors. Portraits of pioneers, objects used in frontier homes, books, and documents were included in the display.

Life among the early Czech settlers of McLeod County was recalled by some of their descendants at a meeting of the Hutchinson chapter of the McLeod County Historical Society on July 21. Among the speakers were Mrs. Josephine Miska and Mrs. Erick Fratzke.

More than six hundred people gathered at Fairmont on August 30 for the fourteenth annual summer meeting of the Martin County Historical Society, which centered about a program of wartime interest. The international situation was discussed by the principal speaker, Professor Harold Deutsch of the department of history in the University of Minnesota. A second speaker, Major Arthur M. Nelson, surveyed the role of Martin County in wars of the past.

A meeting of the Meeker County Historical Society, held on August 16 near Grove City, commemorated the eightieth anniversary of the beginning of the Sioux War of 1862. Among the speakers who addressed the gathering was Mrs. Martha Merrill of Hutchinson, one of the few people still living who remembers some of the events of the massacre. Articles in the *Meeker County News* of Litchfield for August 20 and 27 relate the story of the murders in Acton Township that marked the beginning of the outbreak.

An appeal for the preservation of "pioneer landmarks," physical and spiritual, was made by James R. Crawford of Beaver Creek when he spoke before the tenth annual meeting of the Nobles County Historical Society at Worthington on August 16. About a hundred people were present. Mrs. C. R. Thompson was elected president of the organization, G. M. Walker, vice-president, Mrs. A. G. Satre, treasurer, and Stanley E. Nelson, secretary.

Members of the Washington County Historical Society gathered at Forest Lake for a picnic meeting on August 11. A paper on the history of Forest Lake was presented by Mrs. Clara Telander. For residents of the southern part of Washington County, a special meeting was arranged at the home of Mr. and Mrs. J. V. Bailey near Newport on August 25. Mrs. Grace McAlpine read a historical sketch of Newport, prepared by Mrs. Mary E. Keck, and Mrs. Mary Bailey reviewed the history of the Bailey family.

LOCAL HISTORY ITEMS

A brief history of Pleasant Mound Township in Blue Earth County, appearing in the *Amboy Herald* for September 11, was contributed by W. O. Wiederhoeft. It consists for the most part of lists of names of early settlers and of township and other officers. The various names by which the township has been known since 1865 also are given.

An account of "Coming to America in 1868" from Norway and settling at Hanska in Brown County appears in three installments in *Our Young People,* a weekly issued by the Augsburg Publishing House, for August 9, 16, and 23. The story of the voyage from Norway aboard a sailing vessel and of frontier life in Minnesota has been recalled by Ole K. Broste, and recorded by Petra M. Lien. The narrator was an infant when his parents joined a group emigrating from Romsdalen, Norway. He tells of the journey to the West, and of the hardships of pioneering, such as grasshopper plagues, prairie fires, and blizzards.

A letter written in 1934 by the late A. C. Von Hagen, who settled in Sleepy Eye in 1885 and lived there for many years, is published in full in the *Sleepy Eye Herald-Dispatch* for September 3. In it he tells how the grave of the Sisseton chief for whom the Brown County city is named was located in 1899 with the result that the remains were removed to Sleepy Eye and a monument was erected over the new place of burial.

The historical sketch of Chisago County prepared for *Who's Who in Minnesota* by Bert Merling has been expanded by the author for publication in installments in the *Chisago County Press*. Sections dealing with specific communities appear in some issues. The story of Franconia, a St. Croix Valley ghost town, is published in the *Press* for July 9, and various phases of the history of Taylors Falls are reviewed in installments appearing from July 16 to August 20.

"A History of Newburg Township and the Village of Mabel" in Fillmore County, prepared as a master's thesis in the University of Minnesota by William H. Cartwright, Jr., has been appearing in installments in the *Mabel Record* since August 7. The narrative opens with an account of the acquisition of a section of southeastern Minnesota as the result of Indian treaties and the removal of the Winnebagoes in 1848. Lists of early settlers in the township, particularly the Norwegians who established homes there, accounts of the communities that grew up in the vicinity of Mabel, descriptions of frontier life and customs in the region, and analyses of the census records of 1860 and 1870 are presented in chapters published in the *Record* for August 14 and 29 and September 18 and 25.

A vivid picture of frontier domestic life in southern Minnesota is presented in the *Chatfield News* for September 3 and 10 by Mrs. Edith

Wright of Spring Valley, whose father, James Price, settled near Eyota in 1859. Much attention is given to the food that appeared on the dinner tables of the pioneers, and the methods used in preparing and preserving native products. Household remedies, furniture, cooking and other domestic utensils, lighting equipment, and the arrangement of living quarters are mentioned. Among the well-remembered dishes recalled by Mrs. Wright are "homegrown buckwheat flour pancakes" with bacon drippings and black strap, dried corn, salted cucumbers, salt-rising bread, ginger cake, soda biscuits, maple syrup, and hominy. Her narrative is published in a column devoted to the "Chatfield Quiz," which has presented each week since July 16 questions and answers relating to local history. Another contributor to the column is Miss Margaret Snyder. She outlines the ordinances passed at a meeting of the village council in 1857 in the *News* for August 20, and reviews some early cases handled in the local courts in the issue for August 27. The efforts made from 1910 to 1914 by the local Commercial Club to improve roads in the vicinity of Chatfield are recounted by Miss Snyder in the columns published on September 17 and 24.

Much material about Swedish settlement in Minneapolis is to be found in an anniversary booklet entitled *Seventy-five Years of Christian Service in Minneapolis,* issued by the Augustana Evangelical Lutheran Church of Minneapolis (1941. 75 p.). The founding of the church in 1866 is described, and its growth during three quarters of a century is reviewed. Accounts of the founding and development of church organizations also are presented. An unusual feature of the booklet is a section entitled "What the Archives Contain." There are listed the manuscript records of the church, with brief descriptive statements and notations of the years covered. Printed programs, photographs, and motion pictures made on special church occasions in recent years also are preserved, according to this record. That the church appreciates the value of its archives is evident from the statement that "all inactive records are stored in the vault erected for that purpose."

Under the title "Roaming the Rural Routes of Hubbard County," the *Akeley Herald-Tribune* has been publishing sketches of local historical interest since June 5. The early installments, which deal with exploration and settlement in the vicinity of Akeley, the organization of the county, industrial beginnings, and similar matters, were prepared by Charles F.

Scheers. The narratives published after July 31 present descriptions of local farms and their owners, some of whom are original settlers or their descendants. Sara Ellen Tandy is the author of the later installments.

Fathers Francis Pierz, Joseph Buh, Thomas Borgerding, Simon Lampe, Roman Homar, and Felix Nelles are among the Catholic missionaries who figure in a history of St. Joseph's Mission at Ball Club, published in the *Deer River News* for July 2. A picture of the mission church and guild hall, where a Catholic Indian congress was held late in June, appears with the article. Some information about the Chippewa for whom the mission was established and about the building of the church also is included.

The "first mention of an Itasca county fair, in old files of county newspapers, is in the Grand Rapids Magnet for August 16, 1892," according to the *Grand Rapids Herald-Review* for August 19. The column of that paper entitled "Up in This Neck of the Woods" is devoted to the early history of the county fair. According to this account, several annual fairs were held before the Itasca County Agricultural Association was incorporated in May, 1895. In the same column for September 30, the ruins of some cabins, believed to have been used by early trappers in Itasca County, are described.

The "Old Roche Ranch," a pretentious establishment maintained on the shores of Round Lake in Jackson County in the late decades of the nineteenth century, is the subject of an article in the *Worthington Daily Globe* for September 4. On a tract of two thousand acres purchased in 1879, Owen H. Roche of Chicago erected elaborate buildings, including a "magnificent 26-room 'farm house' in a region where the ordinary settlers were only just beginning to timidly emerge from their dugouts and sod houses." There Roche lived in "baronial fashion," raising blooded beef cattle and "fine porkers," and entertaining large numbers of friends for the hunting season. The writer of the present account reports that in 1901, shortly before his death, Roche sold his Minnesota holdings. The huge barn and some of the other structures on his ranch still are standing, and they are pictured with the article. Some local transportation history is recounted in the *Jackson County Pilot* for July 9, which tells of the improvement of a road that has been in use in Belmont Township since the 1850's. The road, which included a steep grade over the Kilen

Hills, was used as an overland mail route as early as 1856, but it was considered unsafe for modern motor vehicles.

The removal to the Lincoln County fair grounds of a frontier log cabin built in Royal Township in 1873 is announced in the *Ivanhoe Times* for June 10. The structure was presented to the county fair association by the grandchildren of Jonas Swenson, a Swedish immigrant who erected the cabin and lived in it for many years. Its preservation makes available an example of a typical frontier dwelling. A picture of the cabin accompanies the description of the structure.

The site of Fort Ridgely was the scene of a celebration on August 22 commemorating the eightieth anniversary of the siege of the fort in the Sioux War of 1862. The principal address was presented by Senator Joseph H. Ball, and a talk on the early history of the region was given by Mr. A. A. Davidson of Renville.

"Fish stories" that tell of catching "85 black bass of uniformly large size" in three hours in 1874, of taking "507 sunfish, not counting some large fish" in 1889, and of hooking "96 bass and five pike in two and a half hours" as late as 1904 are included in a collection of fishing yarns culled from early Fergus Falls newspapers and reprinted in the *Fergus Falls Journal* for August 24. Records of the landing of salmon trout and of huge sturgeon in the Red River also are presented.

The activities of pioneer musical organizations in St. Paul are reviewed briefly by Albert L. Eggert in an article entitled "When St. Paul Was Young," which appears in two installments in the *St. Paul Shopper* for July 1 and 9. Special attention is given to the Great Western Band organized by George Siebert, Sr., and to the band concerts held for many years in Como Park.

The issue of the *Buffalo Lake News* for July 16 is an illustrated "golden anniversary edition," which contains numerous articles of local historical interest and gives special attention to the development of commercial projects in the Renville County community. It is interesting to note that a number of local business concerns are as old or older than the paper. The editorial page is devoted to a history of the *News,* which was established in 1892 by John Riebe. Some reminiscences of J. R. Landy, who edited the paper from 1899 to 1907, are included in this account.

Some of the backgrounds of the Northwest Angle country are brought out by Herbert L. Mueller in an article calling attention to the district's possibilities as a "paradise for sport fishermen," appearing in the *Minneapolis Sunday Tribune* for September 20. Mentioned in the account are La Vérendrye and Fort St. Charles, the marker on its site, and the old Dawson trail. Some description of the modern community in this northernmost section of the United States also is given.

The fact that the present year marks the ninetieth anniversary of the founding of Henderson is noted in a review of its early history appearing in the *Henderson Independent* for July 24. Emphasis is given to the role of Joseph R. Brown in founding the community and establishing its early business concerns, including a local newspaper. In another column appears an account of the services of Mr. G. A. Buck, who this year celebrates the completion of half a century as owner and editor of the *Independent*.

The seventy-fifth anniversary of the German Farmers' Mutual Fire Insurance Company, which was organized in Washington County in the spring of 1867, is commemorated in a series of interesting articles about the company's origin and history in the *Stillwater Post-Messenger* for August 20. An article by the company's president, Mr. Louis Pagel, sketches the background of German settlement in Woodbury, Oakdale, Afton, Lakeland, Baytown, and Grant townships which preceded the organization of the company. Many of the German pioneers who settled in Washington County had lived earlier in New York state, where they had organized for "mutual assistance," and when they "came to Minnesota, they carried on" that policy, writes Mr. Pagel. He presents also an outline of the financial growth of the company, based upon its manuscript records. Other items relating to the history of this organization are biographical sketches of members of its board of directors, a list of the signers of its first constitution, and a copy of the articles of incorporation drawn up in 1879.

PUBLICATIONS OF THE

MINNESOTA HISTORICAL SOCIETY

OFFICERS

LESTER B. SHIPPEE, *President*

JULIUS E. HAYCRAFT, *Vice-president*

KENNETH G. BRILL, *Vice-president*

ARTHUR J. LARSEN, *Secretary*

JULIAN B. BAIRD, *Treasurer*

MINNESOTA HISTORY

ARTHUR J. LARSEN, *Editor*

BERTHA L. HEILBRON, *Assistant Editor*

VOLUME XXIII

1942

THE MINNESOTA HISTORICAL SOCIETY

Saint Paul

CONTENTS OF VOLUME XXIII

REVIEWS OF BOOKS

ILLUSTRATIONS